Thomas Mann Studies

Volume II

A BIBLIOGRAPHY OF CRITICISM

University of Pennsylvania Studies
in Germanic Languages and Literatures

Edited by
ANDRÉ VON GRONICKA : OTTO SPRINGER

With the cooperation of
Adolph C. Gorr
Adolph D. Klarmann
Egbert Krispyn
Albert L. Lloyd
Heinz Moenkemeyer
George C. Schoolfield
Alfred Senn

George C. Avery
Inquiry and Testament:
A Study of the Novels and Short Prose of Robert Walser

John Gearey
Heinrich Von Kleist: A Study in Tragedy and Anxiety

Klaus W. Jonas and Ilsedore B. Jonas
Thomas Mann Studies, Volume II

Edmund K. Kostka
Schiller in Russian Literature

Kenneth Negus
E.T.A. Hoffman's Other World:
The Romantic Author and His "New Mythology"

William H. Rey
Weltentzweiung und Weltversöhnung
in Hofmannsthals Griechischen Dramen

Thomas Mann Studies
Volume II

A Bibliography of Criticism

By
Klaus W. Jonas and
Ilsedore B. Jonas

Philadelphia
University of Pennsylvania Press

7527
Printed in the United States of America

To
Caroline Newton
In Gratitude and Friendship

Acknowledgement

It is a pleasure to express my appreciation to the Yale University Library for the award of the Caroline Newton Grant; to the American Council of Learned Societies for assisting me through a research grant; and to the University of Pittsburgh for awarding me a Charles E. Merrill Faculty Fellowship in the Humanities in support of this book.

I also wish to thank numerous colleagues and librarians all over the world who have generously assisted me with materials and information. I owe a particular debt of gratitude to several Thomas Mann experts in Europe without whose help this book would not have been completed: Dr. Hans-Otto Mayer of Düsseldorf; Mr. Heinz Saueressig of Biberach an der Riss; Dr. Paul Raabe and Dr. Bernhard Zeller of the Schiller Nationalmuseum at Marbach; Mr. Erich Neumann, former Director of the Thomas Mann Archive of the Deutsche Akademie der Wissenschaften zu Berlin; his successor, Dr. Georg Wenzel, and the staff members of the Archive. In Switzerland, Dr. Hans Wysling and the staff of the Thomas Mann Archive of the Eidgenössische Technische Hochschule in Zurich have been most helpful. And finally, in this country,

I thank Dr. Bernhard Blume and Dr. Henry Hatfield, both
of Harvard University; Dr. André von Gronicka of the
University of Pennsylvania; Dr. Victor Lange of Princeton
University; and Dr. Oskar Seidlin of Ohio State University
for their many kindnesses, their infinite patience, and
encouragement.

K. W. J.

I am deeply indebted to Carnegie-Mellon University for
awarding me a research grant from The Maurice and Laura
Falk Endowment for Research in the Humanities in support
of this bibliography.

My gratitude also belongs to Dr. Erwin R. Steinberg
and Dr. Fred Genschmer, both of Carnegie-Mellon University, and to Dr. J. Alan Pfeffer of the University of Pittsburgh
for their kind interest and assistance in my Thomas Mann
studies.

I. B. J.

Preface

In the spring of 1955, the first part of this bibliography of criticism, entitled *Fifty Years of Thomas Mann Studies,* was published by the University of Minnesota Press. It was introduced by Thomas Mann's good wishes, as expressed in April 1953 in the form of a brief but thoughtful preface, "Ein Wort hierzu," valuable for its autobiographical observations. Although the first volume was by no means intended as anything like a definitive bibliography and was, de facto, rather deficient in certain areas, especially in the coverage of Slavic and Near Eastern tongues, it was yet reasonably comprehensive and international in scope. Thus the book achieved its purpose in facilitating throughout the world research in the rapidly growing area of Thomas Mann studies. Even then it was no surprise that a supplementary volume would become mandatory, especially in view of the fact that *Fifty Years* appeared shortly before the 80th birthday of the author on June 6, 1955, and about three months before his death on August 12 of that year. Since those two memorable events, both of which were the occasion for innumerable articles and books, Thomas Mann studies have reached a triumphant, all-time peak, and never before has the need for a survey such as this become as urgent as at this time. Thus the second volume now appears as the long-promised continuation and supplement (but *not*, it should be made clear to every user, as the revised and improved second edition) of *Fifty Years*. It is designed not only to bring the bibliographical record of the critical literature on Mann up to date through the first part of 1965, but also to fill the gaps found in my initial effort.

While preparing *Fifty Years* in the early fifties, there were in existence between 6,000 and 8,000 items on Thomas Mann, if one included such ephemeral publications as newspaper articles. In view of this vast mass of material extant, a degree of intelligent selectivity was required, and it was not easy to determine where to draw the line. Inasmuch as I was forced by circumstances beyond my control to work against considerable odds and had no access to materials located in any country except the United States (which I did not leave once in the seven years between 1948 and 1955), I had only too often to rely on secondary sources and informants in other countries. This, of course, will explain the number of gaps and also inaccuracies or inconsistencies which are now to be found in *Fifty Years*. Although I wish that I could have checked each item personally, alas, this was by no means possible, especially since the majority of the German newspaper and older periodical items were hard enough to locate anywhere, let alone in this country. A number of ephemeral items have managed to find their way into the book which I would exclude in a future revised edition, to be mentioned presently, while on the other hand some more important materials were overlooked and inadvertently excluded. My apologies not only to their authors, but to all users of *Fifty Years*.

In spite of these faults, however, the book achieved reasonably complete coverage for the years 1902 to 1951, supplemented by the inclusion of a few earlier and later references. Seventeen languages were represented, and a total of 3,010 items, all consecutively numbered, were included. My prime goal in organizing these almost overwhelming masses of paper was for convenient reference, to be approached from any conceivable angle, and thus I chose to divide the items systematically into 17 categories, some of them again subdivided, so that there was a total of 81 subheadings.

By far the majority of the items were articles from newspapers, especially German ones, and periodicals, but 90 items were monographs or separately published essays or pamphlets dealing exclusively with Thomas Mann. More than 100 were dissertations, and about 250 books containing either a chapter or else an important mention of Thomas Mann, even though his name did not appear on their title pages. Reviews of books on Mann were also listed along with the work in question, in order to avoid getting into astronomical figures. A system of cross-references was employed which, I hope, has made it impossible for the user to miss any entry.

Some critics have taken me to task for the organization of the 3,010 items. Obviously no one can please every reader, and I gladly take the responsibility for my system of arranging these items, in most chapters, alphabetically. This, of course, makes for easier use—my chief objective—while, admittedly, it lessens the value of the work as literary history. Only in certain chapters was a chronological arrangement preferred, e.g. "Autobiographical Writings" (Ch. IV) and "Thomas Mann as an Emigré."

When *Fifty Years* appeared, the publisher did not wish to print a large edition. Since then the book has gone entirely

out of print and is now hard to obtain. If it can be found at
all, it can only be accomplished with infinite patience by an
antiquarian dealer. In certain countries with a shortage of
hard currency it has been a "rare book" from the very beginning and has found its way only into major research
libraries, so that their Thomas Mann scholars often have to
make a trip to some other city in order to consult the book.

This second volume, completed eleven years after the
first one, is again a labor of love and a visible expression of
our devotion and gratitude to Thomas Mann. During his last
years, he had taken a warm personal interest in this work and
had contributed generously to our collection, both of his own
works and the literature about him, and in the weeks following his 80th birthday it had been our good fortune to be
granted access to all the research materials in his home in
Kilchberg near Zurich. In that summer the ground work was
laid for this volume, but nine subsequent trips of the two
editors to Europe were necessary to check as many as possible
of the items that were included in this second part. And yet,
we fully realize that the result of our researches is far from
perfect.

Thomas Mann Studies Volume II is intended, first of all,
as the bibliographical record for the period from 1954 to
1965. At the same time, however, this book presents an effort
to fill the gaps found in *Fifty Years*. As a matter of fact, about
1,000 items published prior to 1954 had escaped my attention;
all of these should have gone into the first volume and are
now included in the second, along with 2,500 items actually
covering Mann studies of the last decade. Many of the older
items represent newspaper articles not available to me in the
early fifties; I could check them only after the Ida Herz
Collection had been transferred to the Archive in Zurich
where they became accessible to me a few years ago.

Of the total of 3,500 items listed in the present volume, about 120 are monographs and some 75 are unpublished academic studies such as doctoral dissertations, most of them produced during the past ten years. By far the majority, 2,275 items, are in German, followed by 585 in English, 190 in French, 165 in Italian, and 156 in Swedish. Other languages represented are Japanese (64 items), Dutch (31), Spanish (28), followed by Rumanian (24), Hungarian (21), Czech (17), Danish (14), Polish (11), Russian (10), Hebrew (9), Latvian (3), Norwegian and Serbo-Croatian (2 each), and Finnish and Portuguese (1 item each).

While this book had been in the making for the past ten years, two other related projects had been concurrently in progress by the first editor, both of them unduly delayed and still not completed because of a lack of time, or rather of the necessary research funds. The first of them, listed in *Fifty Years* as item #2981, is a *History of Thomas Mann Criticism*. It is a strange phenomenon that, in spite of a huge body of critical literature that has been written about Thomas Mann, no attempt has thus far been made by any scholar to publish a well-organized analysis and evaluation of the important critical and biographical studies, indicating which aspects and themes have been sufficiently and adequately treated and where the need for detailed investigations is particularly urgent. It is true that the critical reception of Mann's writings has been examined for certain countries, but such studies, limited in character and scope and restricted to periods of two or three decades only, exist for no more than three countries: Germany, England, and the United States. The first of them was a work by M. C. Morris, "A History of Thomas Mann Criticism in Germany, 1900-1930," Ph.D. diss., University of Wisconsin, 1940; followed by D. A. R. H. Webster, "The Reception of Thomas Mann in England and America, 1915-

1938," M.A. thesis, University of London, 1940; and H. Ramras, "Main Currents of American Criticism of Thomas Mann," Ph.D. diss., University of Wisconsin, 1950.

Different from these unpublished academic studies, available to very few scholars, are surveys which discuss and evaluate selected books, essays, and articles not restricted to one particular country, but covering Thomas Mann studies published either during one year, 1954-1955, e.g. R. Thieberger, "Les derniers travaux sur Thomas Mann," *L'Allemagne d'Aujourd'hui*, 4 (August 1955), 98-105, or during a period of seven years, 1948-1955, e.g. H. Hatfield, "Recent Studies of Thomas Mann," *MLR*, 51 (July 1956), 390-403.

But it is the over-all survey and history of Thomas Mann scholarship which has yet to be written, and it is this gap which my first project is intended to fill. All monographs, dissertations, and pamphlets, in addition to serious articles in books, periodicals, and even selected newspapers, have already been located and will have to await the critical scrutiny and evaluation of the historian.

My second project is entitled *Die literarische Entwicklung Thomas Manns* and is meant to present, in bibliographical form, the *Wirkungsgeschichte* of Thomas Mann. Accepted for publication by J. B. Metzler in Stuttgart and scheduled to appear some day in the series of "Repertorien zur deutschen Literaturgeschichte," edited by Paul Raabe, this book will be written in German. The idea of the publisher, the editor of the series, and myself has been to combine, in one volume, the more important critical materials on Mann, along with all available references to the author's own discussion of his works or aspects of his writings. Thus, a chapter dealing with any given book, say *Königliche Hoheit* or *Der Zauberberg,* will, first of all, describe briefly its first and subsequent publications in German and then the various foreign editions to indicate its influence upon, and availability among readers in other countries. This will be followed by the more important statements of the author himself regarding such work, e.g. prefaces, introductions, comments on *Sprechplatten* (phonograph records) and references to diaries or letters, published as well as unpublished. To be sure, the moment has not yet come to bring out this book since too many items in the latter categories have not yet come to light, so that a few years will have to pass before it can be completed. This book should reveal the range of interest of readers in each and every book by Thomas Mann and describe the author's literary career, based upon details as to his own attitude toward a certain book or subject.

The next portion—where greater selectivity has to be applied—will contain the actual critical items, arranged in chronological order by subject. Each chapter will be subdivided into two sections, both of them showing this chronological arrangement. The first part of any chapter will be a listing of all scholarly studies such as monographs, dissertations, essays, chapters in books, or articles in learned journals, dealing with a particular book or some aspect of the author's work. To differentiate these actual contributions to scholarship from the more ephemeral items such as book reviews and shorter references in newspapers and books, the latter will be grouped together in a second category. It is important, again, to indicate the *Wirkungsgeschichte,* the increase or decrease, as the case may be, of interest in the scholarly or journalistic treatment of the author.

A word of explanation may be necessary to say why the present volume had to take precedence over the completion of the two other long-range projects as outlined on the previous pages. During the past years an ever-increasing flow of requests for bibliographical information on modern German authors has reached me—more than I could possibly handle. Many of them dealt with Thomas Mann, and three types of questions have been the most frequent. In an effort to provide for a central clearing house that could handle such matters, I have proposed the establishment of a Bibliographical Center for Modern German Literature, in which these three areas of research would be concentrated: (1) The study of original source materials, i.e., above all German literary manuscripts of the past one hundred years, (2) The bibliographical coverage of secondary or critical literature, and (3) The control of all major research projects, including doctoral dissertations, currently in progress.

Because of the greatest need for early completion of this present volume of Thomas Mann Studies, work on the two related projects had to be delayed. In view of the chronological arrangement to be found in the book on Mann's literary career, there was no reason why I had to deviate from the alphabetical organization of the present volume. It can be consulted as a kind of "Who Is Who in Thomas Mann Scholarship" and will also serve any student of literature or collector anxious to locate materials on a given subject. Ample cross-references have been provided, not only within this second volume, but also many which lead the reader back to *Fifty Years,* abbreviated simply as Vol. I.

K. W. J.

Contents

A Note on
Thomas Mann's Manuscripts
and the
Major Research Collections

AMERICA

Seldom, if ever, has there lived in the United States a foreign-born writer who has won such universal acclaim and made such an impact on the American literary scene as Thomas Mann. The unusual success of his books in this country, the interest they evoke in readers with no knowledge of German, may be compared to that of such fellow-emigrés as Lion Feuchtwanger, Erich Maria Remarque, or Franz Werfel.

In many ways Mann's relationship to America during his lifetime was a very happy one. He was extremely fortunate in having Alfred A. Knopf of New York as his American publisher, beginning in 1916, and, for over thirty years, Helen T. Lowe-Porter as his major translator. But even before she took on the demanding task of translating his works into English, there had been others so engaged, and while Mrs. Lowe-Porter remained the most competent and faithful of all, individual works continued to be translated by others.

Not only have Mann's works, with very few exceptions, been translated and thus made available to American readers, he is also one of the most eagerly collected of modern authors. Practically all of the Mann collections which have been formed in this country are now owned by libraries; only one of them is still in private hands.

In spite of the existence of several major Thomas Mann archives in Europe, the United States is, and will remain, the one country to which scholars and collectors will turn for most of the original documents relating to Mann's residence in this country. The 14 years spent at Princeton (1938-1941), and Pacific Palisades, near Los Angeles, (1941-1952) saw the publication of *Lotte in Weimar, Doctor Faustus,* the last two volumes of the Joseph Tetralogy, *The Black Swan,* and *The Holy Sinner.* During this period, no country gave more genuine respect and admiration for Thomas Mann both as a man and as an artist than the United States. As visible expression of the high regard in which he has been held on this continent, there have been various successful efforts to organize commemorations and exhibitions in his honor, and to cultivate his lasting contributions to world literature by the establishment of special collections.

As early as 1937, the first of these collections in an American library was established at Yale through the initiative and vision of Joseph W. Angell, Jr., its present curator, and the interest and assistance of Thomas Mann himself. In September of that year a large number of his manuscripts came to Yale. They were accompanied by numerous first editions, first publications of his writings in newspapers and journals, foreign language editions, critical literature, as well as source materials used by Mann in the preparation of his works. By far the most precious part was a group of some 38 manuscripts, among them first drafts of his essay "Goethe und Tolstoi," the first notes for *Buddenbrooks* and *Death in Venice,* as well as the final manuscript versions of essays on such literary personalities as Joseph Conrad, André Gide, Lessing, and Nietzsche. Moreover, there were important political addresses and essays, above all that world-famous document, Mann's open letter to the Dean of the Philosophical Faculty of Bonn University of January 1, 1937, his first public attack on the Nazi regime. One of the highlights of this first collection was the original manuscript of the first two volumes of Mann's Joseph novels, purchased from the author by Mr. and Mrs. Wilmarth S. Lewis and presented to the Yale Library. Finally, there were 70 manuscript pages from *The Magic Mountain,* withdrawn before publication and unpublished, strangely enough to this very day despite numerous requests from Thomas Mann scholars all over the world to have them edited and thus made available.

On February 17, 1938, President Charles Seymour of Yale announced the establishment of the Thomas Mann Library; the Rare Book Room organized a display of some of the choicest items of this collection, and Thomas Mann himself came to Yale to give one of the Francis Bergen Lectures, choosing as his subject "The Position of the Artist in the Present Time."

Soon after this event, friends and supporters added to these materials: in March, 1938, Alfred A. Knopf presented the 34-page manuscript of Mann's lecture "Freud und die Zukunft," Gabriel Wells donated the 22-page manuscript of

"Dieser Friede," a lecture delivered in English as "This Peace" in October, 1938 in several American cities, and Mann himself presented to Yale the original of his speech made at the opening of the collection.

During the following years, the materials at Yale were strengthened by various important acquisitions, e.g. the archive of Klaus Mann's short-lived periodical *Decision* (1941), containing numerous letters from such contributors as Albert Einstein, Bruno Frank, Stefan Zweig and, of course, Thomas Mann himself, who had lent practical support as well as moral encouragement to his son's efforts. Oddly enough, this gold mine of valuable data on German literature in exile during the Nazi regime has not been explored or described to this day.

Mrs. Helen T. Lowe-Porter presented her important collection to Yale some years before her death in 1963. Included among her papers were typescripts of her English translations of ten larger and 45 smaller works of Thomas Mann, all bearing marginal notes, questions and comments in the author's own hand, thus testifying to the high degree of co-operation between the poet and his translator. There are also more than 100 original letters to Mrs. Lowe which were written between 1924 and 1955, plus numerous dedication copies of Mann's books, and a large number of assorted critical and biographical items.

The last important collection to be presented to Yale is that of Mrs. Agnes E. Meyer. In 1957 she gave to the Library more than 300 original letters, cards, and telegrams, received from Mann between 1935 and 1955, in addition to 23 letters from various members of his family, and manuscript notes in her own hand about conversations with the author from the time of the composition of his novel *Doctor Faustus*. The original manuscript of a 22-page essay "Mass and Wert," translated by her into English, was also given. It had first been published in the Swiss periodical of the same title, which was edited by Thomas Mann and Konrad Falke and financed, to a large extent, through the generosity of Eugene and Agnes E. Meyer. While it is true that no less than 110 of these letters have now appeared in Vol. II of Erika Mann's edition of her father's letters (Frankfurt, 1962), by far the larger part remains unpublished.

These, then, are among the treasures to be found in the Beinecke Rare Book and Manuscripts Library at Yale, along with numerous Thomas Mann letters to Joseph W. Angell, Hermann J. Weigand, and many other recipients.

Next in importance, without doubt, is the collection in the Princeton University Library, which deserves our special attention as a major center for the study of Mann's life and work during the years of his residence in New Jersey, between 1938 and 1941. To a large extent, its establishment is due to the generosity of Miss Caroline Newton, a friend of Thomas Mann and his family, and a passionate collector in her own right. During all the years of Mann's American residence she was in close contact with him, and maintained regular correspondence with Mann until his death. Thomas Mann scholarship in the United States has greatly benefited from Miss Newton's enthusiasm for the author. The five Thomas Mann Commemorations organized by her will long be remembered.

Miss Newton's collection includes a 29-page manuscript of the essay "Richard Wagner und 'Der Ring des Nibelungen,'" completed in Zurich on November 16, 1937, some 53 Thomas Mann letters addressed to her, and a somewhat larger number of letters from his wife Katja. During the last decade, Miss Newton's Mann collection was enriched by numerous acquisitions, including some 50 letters to the critic and Hauptmann biographer Hans von Hülsen, 64 letters to the

French translator-critic Félix Bertaux, 62 letters to the author
Alexander M. Frey, a number of letters to his brother Viktor
Mann, his publisher Samuel Fischer, the American journalist
George Sylvester Viereck, and one letter to a Hamburg critic,
Dr. Paul Raché, dated July 2, 1902, thanking him for a splen-
did review of *Buddenbrooks* which, oddly enough, has not
yet come to light and has not been traced to this very day.

Apart from the Thomas Mann materials presented by
Miss Newton, the collection in the Princeton Library contains a manuscript of Mann's address of May 18, 1938, when
he was awarded a Doctor of Laws degree by Princeton University, letters to Frank J. Mather, Jr. (May 8, 1940), to
Julian P. Boyd, former Librarian at Princeton (September
26, 1942), to Harold W. Dodds, then President of the University (May 24, 1939), seven letters to Professor George M.
Priest (1939-1941), as well as materials in the papers of
former Dean Christian Gauss, including several letters relating to Mann's tenure in Princeton.

Also in Princeton, but still in the recipient's possession,
are some 55 autograph letters from Thomas Mann to his
friend Erich von Kahler, as well as dedication copies of the
German and English editions of Mann's books published
after 1933, and finally, the manuscript of the address delivered by the author as a tribute to Erich von Kahler on the
occasion of the latter's 60th birthday in 1945.

There are, of course, other libraries in this country which
have extensive German literature collections with an emphasis on Thomas Mann. Strangely enough, despite the author's
residence in California for over a decade, no special collection
of his works has been developed on the Pacific Coast. All of
them are located along the Eastern Seaboard or in the Middle
West.

Harvard was the first university in this country to honor

Thomas Mann on November 20, 1935. The eminent refugee from Hitler's Germany was made an honorary doctor of letters of America's oldest university. In order to express his appreciation for this distinction, Mann presented the manuscript of "Meerfahrt mit Don Quichote," written during his first crossing of the Atlantic, to the Harvard Library. Professor Henry Hatfield has presented to Harvard all his personal letters from the author, and the Widener Library contains a very large collection of Mann's printed works and the secondary literature about him.

Among the honors bestowed upon Mann in America was his appointment, on January 16, 1942, as Consultant in Germanic Literature by the Library of Congress. Mann never considered this office merely a sinecure. On the contrary, he took his duties seriously and was eager to earn, through his work, the annual stipend of $3,000 (granted for this purpose, without his knowledge, by his generous friends and benefactors, Eugene and Agnes E. Meyer). After three years of service, he remained associated with the Library of Congress as a Fellow in Germanic Literature from 1945 until his death on August 12, 1955. Therefore, hardly any of Mann's visits to the Washington home of the Meyers went by without his delivering a lecture in the Coolidge Auditorium. In order to express his feeling of belonging to our national library, he used to write many of his letters in those years on official library stationery, and he also presented the various manuscripts or corrected typescripts of his addresses delivered under the Library's auspices to its permanent collection of manuscripts: "The Theme of the Joseph Novels" (November 17, 1942), "The War and the Future" (October 13, 1943), "Germany and the Germans" (May 29, 1945), Nietzsche's Philosophy in the Light of Contemporary Events" (April 29, 1947), as well as the holograph manuscript of his story "Das

Gesetz." In 1947, the Library's collection was further enriched by the acquisition of Mann's correspondence with the
German-born critic Julius Bab of New York, consisting of
eight letters and one card from the years 1909 until 1928.

The New York Public Library is rich not only in printed
materials by and about Mann, but thanks to the assistance of
an anonymous donor, it acquired at an auction the 42-page
holograph manuscript of Mann's famous lecture, "Der
Zukünftige Sieg der Demokratie," delivered under the title,
"The Coming Victory of Democracy," in the Spring of 1938
in numerous American cities.

Hardly any student of German literature in America
would expect to find one of Mann's original manuscripts in
a special "Klaus Mann Literary Collection" brought together
by the author's oldest son during the second World War. This
collection of valuable manuscripts and inscribed first and
rare editions of many American and European authors and
artists was sold in an auction for the benefit of the War Bonds
effort. Acquired for a total of one million dollars by the
executive of an insurance company, W. T. Grant, it was
presented, in October 1943, to the Library of the University
of Kansas City in Missouri, where Thomas Mann had addressed the students and faculty. In addition to several
inscribed editions of books—*Royal Highness, Listen, Germany!* and a Hungarian translation of his *Lotte in Weimar*
—this collection contains the original manuscript of his
article "Germany's Guilt and Mission."

All of the collections described thus far are now owned
by institutions. Extensive materials still in private hands in
this country are hard to find. A private archive, located at the
University of Pittsburgh, was started by this writer in 1949
with the active support of Thomas Mann himself, and Helen
T. Lowe-Porter. It contains Mann's single and collected works

in German and in English, many of them rare first editions with personal dedications from the author, translations into numerous languages including Japanese, letters received from Thomas Mann in the last six years of his life and those from various members of his family, a great many personal letters from his circle of friends, the final version of his introduction to this writer's *Fifty Years of Thomas Mann Studies,* and a pictorial record of Mann's life. Of his contemporaries there are letters and cards from such men as Francis Biddle, Benedetto Croce, Albert Einstein, Felix Frankfurter, André Gide, Hermann Hesse, Erich von Kahler, Hans Reisiger, Jules Romains, and Albert Schweitzer, to mention only a few.

Also represented are documents from Mann's bitter enemies and critics such as Manfred Hausmann, Kurt Hiller, Bernd Isemann, and two well known members of the so-called "Inner Emigration," Walter von Molo and Frank Thiess. A number of unpublished letters and cards from Thomas Mann to other recipients are also in the collection.

Special efforts are being made to concentrate here what should amount to the complete record of critical, secondary literature about Mann, published as well as unpublished, from all parts of the world. Thus, all items from the first volume of the bibliography of criticism as well as the more than 4,000 items from the second volume should be represented among his materials. It is the writer's purpose that this collection, supplemented, of course, by the others described later in this paper, should serve as the basis for writing a "History of Thomas Mann Criticism." This gigantic task intends to bring order into presently prevailing chaos by a systematic review and analysis of all serious studies about Mann. Organized along the same lines as the Center of Maugham Studies, this writer's Thomas Mann Archive is one of six special research collections of contemporary writers

currently being built at the University of Pittsburgh as part
of a major effort toward the bibliographical control of the
vast field of modern German literature.

EUROPE

A survey of Mann's manuscripts located in Europe
should rightly start with his birth place, the old Hanseatic
city of Lübeck, which is so rich in memories of her great son.
The materials now assembled here are distributed in three
historic buildings in the heart of the city. There is, first of
all, the "Buddenbrook House," located on Mengstrasse 4.
Acquired by Mann's ancestors in 1841, it served as the family
residence until 1881, when Senator Mann built his own house
on Beckergrube 52. Severely destroyed during the 1942 air
raids, only the façade has survived, while the rest of the
building has been entirely reconstructed. In the entrance hall
a bronze plaque of Thomas Mann and a copy of the Nobel
diploma remind the visitor of the author who spent his youth
in this building.

Nowhere can one breathe so well the atmosphere and
spirit of the old Lübeck merchant-aristocracy as in the
"Schabbel-House," also located on Mengstrasse. Dating to
the 14th and 15th centuries and completely restored after its
destruction in 1942, it is now owned by the merchant's association and, since 1962, has been the seat of a small Thomas
Mann Museum. There is a permanent exhibit of portraits,
autograph letters, documents relating to Mann and his ancestors, and, as a gift from the author's widow, the old Family
Bible often mentioned in *Buddenbrooks*.

A truly impressive, rapidly growing Thomas Mann collection was built up in recent years by the City Library

(*Stadtbibliothek*) of Lübeck with the active support of the Dr. Heinrich Dräger Foundation. Apart from Mann's printed works, the collection is rich in manuscript materials, including one early essay, "Das Ewig-Weibliche" (1902), and a large number of letters. There is most of the correspondence with Dr. Paul Amann, in addition to some 164 manuscript pages written by Thomas Mann to his lawyer and friend, Dr. Maximilian Brantl between 1909 and 1951, some 40 letters to Dr. Käte Hamburger (between 1932 and 1955) and 17 letters to Dr. Walter A. Berendsohn. Individual letters to Mann's former classmate at the *Katharineum*, Felix Neumann, to S. Fischer, Moritz Heimann, Frank Mockrauer, Oskar A. H. Schmitz, Dr. Guido Schoenberger, and to Dr. Alfons Spielhoff round out the collection.

Another major center for the study of Thomas Mann, open to all interested students, is located in the Schiller Nationalmuseum in Marbach on Neckar. Here we find his autograph manuscript of "Nachruf auf Bruno Frank" (1945), the complete correspondence from 1910 to 1955 with Ernst Bertram (256 items in Thomas Mann's own hand), and finally some 70 unpublished letters to various recipients including Erwin Ackerknecht, Hermann Beuttenmüller, Max Herrmann-Neisse, Wilhelm Hoffmann, Arthur Kutscher, Emil Ludwig, Erich Pfeiffer-Belli, Anna and René Schickele, and Herbert Steiner. Thus, Marbach has succeeded in the past two decades in building up a strong Thomas Mann collection of both manuscripts and printed works which is worthy of the Museum's tradition and plays a prominent role along with similar archives in the study of Mann's great contemporaries, Gerhart Hauptmann, Rainer Maria Rilke, and Hermann Hesse. Dr. Bernhard Zeller, the Museum's director, as well as Dr. Paul Raabe, its Chief Librarian, are to be congratulated on their truly remarkable accomplishments in creating these collections within the framework of the "Deutsche Literatur-Archiv."

Apart from these two major collections, a number of smaller ones are located in public institutions. The City Library in Aachen received, as part of the Josef Ponten literary estate, several dozens of letters from Thomas Mann. The Freie Deutsche Hochstift in Frankfurt on the Main possesses the manuscript of Mann's remarks spoken at the dedication ceremonies in the Goethehaus in 1932, as well as several letters addressed to Otto Hauer, Ludwig Fulda, and Richard Tauber. The City and University Library of Hamburg possesses in its Dehmel-Archive, 12 letters and three cards to Richard and Ida Dehmel. After the war the University Library of Tübingen received the manuscript of "Der Literat," formerly owned by the Prussian State Library in Berlin.

Few cities are as rich in Thomas Mann documents, above all autographs, as is Munich which, for almost four decades (1894-1933), served as the author's permanent residence. While the Bavarian State Library has but a few Thomas Mann letters, there is an important collection of his manuscripts in the City Library. Among its treasures is the original manuscript of the Renaissance drama *Fiorenza* (1905), Mann's introduction to a Russian anthology entitled "Zum Geleit," and his speech in memory of Berthold Litzmann (1926). Finally, there are more than 150 autograph letters, some 120 of them addressed to Kurt Martens, a friend from his youth in Munich, 26 to Alfred Neumann, seven to Josef Ruederer, and five to Regina Ullmann.

Until Mann's emigration from Nazi Germany in 1933, practically all existing manuscripts were in the author's home in Munich, beginning with his first story, "Gefallen" (1894) and including, in addition to his published works, a large

number of unpublished letters to his wife Katja, dating back
to the time of their engagement in 1904. Among them were
numerous letters written by her from a Swiss sanatorium
where she was forced to stay for extended periods in the years
immediately preceding World War I and which exercised a
strong influence on Mann's composition of *Der Zauberberg*.

Some of the manuscripts—above all that of the Joseph
Novels, on which Thomas Mann was working—were rescued
in 1933 by his courageous daughter Erika from their Munich
villa, already guarded by the Gestapo. But the bulk of the
manuscripts of his completed and published works as well as
all the unpublished letters remained in the house, and were
later moved to the office of Mann's attorney in Munich, Dr.
Valentin Heins, and are feared to have been lost during the
war.

In a survey such as this, it is important to point out those
individuals who, although not collectors, do own autographs
or have been entrusted with their care. A few years after Dr.
Heins had received Mann's manuscripts for safekeeping, he
refused to turn them over to an emissary with a personal
handwritten authorization from Thomas Mann, and later he
assured the author's family that all these precious items had
been destroyed as a result of the air raids on Munich. At the
time of the invasion of Europe by Allied forces, Thomas
Mann expressed his anger in a letter to the Librarian of Yale
University, hoping "to be able soon to send an Allied lieu-
tenant with five men to the faithless lawyer who always kept
the manuscripts from me." A full report about this sad chapter of the fate of the self-exiled poet's property has been given
by Erika Mann.

It is not known exactly how many Thomas Mann manuscripts have found their way into Austria, but the existence
of at least two can be accounted for in the Austrian National

Library in Vienna. In the Stefan Zweig Collection we find the manuscript of Mann's early story "Die Hungernden," which the author had presented to Stefan Zweig, an avid collector of manuscripts. And among the papers of Bruno Walter there is the original of Mann's address honoring the great friend and conductor on his 70th birthday.

One city outside the German-speaking countries deserves to be mentioned in this paper: the capital of Czechoslovakia. Two manuscripts by Mann have found their way into Prague's Naródni Museum, that of an early story, "Luischen," as well as a corrected typescript of his "Amsterdamer Tischrede."

Among private collections of Thomas Mann in Germany, none can compete with those of Dr. Hans-Otto Mayer and Dr. Herbert Rauter. Dr. Mayer's materials are located in a special room in a private residence in Düsseldorf and contain some 1,500 books, 460 complete issues of journals, and approximately 1,200 newspaper and periodical articles. Apart from 12 autograph letters and cards from Thomas Mann, one original manuscript is to be found here, Mann's "Erklärung zu der Aufforderung der 'Gesellschaft zur Bekämpfung der Unmenschlichkeit,' Buchenwald zu besuchen."

Mann's works are well represented in all individual first and subsequent editions, collected works and special limited or de luxe editions signed by the author. There are also 300 volumes of translations representing 22 different languages.

This collection, which also includes the writings of Heinrich, Klaus, Erika, Monika, Golo, and Julia Mann, is especially rich in critical studies, and there is also an impressive record of over 100 photographs and other illustrations. The materials, totalling about 4,000 items, are easily accessible by means of a comprehensive author and subject index and contain almost everything ever written and published by Thomas Mann. They have been invaluable to this writer in preparing the second volume of his Bibliography of Thomas Mann Studies.

Probably the most precious bibliophile's collection in Germany is owned by Consul Herbert Rauter, an industrialist in Säckingen. Surrounding Mann's bust by the Stuttgart artist W. Hager, one may find all his works in first editions with only two exceptions *(Tristan* and *Fiorenza),* a large number of beautifully bound limited editions, the various collected works, as well as Mann's publications in miscel laneous newspapers and periodicals.

Not only are all German editions eagerly collected, but all foreign translations as well, especially from Italy, France, and the English-speaking world. Also included are Mann's innumerable scattered announcements of new books to be found in dealers' catalogues or on dust jackets, in which he recommends the works of other writers to the reading public.

Most valuable in this collection are, of course, the manuscripts. Dr. Rauter possesses the film manuscript of "Tristan und Isolde" from the year 1923, four pages of text in Mann's own handwriting accompanied by a letter of October 17, 1923, to his brother Viktor dealing with the latter's work in the movie industry. There is also the original 20-page manuscript of the essay on Chamisso from June 1911, the original of "Ein Schriftstellerleben" (1924), and a three-page manuscript entitled "Fragment als Beitrag" (1927). The pride of the collector, however, are some 75 autograph letters, most of them addressed to Maximilian Harden and to Moritz Heimann.

Apart from the two outstanding private collections of Dr. Mayer and Dr. Rauter, a number of smaller ones in private hands deserve our attention. For almost 40 years Dr. Hans Bürgin of Kappeln/Schlei has been collecting the literary production not only of Thomas Mann, but of the entire Mann family. His materials miraculously survived World War II and have served as the basis for his *magnum opus* entitled *Das Werk Thomas Manns,* a bibliography of primary works compiled in cooperation with Walter A. Reichart and Erich Neumann. Bürgin's collection includes over 500 books, more than 300 whole issues of newspapers and periodicals, some 2,000 clippings arranged under various subject headings, more than 50 autographs, and a great many photocopies of rare printed materials. Two other private collections, both formed after the war and consisting primarily of printed items by and about Mann which are now hard to locate, are owned by Mr. Heinz Saueressig of Biberach/Riss, and Dr. Hans Waldmüller of Darmstadt.

Finally, two of Thomas Mann's friends treasure manuscripts presented to them by the author himself, but are not, otherwise, to be called collectors: Frau Kitty Neumann of Munich, the widow of Alfred Neumann, has the manuscript of Mann's "Nachruf," his last tribute to her husband. Mr. H. B. Dellefant of the same city received from the author the original manuscript of his speech delivered at ceremonies in connection with the award of the Order of Oranje-Nassau, on July 1, 1955 by Queen Juliana of the Netherlands.

Mention must also be made of several publishers who became personal friends of Mann. There is, first of all, Dr. Gottfried Bermann-Fischer, for more than 30 years director of the S. Fischer Verlag in Frankfurt. In spite of numerous losses during his long exile from Germany, he still owns the complete correspondence to him from Mann for the years 1932–1955. On his 60th birthday, Frau Katja Mann presented to him the original manuscript of the essay "Die

Erotik Michelangelos." Other unpublished materials, mostly letters, are to be found in the archives of Tor Bonnier of Stockholm, Dr. Martin Flinker of Paris, and Mrs. Emmie Oprecht of Zurich.

Ten years ago, on the occasion of Mann's 80th anniversary, the Deutsche Akademie der Wissenschaften zu Berlin founded, as part of its Institute for Germanic Language and Literature, a special Thomas Mann Archive. In March 1955, the Academy announced that its scholarly activities would be in the hands of a committee of literary historians elected from both parts of Germany. In the past decade, a number of foreign Thomas Mann scholars have been invited to join this group, which is charged with the responsibility of preparing as their ultimate goal, the publication of a complete historical-critical edition of everything Thomas Mann has ever written. The man to whose vision and enthusiasm the establishment of this archive is largely indebted is Erich Neumann, who had known Mann since 1924 and has long been familiar with the vexing problems of textual criticism and the *Verwilderung* (corruption) of Mann's printed texts. In one novel alone, *Lotte in Weimar,* he counted and corrected no less than 1450 misspellings. No wonder that Thomas Mann affectionately referred to him as *mein Wortgetreuer* and that he was entrusted with the responsibility for establishing a reliable text of Mann's writings.

The original manuscript of Mann's lecture on Goethe, delivered in Weimar and Frankfurt in 1949, is in the private collection of Georges Motschan of Basel, to whom the author presented it after their trip to the *Deutsche Demokratische Republik,* and the same collector possesses the corrected typescript of an unpublished address delivered by Thomas Mann during a banquet given in his honor by the City of Weimar.

A number of autographs by the author, including the manuscript of his great essay "Gothe und Tolstoi" (1922), are believed to be in the private autograph collection of Dr. Louis Glatt of Geneva, and in nearby Cologny, in the Bibliotheca Bodmeriana, Dr. Martin Bodmer possesses the 558-page manuscript of the Goethe novel, *Lotte in Weimar* (*The Beloved Returns*).

At the time of Mann's death in August, 1955, the bulk of his manuscripts, valued at about $100,000, was in his home in Kilchberg near Zurich. For the following two months, attempts were made in the United States to secure his entire literary estate, along with his personal library and the furniture of his last study. These efforts, however, were soon thwarted by the announcement that all these items had been presented by his heirs to the Swiss Institute of Technology in Zurich which promised to set up a special Thomas Mann Archive.

Of all places in Europe where Mann's manuscripts are being collected, this Archive is by far the most important. In August, 1955, his family first expressed a desire to leave to posterity *als unteilbares Gut* all of the author's papers and to present them to the Eidgenössische Technische Hochschule in Zurich, which, a few months before, had awarded him an honorary degree as doctor of natural sciences. Inasmuch as Mann had made no decision in his will about the future of his manuscripts, it was entirely up to his wife and children to reach an agreement satisfactory to them as his heirs. The document legalizing the transfer of his papers to the Swiss Federation is dated June 11, 1956, and on October 31 of that year, Thomas Mann's manuscripts, his library, and the furniture of his Kilchberg study became a part of the Institute's Library. Thus, the Thomas Mann Archive came into being according to the wishes of the author's heirs, who wanted it to be more than just a final tribute to his memory. Above all, it was to be the center for all aspects of Thomas Mann scholarship, where all the documents concerning his life and career would be collected. But the bequest to the only Federal institution of higher learning in Switzerland had still another purpose. It was to symbolize the gratitude Thomas Mann had felt for the hospitality which that country had twice offered him and his family, and was meant as an expression of appreciation and a feeling of *Zugehörigkeit* and *Verbundenheit* of his heirs, who continued to make their home in Switzerland.

During the first four years of the Archive's existence, its materials were housed in a provisional environment in the Library of the Institute of Technology, and although its quarters were crowded and working space was limited, visitors were freely admitted and a few *bona fide* scholars were privileged to pursue their studies on Thomas Mann. With its final move in February, 1961, however, a new phase in the history of the Archive began. The "Obere Schönenberg" or "Bodmerhaus" with its long literary tradition is a 300-year old Patrician villa adjoining the University of Zurich. A memorial plaque above its entrance door recalls the names of former inhabitants and visitors intimately connected with German literature. In the 18th century, when Johann Jakob Bodmer lived there for 44 years, it became a center of literary and cultural life; in 1750, Klopstock came to it for several weeks as Bodmer's guest, and Goethe himself visited it twice with his friends Count Stolberg (1775) and Duke Karl August (1799). In the last century, Gottfried Keller spent part of his youth in it as an apprentice to the painter Ludwig Vogel. In 1911, it became the property of the Canton of Zurich.

Until 1961, the direction of the Archive was entrusted
to the Director of the Library of the Federal Institute of
Technology, Dr. Paul Scherrer. A Germanist by training and
a former student of Fritz Strich, Franz Muncker and Carl
von Kraus, he worked in close cooperation with a supervising
committee or *Aufsichtskommission* under the chairmanship
of Richard Schweizer, and with the Thomas Mann Society
in Zurich, which was formed to support the activities and
acquisitions of the Archive and which counts a number of
Americans among its members. Some months after its
move, in February 1961, into the Bodmerhaus, the Archive
announced the appointment of a new curator, Dr. Hans
Wysling. At the same time it became an independent division of the Eidgenössische Technische Hochschule and is no
longer part of its Library.

The development and growth of the collection in Zurich
is truly amazing and can best be illustrated by mentioning
the acquisitions of a record year such as 1960: a total of 5,668
items, of which 1,454 were books and pamphlets, 84 manuscripts, 466 letters, the rest photostats, film-strips, microfilms,
newspaper clippings, graphic materials, tape recordings,
medals, and memorabilia of all sorts. Considering the
Archive's modest beginnings, it is hard to visualize how
much has been accomplished in a relatively short period.
At the time of the move into its present quarters, it possessed
no less than 331 original autograph manuscripts, as well as
266 typescripts, often with autograph corrections in Mann's
own hand. All of these typescripts represented works whose
originals are no longer extant. There were also eight manuscripts in photocopy. Moreover, the Archive possessed a total
of 2,613 letters, 1,638 of which are by Thomas Mann, 829
addressed to him, and the rest received by other members of
his circle.

The bulk of Mann's personal library is now in the Zurich Archive, where it is growing steadily due to additional bequests from his estate, presented by his heirs. Altogether, it now amounts to 2,762 volumes, many of which contain marginal notes in pencil. Through the serious losses in Germany his original library was greatly reduced, and his subsequent moves to Zurich, Princeton, and California resulted in further losses. An invaluable tool for researchers, the only existing copy of a hand-written catalog of his library made in the summer of 1925 in his home in Munich by Miss Ida Herz, was lost in Germany. In an attempt to fill the many gaps, the Archive has started a special working collection of materials necessary for any serious researcher. The various editions of Mann's writings, reference works, dissertations, all published as well as unpublished studies, essays, periodical articles, newspaper clippings, and photographs are systematically collected, in addition to every item in which references to Thomas Mann are to be found. Antiquarians and bookdealers all over the world are constantly looking for materials to supply to the Archive, and its present collection of books and pamphlets by and about Mann undoubtedly represents the most comprehensive library of its kind.

It is not yet possible to present a detailed inventory of the treasures assembled in Zurich. To mention but a few items, there are fragments from the manuscripts of *Buddenbrooks, Tonio Kröger,* and *Königliche Hoheit,* preliminary notes, working materials for many of his books, and finally, the complete holograph manuscripts of *Joseph in Ägypten, Joseph der Ernährer, Doktor Faustus, Der Erwählte, Die Entstehung des Doktor Faustus, Die Betrogene,* and *Felix Krull.* Of unique importance are Mann's notebooks, beginning in 1893, which are open to selected researchers. The same, however, cannot be said of the diaries beginning with his exile in 1933. There are four sealed packages preserved in a fireproof steel cabinet, which bear the inscription in Thomas Mann's own hand: "Without literary value." According to his will, these *Tagebücher* must not be opened before August 12, 1975, twenty years after his death, and before they become available, together with the bulk of his letters, no truly definitive biographical study can be undertaken.

No one can be more aware of the invaluable assistance provided by the Archive to researchers than this writer. From personal experience gained over the past nine years since its humble beginnings, he can testify to the splendid co-operation granted by the Archive's director and his indefatigable librarians, to visitors in search of specific information or materials. American admirers and friends of Thomas Mann have every reason to thank them for their efforts and will, I am sure, show their appreciation by more active support of this unique research center.

It is a pleasure for this writer to express his deep appreciation to all those friendly helpers both in the United States and abroad who have assisted him in his efforts to locate Thomas Mann's original manuscripts. He sincerely hopes that this world-wide search may continue, and that its results will contribute toward the publication of that comprehensive critical-historical edition of Mann's works for which all his admirers have so long been waiting.

Thomas Mann Studies

Volume II

1. Abbate, Michele. "Felix Krull," *Gazzetta del Mezzogiorno,* October 22, 1963, p. 3.
2. Abbé, Derek Maurice van. "Th. M.," in his *Image of a People,* pp. 161-171. London: G. Harrap, 1964.
3. Abbeg, Emil. "Oedipus in Indien," *NZZ,* Vol. 172, No. 706 (April 3, 1951), Bl. 1. [*Der Erwählte*]
4. Abendroth, Walter. "Th. M.," in his *Hans Pfitzner,* pp. 222-223 et al. München: Langen-Müller, 1935. [With a letter from Th. M.]
5. Abusch, Alexander. "Th. M. und das freie Deutschland," *Sinn und Form: Sonderheft Th. M.,* 1965, pp. 61-73.
6. Ackermann, Paul Kurt. "Introduction," in his *ed.* of Th. M., *Bekenntnisse des Hochstaplers Felix Krull,* pp. v-ix. Boston: Houghton Mifflin [1958]
7. ———. "Comments on 'Joseph und seine Brüder' in Some Unpublished Letters from Th. M. to René Schickele," *Monatshefte,* 54 (April-May, 1962), [197]-200.

7a. Adams, J. Donald. "Th. M. and the Mountain," in his
    Speaking of Books — and Life, pp. 168-170. New York: Holt
    [1965] [*The Magic Mountain*]

8. *Admoni, Vladimir G., [and] Tamara I. Silman. *Th. M.*
    Leningrad: Izd. 'Sovetskij pisate,' 1961. 352 pp. [In Russian]
    Reviews: Pietsch, #2,550, Rotsch, #2,777

9. ———., [and] Tamara I. Silman. "Wandlungsmöglichkeiten
    der Erzählweise Th. M's," in G. Wenzel, item #3,472,
    pp. 120-130.

10. Adorno-Wiesengruhd, Theodor. "Aus einem Brief über 'Die
    Betrogene' an Th. M.," *Akzente*, 2 (June 1955), 284-287.

11. ———. "Zu einem Porträt Th. M's," *Neue Rundschau*, 73
    (1962), 320-327. Also in *Frankfurter Allgemeine Zeitung*,
    No. 127 (June 2, 1962), Feuilleton, and in his *Noten zur
    Literatur III*, pp. 18-29. [Frankfurt a. M.] Suhrkamp [1964]
    [Subtitle: "Ansprache gehalten bei der Eröffnung der Th. M.-
    Ausstellung in Darmstadt am 24. März"] Also in Italian, "Per
    il ritratto di Th. M.," *Questo e altro*, No. 2 (1963), pp. 101-
    105. Translated into French by Jacques Chavy, "Portrait de
    Th. M.," *Mercure de France*, Vol. 4, No. 1206 (April 1964),
    pp. [590]-569.

12. Agoston, Gerty. "Der unerschöpfliche Born: Zu Th. M's
    neuem Roman 'Der Erwählte,' " *Staats-Zeitung und Herold*,
    May 13, 1951, Sonntagsblatt, p. 6 C.

13. Ahl, Herbert. "Literarische Marginalien: Zu Th. M's 80.
    Geburtstag," *Diplomatischer Kurier*, 4 (1955), 398-400.

14. ———. "Literarische Marginalien: Th. und Klaus M.,"
    Diplomatischer Kurier, 5 (1956), 605-608.

15. ———. "Genie ist Fleiss: Th. M.," in his *Literarische
    Porträts*, pp. 280-292. München: A. Langen [1962]
    [*Felix Krull*]

16. Ahlberg, Alf. "Th. M's tal till Europa," *BLM*, 7 (December
    1938), 753-761. [*Achtung, Europa!*]

17. Ahnlund, Knut. "Doktor Faustus," *Svenska Dagbladet*, April
    27, 1963. [Review of G. Bergsten, item #292]

18. Aiken, Conrad. "Th. M.," in his *Reviewer's ABC*, pp. 288-290. New York: Meridian Books, 1958. [Reprint of I, item #2017. Review of Th. M's *Children and Fools*]

19. Airó, Clemente. "Th. M.," *Espiral*, Vol. 6, No. 58 (August 1955), pp. 4, 18. [80th birthday]

20. Aita, Antonio. "Th. M.," in his *Comentarios*. Buenos Aires: Pesce, 1938.

21. ———. "Th. M.," in his *Cuatro Ensayos*, pp. 127-130. Buenos Aires [Pesce] 1939. [Th. M. as a novelist]

22. Albérès, R. M. "Th. M." in his *Geschichte des deutschen Romans*, pp. 236-238 et al. Düsseldorf: E. Diederichs, 1964.

23. Albrecht, Gertrude. "Heimatrecht für die Brüder Mann," *NDL*, 5 (1957), 157-159. [Heinrich and Th. M.]

24. ———. "Zásluhy obce Prosece o německou literaturu," *CpMF*, Vol. 39, No. 1 (1957), pp. 63-64.

25. ———. "Th. M. —,Staatsbürger der Tschechoslowakei," in G. Wenzel, item #3461, pp. 118-[129] [Based on the author's unpublished study "Die Tschechoslowakei als Asyl der deutschen antifaschistischen Literatur"]

26. Aler, Jan. "Dr. Faustus Redivivus," in *Vijf eeuwen Faust*, pp. 187-203. Den Haag: Servire, 1963.

26a. ———. "De mythe in de hedendaagse kunst," in *Mythe en realiteit*, pp. 76-81. Amsterdam: Wereldbibliotheek, 1963. [*Der Zauberberg*]

27. Alker, Ernst, "Th. M.," in his *Die deutsche Literatur im 19. Jahrhundert*, pp. 785-794. Stuttgart: Kröner [1961]

28. Allemann, Beda. "Th. M.," in his *Ironie und Dichtung*, pp. 137-175. [Pfullingen] Neske [1956]

29. Altenberg, Paul. "Th. M's letztes Werk," *Schweizer Monatshefte*, 36 (January 1957), 790-797. [*Felix Krull*]

30. ———. "Nachwort," in Th. M., *Bekenntnisse des Hochstaplers Felix Krull*, pp. 421-431. Zurich: Büchergilde Gutenberg, 1957.

31. ———. "Th. M's 'Lotte in Weimar,' " *Schweizer Monatshefte*, 37 (August 1957), 409-415.

32. ———. "Bücher von und über Th. M.," *Schweizer*
      Monatshefte, 38 (January 1959), 898-899. [Review of
      Nachlese, and H. M. Wolff, #3,532]

33. ———. "Die Joseph-Romane," *Schweizer Monatshefte*, 40
      (April 1960), 84-91.

34. *———. *Die Romane Th. M's: Versuch einer Deutung.* Bad
      Homburg: Gentner [1961] 373 pp.
      Reviews: Endres, #777 — Haile, #1,154 — Hellmann,
      #1,298 — Konrad, #1,767 — Koopmann, #1,770 —
      Leibrich, #1,902 — Lindsay, #1,972 — Poschmann, #2,593a
      — Remak, #2,684 — Storck, #3,163 — Wenzel, #3,460.

35. Alter, Robert. "Heirs of the Tradition," in his *Rogue's*
      Progress: Studies on the Picaresque Novel, pp. 106-132.
      Cambridge: Harvard University Press, 1964. [On Th. M. *see*
      esp. pp. 125-129]

36. Altmann, Rüdiger. "Felix oder der letzte Europäer," in his
      Die neue Gesellschaft, pp. 16-21. Stuttgart: Vorwerk [1958]
      [*Felix Krull*]

37. Amado, Jorge. "La madre brasiliana di Th. M.," *Il*
      Contemporaneo, Vol. 2, No. 23 (June 4, 1955), p. 9.

38. Amadori, Maria Grazia. "I due volti di Th. M.," *Fiera*
      Letteraria, Vol. 16, No. 38 (1961), pp. 4, 6.

39. Amann, Paul. "Deux romanciers allemands: E[mil] Strauss et
      Th. M.," *L'Effort Libre*, 1 (September 1912), [513]-540.

40. Améry, Jean. "Der Zauberer," in his *Karriere und Köpfe*,
      pp. 71-76. Zurich: Thomas 1955.

41. Amoroso, Ferruccio. "Appunti sulla poesia di Th. M.," *Ponte*,
      11 (June 1955), 878-887.

42. Amory, Frederic. "The Classical Style of 'Der Tod in
      Venedig,' " *MLR*, 59 (July 1964), 399-409.

43. Amrein, O. "Aus den 'Zauberbergen,' " *Münchner Medizinische*
      Wochenschrift, No. 21 (1928), pp. 908-916.

44. Amunategui, Francisco. "Th. M.: La Mort à Venise," *La Revue*
      Nouvelle, Vol. 2, No. 13 (December 15, 1925), pp. 45-48.

45. Anders, Hellmuth. "Adrian Leverkühn: Vorschau auf Th. M's
      neues Werk," *Neue Zeitung*, April 15, 1946 [*Doktor Faustus*]

46. Andersch, Alfred. "Th. M. als Politiker," *Texte und Zeichen,*
    1 (1955), 85-100. Reprinted as "Th. M. und die Politik" in his
    Die Blindheit des Kunstwerks und andere Aufsätze, pp.
    [41]-60. Frankfurt a. M.: Suhrkamp [1966] Also in French,
    "Th. M. et la politique," *Documents,* 10 (September 1955),
    1092-1108. Excerpted as "Prefazione" in Th. M., *Scritti
    Storici e Politici,* pp. [17]-30. [Milano] Mondadori [1957]
    [Italian translation by Adele Cortese Rossi] [Cf. #3,674]

47. ———. "Kulturbrief aus Rom," *Konkret,* No. 5 (May 1963),
    p. 13. [Lavinia Mazzucchetti]

48. *Anderson, Edna. *The Anticipatory Way: A Letter to Th. M.*
    [Los Angeles] Los Angeles City College, 1954. 9 pp.

49. Andrea, O. "Die Bedeutung von Krankheit und Kranksein in
    den Werken Th. M's," *Deutsches Gesundheitswesen,* 19
    (1964), 36-39.

50. Andrea Consalvo, Clara d'. "Omaggio a Th. M.," *Procelleria,*
    Vol. 3, No. 5 (September-October, 1955), pp. 1-4. [Obit.]

51. Angell, Joseph W. "The 1950 Th. M. Exhibition," *YULG,* 25
    (April 1951), 146-154.

52. Angelloz, Joseph François. "Deux grands anniversaires:
    Schiller et Th. M.," *Mercure de France,* No. 325 (1955),
    134-137.

53. ———. "Th. M.," *Larousse Mensuel,* 48 (December 1955),
    757-759.

54. ———. "La genèse d'une oeuvre romanesque: *Le Journal du
    Docteur Faustus,*" *Mercure de France,* No. 331 (June 1962),
    pp. 331-334.

55. Angioletti, Giovan Battista. "Th. M. a Palestrina," *Stampa,*
    Vol. 93, No. 51 (February 28, 1959), p. 3. Also in his *I grandi
    ospiti,* pp. 159-163. Firenze: Vallecchi, 1960.

56. Anon. "Un message de Th. M.," *Allemagne d'Aujourd'hui,*
    No. 7 (November 1954), pp. 659-662. [Concerns M's message
    on Franco-German relations. Cf. *L'Exprès,* October 23, 1954]

57. Anon. "Ein konsequenter Humanist," *Allgemeine
    Wochenzeitung der Juden in Deutschland,* Vol. 7, No. 3
    (November 7, 1952), p. 5. [Concerns interview in Munich]

58. Anon. "Unruhe des Lebens: Zum Erscheinen von Th. M's Erzählung 'Thamar,' " *Allgemeine Wochenzeitung der Juden in Deutschland,* Vol. 11, No. 16 (July 20, 1956), Feuilleton.

59. Anon. "Vom Zauberer Th. M.," *Allgemeine Wochenzeitung der Juden in Deutschland,* Vol. 11, No. 27 (October 5, 1956), Feuilleton. [*Joseph und seine Brüder*]

60. Anon. "Th. M., grand écrivain et homme libre," *Appréciation,* 45 (October 8, 1955), 1-4. [Obit.]

61. Anon. "Pour le Mérite für Gegner des Dritten Reichs," *Aufbau* (New York), Vol. 21, No. 33 (August 19, 1955), p. 2. [Awards for Th. M., Werner Jaeger and Hans Purrmann]

62. Anon. "Abschied von Th. M.," *Aufbau* (New York), Vol. 21, No. 34 (August 26, 1955), p. 4. [Obit.]

63. Anon. "Th. M.," *Befreiung,* No. 10 (1955), pp. 224-226.

64. Anon. "Th. M.-12. August: 5. Todestag," *Bibliographische Kalenderblätter,* Vol. 2, No. 8 (1960), pp. 30-41.

65. Anon. "Th. M. unterwegs," *Büchergilde,* No. 9 (September 1952), pp. 186-187. [Biog.]

66. Anon. "Th. M.: Zynismus und Anbetung," *Christ und Welt,* Vol. 4, No. 33 (August 16, 1951), p. 8. [*Der Erwählte*]

67. Anon. "Omaggio a Th. M.," *Il Contemporaneo,* Vol. 2, No. 23 (June 4, 1955), p. 1. [80th birthday]

68. Anon. "Grabow: Die Heimat der Familie Mann," *Demokrat,* September 24/25, 1954, p. 223. [Biog.]

69. Anon. "Th. M. à Paris," *L'Eclair,* 13 (January 20, 1926), 4. [*See also* Treich]

70. Anon. "Th. M. à Paris," *L'Europe Nouvelle,* 9 (February 6, 1926), 164.

71. Anon. "Weitere Ausbürgerungen; eine neue Liste," *Frankfurter Zeitung,* No. 621 (December 4, 1936), p. 2. [Loss of Th. M's citizenship and confiscation of his property in Nazi Germany]

72. Anon. "Nicht leicht zu folgen," *Gegenwart,* Vol. 9, No. 198 (January 1954), pp. 5-6. [Concerns Th. M's radio message "Sprache und Humor"]

73. Anon. "Das Dauernde und der Augenblick," *Gegenwart,* 11 (June 28, 1958), [405] 406. [Th. M.-Archive in Zurich]

74. Anon. "Tonio Kröger in der Emigration," *Geist und Zeit,* April 1937, pp. 305-306. [Concerns Th. M's *Ein Briefwechsel.* Cf. F. E. Roth, item #2,775, and Obenauer, item #2,436]
75. Anon. "Th. M. in Weimar," *Das Goethejahr 1949,* pp. 40-56. Weimar, 1950. [Biog.]
76. Anon. "Briefe von draussen — Antworten von drinnen," in Grosser, item #1,090, pp. 42-50. [Cf. I, item #1442]
77. Anon. "Th. M. à la Dotation Carnegie," *Journal des Débats,* 138 (January 22, 1926), 2.
78. Anon. "Gespräch mit Th. M.," *Komödie,* Vol. 3, No. 5 (1922), pp. 3-4. [Interview]
79. Anon. "Literary Giant: Th. M.," *MD,* 7 (January 1963), 140-144. [Biog.]
80. Anon. "A German Genius, *"Manchester Guardian,* June 6, 1955. [80th birthday]
81. Anon. "L'écrivain allemand Th. M. a fait hier une conférence à Paris," *Le Matin,* 43 (January 21, 1926), 1.
82. Anon. "Th. M. als Agitator," *National-Zeitung Basel,* Abendblatt No. 568 (December 7, 1945), p. 1. [*Deutsche Hörer*]
83. Anon. "Th. M. in der Münchner Revolution," *National-Zeitung Basel,* No. 384 (August 21, 1955). [Biog. — Politics]
84. Anon. "Th. M.†," *NDH,* No. 18 (September 1955), pp. 401-402. [Obit.]
85. Anon. "Th. M.: 6. Juni 1875-12. August 1955," *Neue Rundschau,* 76 (Summer 1965), [169] [Tenth anniversary of M's death]
86. Anon. "Th. M.-Kundgebung im Mecca-Tempel: Die Welt braucht mehr Demokratie," *Neue Volkszeitung,* Vol. 6, No. 17 (April 24, 1937), pp. 1-2. [Politics]
87. Anon. "Vom Th. M.-Archiv," *NZZ,* Vol. 184, No. 397 (February 1, 1963), Bl. 6. [Th. M.-Archive in Zurich]
88. Anon. "Mr. W. J. Turner and Th. M.," *New Statesman and Nation,* N. S., 6 (1933), 413. [Letter to the Editor in reply to a letter by Cecil Winter, item #3,506]

89. Anon. "Th. M., 80, dies in a hospital at Zurich," *New York Herald Tribune,* August 13, 1955, pp. 1, 10. [Obit.]

90. Anon. "Welcome to Th. M.: New American Citizen," *New York Post,* May 9, 1938. [Biog.]

91. Anon. "In Exile," *New York Times,* April 23, 1937. [Editorial]

92. Anon. "Th. M. at 80," *New York Times,* June 6, 1955.

93. Anon. "Th. M. dies at 80," *New York Times,* August 13, 1955, pp. 1, 13. [Obit.]

94. Anon. "Das Festmahl zu Ehren Th. M's: Die Reden der polnischen Schriftsteller," *Pologne Littéraire,* Vol. 2, No.7 (April 15, 1927), p. 2. [Biog.]

95. Anon. "Introduzione," *Ponte,* 14 (1958), 374-375. [Followed by Th. M's "Soffrendo per la Germania, 1933-1934" — *Leiden an Deutschland*]

96. Anon. "Rotarian Wins Nobel Book Award," *Rotarian,* Vol. 36, No. 2 (February 1930), p. 6. [Nobel Prize — with a message by Bruno Frank]

97. Anon. "Eine Art Nekrolog: Wer war Th. M.?" *Das Schwarze Korps,* No. 36 (July 29, 1937), p. 16. [Nazi defamation — Politics]

98. Anon. "Zur Kritik des bürgerlichen Jahrhunderts in den Werken von Heinrich und Th. M.," *Ein Sechstel der Erde,* Vol. 2, No. 5 (1953), pp. 7-10.

99. Anon. Review of H. Saueressig, #2,844, *Selecta,* No. 50 (December 1965), p. 2214.

100. Anon. "Th. M.: Zum 60. Geburtstag des grossen Dichters am 6. Juni," *Sie und Er,* No. 23 (June 8, 1935), pp. 582-583. [60th birthday]

101. Anon. "Th. M.: Der Zauberer," *Spiegel,* Vol. 8, No. 52 (December 22, 1954), pp. 32-45. [Biog.]

102. Anon. "Protokollchef Erika," *Spiegel,* Vol. 10, No. 31 (August 1, 1956), pp. 40-42. [Review of E. Mann, #2,059; Monika Mann, #2,100]

103. Anon. "Schriftsteller Th. M.," *Spiegel,* Vol. 14, No. 29 (July 13, 1960), pp. 55-56. [Concerns Flinker, #887; E. Heller, #1,278; Amann, #3,426]

104. Anon. "Th. M.: Verlorene Handschrift," *Spiegel*, Vol. 16, No. 20 (May 16, 1962), pp. 81-84. [Concerns *Briefe I*, # 2,062, and the fate of M's *Nachlass* in Munich]

105. Anon. "Wälsungenblut: Nicht die Bohne," *Spiegel*, Vol. 17, No. 35 (August 28, 1963), p. 62. [Controversy Klaus Pringsheim vs. W. E. Süskind, # 2,607-2,608; # 3,215-3,216]

106. Anon. "Erika Mann über Th. M.: *Briefe 1948-1955* und *Nachlese*," *Spiegel*, December 8, 1965. [Concerns *Briefe III*, item #2,071]

107. Anon. "Le Docteur Faustus," *La Table Ronde*, No. 28 (1950), pp. 9-28.

108. Anon. "Germany: Kultur Man," *Time*, Vol. 66, No. 8 (August 22, 1955), pp. 24-27. [Obit.]

109. Anon. "Some Recent German Literature," *TLS*, July 3, 1903. [*Tristan*]

110. Anon. "Th. M's New Novel," *TLS*, No. 1208 (March 12, 1925), p. 170. [*The Magic Mountain*]

111. Anon. "A Modern Faustus," *TLS*, Vol. 47, No. 2,402 (February 14, 1948), p. 96. [*Doktor Faustus*]

112. Anon. "Dr. Th. M.," *TLS*, Vol. 50, No. 2,602 (December 14, 1951), p. 803. [Review of Neider, I, item # 297]

113. Anon. "Dr. Mann's Fiction," *TLS*, Vol. 51, No. 2,613 (February 29, 1952), p. 160. [Review of H. Hatfield, I, item # 199]

114. Anon. "Th. M. and His Art," *TLS*, Vol. 55, No. 2,854 (November 9, 1956), p. 667. [Review of R. Hinton Thomas, item # 3,273]

115. Anon. "Mann and His Brethren," *TLS*, Vol. 57, No. 2,953 (October 3, 1958), p. 560. [Concerns E. Heller, item # 1,278, and F. Kaufmann, item # 1,683. *See also* E. Heller's reply, item # 1,280]

116. Anon. "Perpetuating Themes," *TLS*, Vol. 60, No. 3,103 (August 18, 1961), p. 545. [*Stories of a Lifetime*]

117. Anon. "The Birth of Dr. Faustus," *TLS*, Vol. 60, No. 3,117 (November 24, 1961), p. 846. [*The Story of a Novel*]

118. Anon. "Letters of a Professional Writer," *TLS*, Vol. 61, No. 3,114 (June 1, 1962), p. 388. [*Briefe I*, item #2,062]

119. Anon. "Mann's Talk," *TLS*, Vol. 62, No. 3,225 (December 19, 1963), p. 1044. [Review of *Addresses 1942-1949;* Koopmann, item #1,769; Pütz, item #2,620]

120. Anon. "Mann in America — and Switzerland," *TLS*, Vol. 63, No. 3,232 (February 6, 1964), p. 108. [Review of *Briefe II*, item #2,066, Th. M.-Faesi, item #833]

121. Anon. "Novels and Ideas," *TLS*, Vol. 63, No. 3,255 (July 16, 1964), p. 625. [Reviews of G. Brennan, item #451]

122. Anon. [R. St.] Review of H. Saueressig, item #2,844, *Zeitschrift für Ärztliche Fortbildung*, No. 10 (1965), p. 808.

123. Anstett, J. J. Review of A. Hellersberg, item #1,285, *Erasmus*, 17 (March 25, 1964), 165-167.

124. Antal, László. "Th. M.," *Dunántúl*, No. 15, pp. 47-51; No. 16, pp. 66-71; No. 17, pp. 53-55 (1956).

125. Anthes, Otto. *"Fiorenza:* Eine Erinnerung," *Lübeckische Blätter*, 67 (May 31, 1925), 404.

126. Aoki, Junzo, [and] T. Shigi. Review of K. Sato, item #2,842, *Germanistik*, 5 (April 1964), 381.

127. Aoyagi, Kenji. "Über das Problem der Parodie bei Th. M.," *Doitsu Bungaku —Die deutsche Literatur*, No. 24 (1960), pp. 14-21. [Japanese text with German resumé]

128. Aram, Kurt. "Th. M. als Schriftsteller," *Zeit* (Berlin), December 6, 1921. [*Rede und Antwort*]

129. Aramus, Rudolf. "Das Versagen des modernen Dichters: Zu Th. M's 'Joseph der Ernährer," *Die Kommenden*, Vol. 3, No. 1 (January 10, 1949), p. 5.

130. *Arens, Hans. *Analyse eines Satzes von Th. M.* Düsseldorf: Schwann, 1964. 72 pp. [Beiheft zur Zeitschrift *Wirkendes Wort*, No. 10]

131. Arias, A. Fernández. "Resulta difícil soportar el Gran Peso del Premio Nobel," *Crítica*, December 25, 1929.

132. Arnheim, Rudolf. "Th. M.," in his *Film als Kunst*, pp. 154-157 et al. Berlin: Rowohlt, 1932.

133. Arnold, Armin. "D. H. Lawrence und Th. M.," *NZZ*,
     Vol. 180, Sonntagsausgabe No. 3696 (November 29, 1959),
     Bl. 5. Also in English in *CL*, 13 (Winter 1961), 33-38.
     Revised version in his *D. H. Lawrence and German Literature*,
     pp. [49]-58. Montreal: H. Heinemann, 1963.

134. *Arnold, Ludwig. *Das Wagnererlebnis Th. M's.* Giessen:
     J. Christ, 1934. 33 pp.

135. Arnold, Maria. "Begegnung mit alten Büchern," *Wort*, 3
     (February 1938), 123-124. [*Felix Krull*]

136. Arntzen, Helmut. "Th. M's 'Buddenbrooks,' 5. Teil, 5.
     Kapitel," in his *Satirischer Stil: Zur Satire Robert Musils im
     'Mann ohne Eigenschaften,'* pp. 31-35. Bonn: Bouvier, 1960.

137. ———. "Th. M.: Der Zauberberg," in his *Der moderne
     deutsche Roman*, pp. 37-57. Heidelberg: W. Rothe [1962]

138. Arzeni, Bruno. "Introduzione," in Th. M., *Nobiltà dello
     Spirito*, pp. [xv]-xxvii. [Milano] A. Mondadori [1953]

139. ———. "Introduzione," in Th. M., *Giuseppe e i suoi fratelli*,
     pp. [xvii]-xxxv. [Milano] A. Mondadori [1954]

140. Asbeck, Leni. "Th. M. und die Blume des Bösen:
     Bekenntnisse des Hochstaplers Felix Krull als Buch und
     Film," *SZ*, 83 (1957/58), 466-468.

141. Asher, John Alexander. "Th. M's 'Unio Mystica' with
     Goethe," *PEGS*, 25 (1956), 1-20.

142. ———. "Th. M. and Goethe: A Rejoinder," *PEGS*, 26
     (1957), 92-98. *See also* H. Eichner, item #749.

143. Aspelin, Kurt. "Th. M. pardistans," *Aftonbladet*, September
     17, 1964, p. 4. [Review of H. Levander, item #1,958]

144. Attorps, Gösta. "Far och son," *Svenska Dagbladet*, February
     4, 1950. [Concerns Klaus Mann, *Der Wendepunkt*, see I,
     item #664]

145. ———. "Buddenbrooks i verkligheten," *Svenska Dagbladet*,
     August 24, 1950. [Concerns Viktor Mann, *Wir waren fünf*,
     see I, item #666. Cf. #2,106]

146. ———. "Völsungablod," *Svenska Dagbladet*, December 8,
     1958. [Concerns Th. M's shorter fiction]

147. Audiat, Pierre. "La Montagne Magique," *L'Européen*,
      August 1931.

148. Auer, Annemarie. "Auswirkungen der Oktoberrevolution in
      Th. M's Werk und Weltanschauung," *NDL*, Sonderheft,
      November 1952, pp. 173-181.

149. Augustin, Elisabeth. "Van chaos naar orde. Th. M.: *Der
      Erwählte*," *Critisch Bulletin*, 20 (April 1953), 166-771.

150. Aust, Hans W. "Th. M's Weg zur Demokratie," *Neue Welt*,
      Vol. 2, No. 13 (July 1947), pp. 76-87.

151. Avenarius, Ferdinand. "Unsere Fürsten und wir," *Kunstwart*,
      Vol. 23, No. 13 (April 1910)., pp. 7-11. [Cf. I, item #2170.
      See also F. von Schleswig-Holstein, item #2,905. Concerns
      Königliche Hoheit]

152. Ayrenschmalz, Armin. "Stirbt der Abenteuerroman aus?
      Betrachtungen über die Entwicklung der Abenteuertypen,"
      Welt und Wort, 18 (January 1963), 1-6. [*Felix Krull*]

153. Bab, Julius. "Von der Feindschaft gegen Wagner,"
      Schaubühne, 7 (September 7, 1911), 171-180. *See* esp.
      pp. 178-179.

154. ————. "Der Knabe Henoch," *Morgen*, 10 (June 1934),
      127. [*Joseph und seine Brüder*]

155. ————. "Neudeutsche Klassiker: Th. M.," *Staats-Zeitung
      und Herold*, November 23, 1947, p. 4 C.

156. ————. "Goethe und die Demokratie: Vortrag von Th. M. im
      Hunter College," *Staats-Zeitung und Herold*, May 9, 1949.

157. ————. "Th. M.: Der Zauberberg," in his *Über den Tag
      hinaus*, pp. 127-139. Heidelberg: L. Schneider, 1960.
      [Cf. I, item #2223]

158. ————. "Th. M's 'Doktor Faustus,' " in item #157,
      pp. 139-149. [Cf. I, item #2668]

159. Babler, O. F. Review of K. W. Jonas, item #1,605,
      Antiquariat, 12 (1956), 197.

160. Bach, Anneliese. "Das epische Bild im Bildungsroman von
      Goethe bis Th. M.," *GRM*, N. F., 12 (October 1962),
      371-386.

161. Bach, Hans. "Mythische Geschichte: Th. M." *Morgen*, 10 (April 1934), 46-47. [*Der Junge Joseph*]

162. Bachler, Karl. "Kunstvoll und künstlich," *Industriekurier*, October 10, 1953. [*Die Betrogene*]

163. ————. ' Th. M. und die Ironie," *Lübecker Nachrichten*, No. 116 (May 19, 1955), p. 11. Reprinted as "Th. M., der Meister der kritischen Ironie," *Weser-Kurier*, No. 127 (June 4, 1955), p. 15. [80th birthday]

164. ————. "Th. M., der Weltdeutsche," *Weser-Kurier*, No. 186 (August 13, 1955), p. 17. [Obit.]

165. ————. "Th. M's Ironie," *Westdeutsche Rundschau*, August 5, 1961.

166. Bänsch, Dieter. Review of H. Koopmann, item #1,769, *Archiv*, 199 (February 1963), 412-414.

167. Baeumler, Alfred. "Metaphysik und Geschichte: Brief an Th. M.," *Neue Rundschau*, 31 (October 1920), 1113-1129.

168. Bahr, Hermann. "Th. M.: Zum 50. Geburtstag," *Tagebuch* (Berlin), 6 (June 6, 1925), 828-831.

169. Baker, Carlos. "Education by Escapade," *Nation* (New York), 181 (October 1, 1955), 286-287. [*Felix Krull*]

170. Balan, George. "Presenţa lui Wagner in opera lui Th. M.," *Secolul XX*, No. 6-7 (June-July, 1963), pp. 39-59. [Concerns Richard Wagner and Th. M.]

171. Baldacci, Gaetano. "Th. M. inquieto profeta rifugge oggi da una 'scelta,' " *Corriere della Sera*, Vol. 79, No. 83 (April 7, 1954), p. 3. [Interview — Politics]

172. Baldauf, Anita. "Das Th. M.-Archiv," *Börsenblatt* (Leipzig), 127 (June 4, 1960), 363-364. [Archive in East Berlin]

173. Baltzer, Peter. Review of Th. M. — Faesi, Briefwechsel, item #833, *Deutsche Zeitung*, November 8, 1962.

174. ————. Review of E. Keller, item #1,696, *Bücherkommentare*, September 15, 1965, p. 126.

175. Bamm, Peter. "Der Adam der Wissenschaft," in his *Ex Ovo: Essays über die Medizin*, pp. 101-[113] Stuttgart: DVA [1961] [*Doktor Faustus*]

176. Banitz, Erhard. "Das Bild des Geologen in der schönen Literatur," *Jahrbuch des Staatlichen Museums für Mineralogie und Geologie* (Dresden), 1956/57, pp. 70-115. [*See esp.* pp. 94-99 on *Felix Krull*]

177. Bantel, Otto. "Th. M's 'Doktor Faustus' und seine Erarbeitung in der Schule," *Deutschunterricht* (Stuttgart), Vol. 16, No. 2 (June 1964), pp. [26]-40.

178. Banuls, André. "Ironie und Humor bei Th. M.," *Annales Universitatis Saraviensis*, 8 (1959), [119]-131.

179. Baranowsky, Wolfgang. "Th. M. und die Politik," *Freiheit*, December 1960.

180. Barbu, Eugen, [and] Andrei Ion Deleanu. "Serenus Zeitblom," *Sinn und Form: Sonderheft Th. M.*, 1965, pp. 134-143.

181. Barilli, Renato. "Th. M. e la tragedia dell'arte moderna," *Convivium*, 26 (1957), 89-93. [Review of Lukács, #2,031]

182. Barnasch, Hellmuth. "Th. M. im Deutschunterricht der demokratischen Oberschule," *Deutschunterricht* (Berlin), 7 (December 1954), 719-724.

183. Barski, Sergej. "Doktor Faustus: Eine sowjetische Kritik zu Th. M's Buch über den Verfall der bürgerlichen Kunst," *Neues Deutschland*, Vol. 8, No. 86 (April 14, 1953), p. 4.

184. Barth, Max. "Abschied von Th. M.: Ein unfreundlicher Kommentar zu einer unfreundlichen Erklärung," *Neue Volkszeitung*, Vol. 15, No. 37 (September 15, 1945), p. 2. [Th. M. as an emigré] [*See* comment by O. Meyer, #2,248]

185. Basler, Otto. "Goethe und die Demokratie," *National-Zeitung Basel*, Sonntags-Beil. No. 479 (October 16, 1949).

186. ———. "Fünfzig Jahre 'Buddenbrooks,'" *National-Zeitung Basel*, Sonntags-Beilage No. 473 (October 14, 1951), p. 2.

187. ———. Review of J. Lesser, I, item #1865, *National-Zeitung Basel*, No. 109 (March 8, 1953).

188. ———. "Altes und Neues von Th. M.," *National-Zeitung Basel*, Sonntags-Beilage No. 197 (May 3, 1953), p. 2.

189. ———. "Th. M's neue Erzählung: 'Die Betrogene,'" *National-Zeitung Basel*, Sonntags-Beilage No. 480 (October 18, 1953), p. 1.

190. ———. "Th. M.," *National-Zeitung Basel,* No. 1 (January 3, 1954), p. 2. [Review of H. Eichner, I, item #159. *See also* #750]

191. ———. "Th. M.: Ehrenbürger von Lübeck. Die dichterische Beseelung einer Stadt," *Sie und Er,* April 23, 1955, p. 12.

192. ———. "Th. M. zum 80. Geburtstag," *National-Zeitung Basel,* Sonntags-Beilage (June 5, 1955), p. 2. Also in G. Wenzel, item #3,453, pp. 49-55.

193. ———. "Das Werk Th. M's," *National-Zeitung Basel,* Sonntags-Beilage No. 384 (August 21, 1955), pp. 1-2. [Obit.]

194. ———. "Th. M.: *Nachlese,*" *Aargauer Tageblatt,* December 8, 1956.

195. ———. "Mystik der Gottesferne," *Der Bund; der kleine Bund,* Vol. 111, No. 253 (June 17, 1960), p. 1. [Review of A. Hellersberg, item #1,285]

196. ———. "Th. M's Briefe: Der zweite Band," *Aargauer Tageblatt,* No. 61 (March 13, 1964). [Review of item #2,066]

197. ———. "Briefe von Th. M.," *Blätter der Th. M.-Gesellschaft Zürich,* No. 5 (1965), pp. 5-15. [With text of 15 letters from Th. M. written between 1948 and 1955]

198. Bauer, Arnold. "Verbannte und Verkannte," *Aufbau* (Berlin), 1 (1946), 315-317.

199. ———. "Der fröhliche Hochstapler Felix Krull," *Berliner Morgenpost,* October 31, 1954. [*Felix Krull*]

200. *——— *Th. M.* Berlin: Colloquium-Verlag, 1960. 92 pp. Reviews: Hellmann, item #1,292.

201. Bauer, H., [and] K. Rauch. "Der Humor und seine Grenzen," *Aussprache,* 3 (1951-52), 74-76 [*Der Erwählte*]

202. Baukloh, Friedhelm. " 'Buddenbrooks' und Familie Mann: *Sinn und Form* veröffentlicht ein wichtiges Dokument," *Mittag,* No. 197 (August 27, 1963). [Concerns Julia Mann, item #2,085] *See also* item #679.

203. Baum, Werner. "Th. M.: Zum 80. Geburtstag des Dichters am 6. Juni 1955," *Bibliothekar,* 9 (1955), 273-283.

204. *Baumgart, Reinhard. *Das Ironische und die Ironie in den Werken Th. M's.* München: Carl Hanser [1964] 131 pp.

[Rev. version of Ph. D. diss., Freiburg i. Br., 1953]
Reviews: Dickson, #669 — Hatfield, #1,232 — Müller-
Seidel, #2,324 — Richter, #2,712 — Zimmermann, #3,595.

205. ———. "Th. M. — aus der Ferne gesehen," *Spandauer
Volksblatt,* Vol. 20, No. 5,780 (June 6, 1965), p. 19.
[90th birthday]

206. ———. "Beim Wiederlesen Th. M's," *Sinn und Form:
Sonderheft Th. M.,* 1965, pp. 178-185. [Cf. #3,814]

207. Becher, Hubert. "Rückblick auf Th. M.," *SZ,* 167 (November
1960), 147-152. [Review of *Nachlese;* E. Heller, item #1,278,
and A. Hellersberg, item #1,285]

208. ———. "Th. M. als Briefschreiber," *SZ,* 170 (August 1962),
384-386. [Review of *Briefe I,* item #2,062; Bertram, item
#1,575, and Sontheimer, item #3,097]

209. Becher, Johannes R. "Glückwunsch an Th. M. zum 79.
Geburtstag," *Tägliche Rundschau,* Vol. 10, No. 129 (June 6,
1954), p. 2.

210. ———. "Ansprache . . . vor Th. M. am 14. Mai 1955 . . . in
Weimar," *National-Zeitung,* Vol. 8, No. 114 (May 17, 1955).
Also in #296.

211. ———. "Für Th. M., Ruhm der Nation und ihrer Literatur,"
Tägliche Rundschau, Vol. 7, No. 129 (June 5, 1955), p. 5.
[80th birthday]

212. ———. "Gruss an Th. M.," *Sinn und Form,* 7 (1955), 345.
Also in *Aufbau* (Berlin), 11 (June 1955), 486-487.
[80th birthday]

213. ———. "Th. M.," *NDL,* 3 (June 1955), 12. This poem also
appeared in G. Wenzel, item #3,453, p. 7, and in *Spektrum,*
11 (1965), p. [139]

214. ———. "Der deutsche Dichter unseres Jahrhunderts,"
Volksstimme (Stuttgart), August 15, 1955. [Obit.]

215. ———. "Trauer um Th. M.," *BZ am Abend,* Vol. 7, No. 190
(August 16, 1955), p. 3. [Obit.]

216. ———. "In memoriam Th. M.: Dem grossen Künstler und
Humanisten," *Sonntag,* No. 34 (August 21, 1955), p. 7.
[Obit.]

217. ———. "Hochverehrter Thomas Mann: Aus der Rede anlässlich der Überreichung des Goethepreises 1949 in Weimar," *Land und Leute,* 9 (1958), 252-253.

218. ———. "Aus dem Briefwechsel Th. M. — Johannes R. Becher," *NDL,* 8 (July 1960), 17-20.

219. ———. "Sehr geehrter Herr Thiess," letter of January 26, 1946, in Grosser, item #1,090, pp. 97-101.

220. Becher, Lilly. "Vorbild und Vollender: Th. M. zum 80. Geburtstag," *Wochenpost,* Vol. 2, No. 23 (June 4, 1955), p. 5. [80th birthday]

221. †Beck, Helmut. Epische Ironie als Gestaltungsprinzip in Th. M's Joseph-Tetralogie. Ph. D. diss., Jena, 1960. 171 pp.

222. ———. "Epische Ironie: Einige Bemerkungen zu Th. M's Joseph-Tetralogie," *Forschungen und Fortschritte,* 36 (1962), 141-143.

223. ———. "Th. M's Joseph-Tetralogie und das Gestaltungsprinzip der epischen Ironie," in G. Wenzel, item #3,472, pp. 11-106.

224. Beck Kurt. "Th. M.," in his *Prominente und unsere Zeit,* pp. 275-277. Wien: Alfa [1957]

225. †Becker-Frank, Sigrid W. Untersuchungen zur Integration der Zitate in Th. M's 'Doktor Faustus' mit Berücksichtigung der anderen späten Romane. Ph. D. diss., Tübingen, 1963. 161 pp.

226. Beharriell, Frederick J. "Freud and Literature," *QQ,* 65 (Spring 1958), 118-125. [Concerns D. H. Lawrence, James Joyce, T. S. Eliot, Kafka, and Th. M.]

227. ———. "Psychology in the Early Works of Th. M.," *PMLA,* 77 (March 1962), 149-155.

228. Beheim-Schwarzbach, Martin. "Der schwarze Schwan," *Tagesspiegel,* September 27, 1953. [*Die Betrogene*]

229. "———. "Th. M's Werk und Gesinnung," *Leserzeitschrift,* No. 5 (1961), pp. 1-8.

230. Behn, Fritz. "Th. M.," in his *Professor Behns 'Tierleben,'* pp. 8, 17. Darmstadt: Hoppenstadt [1961]

231. Behrens, Georg. "Th. M. in Zürich und Lübeck," *Lübeckische Blätter,* 119 (April 24, 1959), 81-83. [Concerns P. Scherrer, item #2,873]

Békassy, Imre. *See* Rudolf Fleischmann.

232. Belfrage, Kurt. "Th. M.," *Der Rotarier für Deutschland und Österreich*, 1 (1930), 171-172. [Address in the Stockholm Rotary Club, December 11, 1929]

233. Bellessort, André. "Un roman de Th. M.," *Le Correspondant*, September 10, 1931, pp. 769-779.

234. Belzner, Emil. "Der Brief," *Rhein-Neckar-Zeitung*, August 9, 1947.

235. ———. "Neue Studien: Gruss Th. M's an Deutschland," *Rhein-Neckar-Zeitung*, Vol. 4, No. 80 (July 13, 1948), p. 2. [*Neue Studien*]

236. ———. "Besuch aus Kalifornien," *Rhein-Neckar-Zeitung*, November 6, 1948.

237. ———. "Zum Besuch Th. M's in Frankfurt," *Rhein-Neckar-Zeitung*, July 24, 1949.

238. ———. "Ehrentag in der Paulskirche," *Rhein-Neckar-Zeitung*, July 27, 1949.

239. ———. "Goethe und Lotte," *Rhein-Neckar-Zeitung*, May 27, 1950. [*Lotte in Weimar*]

240. ———. "Gespräch in Lugano," *Rhein-Neckar-Zeitung*, October 10/11, 1953.

241. ———. "Th. M.," *Rhein-Neckar-Zeitung*, No. 188 (August 15, 1955), p. 2. [Obit.]

242. Ben-Chorin, Schalom. "Die Jahre des Exils: Th. M. zum 65. Geburtstag am 6. Juni 1940," *Hashavua*, June 7, 1940, pp. 19-20. [65th birthday]

243. Bender, Hans. "Wie in einer Glaskugel: Zum Tode von Ferdinand Lion," *Merkur*, 19 (March 1965), [298]-300. [Concerns in part his activities for Th. M's journal *Mass und Wert*]

244. ———. "Das Mass verehren, den Wert verteidigen: Th. M. und seine Zeitschrift *Mass und Wert*," *Weltwoche*, No. 1649 (June 18, 1965), p. 25.

245. Benn, Gottfried. "Th. M.," in his *Ausgewählte Briefe*, pp. 290-293 et al. Wiesbaden: Limes [1957]

246. Bennett, Joseph. "A Bourgeois Eros," *Hudson Review*, 8

(Spring 1955), 617-620. [*Felix Krull*]

247. Bense, Max. "Der Geist der Erzählung: Bemerkungen zum späten Th. M.," in his *Rationalismus und Sensibilität: Präsentationen*, pp. 36-43. Krefeld: Agis [1956]

248. *Bentmann, Friedrich. *Goethe in der Sicht Th. M's.* [Karlsruhe: Faass, 1962] 23 pp.

249. Deleted

250. Berendsohn, Walter A. "Ein Däne über Th. M.," *Litterär kritik*, 5 (March 3, 1939), pp. 5-6. [Review of Kragelund, I, #241]

251. ————. "Der Humanist Th. M.," *Freies Deutschland*, Vol. 1, No. 1 (1944), pp. 12 32.

252. ————. "Th. M.: Das deutsche Gewissen," *Politische Information*, Vol. 3, No. 19 (1945), p. 12. [*Deutsche Hörer*]

253. ————. "Th. M.: Adel des Geistes," *Erasmus* (Brussels), 1 (1947), 545-555. [*Adel des Geistes*]

254. ————. "Th. M. och humanitetens problem," *Ord och bild*, 57 (1947), 304-310.

255. ————. "Th. M. och Tredje riket," *Dagens Nyheter*, December 30, 1947. [Not identical with his 1956 article in *Värld och vetande*, #267]

256. ————. "Blå böckerna och *Doktor Faustus*," *Dagens Nyheter*, March 15, 1948. [Comparison with Strindberg's *Blaubüchern*]

257. ————. "Th. M.," in his *Martin Andersen Nexø, hans vej til verdenslitteraturen*, pp. [119]-133. Copenhagen: Gyldendal, 1948. German version entitled "Einzelschicksal und Menschenschicksal in der Literatur der Gegenwart: Th. M. und Martin Andersen Nexö," in his *Martin Andersen Nexös Weg in die Weltliteratur*, pp. 130-145. Berlin: Dietz [1949]

258. ————. "Th. M. som andens äventyrare," *Samtid och framtid*, 6 (May 1949), 219-222.

259. ————. "Th. M. og religionen," *Varlösen*, 40 (June-July, 1949), 182-185.

260. ————. "Heinrich und Th. M's jüngerer Bruder," *Argentinisches Tageblatt*, April 11, 1950. [Review of V. Mann, I, #666. See also #2,106]

261. ———. "Faustsage und Faustdichtung bis zu Th. M's 'Doktor Faustus,' " *Edda,* 50 (Spring 1951), 371-382.
262. ———. "Th. M. und Goethe," *Edda,* 54 (Spring 1955), 351-359.
263. ———. "Ansprache an Th. M. in Lübeck am 20. Mai 1955," *Die andere Zeitung,* No. 4 (June 2, 1955), p. 14. [80th birthday]
264. ———. "Th. M. och tredje riket," in #2,431, pp. 13-25.
265. ———. "Der Dichter der Humanitas ging von uns," *Hamburger Echo,* August 13, 1955, p. 6. [Obit.]
266. ———. "Zum Tode von Th. M.: Die Verantwortung des geistigen Menschen," *Die andere Zeitung,* No. 15 (August 18, 1955), p. 12.
267. ———. "Th. M. och Tredje riket," *Värld och vetande,* 6 (1956), 281-288. German version, "Th. M. und das Dritte Reich," *Das Parlament,* Beilage *Aus Politik und Zeitgeschichte,* 16 (April 18, 1956), [245]-248.
268. ———. Review of E. Heller, #1,278, *Erasmus* (Darmstadt), 12 (May 25, 1959), 275-276.
269. ———. "Th. M. zum Problem des Antisemitismus: Einleitung zur Erstveröffentlichung von Th. M's Vortrag in der Vereinigung KADIMAH," *Allgemeine Zeitung der Juden in Deutschland,* Vol. 14, No. 38 (December 18, 1959), pp. 17-19. Also in French, "Un texte inédit de Th. M.," *Evidences,* Vol. 11, No. 81 January-February, 1960), pp. 26-32.
270. ———. "Th. M's Hinterlassenschaft," *Orbis Litterarum,* 14 (1960), [215]-222. [Th. M.-Archive in Zurich]
271. ———. Review of K. W. Jonas, #1,605, and H. Bürgin, #502, *Moderna språk,* 55 (July 1961), 99-100.
272. ———. "Th. M's frühe Meisterschaft," in *Festgabe für L. L. Hammerich,* pp. [1-6] Copenhagen: Kulturmetodens Sproginstitut, 1962.
273. ———. "Bekenntnis zu Th. M.," *Lübeckische Blätter,* Vol. 123, No. 5 (March 2, 1963), pp. 67-68.
274. ———. "Th. M.: Sein Lebenswerk und seine Stellung in der Weltliteratur," *Universitas,* 18 (May 1963), 469-480.

275. ————. "Th. M's Tonio Kröger," *Lübeckische Blätter*, Vol. 123, No. 18 (November 2, 1963), pp. 253-260.

276. ————. Review of H. Stresau, #3,181, *Lübeckische Blätter*, Vol. 124, No. 1 (January 11, 1964), pp. 11-12. Also in *Orbis Litterarum*, 20 (1965), 225-227.

277. ————. "Ist Th. M. ein Gralssucher?," *MB*, Vol. 32, No. 2 (January 10, 1964), pp. 5-6.

278. ————. "Th. M's moralischer Mut," *Lübeckische Blätter*, Vol. 124, No. 5 (September 12, 1964), pp. 231-233. Also in item #284, pp. 9-19.

279. ————. Review of K. Schröter, #2,971, *Lübeckische Blätter*, Vol. 124, No. 5 (September 12, 1964), pp. 239-240.

280. ————. "Th. M's 'Bekenntnisse des Hochstaplers Felix Krull.' Struktur- und Stilstudien," *Acta Universitatis Stockholmiensis*, N. S., 2 (1964), 57-[115]

281. ————. "Th. M. erfüllt die Forderungen des Tages," *MB*, Vol. 32, No. 46 (November 13, 1964), pp. 5-6; No. 47 (November 20, 1964), pp. 5-7.

282. *———— *"Th. M's Goethe-fernstes Werk 'Doktor Faustus'*. Saltsjö-Duvnäs: Moderna språk [1964] 16 pp. (Language monographs No. 5). [Concerns G. Bergsten, item #292] Also in *Lübeckische Blätter*, Vol. 125, No. 12 (June 5, 1965), pp. 183-188; No. 13 (June 19, 1965), pp. 199-202.

283. *————. *Th. M.: Künstler und Kämpfer in bewegter Zeit*. Lübeck: Max Schmidt-Römhild [1965] 259 pp.

284. ————. "Nachwort," in his *ed*. of Th. M., *Sieben Manifeste zur jüdischen Frage, 1936-1948*, pp. 89-92. Darmstadt: J. Melzer [1966] [*See also* his "Quellennachweis und Kommentar," pp. 95-97] Reviews: Johann, item #1,596

285. Bergengruen, Werner. "Zum Tode Th. M's," in his *Mündlich gesprochen*, pp. 158-160. München: Nymphenburger Verlagsanstalt, 1963.

286. Bergenthal, F. "Faust oder Doktor Faustus?," *Theologie und Glaube*, 39 (1949), 351-357. [Goethe — *Doktor Faustus*]

287. Berger, Bertha. "Der Held des Bildungsromans —ein Exponent des bürgerlichen Verfalls und Kriegsgeschehens," in her *Der*

moderne deutsche Bildungsroman, pp. 22-27. Bern: P. Haupt,
1942. [Concerns *Der Zauberberg*]

288. Berger, Bruno. "Th. M.," in his *Der Essay: Form und
Geschichte,* pp. 90-91 et al. Bern: Francke [1964]

289. Berger, Erich. "Eine Dantestelle in Th. M's 'Doktor Faustus,' "
Monatshefte, 49 (April-May 1957), [212]-214. Also in his
Randbemerkungen zu Nietzsche, George und Dante, pp. 55-
58. Wiesbaden: Limes, 1958.

290. Bergmann, Olga. Review of E. Heller, item #1,278, *Moderna
språk,* 54 (July 1960), 88-91.

291. Bergsten, Gunilla. "Musical Symbolism in Th. M's 'Doctor
Faustus,' " *Orbis Litterarum,* 14 (1959), 206-214.

292. *———. *Th. M's Doktor Faustus: Untersuchungen zu den
Quellen und zur Struktur des Romans.* [Stockholm] Bonnier
[1963] xii, 308 pp. [Ph. D. diss., Uppsala, 1963] Translated
into German by Hannelore Zeitler. Reviews: Ahnlund, #17 —
Berendsohn, #282 — Cremer, #605 — Dickson, #668 —
Gustafsson, #1,105 — Hamburger, #1,184 — Jansson,
#1,570 — Levander, #1,957 — Olofsson, #2,458 — Schiffer,
#2,892 — J. Steiner, #3,133 — Svanberg, #3,224 —
Tracy, #3,302a — Wysling, #3,546

293. ———. "Mann och hans värld," *Upsala Nya Tidning,*
February 24, 1965. [Review of H. Levander, item #1,958]

294. Berl, Heinrich. "Der letzte Bürger in der Literatur: Th. M.,"
in his *Gespräche mit berühmten Zeitgenossen,* pp. 37-41.
Baden-Baden: Bühler, 1946.

295. Berland, Alwyn. "In Search of Th. M.," *Symposium,* 18
(Fall 1964), 215-227. [*Der Zauberberg*]

296. *Berlin. Stadtbibliothek. *Das Werk Th. M's: Ein
Literaturverzeichnis anlässlich seines 80. Geburtstags.*
[Berlin, 1955] 13 pp. Includes speech by J. R. Becher,
item #210.

297. *Berlin. Zentralinstitut für Bibliothekswesen. *Th. M.: Leben
und Werk.* [Berlin, 1955] 23 pp. Includes Arnold Zweig's
"Abschied von Th. M.," item #3,616.

298. Bermann-Fischer, Gottfried. "Vom Verlegen von Büchern," *Almanach: das 68. Jahr*, pp. 99-116. [Frankfurt a. M.] S. Fischer, 1954. [*See* pp. 107-108 on *Buddenbrooks*]

299. ————. "Zueignung: Th. M. zum 80. Geburtstag," *Neue Rundschau*, 66 (June 1955), 253-254.

300. ————. "Th. M.," in his *In memoriam S. Fischer*, pp. 81, 113 et al. [Frankfurt a. M.: S. Fischer, 1960]

301. Bernardelli, Francesco. "L'ultimo anno di Th. M.," *Stampa*, Vol. 95, No. 28 (February 2, 1961), p. 3. [Review of Erika Mann, item #2,059]

302. Bernari, Carlo. "Mann 'e' noi," *Il Contemporaneo*, Vol. 2, No. 23 (June 4, 1955), p. 8. [80th birthday]. Enlarged version under the same title in *Paragone*, Vol. 17, No. 192/12 (February 1966), pp. [39]-52.

303. Bernd, Clifford A. "Th. M's 'Meerfahrt mit Don Quichote,'" *GQ*, 38 (November 1965), 252-259.

304. ————. "Keller's Comment on the *Schimmelreiter* in Th. M's Essay *Theodor Storm*: Fact or Fiction?," *MLN*, 80 (December 1965), 635.

305. Bernhard, Georg. "Im Hause der Buddenbrooks," *B. Z. am Mittag*, No. 182 (August 6, 1913), 1. Beiblatt.

306. Bert, Jack. "Th. M's politisches Bekenntnis," *Lübecker Volksbote*, Vol. 37, No. 288 (August 10, 1930). [*Deutsche Ansprache*]

307. Bertaux, Félix. "Der Zauberberg," *Nouvelle Revue Française*, 13 (October 1, 1925), 508-510.

308. ————. "Th. M. à Paris," *Europe Nouvelle*, February 6, 1926.

309. Bertaux, Pierre. "La correspondance de deux humanistes: Th. M.-Karl Kerényi," *Critique*, March 1961, pp. 216-220. [Review of item #1,700c]

310. Bertel's, D. E. "Th. M. i Cechov," in his *Problemy meždunarodnych literaturnych svjazei*, pp. 144-161. Leningrad, 1962.

311. Bessie, Alvah C. "Th. M.: The Artist in Exile," *Brooklyn Daily Eagle*, April 18, 1937, p. C 13. [Interview-Biography]

312. Bestaux, E. "Th. M.: Prix Nobel de Littérature," *Nouveau Monde*, 11 (1932), 758-763.

313. Bethge, Hans. "Th. M's 'Fiorenza,'" *Breslauer Zeitung*, November 12, 1905. Also in *Das Blaubuch*, 1 (1906), 117-118.

314. Bettex, Albert. "Th. M.: Der Zauberberg," in his *Spiegelungen der Schweiz in der deutschen Literatur 1870-1950*, pp. 90-91, 164-166. Zürich: M. Niehans [1954] Berlin: W. de Gruyter [²1962]

315. ———. "Th. M. und Otto Flake," in item #314, pp. 182-185.

316. ———. "Th. M.," *Du*, Vol. 15, No. 6 (June 1955), pp. 15-16. [80th birthday]

317. ———. "Die moderne Literatur: Von 1880 bis zur Gegenwart," in Bruno Boesch, *ed., Deutsche Literaturgeschichte in Grundzügen*, pp. 430-433 et al. Bern: Francke, ²1961. [Cf. I, item #418]

318. Bettiza, Enzo. "L'esecrabile Naphta; i marxisti e Th. M.," *Tempo Presente*, Vol. 2, No. 3 (March 1957), [223]-228.

319. Beutner, Roland. "Th. M.," *Einheit*, No. 9 (1949), pp. 855-856.

320. Bianchi Bandinelli, Ranuccio. "Un incontro a Roma," *Il Contemporaneo*, Vol. 2, No. 23 (June 4, 1955), p. 4. Also in *Unità*, August 14, 1955. [Concerns Th. M's visit in Rome, 1953]

321. Bianquis, Geneviève. "Problèmes sociaux dans le roman allemand contemporain," *Revue des Cours et Conférences*, 39 (1938), 395-405.

322. ———. Review of F. Lion, I, item #263, *EG*, 4 (1948), 445-446. Also in *Erasmus* (Darmstadt), 3 (1950), 343. [Cf. item #1,979]

323. ———. "Th. M. et le 'Faust-Buch' de 1587," *EG*, 5 (1950), 54-59. Also in her *Etudes sur Goethe*, pp. 163-168. Paris, 1951.

324. ———. Review of H. Mayer, I, item #278, *Erasmus* (Darmstadt), 5 (1952), 238-240. [Cf. item #2,172]

325. Bie, Richard. "Der Fall Th. M.," in his *Diagnose des Zeitalters*, pp. 16-19. Weimar: Duncker [1928] [*Betrachtungen eines Unpolitischen*]

326. ———. "Die Stellung der Akademie: Th. M. und Max
     Liebermann," in item #325, pp. 121-128.
327. ———. "Die Generation der Dichter: Gerhart Hauptmann,
     Die Brüder Mann, Hanns Johst," in item #325, pp. 191-194.
328. Biedrzynski, Richard. "Heroische Passion: Die Festrede von
     Th. M. im Grossen Haus," *Stuttgarter Zeitung,* Vol. 11, No.
     105 (May 9, 1955), p. 9. [Schiller]
329. Biergann, Armin. " 'Ihr Herz ist hart geworden': Ein
     Briefwechsel um Deutschland zwischen Walter von Molo und
     Th. M.," *Kölnische Rundschau,* September 7, 1963, Feuilleton.
     [Review of Grosser, item #1,090]
330. Biermann-Ratjen, Hans. "Über Th. M.," *Volksbühne, 6*
     (January 1956), 124-129.
331. Biging, Curt. "Th. M's 'Okkulte Erlebnisse,' " *Berliner
     Volkszeitung,* Morgenausgabe, December 14, 1923.
332. Bihalji-Merin, Otto. "Faustus und Ulysses: Gespräch mit Th.
     M.," *NIN-Wochenzeitung,* August 9, 1953.
333. ———. "Geist und Persönlichkeit in der Despotie: Gespräch
     mit Th. M.," *Knjizevne novine,* Vol. 1, No. 8 (March 4, 1954).
334. ———. "Vorwort zum 'Zauberberg,' " *Knjizevnost,* Vol. 9,
     No. 1 (1954), pp. 3-22. [In German and Serbo-Croatian]
335. ———. "Vorwort zum 'Doktor Faustus,' " *Knjizevne novine,*
     Vol. 2, No. 3-4 (April 1, 1955), pp. 4, 10.
336. ———. "Th. M.: Anlässlich des Ablebens eines grossen
     Dichters," *Internationale Politik,* 6 (September 1955), 29-30.
337. ———. "Th. M. — Weltsicht und Selbstvollendung," *Sinn
     und Form: Sonderheft Th. M.,* 1965, pp. 85-111.
338. Binding, Rudolf G. "Briefe an Th. M.," in his *Die Briefe,*
     pp. 185-186 et al. Hamburg: Dulk, 1957.
339. Birnbaum, Immanuel. "Th. M. und die Münchner Revolution,"
     Süddeutsche Zeitung, No. 197 (August 20, 1955).
340. Birrer, Emil. "Zum 80. Geburtstag Th. M's: Eine Reise nach
     Lübeck," *Du,* Vol. 15, No. 6 (June 1955), pp. 3-4, 13-14.
341. Birven, Henri. "Th. M's 'Doktor Faustus' und das Faustbuch
     von 1587," *Blätter der Knittlinger Faust-Gedenkstätten und
     des Faust-Museums,* 3 (1956), 36-39. Also in his *Der*

historische Doktor Faust: Maske und Antlitz. Gelnhausen: H.
Schwab [1963] and in his *Faust im 20. Jahrhundert:
Festschrift für Karl Theens.* Knittlingen/Württ.:
Stadtverwaltung, 1964.

342. *Bitterli, Urs. *Th. M's politische Schriften zum Nationalsozialismus 1918-1939.* Aarau: Keller-Verlag, 1964. 108 pp.

342a. Bizám, Lenke. "Mythe et mysticisme: Le roman Joseph de
Th. M. et les mythes d'avant-garde," *Filológiai Közlöny,* 10
(1964), 345-370.

343. Blackmur, Richard P. "Parody and Critique: Notes on Th. M's
'Doctor Faustus,' " in *The Kenyon Critics,* pp. 180-200.
Cleveland: World [1951] Also in his *Eleven Essays in the
European Novel,* pp. 97-116. New York: Harcourt, Brace
[1964] Also under the title "Artist as Hero: A Disconsolate
Chimera," in his *The Lion and the Honeycomb,* pp. 43-50.
New York: Harcourt, Brace 1955. [Cf. I, #1173]

344. ———. "The Lord of Small Counterpositions: Mann's 'The
Magic Mountain,' " in his *Eleven Essays in the European Novel,*
item #343, pp. 75-96 [Cf. I, item #2231]

345. Blanchot, Maurice. "Le Rencontre avec le démon," in
item #1,493 pp. 83-102.

346. Blanzat, Jean. "Th. M.: Mario et le magicien," *Europe,* No. 123
(1933), p. 445.

347. Blauhut, Robert. "Wandel des Bildes von deutschen Menschen:
Zu Th. M's 'Doktor Faustus,' " *Furche,* Vol. 4, No. 24
(June 12, 1948), Beilage 'Die Warte,' p. 2.

348. Bleckmann, Theodor. "Th. M. und die Deutschen," *Vorwärts,*
Vol. 8, No. 33 (August 19, 1955), p. 11. [Obit.]

349. Blei, Franz. "Th. M.," in his *Schriften in Auswahl,*
pp. 575-576. München: Biederstein [1960]

350. Blieffert, Hans Jürgen. "Die Josephsgeschichte in Dichtung und
Wissenschaft: Eine Untersuchung zu Th. M's Josephroman,"
Zeichen der Zeit, Vol. 9, No. 8-9 (1955), pp. 304-308.

351. ———. "Humanismus und Christentum bei Th. M.," *Zeichen
der Zeit,* Vol. 11, No. 2 (1957), pp. 53-60.

352. Blissett, William. "Th. M.: The Last Wagnerite," *GR,* 35 (February 1960), [50]-76.

353. Bloch, Adèle. "The Archetypal Influences in Th. M's 'Joseph and His Brothers,' " *GR,* 38 (March 1963), [151]-156.

354. Bloch, Ernst. "Th. M's Manifest,'" *Neue Weltbühne,* 33 (September 9, 1937), 1153-1158. [*Mass und Wert*]

355. Bloch, Martin. "Keine neuen Gesichtspunkte," *Die andere Zeitung,* April 4, 1960. [Correspondence Th. M.-Amann, item #3,426]

356. Blochmann, Elisabeth. "Pessimistischer Humanismus?," *Sammlung,* 3 (October 1948), 577-583. [Th. M. and Schopenhauer]

357. Block, Paul. "Th. M. in Paris," *Berliner Tageblatt,* January 21, 1926.

358. Blöcker, Günter. "Mythos plus Psychologie," *Athena,* Vol. 1, No. 4 (1946/47), pp. 29-33. [Review of K. Kerényi, I, item #1,247. Cf. #1,700c]

359. ———. "Die Heimkehr des Romans: Gedanken über den Mythos bei Th. M.," *Das ganze Deutschland,* Vol. 7, No. 24 (1955), p. 5. Also in *Tagesspiegel,* No. 2959 (June 5, 1955), p. 5.

360. ———. "Die endgültige Gegenwart: Zum Gedenken an Th. M.," *Das ganze Deutschland,* Vol. 7, No. 34 (1955), p. 5. [Obit.]

361. ———. "Th. M. und das Theater: Zum Tode des Dichters," *Theater und Zeit,* Vol. 3, No. 1 (September 1955), pp. 1-3.

362. ———. "Th. M.," in his *Die Neuen Wirklichkeiten,* pp. 339-352. Berlin: Argon [1957]

363. ———. "Schöpfer und Helfer: Zu drei Briefbänden Th. M's," *Merkur,* 15 (April 1961), 386-389. Also in his *Kritisches Lesebuch,* pp. 130-137. Hamburg: Leibniz [1962] Shorter version, entitled "Th. M. in eigner Sache," in *Tagesspiegel,* Vol. 17, No. 4750 (April 23, 1961), p. 41. [Review of Amann, item #3,426; Bertram, item #1,575; Kerényi, item #1,700 c]

364.   ———. "Symbolisches Dasein," *Merkur,* 16 (1962),
183-184. Also in his *Literatur als Teilhabe,* pp. 276-287.
Berlin: Argon [1966] [*Briefe I,* item #2,062]

365.   ———. "Heroische Geduld," *Merkur,* 17 (1963),
1,207-1,209. Also in his *Literatur als Teilhabe,* item #364.
[*Briefe II,* item #2,066]

366.   ———. "Nach dem 'Doktor Faustus,' " *Merkur,* 19 (1965),
1207-1209. Also in his *Literatur als Teilhabe,* item #364.
[*Briefe III,* item #2,071]

367. †Blomster, Wesley Vernon. 'Wagner und kein Ende.' Richard
Wagner in the Life and Works of Th. M. M.A. thesis,
University of Colorado, 1958.

368. †———. Th. M's Commentary on His Own Works. Ph. D.
diss., University of Colorado, 1960. 356 pp.

369.   ———. "Textual Variations in 'Doktor Faustus,' " *GR,* 39
(May 1964), [183]-191.

370.   ———. Review of Th. M., *Briefe I* and *Briefe II,* items
#2,062 and 2,066, *GQ,* 37 (November 1964), 543-545.

371.   ———. Review of Th. M., *Addresses . . . Library of Congress,*
GQ, 38 (November 1965), 708-709.

371a. †Blühm, Reimund. Studien über den Beitrag Th. M's zur
Selbsterhellung des Christentums im spätbürgerlichen Zeitalter
Ph. D. diss., Greifswald, 1962.

372.   Blume, Bernhard. "Perspektiven des Widerspruchs: Zur
Kritik an Th. M.," *GR,* 31 (October 1956), 176-190. Translated
into English by H. Hatfield as "Aspects of Contradiction: On
Recent Criticisms of Th. M.," in item #1,229, pp. 155-169.

373.   ———. "Th. M's Briefe," *Stuttgarter Zeitung,* No. 22
(January 27, 1962), p. 74. [*Briefe I,* #2,062]

374.   ———. "Leiden an Deutschland: Zu Th. M's Briefen,
1937-1947," *Stuttgarter Zeitung,* No. 32 (February 8, 1964),
p. 84. [*Briefe II,* #2,066]

375.   ———. "Motive der frühen Lyrik Bertolt Brechts: I. Der Tod
im Wasser," *Monatshefte,* 57 (March 1965), [97]-112. [*See*
esp. pp. 101-102 for a comparison of B. Brecht and Th. M.]

376. Blume, Gustav. "Offener Brief an Th. M.," *DAZ*, December
     4, 1924.

377. Blumenberg, Hans. "Zauberberg und geteilte Welt,"
     Düsseldorfer Nachrichten, Vol. 76, No. 128 (June 4, 1955).
     [80th birthday]

378. Blunck, Hans Friedrich. "Grüsse Hamburger Dichter an Th.
     M.," *Hamburger Anzeiger*, No. 129 (June 6, 1925). [50th
     birthday]

379. Bo, Carlo. "Le lettere di Mann," *Corriere della Sera*, Vol. 88,
     No. 262 (November 10, 1963), p. 9. [Review of *Briefe II*,
     item #2,066]

380. †Bock, Klaus. Geschichtsbegriff und Geschichtsbild bei Th. M.
     Ph. D. diss., University of Kiel, 1959. 202 pp.

381. Bodart, R. "Marcel Proust, Th. M. et l'idée de temps,"
     Cahiers du Sud, 26 (1939), 198-205.

382. Bode, Helmut. "Th. M. und sein Werk: Zum 80. Geburtstag
     des Dichters," *Bücherschiff*, Vol. 5, No. 6 (June 1955),
     pp. 1-3.

383. Böckmann, Paul. "Die Bedeutung Nietzsches für die Situation
     der modernen Literatur," *DVJS*, 27 (1953), 78-101.

384. †Boeddinghaus, Walter. Mythos und Ironie im Werke Th. M's.
     Ph. D. diss., University of Cape Town, 1960. 395 pp.

385. Boehlich, Walter. "Der Unpolitische und der Bücherverbrenner:
     Noch einmal Th. M. als Briefsteller," *Monat*, Vol. 13, No. 150
     (March 1961), pp. 74-75, 78-80. [Review of E. Bertram,
     item #1,575]

386. ———. "Nationale Echtbürtigkeit: Th. M's Briefe, 1889-
     1936," *Frankfurter Hefte*, 17 (December 1962), 854-856.
     [Review of item #2,062]

387. ———. "Eine öffentliche Figur," *Frankfurter Hefte*, 20
     (February 1965), 137-139. [Review of *Briefe II*, item #2,066]

388. *Böhmer, Gunter. *Th. M. an seinem 80. Geburtstag:
     Malernotizen*. Konstanz: Rosgarten [1958] 21 pl. [For
     commentary by B. Zeller see item #3,580]

389. Böhmer, Jürgen. "Th. M's Briefe an Paul Amann," *Welt und
     Wort*, 16 (March 1961), 88. [Review of item #3,426]

390. Boekhoff, Hermann. "Betrachtungen eines Unpolitischen," *Westermanns Monatshefte*, Vol. 98, No. 4 (1957), pp. 88, 90.
391. Boeninger, Helmut R. "Zeitblom, Spiritual Descendant of Goethe's Wagner and Wagner's Beckmesser," *GLL*, N. S., 13 (October 1959), 38-43. [*Doctor Faustus*]
392. Böök, Fredrik. "Th. M's nya roman," *Svenska Dagbladet*, August 25, 1925. [*Der Zauberberg*]
393. ———. "Th. M.," *Svenska Dagbladet*, No. 191 (July 16, 1928). [Review of M. Havenstein, I, #201]
394. Börner, H. "Das Goethebild Th. M's," *Die Kommenden*, Vol. 9, No. 16 (1954), p. 6.
395. Böse, Georg. "Th. M. als politisches Ärgernis," *Mannheimer Morgen*, April 7, 1962.
396. *Böttcher, Kurt, ed. *Th. M*. Berlin: Volk und Wissen, 1954. 121 pp.
397. Bolz, Lothar. "Th. M.," *Nation* (Berlin), 5 (1955), 603-606. Also under the title "Sein Volk wird sein Werk vollenden: Ansprache auf der Trauerfeier der Regierung der DDR," in his *Für die Macht des Volkes und des Friedens*, pp. 19-25. [Berlin] Verlag der Nation [1959]
398. Bondy, François-Gil. "Th. M.," *Preuves*, No. 55 (September 1955), pp. 76-77. [Obit.]
399. Boni Fellini, Paola. "La 'Montagna Incantata' a Davos," *Nuova Antologia*, 95 (April 1960), [525]-536. [*Der Zauberberg*]
400. Booth, Friedrich von. "Der Meister von der Trave," *Marburger Presse*, No. 127 (June 3, 1950). [Cf. I, #858 — 75th birthday]
401. Borcherdt, Hans Heinrich. "Th. M's 'Königliche Hoheit,' " *Schlesische Heimatblätter*, 2 (1910), 316-317.
402. ———. "Das 'Vorspiel' von Th. M's 'Königliche Hoheit,' " *Wirkendes Wort*, 4 (September 1954), 359-365.
403. ———. "Gerhart Hauptmann und seine Dramen," in H. Friedmann [and] Otto Mann, eds., *Deutsche Literatur im 20. Jahrhundert*, pp. 381-404. Heidelberg: W. Rothe [⁴1961] *See* esp. pp. 381-384.

404. ———. "Das Faustproblem bei Th. M.," *Jahrbuch des Wiener Goethe-Vereins*, N. F., 65 (1961), 5-12.

405. Borgese, Elisabeth Mann. "Infanzia con mio padre," *Ponte*, 11 (June 1955), 899-902. [Translated from English by Glauco Cambon]

406. ———. "Lettera all 'Editore," *Tempo Presente*, Vol. 3, No. 3 (March 1958), pp. [219]-221. [Reply to I. Silone, #3,069, incorporated in #3,070]

407. Borgese, Giuseppe Antonio. "L'ultimo Mann," in his *Da Dante a Th. M.*, pp. [298]-305. [Milano] A. Mondadori [1958] [Cf. I, #2,876 — *Der Erwählte*]

408. Bormann, H. H. "Th. M.," *Germania*, No 34 (January 21, 1926). [Review of A. Eloesser, I, item #619]

409. Bornkamm, Heinrich. "Th. M.," in his *Luther im Spiegel der deutschen Geistesgeschichte*, pp. 95-96. Heidelberg: Quelle & Meyer, 1955.

410. Borrmann, Martin. "Th. M.," *Kölner Tageblatt*, December 23, 1916.

411. *Boss, W. *Einführung in den Roman 'Doktor Faustus' von Th. M.* Bonn: Univ.-Druckerei [1948] 31 pp.

412. Boucher, Maurice. "Lettres allemandes: L'Elu," *Hommes et Mondes*, 22 (June 1951), 143-145. [*Der Erwählte*]

413. ———. "Lettres allemandes: Le Mirage," *Hommes et Mondes*, 25 (August 1954), 145-147. [*Die Betrogene*]

414. ———. "Lettres allemandes: Les Confessions du Chevalier d'industrie Felix Krull," *Hommes et Mondes*, 26 (March 1955), 605-607.

415. ———. "En attendant un message d'espérance," in item #1,493, pp. 117-121.

416. ———. "La Montée du doute," in his *Le Roman Allemand 1914-1933 et la Crise de l'Esprit*, pp. [11]-42. Paris: Presses Universitaires de la France, 1961. [Cf. I, item #420]

417. Boulez, Pierre. "Docteur Faustus, chapitre XXII," in item #1,493, pp. 107-109.

418. Boy-Ed, Ida. "Zwei Idyllen von Th. M.," *Lübeckische Blätter*, Vol. 62, No. 25 (April 7, 1920), pp. 361-362.

419. ———. "Th. M.: Versuch einer Deutung," *Lübeckische Blätter*, 67 (May 31, 1925), 397-399.

420. ———. "Th. M.: Lübeck als Geistesform," *Zeitschrift des Vereins für Lübeckische Geschichte und Altertumskunde*, 24 (1928), 201-204. [*Buddenbrooks*]

421. Braak, Menno ter. "Maat en waarde," *Het Vaderland*, August 18, 1937. [*Mass und Wert*]

422. Brachfeld, F. Oliver. "Prólogo: Señor y Perro," in *Los Premios Nobel de Literatura*, pp. 161-167. Barcelona: Janés, 1963.

423. Braemer, Edith. "Aspekte der Goethe-Rezeption Th. M's," in G. Wenzel, item #3,461, pp. 162-195.

424. Brandell, Gunnar. "Th. M's nya roman," *BLM*, 9 (February 1940), 138-140. [*Die Vertauschten Köpfe*]

425. ———. "Th. M. som politiker," *BLM*, 11 (September 1942), 550-553. [Review of O. Holmberg, I, item #1405]

426. ———. "Th. M. ofullbordade," *Svenska Dagbladet*, October 12, 1955. [*Felix Krull*]

427. Brandenburg, Hans. "Th., Klaus und Heinrich Mann," *Eckart*, 1 (1925), 278-280.

428. ———. "Th. M.," in his *München leuchtete: Jugenderinnerungen*. München: Neuner [1953]

429. ———. "Th. M.," in his *Im Feuer unserer Liebe*, pp. 208-222 et al. München: Neuner [1956]

430. Brandstetter, Alois. Review of A. Wolf, item #3,531, *Germanistik*, 6 (January 1965), 78-79. [*Der Erwählte*]

431. Brandt, Thomas O. "Narcissism in Th. M's 'Der Erwählte,'" *GLL*, N. S., 7 (1954), 233-241.

432. ———. Review of A. Wolf, item #3,531, *GQ*, 38 (March 1965), 213-214.

433. Brann, Henry Walter. "Th. M's Humanist Mission," *Books Abroad*, 24 (Autumn 1950), 365-366.

434. ———. "Th. M. und Arthur Schopenhauer," in Arthur Hübner, ed., *Schopenhauer-Jahrbuch*, Vol. 43, pp. 117-126. Frankfurt a. M.: Kramer [1962]

435. Braun, Felix. "Zeitgenössische Bücher für Weihnachten,"
     Die lit. Welt, Vol. 2, No. 50 (1926), pp. 5-7. [*Unordnung
     und frühes Leid*]
436. ———. "Gedanken über die Kunst Th. M's," *Badische Presse*,
     July 1, 1929. Expanded version in his *Die Eisblume:
     Ausgewählte Essays*, pp. 195-200. Salzburg: Otto Müller
     [1955) Entitled "Augenblicke mit Th. M" in his *Zeitgefährten*,
     pp. 141-155. München: Nymphenburg, 1963. [Cf. I, item
     #137]
437. Braun, Frank X. "Th. M's Canine Idyl," *Monatshefte*, 49
     (April-May 1957), [207]-211. [*Herr und Hund*]
438. ———. Review of K. Weimar, item #3,435, *GQ*, 35 (May
     1962), 345. [*Tristan*]
439. Braun, Hanns. "Im Schauspielhaus: Matinée mit Th. M.,"
     Süddeutsche Zeitung, No. 242 (October 20, 1952). [*Felix
     Krull*]
440. Braun, Harald. "Naphta und Settembrini: Ost und West in
     Th. M's Zauberberg," *Eckart*, 2 (1925/26), pp. 52-54.
441. ———. "Th. M.: Mario und der Zauberer," *Eckart*, 6 (1930),
     448-449.
442. Bredel, Willy. "Wir hüten sein Vermächtnis," *Neues
     Deutschland*, Vol. 10, No. 189 (June 14, 1955), p. 4.
     [80th birthday]
443. Brehme, Siegfried. "Seine Sorge um die Menschen," *Tag*,
     June 5, 1955. [80th birthday]
444. Breitbach, Joseph. "Hommage à 'Altesse Royale,' " in item
     #1,493, pp. 59-63.
445. Breitenstein, Jørgen. "Th. M. og Kielland," *Edda*, 50 (1963),
     157-160.
446. Breiter, Emil. "Na Przyjazd Tomasza Manna," *Wiadomósci
     Literackie*, Vol. 4, No. 11 (167), March 13, 1927.
447. Bremser, Horst. "Th. M. und die Deutschen," *Rheinische
     Post*, February 3, 1962. [Review of item #3,097]
448. ———. "Ein Schweizer Idyll: Zum Briefwechsel Th. M. —
     Robert Faesi," *Rheinische Post*, January 5, 1963. [Review
     of item #833]

449. †Brener, Bernard J. The Interrelationship of Mann's Essays and
     the Fiction of Th. M. as Revealed through Selected Works.
     Ph. D. diss., New York University, 1958.

450. *Brennan, Joseph Gerard. *Th. M's World.* New York:
     Russell & Russell, 1962. 206 pp. [Cf. I, item #140. *See also*
     additional reviews of first edition: Buck, item #499; Pfeiler,
     item #2,540; Zeydel, item #3,585]

451. ———. "Th. M.," in his *Three Philosophical Novelists:
     Joyce, Gide, Mann,* pp. [113]-172. New York: Macmillan
     [1964] [See comments in item #121.]

452. Brentano, Bernard von. "Antwort an Th. M.," *Frankfurter
     Zeitung,* Literaturblatt, August 5, 1928. [Cf. I, item #1272,
     concerning Th. M's "Politische Novelle"]

453. ———. "Th. M. und Gerhard [*sic*] Hauptmann," *Allgemeine
     Zeitung. Mainz,* October 14, 1961. [About Th. M. and G.
     Hauptmann in Zurich and their unwillingness to meet]

454. ———. "Das Menschenbild in der modernen Literatur," in his
     Schöne Literatur und öffentliche Meinung, pp. 54-81.
     Wiesbaden: Limes [1962] [On Th. M's *Der Zauberberg* see
     pp. 66-69]

455. Brettschneider, Rudolf. "Die Entdeckung des 'Wälsungen-
     blut,'" *Bücherstube,* 1 (October 1920), 110-112.

456. Brewster, Robert R. Review of Thomas A. Riley, item #2,728,
     MLJ, 50 (March 1966), 181-182.

457. Brill, Hermann. "Staatsrecht und Literatur: Ein Beitrag zu
     Th. M's 80. Geburtstag," *Gewerkschaftliche Monatshefte,*
     6 (June 1965), 364-368.

458. Briner, Andres. "Wahrheit und Dichtung um J. C. Beissel:
     Studie um eine Gestalt in Th. M's 'Doktor Faustus,'"
     Schweizerische Musikzeitung, 98 (1958), 365-369. Also in
     English as "Conrad Beissel and Th. M.," *AGR,* Vol. 26, No. 2
     (December 1959-January 1960), pp. 24-25, 38. [*Doktor
     Faustus*]

459. ———. "Th. M. and *The American-German Review,*" *AGR,*
     Vol. 30, No. 3 (March 1964), p. 33. [Concerns Conrad
     Beissel in *Doctor Faustus*]

460. *Brinkmann, Karl. *Erläuterungen zu Th. M's Novellen Tristan, Tonio Kröger, Mario und der Zauberer.* Hollfeld/Obfr.: C. Bange [1962] 80 pp.

461. Brion, Marcel. "Th. M.," *Les Cahiers du Sud,* 16 (October 1929), [857]- 862. [Nobel Prize]

462. ———. "Présence du fantastique dans l'oeuvre de Th. M.," in item #1,493, pp. 49-57.

463. ———. "Th. M.," *Les Nouvelles Littéraires,* No. 1459 (August 18, 1955), pp. 1-2. [Obit.]

464. ———. "In memoriam Th. M.," *Revue des Deux Mondes,* No. 18 (1955), pp. 348-358. [Obit.]

465. ——— "Préface," in Louis Leibrich, *Th. M.,* item #1,894, pp. [7]-10. [Cf. I, item #251]

466. ———. "Préface," in Th. M., *Le Journal du Docteur Faustus,* pp. i-xvi. Paris: Plon, 1962.

467. ———. "Regard sur les lettres allemandes," *Revue des Deux Mondes,* No. 325 (March 1, 1962), pp. 123-129. [Review of *Briefe I,* item #2,062]

468. Broadhurst, Patricia. "An Old Master," *QQ,* 64 (Winter 1957/58), 625-627. [*Felix Krull*]

469. Broch, Hermann. "Philiströsität, Realismus, Idealismus der Kunst," *Brenner,* 3 (February 1, 1913), 399-415. Also in his *Gesammelte Werke,* Vol. 10, pp. 237-250. Zurich: Rhein [1961] [*Der Tod in Venedig*]

470. ———. "Brief an Elisabeth Langgässer," in his *Briefe,* pp. 315-316. Zurich: Rhein [1957]

471. Brock, Erich. "Th. M's Manifest zum Schutz der Republik," *Gewissen,* 5 (July 23, 1923). [*Von Deutscher Republik*]

472. ———. "Th. M. als Prophet des Westens," *Gewissen,* 7 (June 8, 1925). [Th. M. and Troeltsch]

473. ———. "Die Brüder Mann auf der Wallfahrt nach Europa," *Gewissen,* 8 (April 5, 1926). [Heinrich and Th. M.]

474. ———. "Th. M. zum 60. Geburtstag," *NZZ,* Vol. 156, Fernausgabe No. 958 (June 2, 1935), Bl. 4.

475. ———. "Th. M., der Bewahrer," *Thurgauer Zeitung,* Sonntagsblatt No. 128 (June 4, 1955). [80th birthday]

476. ———. "Th. M.," *Hochland,* 48 (October 1955), 79-81. [Obit.]

477. ———. "Versuch über Schiller," *Schweizer Monatshefte,* 36 (July 1956), 323-325.

478. ———. "Ein gern vergessenes Buch Th. M.'s," *Orbis Litterarum,* Vol. 13, No. 1-2 (1958), pp. 3-6. [Concerns #2,058—*Betrachtungen eines Unpolitischen*]

479. Brod, Max. "Das neue Buch von Th. M.," *Dawar,* December 27, 1940. [*Die Vertauschten Köpfe*]

480. ———. "Th. M. ben 80," *Ma' arib,* June 3, 1955. [80th birthday]

481. Brome, Vincent. "The Ironic German," *Time and Tide,* 39 (1958), 1167-1168. [Review of E. Heller, #1,278]

482. Bronnen, Arnolt. "Wie es war — und wie es ist," *DAZ,* No. 515 (November 4, 1930). [*Deutsche Ansprache. See also* Hacker, #1,136]

483. Brown, Calvin S. "The Entomological Source of Mann's Poisonous Butterfly," *GR,* 37 (March 1962), [116]-120. [*Doctor Faustus*]

484. Brown, Ivor. "Th. M.," *Observer,* June 12, 1955, p. 3. [80th birthday]

485. Browning, Robert M. Review of K. W. Jonas, #1,605, *Symposium,* 9 (Fall 1955), 360-362.

486. Brück, Max von. "Über das Parodistische," *Gegenwart,* 10 (June 4, 1955), 379-380. [80th birthday]

487. ———. "Spielfeld der Ironie," *Frankfurter Allgemeine Zeitung,* February 13, 1960. [Review of E. Heller, item #1,278]

488. ———. "Th. M. in Italien," *Merkur,* 18 (June 1964), 534-545. Also in *Römische Reden: Zehn Jahre Deutsche Bibliothek Rom,* pp. 72-88. München: Süddeutscher Verlag, 1965.

489. Brües, Otto. "Fünfzig Jahre Buddenbrooks," *Mittag,* July 3-4, 1952.

490. ———. "Essayistik, Virtuosität und Humor," *Industriekurier,* June 4, 1955.

491. ———. "Auf römischen Spuren Th. M's: Wo die *Buddenbrooks* entstanden," *Nürnberger Nachrichten,* August 10-11, 1957, p. 18.

492. ———. "Th. M. und das Seemannsgarn," *Westfälische Rundschau,* June 4, 1960. [85th birthday]

493. ———. "Eine Stimme ohne Gegenstimme; über Briefe Th. M's an Ernst Bertram," *Mittag,* November 19, 1960 [Review of #1,575]

494. ———. "Virtuoser Interpret seiner selbst: Zum 90. Geburtstag von Th. M. am 6. Juni, *"Augsburger Allgemeine,* June 5, 1965; also in *Nürnberger Nachrichten,* June 5, 1965.

495. Brüll, Oswald. "Th. M. und der Ruhm," in *Th. M.: Zur Erinnerung an seinen Vortragsabend am 8. Juni 1926,* pp. 15-23. Altona: [Lübkert] 1926. [Excerpt from I, item #145]

496. Bruhn, Christian. "Th. M's Hypnotiseur," in his *Gelehrte in Hypnose,* pp. 25-36. Hamburg: Parus [1926] [*Der Zauberberg — Okkulte Erlebnisse —* Dr. Freiherr von Schrenck-Notzing]

497. Bruyn, J. de. "Th. M.," *Dietsche Warande en Belfort,* 30 (1934), 53-64.

498. Buchner, Hartmut. "Philologie ohne Verachtung: Zur Edition der Briefe Th. M's an Ernst Bertram," *Doitsu Bungaku — Die deutsche Literatur,* No. 27 (1961), pp. 127-134. [Review of #1,575]

499. Buck, Philo M. Review of J. G. Brennan, I, #140, *Monatshefte,* 35 (1943), 236. [Cf. #450]

500. Bülow, Joachim von. "Ein Brief Th. M's," *Auslese,* Vol. 2, No. 90 (1915). [Concerns Th. M's letter "An die Redaktion von *Svenska Dagbladet"*]

501. Bürgin, Hans. "Th. M's Alterswerke," *Westfälische Nachrichten,* November 27, 1947.

502. *———., Walter A. Reichart [and] Erich Neumann. *Das Werk Th. M's: Eine Bibliographie.* [Frankfurt a. M.] S. Fischer [1959] 319 pp. Reviews: Berendsohn, #271 — Fratzscher, #922 — Halász, #1,161 — Johann, #1,593 — Jonas, #1,608 — Krammer, #1,784 — Krueger, #1,809 — Leibrich, #1,896

— H. Schmidt, #2,914 — Siebenschein, — #3,043 — E. E. Stein, #3,118.

See also supplement by K. Schröter, #2,971.

503. ———. "Editionsbericht," in Th. M., *Gesammelte Werke in Zwölf Bänden,* Vol. 12, pp. 987-[994] [Frankfurt a. M.] S. Fischer [1960] [Concerns Th. M's miscellaneous essays collected in vols. 9-12]

504. *———, [and] Hans-Otto Mayer. *Th. M.: Eine Chronologie.* [Frankfurt a. M.] S. Fischer, 1965. 283 pp. Reviews: Fontana, #897 — Hack, #1,135 — Johann, #1,595 — Lindemann, #1,969 — Niderlechner, #2,413a — Saueressig, #2,849 — Speckner, #3,106 — Wallmann, #3,386. ———. See also #2,389 and #3, 901.

505. Buesche, Albert. "Begräbnis eines Sonntagskindes: Zum einjährigen Todestag Th. M's," *Mittag,* August 10, 1956.

506. Buisonjé, J. C. de. "Th. M.: 1875-1955," *Duitse Kroniek,* 7 (November 1955), 91-93. [Obit.]

507. ———. "Bemerkungen über Th. M's Werk 'Doktor Faustus,' " *Neophilologus,* 41 (July 1957), 185-199.

508. ———. "Zu Th. M's Novelle 'Wälsungenblut,' " *Revue des Langues Vivantes — Levende Talen,* 24 (1958), 515-536.

509. *Bulhof, Francis. *Transpersonalismus und Synchronizität: Untersuchungen zur Wiederholung als Strukturelement im 'Zauberberg' von Th. M.* Groningen, 1966. [Ph. D. diss., University of Utrecht, 1966] [See also #3,629]

510. *Bundesrepublik Deutschland. Auswärtiges Amt, [and] Magistrat der Stadt Darmstadt. *Th. M.-Ausstellung: Leben. Umwelt. Werk.* Darmstadt, 1956. [This catalogue was also issued in English and in Italian. See also Martin Gregor-Dellin, item #1,067, and R. Clemens, #588]

511. Bunsen, Douglas P. "Unveröffentlichtes aus dem Leben des jungen Castorp," *Annalen,* 2 (1927), 751-754. [Parody — *Der Zauberberg*]

512. Burger, Erich. "Das neue Buch von Th. M.," *Berliner Tageblatt,* November 13, 1929. [*Die Forderung des Tages*]

513. Burgert, Helmuth. "Verborgene Christlichkeit: Eine Anmerkung zu Th. M.," *Zeichen der Zeit*, 7 (1953), 338-340.

514. Deleted

515. Burgmüller, Herbert. "Th. M. und die Deutschen," *Volksecho*, June 3, 1947. [Cf. I, item #1,602]

516. ————. "Th. M's 'Doktor Faustus,'" *Freies Volk*, April 8, 1949.

517. ————. "Zwischen Ende und Anfang: Die geistige Gestalt Th. M's," *Heute und Morgen*, No. 6 (1953), pp. 448-452.

518. ————. "Glückwunsch," in K. Saller, item #2,833, pp. 4-5.

519. Burwick, Hildegard. "Th. M. und das Abitur," *Fuldaer Volkszeitung*, February 23, 1961.

520. Busch, Günther. "Appetit auf Briefe," *Forum* (Wien), 8 (December 1961), 465-466. [*Briefe I*, item #2,062]

521. Butler, E. M. "The Traditional Elements in Th. M's 'Doctor Faustus,'" *PEGS*, 18 (1948), 1-33.

522. ————. "The Faust Legend and the Youth of Germany," *Listener*, Vol. 40, No. 1014 (July 1, 1948), pp. 16-17.

523. ————. Review of E. Heller, item #1,278, *GLL*, N. S., 12 (July 1959), 314-316.

524. Caballero, Agustín. "Th. M.," in Th. M., *Obras Escogidas*, pp. [11]-25. [Madrid] Aguilar [³1961] [*Buddenbrooks — Königliche Hoheit — Herr und Hund*]

525. Cahn, Alfredo. "Th. M.," in his *Literaturas germanicas*, pp. 5-187. [Buenos Aires] Fabril, 1961.

526. Calamandrei, Piero. "Saluto a Th. M.," *Ponte*, 11 (June 1955), 865-867. [80th birthday]

527. Calker, Andrea van. "Ein Leben in Allsympathie," *Offene Welt*, No. 38 (1955), 62-66.

528. Calvino, Italo. "Manniano all'incontrario," *Il Contemporaneo*, Vol. 2, No. 23 (June 4, 1955), p. 7.

529. Cambon, Glauco. "Felix Krull si confessa," *Aut aut*, No. 29 (September 1955), pp. 384-389.

530. Camilucci, Marcello. "Biblismo e razionalismo di Th. M.," *Vita e Pensiero*, 38 (November 1955), [642]-647. [*Joseph und seine Brüder*]

531. Campana, Domenico. "Confessioni di un cavaliere d'industria,"
     Vita e Pensiero, 41 (May 1958), 338-344. [*Felix Krull*]

532. Campbell, Lily B. " 'Doctor Faustus': A Case of Conscience,"
     PMLA, 67 (1952), 219-239.

533. Canby, Henry Seidel. "The Three-Decker," *SRL*, Vol. 18, No. 7
     (June 11, 1938), p. 8. [*Joseph und seine Brüder*]

534. Cannabrava, Euryalo. "Th. M.: 'Avertissement à l'Europe,
     1937,' " *O Jornal*, January 30, 1938. [*Achtung, Europa!*]

535. Capri, Antonio. "Wagner in Th. M.," *La Scala*, No. 56 (July
     1954), pp. 21-25, 86-[88]

536. Caracciolo, Alberto. "Arte e umanità nel 'Doktor Faustus'
     di Th. M.," *Lettere Italiane*, 5 (October-December, 1953),
     248-255.

537. Carlsson, Anni. "Th. M.: 'Altes und Neues,' " *Universitas*, 9
     (October 1954), 1116-117.

538. ———. "Der Meeresgrund in der neueren Dichtung:
     Abwandlungen eines symbolischen Motivs von H. C. Andersen
     bis Th. M.," *DVJS*, 28 (1954), [221]-233. Also in #2,431,
     pp. 93-112.

539. ———. "Das Wesen der Erzählung bei Th. M.," *NZZ*,
     Vol. 176, Sonntagsausgabe No. 1,497 (28), June 1, 1955,
     Bl. 3.

540. ———. "Zu einer Schiller-Studie von Th. M.," *NZZ*, Vol. 176,
     No. 2258 (August 30, 1955). Also in Fernausgabe No. 241
     (September 2, 1955), Bl. 2. [*Versuch über Schiller*]

541. ———. "Die deutsche Sprache und Th. M.," *Universitas*, 12
     (June 1157), 617-628.

542. ———. "Roman als Zeitbild: *Doktor Faustus* und *Hundejahre*,"
     Stuttgarter Zeitung, November 27, 1964. [Th. M. and Günter
     Grass]

543. ———. "Der Kritiker Th. M.," *NZZ*, Vol. 186, Fernausgabe
     No. 159 (June 12, 1965), Bl. 21. Also *NZZ*, Vol. 186,
     No. 2533 (June 13, 1965), Bl. 6.

544. Carlsson, Leif. "Häxmästaren som demokrat," *Svenska
     Dagbladet*, March 18, 1965. [Review of H. Levander, item
     #1,958]

545. *Caro, Ethel E. *Music and Th. M.* Stanford, California, 1959. 31 pp. (Stanford Honors Essays in Humanities, No. 2).

546. Caro, Herbert. "A mae brasileira de Th. M.," *Comentário,* Vol. 1, No. 3 (1960), pp. 65-72.

547. Carossa, Hans. "Übersiedlung nach München; eine Erinnerung an die Zeit, wo Th. M. in München nahe der Isar wohnte," *Neue Rundschau,* 66 (June 1955), 294-297.

548. Carter, Sydney. "Pact with the Devil," *Books of the Month,* January 1948, pp. 5-6. [*Doctor Faustus*]

549. Cases, Cesare. "L'inganno," *Il Contemporaneo,* May 1, 1954. Also in his *Saggi e Note di Letteratura Tedesca,* pp. 152-166. [Torino] Einaudi, 1963. [*Die Betrogene*]

550. ————. "La Morte di Venezia," *Notiziario Einaudi,* Vol. 3, No. 10 (1954). Also in his *Saggi,* #549, pp. 148-152.

551. ————. "Un romanzo picaresco; l'ultimo libro di Th. M., il *Felix Krull,*" *Il Contemporaneo,* Vol. 2, No. 23 (June 4, 1955), pp. 8-9. Also in his *Saggi,* item #549, pp. 166-175.

552. ————. "Th. M. e lo spirito del racconto," *Notiziario Einaudi,* Vol. 4, No. 6-7 (June-July 1955), pp. 7-9. Also in his *Saggi,* item #549, pp [139]-147. *See* comments by Paci, #2,476.

553. Casmati, Francesco. "Riserva a Th. M.," *Il Quotidiano Sardo,* January 1, 1956. [*Joseph und seine Brüder*]

554. Castellani, Emilio. "Introduzione," in Th. M., *Novelle e Racconti,* pp. [15]-23. [Milano] A. Mondadori [1953]

555. ————. "Introduzione," in Th. M., *Romanzi Brevi,* pp. [xvii]-xxxvi. [Milano] A. Mondadori [1955]

556. Castiglione, Luigi. "Mann: il dito sulla chiaga," *Il Popolo,* February 26, 1961.

557. Castiglioni, Vittorio. "Mario e il Mago," *Teatro alla Scala,* Stagione lirica 1955-1956, pp. 282-289. [Concerns Luchino Visconti's production of "Mario e il Mago" in the Scala of Milan]

558. Cecchi, Emilio. "Doktor Faustus," *Corriere della Sera,* Vol. 75, No. 59 (March 10, 1950), p. 3.

558a. ————. "Colloquio con Th. M.," *Corriere della Sera,* April 29, 1953. [Interview]

559. ———. "Th. M.," *Corriere della Sera,* August 28, 1955.
      [Obit.]

560. ———. "Th. M.: 1875-1955," *Accademia Nazionale dei
      Lincei,* 3 (1962), [132]-136.

561. Chabanna, J. "Th. M. et la Montagne Magique," *Notre Temps,*
      July 19, 1931. [*Der Zauberberg*]

562. Chapiro, Joseph. "Europäertum und Antiromantik: Zu Th.
      M's *Bemühungen,*" *Berliner Tageblatt,* December 14, 1925.

563. Charles, Gilbert. "L'Erreur de Th. M.," *Figaro,* August 12,
      1931. [*Wälsungenblut*]

564. Charney, Hanna, [and] Maurice Charney. " 'Doctor Faustus'
      and 'Mon Faust': An Excursion in Dualism," *Symposium,* 16
      (Spring 1962), 45-53. [Th. M. and Paul Valéry]

565. *Checconi, Sergio. *Th. M.* Firenze: La Nuova Italia, 1966. 219
      pp.

566. Cheval, René. "Th. M. und Romain Rolland im ersten
      Weltkrieg," *Moderna språk,* 53 (1959), 254-269.

567. ———. "Les intellectuels ne veulent pas se couper de
      l'avènement: ainsi Th. M.," in his *Romain Rolland,
      l'Allemagne et la guerre,* pp. 294-297. Paris: Presses
      Universitaires de France, 1963.

568. ———. "Th. M. et ses 'Pensées de guerre' provoquent
      l'indignation de Rolland et de certains allemands," in item
      #567, pp. 351-364.

569. ———. "Le cas de Rolland semble inciter Th. M. à repentir,"
      in item #567, pp. 548-554.

570. Chiarini, Paolo. "Cultura e poesia nell'opera di Th. M.,"
      Società, Vol. 8, No. 4 (December 1952), p. 7. Reprinted in
      his *Romanticismo e realismo nella letteratura tedesca,* pp. 195-
      243. Roma: Edizioni dell'Ateneo [1961] [*Der Zauberberg*]

571. ———. "Th. M. e la crisi del romanzo borghese," *Belfagor,* 8
      (November 30, 1953), 609-617.

572. ———. "Gli studi su Mann nel '55," in #570, pp. 249-262.

573. ———. "Un nuovo ritratto di Mann?," *Belfagor,* 19 (January
      31, 1964), 80-87. [Review of *Briefe I* and *Briefe II,* #2,062
      and 2,066]

574. Chiusano, Italo Alighiero. "Introduzione," in Th. M., *Scritti Moderni,* pp. [13]-26. [Milano] A. Mondadori [1958]

575. Chujo, Sosuke. "Th. M. und die Musik," *Bulletin, University of Aichi,* 5 (1953), 155-165. [In German]

576. Church, Margaret. "Th. M.: Time," *Hopkins Review,* Vol. 3, No. 3 (Spring 1950), pp. 20-29. Reprinted under the title "Th. M.: The Circle of Time," in her *Time and Reality: Studies in Contemporary Fiction,* pp. 131-170. Chapel Hill: University of North Carolina Press, 1963.

577. ————. " 'Death in Venice': A Study of Creativity," *CE,* 23 (1962), 648-651.

578. Cibulka, Hans. "Requiem," *Sonntag,* August 21, 1965. [Obit.]

579. Cioculescu, Şerban. "Doctor Faust," *Secolul XX,* No. 6-7. (June-July, 1963), pp. 29-38.

580. Cisek, Oscar Walter. "Întîlniri cu Th. M.," *Secolul XX,* No. 1 (January 1964), pp. 127-142. Also in German as "Begegnungen mit Th. M.," *Sinn und Form: Sonderheft Th. M.,* 1965, pp. 357-376. [Biog.]

581. Citron, Bernhard. "Bei Th. M.," *Ost-Kurier,* April 15, 1936. [Biog.—concerns visit with Th. M. in Küsnacht]

582. Citroen, Paul. "Wie ich Th. M. zeichnete," *Bulletin Museum Boymans,* Vol. 8, No. 1 (1957), pp. 21-39. [With seven letters from Th. M.]

583. Cives, Giacomo. "Verità, bellezza e psicologia in 'Nobiltà dello Spirito,' " *Aut aut,* No. 29 (September 1955), pp. 440-457. [*Adel des Geistes*]

584. Clar, O. "Th. M's 'Betrachtungen eines Unpolitischen,' " *Eiserne Blätter,* 1 (December 28, 1919), [470]-474.

585. Clark, Alexander Frederick Bruce. "Confessions of Felix Krull, Confidence Man," *Canadian Forum,* 35 (January 1956), 236.

586. Clausewitz, Detlev. "Deutsche Ansprache: Th. M. im Beethovensaal," *DAZ,* October 18, 1930. [*Deutsche Ansprache*]

587. Clemens, C. "Some Glimpses of Th. M.," *Hobbies,* 60 (January 1956), 108-109.

588. Clemens, Roman. "Die Absicht der Th. M.-Ausstellung," in
      #510, p. 6.

589. Clément, Alain. "Politique et création romanesque chez Th. M.,"
      Preuves, No. 128 (October 1961), pp. 17-31.

590. ———. "Th. M.: un épistolier attentif," *Preuves,* September
      1963, pp. 18-19. [Review of item #2,066]

591. Clément, Frantz. "Th. M. in Paris," *Die liter. Welt,* Vol. 2,
      No. 6 (February 2, 1926).

592. Clurman, Harold. "Correction of Life," *Nation* (New York),
      188 (April 11, 1959), 319-320. [*Last Essays*]

593. Cocteau, Jean. "Salut fraternel," in #1,493, p. 103. [facsim.]

594. Cohn, Fritz Harold. "Das Schicksal der Brüder Heinrich und
      Th. M.," *Das junge Deutschland,* 2 (1919), 71-74.

595. Colleville, Maurice. "Nietzsche und der 'Doktor Faustus,' "
      Das Goldene Tor, 3 (1948), 644-648. [Cf. French original, I,
      #1665]

596. Colombo, Beppe. "Il sorriso ironico del vecchio Mann,"
      L'Italia, November 6, 1963, p. 3.

597. Conrad, Michael Georg. "Münchener Briefe: VII," *Neue
      Illustrierte Zeitung,* Vol. 31, No. 59 (August 10, 1926),
      pp. 1-2. [Heinrich and Th. M.]

598. Conrady, Karl Otto. "Nachspiel 1937: Eine kaum bekannte
      Antwort des Bonner Dekans an Th. M.," *Zeit,* No. 47
      (November 27, 1964), p. 10. [Concerns K. J. Obenauer,
      item #2,436]

599. Cordan, Wolfgang. "Öffentliche Lustbarkeit des Meisters,"
      St. Galler Tageblatt, November 6, 1954. [*Felix Krull*]

600. Cornélis. "Th. M.," *Notre Temps,* November 8, 1931, pp. 380-
      81. [*Buddenbrooks*]

601. Corti, Walter Robert. "Lob der Vergänglichkeit," *Du,* Vol. 15,
      No. 6 (June 1955), pp. 54, 56.

602. Costa, Dan. "Th. M.," *Steana,* No. 9 (September 1955),
      pp. 71-76. [Obit.]

603. Courths-Mahler, Helene. "Über Th. M.," *Die lit. Welt,* Vol. 1,
      No. 2 (1925), p. 1. [Interview]

604. Cremer, F. J. Review of G. Bergsten, item #292, *Neophilologus,* 47 (October 1963), 334.

605. Cremers, Paul Joseph. "Die grosse Sache der Gebrüder Mann," *Rheinisch-Westfälische Zeitung,* December 16, 1930. [Heinrich and Th. M.]

606. †Crick, Joyce. The Impact of the Theories of Psycho-Analysis on the Later Works of Th. M. Ph. D. diss., University of London, 1956.

607. ————. "Th. M. and Psycho-Analysis: The Turning Point," *Literature and Psychology,* 10 (Spring 1960), 45-55.

608. ————. "Psycho-Analytical Elements in Th. M's Novel 'Lotte in Weimar,' " *Literature and Psychology,* 10 (Summer 1960), 69-75.

609. Croce, Benedetto. "Th. M.," *Critica,* 18 (May 1920), 182-183. Also in German, translated by Julius Schlosser, as "Th. M's 'Betrachtungen eines Unpolitischen,' " in his *Randbemerkungen eines Philosophen zum Weltkriege, 1914-1920,* pp. 290-293. Zurich: Amalthea [1922]

610. Cronheim, Friedrich. "Th. M.," *Hilfe,* 41 (1935), 286-288.

611. Cronheim, Paul. "Th. M. en Richard Wagner," *De Nieuwe Stem,* 13 (March 1958), 138-147.

612. Crossman, R. H. S. "Th. M.," *New Statesman and Nation,* 50 (August 20, 1955), 208. [Obit.]

613. Csokor, Franz Theodor. "Geburtstagsgruss an Th. M.," *Wiener Zeitung,* June 6, 1955. [80th birthday]

614. ————. "Mehr als ein Dichter: Abschied von Th. M.," *Wiener Zeitung,* August 15, 1955. [Obit.]

615. Curtius, Ernst Robert. "Th. M's 'Zauberberg,' " in H. Saueressig, #2,844, pp. 51-55. [Cf. I, #2244]

616. Dabrowska, Maria. "Weimar po raz trzeci czyli tydzien z Schillerem i Mannem," *Szkice z podrózy,* 1956, pp. 95-144.

617. Dach, Charlotte von. "Bekenntnisse des Hochstaplers Felix Krull," *Der Bund; der kleine Bund,* Vol. 105, No. 601 (December 24, 1954), pp. 7-8.

618. ————. "Lebensgeleit: Th. M. zum Dank," *Der Bund,* Vol. 106, No. 257 (June 6, 1955), pp. 2-3. [80th birthday]

619. ———. "Ein Faksimile von Th. M.," *Der Bund; der kleine Bund,* Vol. 106, No. 266 (June 10, 1955). [*Die Betrogene*]

620. ———. "Die Trauerfeier für Th. M.," *Der Bund,* Vol. 106, No. 383 (August 18, 1955), Morgenausgabe, pp. 2-3 [Obit.]

621. ———. "Th. M's 'Nachlese,' " *Der Bund,* Vol. 107, No. 578 (December 10, 1956), pp. 8-9. [*Nachlese*]

622. ———. "Lebensfeier," *Der Bund,* Vol. 110, No. 498 (November 20/21, 1959), pp. 3-4. [*Gesang vom Kindchen*]

623. ———. "Briefe von Th. M. an Paul Amann," *Der Bund,* Vol. 111, No. 309 (July 22/23, 1960), pp. 3-4. [Review of item #3,426]

624. ———. "Dauer im Geiste: Zur Eröffnung des Th. M.-Archivs in Zürich am 25. Februar," *Der Bund,* Vol. 112, No. 74 (Februar 17, 1961), pp. [1-2]. Reprinted, under the title "Ein Leben und ein Werk in Dokumenten und Bildern," *Welt,* February 21, 1961.

625. ———. "Briefe von Th. M.," *Der Bund,* Vol. 113, No. 502 (November 23/24, 1962), pp. 2-3. [Review of *Briefe I,* item #2,062]

626. †Daemmrich, Horst S. Th. M's Concept of Culture: An Introduction to *Betrachtungen eines Unpolitischen, M. A.* thesis, Wayne State University, 1959. 75 pp.

627. †———. Th. M. und Schiller. Ph. D. diss., University of Chicago, 1964.

628. ———. "Friedrich Schiller and Th. M.: Parallels in Aesthetics," *Journal of Aesthetics and Art Criticism,* 24 (December 1965), [227]-249.

629. Dahl, Hermann. "Dichterehefrauen," *Berliner Tageblatt,* No. 125 (March 15, 1927). [Katja Mann]

630. Dahms, W. "Th. M. in Lübeck," *Lübeckische Anzeigen,* March 7, 1922.

631. Dal, Ingerid. "Humanitesidéen hos Th. M.," in item #2,431, pp. 1-12.

632. Dallago, Carl. "Philister," *Brenner,* 2 (1912), 495-505, 534-542, 575-589. [Concerns in part Th. M's essay on Chamisso]

633. ———. "Gegenüberstellung," *Brenner,* 3 (1913), 442-449. [Th. M's *Der Tod in Venedig* — Hermann Broch]

634. Damisch, Hubert. "L'autre inquisition," *Mercure de France,* No. 349 (October 1963), pp. [426]-432.

635. Dangel, Anneliese. "Th. M.," in Johannes Beer, *ed., Reclams Romanführer,* Vol. 1, pp. [562]-572, 575-577. Stuttgart: Reclam [1962] [Contains resumés of *Buddenbrooks, Tonio Kröger, Tristan, Königliche Hoheit, Der Tod in Venedig, Der Zauberberg,* and *Doktor Faustus*]

636. Daniel, Ion. "Th. M.," *Tînărul Scriitor,* No. 8 (August 1955), pp. 65-68. [Obit.]

637. Dannecker, Hermann. "Eine Stätte der Forschung: Das Th. M.-Archiv in Zürich," *Rheinische Post,* No. 45 (February 22, 1961). [Zurich Archive]

638. ———. "Th. M. und Ernst Bertram," *Badische Neueste Nachrichten,* March 16, 1961. [Review of #1,575]

639. Daudet, Léon. "Th. M.: 'Sang réservé,' " *Candide,* Vol. 8, No. 394 (October 1, 1931), p. 4. Excerpted, in German translation, under the title "Th. M. und Léon Daudet: Der Streit um Wälsungenblut," *Berliner Tageblatt,* November 9, 1931.

640. David, Claude. Review of J. Lesser, I, item #1865, *EG,* 10 (January-March, 1955), 81-82.

641. ———. "Th. M., in his *Von Richard Wagner zu Bertolt Brecht,* pp. 159-169. [Frankfurt a. M.] Fischer-Bücherei [1964] [Cf. French original, #3,837]

642. David, Sante. "L'Italia nell'opera di Th. M.," *Giornale dell'Emilia,* April 11, 1948.

643. ———. "Th. M.: 'Bekenntnisse des Hochstaplers Felix Krull,' " *Ponte,* 11 (February 1955), 250-257.

644. ———. "Th. M.: Dialogo con Goethe," *Ponte,* 13 (1957), 810-812.

645. ———. "Th. M.: Scritti storici e politici," *Ponte,* 14 (1958), 924-925.

646. Debenedetti, Giacomo. "Il grande gioco," *Il Contemporaneo,* Vol. 2, No. 23 (June 4, 1955), p. 6.

647. Decker, Clarence R. [and] Mary Bell Decker. "Th. M. and Klaus M.," in their *A Place of Light: The Story of a University Presidency,* pp. 233-236. New York: Hermitage House, 1954.

648. Deguy, Michel. "La thématique de Th. M.: de 'Joseph' à 'Félix Krull,' " *Critique* 13 (October 1961), 819-843.

649. *————. *Le Monde de Th. M.* [Paris] Plon [1962] 169 pp. Reviews: Faye, #839 — Leibrich, #1,903

650. ————. "Vie et roman," *Nouvelle Revue Française,* 10 (May 1962), 886-894. [*Le Journal du Docteur Faustus*]

651. ————. "Art et consolation selon Th. M.," *Cahiers des Saisons,* No. 30 (Summer 1962), pp. 569-575.

652. Dehoff, E. "Der Zauberberg," *Tuberkulose,* No. 4 (1925), pp. 42-45.

653. Dehmel, Richard. "Brief an Th. M.," in his *Ausgewählte Briefe aus den Jahren 1883-1902,* pp. 184-185. Berlin: S. Fischer, 1922.

654. ————. "Briefwechsel Richard Dehmel — Th. M.," in Paul Johannes Schindler, ed. *Richard Dehmel: Dichtungen. Briefe. Dokumente,* pp. 169-173. [Hamburg] Hoffmann & Campe [1963]

655. Della Volpe, Galvano. "Amor fati," *Il Contemporaneo,* Vol. 2, No. 23 (June 4, 1955), p. 7.

656. Demetz, Peter. "Th. M. war kein Prophet: Ein Brief, keine Besprechung," *Zeit,* Vol. 15, No. 31 (July 29, 1960), p. 8. [Letter to Martin Flinker about his book, item #887]

657. Demetz-Helin, Björn. "Smärtans vår," *Lundagard,* Vol. 35, No. 6 (1954), pp. 9-10. [*Die Betrogene*]

658. De Toni, Gianantonio. "Al lettore di 'Zauberberg,' " *Aut aut,* No. 29 (September 1955), pp. 4-5-422.

659. *Deutsche Akademie der Künste zu Berlin, ed. *Aus den Familienpapieren der Manns: Dokumente zu den 'Buddenbrooks.'* Berlin, 1965. 56 pp. text — 26 pp. facsims. [Ulrich Dietzel, ed.]

660. *Deutscher Kulturbund, ed. *Th. M.: 1875-1955.* Berlin, 1965. 118 pp. [With contributions by Klaus Hermsdorf,

#3,884—Hans Grandi, #3,860, and excerpts from Th. M's
writings]

661. *Devescovi, Guido. *Il 'Doktor Faustus' di Th. M.: Problemi e
considerazioni.* Trieste: E. Borsatti, 1955. 155 pp.
Reviews: Mazzucchetti, #2,198.

662. Devoto, Daniel. "Deux Musiciens russes dans le *Doktor
Faustus* de Th. M.," *RLC,* 33 (January-March 1959), 104-106.
[Tschaikowsky — Strawinsky]

663. De Vries, Theun. "Th. M. in de russische kritiek:
Een samenvatting," *Maatstaaf* 11 (1963), 326-341.

664. ———. "Ein Dichterbild: Th. M. wäre am 6. Juni 90 Jahre
alt geworden," *Sonntag,* No. 23 (June 6, 1965), p. 14. [Review
of E. Hilscher, item #1,420]

665. ———. "Th. M. und der Niedergang des Bürgertums," *Sinn und
Form: Sonderheft Th. M.,* 1965, pp. 218-223.

666. Dibelius, Ulrich. "Kunstverstand im 'Schmerzensfrühling':
Zu Th. M's Erzählung 'Die Betrogene,' " *Frankfurter Neue
Presse,* March 25, 1954.

667. Dickson, Keith. "The Technique of 'musikalisch-ideeller
Beziehungskomplex' in 'Lotte in Weimar,' " *MLR,* 59 (July
1964), 413-424.

668. ———. Review of G. Bergsten, item #292, *MLR,* 60
(January 1965), 157-158.

669. ———. Review of R. Baumgart, item #204, *MLR,* 60
(July 1965), 475.

670. Diebold, Bernard. "Die drei Meister: Carl Spitteler, Gerhart
Hauptmann, Th. M.," *Frankfurter Zeitung,* December 30, 1924.

671. ———. "Zwischen Herrn und Frau Potiphar," *Weltwoche,*
No. 168 (January 29, 1937), pp. 5-6. [*Joseph in Ägypten*]

672. ———. "Lotte in Weimar," *National-Zeitung Basel,* Vol. 21,
No. 9 (January 7, 1940), Sonntags-Beilage, p. 1.

673. Diel, Louise. "Th. M. und der Okkultismus," *Germania,*
December 14, 1923. [*Okkulte Erlebnisse*]

674. †Diersen, Inge. Untersuchungen zur Frage des Realismus im
Werke Th. M's. Ph. D. diss., Humboldt University, Berlin,
1954. 342 pp.

675. ————. "Th. M's Faustkonzeption und ihr Verhältnis zur Faust-Tradition," *WB*, 1 (1955), [313]-330.

676. ————. "Th. M's 'Buddenbrooks,' " *WB*, 3 (1957), 58-86.

677. *————. *Untersuchungen zu Th. M.: Die Bedeutung der Künstlerdarstellung für die Entwicklung des Realismus in seinem erzählerischen Werk*. Berlin: Rütten & Loening [1959] 371 pp.
      Reviews: Gronicka, #1,087 — Haiduk, #1,146 — Hellmann, #1,286 — Leibrich, #1,899 — Siebenschein, #3,044 — Suchsland, #3,202.

678. Dietzel, Ulrich. "Th. M. und der Kulturaustausch," *Heute und Morgen*, No. 9 (1954), 545-546. [*Felix Krull*]

679. ————. "Tony Buddenbrook — Elisabeth Mann: Ein Beitrag zur Werkgeschichte der 'Buddenbrooks,' " *Sinn und Form*, 15 (1963), 497-502. [*See also* Baukloh, #202; Julia Mann, #2,084-2,085 and #659]

680. Deleted

681. Diggelmann, Walter M. "So arbeitete Th. M.: Ein Blick in das neue Zürcher Archiv," *Weltwoche*, No. 1423 (February 17, 1961), p. 23.

682. Dijsterhuis, E. J. "Goethe en Th. M.," *De Lites*, 2 (August 1949), [145]-157.

683. Diller, Inez. "Th. M.: Bekenntnisse des Hochstaplers Felix Krull," *Mädchenbildung und Frauenschaffen*, Vol. 6, No. 2 (February 1956), pp. 68-78.

684. Dima, Alexandru. "Prefaṭa," in Th. M., *Novellen*, Bucharest: Espla, 1960.

685. Dinaux, C. J. E. "Th. M., een meester," *De Groene Amsterdammer*, Vol. 79, No. 23 (June 4, 1955), p. 12. [80th birthday]

686. ————. "Supernationale hulde aan 'chef maître' Th. M.," *Het Boek Van Nu*, 9 (March 1956), 129-130. [Review of item #1,493]

687. ————. "Th. M. na tien jaar," *Het Vaderland,* Weekjournal, December 4, 1965.

688. Dippel, Gerhardt. "Th. M's Beziehungen zum russischen Geistesleben," *Neue Gesellschaft,* 2 (1950), 97-100.

689. ————. "Th. M. und die Musik," *Wissenschaftliche Annalen,* 5 (1956), 687-692.

690. Dirks, Walter. "Der wiedergefundene Brief," *Frankfurter Hefte,* 2 (September 1947), 965-966. [Concerns Th. M's letter to Hitler's 'Innenminister Wilhelm Frick,' 1934]

691. Dittmer, Hans. "Die 'Babenaas'-Strophe," *Eckart,* 7 (1931), 189-190. [Ironic treatment of Protestant clergymen in *Buddenbrooks*]

692. Dneprow, W. "Der intellektuelle Roman Th. M's" *Kunst und Literatur,* No. 8 (1961), pp. 823-834.

693. ————. "Der Umschwung in Th. M's Weltanschauung," *Kunst und Literatur,* No. 9 (1961), pp. 942-952.

694. ————. "Doktor Faust XX veka," *Voprosy Lit.,* 6 (1963), 96-116. [Title transl.: "Doctor Faustus of the Twentieth Century"]

695. Dobbek, Wilhelm. "Th. M's Weg zu einer humanen Musik," in #3,461, pp. 72-86.

696. Doderer, Otto. "Essays und Abhandlungen," *Die Literatur,* 32 (1930), 213-216. [*Pariser Rechenschaft*]

697. Doerne, Martin. "Th. M. und das protestantische Christentum," *Sammlung* (Göttingen), 11 (September 1956), 407-425.

698. ————. "Th. M. und der Protestantismus," *Anstösse,* No. 5 (November 1957), pp. 177-179.

699. Dörrschuh, Hubert. "Schriftsteller-Repräsentant unseres Jahrhunderts," *Badische Neueste Nachrichten,* August 20, 1955. [Obit.]

700. Döscher, K. H. "Okkulte Erlebnisse und okkulte Tatsachen," *Vorwärts,* December 14, 1923.

701. Doflein, Erich. "Leverkühns Inspirator: Eine Philosophie der neuen Musik," *Gegenwart,* Vol. 4, No. 22 (1949), p. 22. [Concerns Adorno's influence on Th. M's *Doctor Faustus*]

702. Dohm, Hedwig. "Der Tod in Venedig; Novelle von Th. M.," *Tag*, February 13, 1913.

703. Dolfini, Giorgio. Review of G. Lukács, item #2,031, *Belfagor*, 11 (November 1956), 714-717.

704. Dorn, Else. "Th. M.-Archiv in Nürnberg," *Nürnberger Zeitung*, August 8/9, August 10, 1931. [Concerns Ida Herz Collection]

705. Dorn, Hans Peter. *War ich wirklich ein Hochstapler?* Berlin: Herbig, 1958. 400 pp. [Parody on Th. M's *Felix Krull* — *See* E. E. Stein, items #3,116-3,117]

706. Dornheim, Alfredo. "Th. M's *Felix Krull:* Modernität und antiker Geist," in his *Vom Sein der Welt*, pp. [295]-326. Mendoza: Sociedad Goetheana Argentina, 1958. Also in Spanish as "Modernidad y espíritu antiguo en el 'Felix Krull' de Th. M.," *Boletín de Estudios Germánicos*, 4 (1960), 85-100.

707. ———. "Goethes 'Mignon' und Th. M's 'Echo': Zwei Formen des 'göttlichen' Kindes im deutschen Roman," in item #706, pp. [329]-389.

708. ———. Review of Scarpa, item #2,852, *DLZ*, 85 (July-August 1964), 671-674.

709. Dort, Bernard, "Le Paradoxe de Th. M.," *Cahiers du Sud*, 42 (October 1955), 460-462.

710. Dosenheimer, Elise. "Th. M.," *Bayerische Lehrerinnen-Zeitung*, 16 (October 1, 1925), [185]-194.

711. ———. "Wie sich Wagner im Werk von Th. M. abspiegelt," *Neue Musik-Zeitung*, 49 (1928), 604-606.

712. Downes, Olin. "Mann on Wagner: Novelist Regards Composer as Supreme Symbol of Nineteenth Century," *New York Times*, April 25, 1937.

713. Drew, David. "Galileo and Palestrina," *New Statesman*, 57 (April 18, 1959), 542-543.

714. Drews, Wolfgang. "Abenteurer des Geistes und Gefühls: Zum Tode von Th. M.," *Feuilleton des Sozialdemokratischen Pressedienstes*, August 16, 1955, pp. 2-4. [Obit.]

715. Drexl, Hildegarde K. Review of K. W. Jonas, #1,605, *GQ,* 32 (January 1960), 85.

716. Drommert, René. "Th. M. und das Plagiat," *Zeit,* Vol. 12, No. 21 (May 23, 1957), p. 6. [Concerns John Kafka's charges of M's alleged plagiarism — *Felix Krull*]

717. †Düwel, Hans. Die Bedeutung der Ironie und Parodie in Th. M's Roman 'Der Erwählte.' Habil.-Schrift, University of Rostock, 1954. 185 pp.

718. Duffy, Charles, and Don A. Keister. "Mario and the Magician: Two Letters by Th. M.," *Monatshefte,* 51 (April-May, 1959), [190]-192.

719. Duhamel, Georges. "Hommage à Th. M.," in item #1,493, p. 115.

720. Dupee, Frederick W. Review of Hatfield, I, item #199, *Perspectives,* 2 (Winter 1953), [160]-162. [Cf. item #1,227]

721. ———. "Th. M's 'The Holy Sinner,' " *Perspectives,* 2 (Winter 1953), 162-164.

722. ———. "Th. M's Farewell," *New Leader,* 38 (December 12, 1955), 25-26. Also in his *The King of the Cats,* pp. 104-106. New York: Farrar, Strauss [1965] [*Felix Krull*]

723. ———. "The More-than-German Mann," *Commentary,* 28 (August 1959), 173-176. Under the title "Th. M.: The Good European," in item #722, pp. [97]-104. [Review of E. Heller, item #1,278, and Th. M., *Last Essays*]

724. Du Rieux, Editha. "Renaissance," *Fremden-Blatt,* No. 285 (October 15, 1905), pp. 17-18. [*Fiorenza*]

725. Durston, John H. "Mann and Maugham: Some Reflections on the Novel and the Nobel Prize," *House and Garden,* 108 (November 1955), 227.

726. Duvignaud, Jean "Métamorphose du Théâtre de Schiller," *Critique,* No. 105 (February 1956), pp. 121-124. [*Versuch über Schiller*]

727. Duwe, Wilhelm. "Th. M.," in his *Deutsche Dichtung im 20. Jahrhundert,* Vol. 1, pp. 363-379. Zurich: Orell Füssli [1962]

728. Dyck, J. W. "Th. M. und Joseph Ponten," *GQ,* 35 (January 1962), 24-33.

729. Eberhardt, Walter. "Th. M.: Der letzte Gruss," *General-Anzeiger der Stadt Wuppertal*, August 18, 1955. [Obit.]

730. Eberle, Josef. "Zu Th. M's Roman 'Lotte in Weimar,' " *Stuttgarter Zeitung*, Beilage 'Die Brücke zur Welt,' Vol. 1, No. 22 (December 1, 1945), p. 5.

731. Ebermayer, Erich. "Eine unbekannte Jugendnovelle Th. M's," *Berliner Börsen-Courier*, September 24, 1926. [Cf. I, item #1890 — "Gefallen"]

732. ———. "Erste Begegnung zwischen zwei Generationen: Th. M.," *Berliner Tageblatt*, No. 38 (January 23, 1927), 4. Beiblatt.

733. ———. "Th. M.," in his *Denn heute gehört uns Deutschland*, pp. 374-376 et al. Hamburg: Zsolnay, 1959.

734. ———. "Der Dichter und die Wirklichkeit," *Almanach 1963*, pp. [65]-71. Köln: G. Heymann, 1963. [Concerns 'Bilse'-Romane — Gerhart Hauptmann — *Der Zauberberg*]

735. Edfelt, Johannes. "Ett diktverk kommer till," *BLM*, 18 (July-August 1949), 483-484. [*Die Entstehung des Doktor Faustus*]

736. Eggebrecht, Jürgen. "Dank an Th. M.," *Augsburger Allgemeine Zeitung*, June 4, 1960. [85th birthday]

737. ———. "Begegnung mit Th. M.," *Süddeutsche Zeitung*, No. 188 (August 7-8, 1965), [Biog. — 10th anniversary of M's death]

737a. Egri, Péter. "Die Novellen von Th. M. und James Joyce vor dem Ersten Weltkrieg," *Filológiai Közlöny*, 9 (1963), 71-86. [In Hungarian]

738. Ehrenstein, Albert. "Der Tod in Venedig," *Sturm*, 4 (1913/14), 44.

739. ———. "Th. M.: 'Die Vertauschten Köpfe,' " in his *Ausgewählte Aufsätze*, pp. 111-112. Heidelberg: L. Schneider, 1961.

740. Ehrentreich, Alfred. "Das Frühwerk Th. M's im Lichte der neueren Philosophie," *Neue Sammlung*, 4 (1964). 474-483.

741. †Ehrentreich, Swantje. Erzählhaltung und Erzählerrolle Hartmanns von Aue und Th. M's, dargestellt an ihren Gregoriusdichtungen. Ph. D. diss., University of Frankfurt a. M., 1963.

742. Ehrenzweig, Stephan. "Der neue Th. M.," *Tagebuch,* 11 (July 5, 1930), 1070-1073. [Nobel Prize — *Mario und der Zauberer*]

743. Eich, Hermann. "Th. M.," in his *Die unheimlichen Deutschen,* pp. 20, 35 et al. Düsseldorf: Econ, 1963.

744. Eichholz, Armin. "Th. M., inszeniert von Th. M.: Bericht von einer Matinée," *Neue Zeitung,* No. 252 (October 25/26, 1952). Also in his *Per Saldo: Glossen zur Zeit,* pp. 7-14. München: Pohl [1955] [*Felix Krull*]

745. ———. "Th. M.: Der wortmächtigste Deutsche unserer Zeit," *Münchner Merkur,* No. 195 (August 16, 1955), p. 9. [Obit.]

746. ———. "Der wortwörtliche Leberknödel, nach Th. M.," in his *In flagranti: Parodien,* pp. 23-27. München: Pohl [1958]

747. ———. "Bei Th. M. auf dem oberen Schönenberg," *Münchner Merkur,* February 25, 1961. [Zurich Archive]

748. Eichhorn, Karl. "Medizinische Romane: Theorie und Gestaltung," *Zeitschrift für Menschenkunde,* Vol. 2, No. 5 (1926), pp. 38-48. [*Der Zauberberg.*]

749. Eichner, Hans. "Th. M. and Goethe: A Protest," *PEGS,* 26 (1957), 81-92. *See also* J. A. Asher, *ibid.,* pp. 92-98 [item #142]

750. *———. *Th. M.: Eine Einführung in sein Werk.* Bern: Francke [²1961] 103 pp. [Cf. First ed., I, item #159] Reviews: Basler, #190 — Leemans, #1,869 — Leibrich, — #1,887 — Schmid, #2,911 — Schultz, #2,978 — Wyss,. #3,553

751. ———. "Th. M.," in his *Four German Writers,* pp. [1]-22, 83-84, 87-88. Toronto: Canadian Broadcasting Corporation [1964]

752. Einstein, Albert. "Th. M.," *Neue Rundschau,* 66 (June 1955), 255. [80th birthday, written on April 2, 1955]

753. Eis, Ruth, [and] Karl S. Guthke. "Naphtas Pietà: Eine Bemerkung zum Zauberberg," *GQ,* 33 (May 1960), 220-223.

754. Elchinger, Richard. "Th. M.," *Welt-Literatur,* No. 38 (1920), p. 3.

755. Elema, J. "Th. M.," *Het Boek Van Nu,* No. 9 (September 1955), pp. 1-2. [Obit.]

756. ———. "Het kunstwerk in verband met zijn tijd," in his *Benaderingen van het literaire werk,* pp. [27]-48. Den Haag: Servire, 1961. [*Buddenbrooks*]

757. ———. "Th. M., Dürer und 'Doktor Faustus,' " *Euphorion,* 59 (1965), 97-117.

758. Eliasberg, Wladimir G. "Okkulte Erlebnisse: Ein Briefwechsel mit Th. M.," *Ruperto-Carola,* 33 (June 1963), 194-196.

759. Eloesser, Arthur. "Neue Bücher," *Neue Rundschau,* 12 (1901), 1281-1290. [*See* esp. pp. 1288-1289 on *Buddenbrooks*]

760. ———. "Th. M.: 'Tristan,' " *Vossische Zeitung,* No. 297 (June 28, 1903. [Cf. I, #1898]

761. ———. "Th. M.," in his *De Duitsche litteratuur sinds 1880,* pp. 76-81. Amsterdam: Elsevier, 1924. [Cf. I, #426. Dutch translation by Martha Leopold]

762. ———. "Th. M.," *Weltbühne,* 21 (1925), 746-750.

763. ———. "Die Th. M-Feier in München," *Berliner Tageblatt,* June 8, 1925; *Vossische Zeitung,* June 8, 1925. [50th birthday]

764. ———. "Th. M., der Deutsche und Europäer," in *Th. M.: Zur Erinnerung an seinen Vortragsabend,* pp. 25-26. Altona, 1926. [Excerpt from I, #619]

765. ———. "Th. M.," in his *Die deutsche Literatur vom Barock bis zur Gegenwart,* Vol. 2, pp. 507-518. Berlin: E. Cassirer, 1931.

766. *Elster, Hanns Martin. "Einleitung," in his *Deutsche Dichterhandschriften,* Vol. 1: *Th. M.,* pp. 7-19. Dresden: Lehmann [1920]

767. ———. " 'Romane der Welt' von Winifred Katzin und Th. M.," *Horen,* 5 (1928), 266-269.

768. ———. "Th. M.: Leben und Werke," in Th. M., *Königliche Hoheit,* pp. 5-[36] Berlin: Deutsche Buch-Gemeinschaft [1928] [Cf. I, item #620]

769. Emig, Erik. "Th. M — K. Kerényi: Gespräch in Briefen," *Freiheit,* July 29, 1960. [Review of item #1,700 c]

770. Emmel, Hildegard. "Das Selbstgericht: Th. M. — Walter Jens; E. Schaper — Günter Grass," in her *Das Gericht in der deutschen Literatur*, pp. 82-119. Bern: Francke, 1963.

771. Emrich, Wilhelm. "Formen und Gehalte des zeitgenössischen Romans," *Universitas*, 11 (January 1956), 49-58. [Th. M., Kafka, Broch, Musil, Proust]

771a. ————. "Th. M.," in his *Das Bild Italiens in der deutschen Dichtung*, pp. 23-24. Köln: Böhlau, 1959.

772. ————. "Die Erzählkunst des 20. Jahrhunderts und ihr geschichtlicher Sinn," in his *Deutsche Literatur in unserer Zeit*, pp. 58-79. Göttingen: Vandenhoeck & Ruprecht [²1959]

773. . "Mythos des 19. Jahrhunderts: Zu Th. M's 'Leiden und Grösse Richard Wagners,' " *Wirtschaftskorrespondenz für Polen*, February 14, 1934, Lit. Beilage. Also in *Zeugnisse: Festschrift für Theodor W. Adorno*, pp. 222-224. Frankfurt a. M.: Europäische Verlagsanstalt, 1963.

774. Emrich, Willi. "Th. M.," in his *Die Träger des Goethepreises der Stadt Frankfurt a. M. von 1927 bis 1961*, pp. 219-225. Frankfurt a. M.: Osterrieth, 1963. [With Th. M's letter to Mayor Walter Kolb and text of his address given on July 25, 1949, pp. 293-302]

775. Enckell, Olof. "Th. M. 80 år," *Hufvudstadsbladet*, June 5, 1955.

776. Enders, Horst. "Der doppelte Beginn mit Hans Castorp: Zu Th. M's 'Der Zauberberg,' " in Norbert Miller, *ed.*, *Romananfänge: Versuch zu einer Poetik des Romans*, pp. 289-316. Berlin: Verlag Lit. Colloquium, 1965.

777. Endres, Elisabeth. "Th. M. — nicht Ironie allein," *Deutsche Zeitung*, November 11, 1961. [Review of Altenberg, item #34]

778. Endres, Fritz. "Th. M.: Zu seinem 50. Geburtstag am 6. Juni," *Hamburger Fremdenblatt*, No. 155 (June 6, 1925), p. 25.

779. *————. *Buddenbrooks*. Lübeck: Buddenbrook-Buchhandlung [1925] 8 pp. pamphlet.

780. ————. "Der Zauberberg," *Lübeckische Blätter*, 67 (May 31, 1925), 402-403.

781. Engberg, Harald. "Th. M.," in Th. M., Døden i Venedig, pp. 5-8. Copenhagen: Gyldendal, 1953. [Der Tod in Venedig]

782. Engel, Eduard. "Die Buddenbrooks," in Rudolf K. Goldschmit, ed., Der kluge Zeitgenosse, p. 203. [Heidelberg] N. Kaupmann [1930] [Concerns Th. M's alleged inability to master his mother tongue]

783. Engelberg, Edward. "Th. M's Faust and Beethoven," Monatshefte, 47 (February 1955), 112-116. [Doctor Faustus]

784. Engeli, Max. "Besuch im Th. M.-Archiv an der E.T.H.," Zürcher Woche, Vol. 10, No. 28 (July 10, 1958), p. 7.

785. Engelson, Suzanne. "Th. M. et la littérature française," Monde, October 1, 1929.

786. Engländer, Richard. "Th. M's Faustroman: Ett verk om ett musikgeni," Musikrevy, 10 (1955), 133-139. [Doktor Faustus]

787. Engler, Winfried. "Der Briefschreiber Th. M.," Stuttgarter Nachrichten, January 27, 1962. [Briefe I,# 2,062]

788. Enns, A. B. "Ein Dichter optisch gesehen: Zur Th. M.-Ausstellung in Lübeck," Lübeckische Blätter, 122 (June 9, 1962), 159-160. [Exhibition]

789. Enright, Dennis Joseph. "Th. M. and the 'Novel of Ideas,' " in his The Apothecary's Shop: Essays on Literature, pp. [113]-120. London: Secker & Warburg, 1957. [The Magic Mountain]

790. ———. "The Anti-Diabolic Faith: Th. M's 'Doctor Faustus,' " in item #789, pp. [121]-144.

791. ———. "The Ironic German. — The Last Year," Essays in Criticism, 9 (July 1959), 300-309. [Review of E. Heller, item #1,278; E. Mann, item #2,059]

792. ———. "My Parsifal: The Genesis of a Novel by Th. M.," New Statesman, (October 27, 1961), 606. [Die Entstehung des Doktor Faustus]

793. ———. "Aimez-vous Goethe? An Inquiry into English Attitudes of Non-Liking Towards German Literature," Encounter, Vol. 22, No. 4 (April 1964), pp. 93-97.

794. Eppelsheimer, Hanns W. "Th. M.," in his Bibliographie der deutschen Literaturwissenschaft, Vol. 1, 1945-1953, pp. 357-

373. Frankfurt a. M.: Klostermann [1957] [See also Köttelwesch]

795. ———. Review of K. W. Jonas, item #1,605, Erasmus (Darmstadt), 11 (1958), 92.

796. ———. "Th. M.," in his Handbuch der Weltliteratur, pp. 623-625. Frankfurt a. M.: Klostermann, ³1960.

797. Eppstein, Irvin. "Th. M. als Repräsentant des humanen Gedankens," MB, Vol. 23, No. 22 (June 3, 1955), pp. 3, 8.

798. Erikson, Erik. "Brief an die Redaktion," Dinge der Zeit, No. 6 (June 1950), pp. 398-399. [Language — Style]

799. ———. "Kritische Revue zum Thema Doktor Faustus," Dinge der Zeit, No. 16 (June 1954), pp. 145-160.

800. ———. "Kritische Revue zum Doktor Faustus: Szenen aus der literarischen Walpurgisnacht," Dinge der Zeit, No. 17 (December 1954).

801. ———. "Kritische Revue zum Doktor Faustus: Prolog im Literaturhimmel," Dinge der Zeit, No. 19 (July/August, 1955).

802. ———. "Kritische Revue: Erster Brief über Kunst und Künstler," Dinge der Zeit, No. 21 (October 1956), pp. 48-72. [Concerns Neider, I, #297]

803. Ernst, Fritz. "Th. M. und der Schelmenroman," NZZ, Vol. 176, Sonntagsausgabe No. 1498 (29), June 5, 1955, Bl. 4. [Felix Krull]

804. Erpel, Fritz. "Th. M's Knowledge of Goethe," GR, 32 (December 1957), 311-313.

805. Esche, Annemarie. "Mythisches und Symbolisches in Th. M's Josephromanen," in G. Wenzel, #3,461, pp. 149-161.

806. Eschenburg, Theodor. "Nachlese zu den Buddenbrooks: Die Hansestadt Lübeck und die letzten Zeitgenossen des Senators Th. M.," Zeit, No. 13 (March 27, 1964), pp. 13-14.

807. Essén, Bengt. "Från bokhyllan," BLM, 18 (May-June, 1949), 390-392. [Der Zauberberg]

808. Esser, Wilhelm Martin. "Grundlinien des Altersstils von Th. M.," Wirkendes Wort, 12 (July 1962), 223-236. [Der Erwählte — Felix Krull]

809. †Essner-Schaknys, Günther. Die epische Wirklichkeit und die
       Raumstruktur des modernen Romans dargestellt an Th. M.,
       Franz Kafka und Hermann Hesse. Ph. D. diss., University of
       Marburg, 1957.

810. Estelrich, J. "Prologo," in Th. M., *Novelas,* pp. [ix]-xxxi.
       Barcelona: J. Janés, 1951.

811. Estorick, Eric. "Th. M.: The Artist as Citizen," *Washington
       Square College Review,* Vol. 1, No. 7 (1937), pp. 3, 32.

812. Eulenberg, Hedda. "Eine Frau dankt Th. M.," *Mittag,* June 7,
       1950. [75th birthday]

813. ———. "Der Erwählte," *Mittag,* March 7, 1951.

814. ———. "Erinnerungen an einen grossen Menschen," *Mittag,*
       August 20, 1955. [Biog. — Obit.]

815. Ewers, Hans. "Lübeck im Kunstwerk Th. M's," *Der Wagen
       1958,* pp. 123-132. Lübeck: Rahtgens, 1958.

816. Ewton, Ralph W., Jr. "The Chronological Structure of Th. M's
       'Die Geschichten Jaakobs,' " *Rice University Studies,* Vol. 50,
       No. 4 (Fall 1964), pp. 27-40.

817. Exner, Richard. "Probleme der Methodik und der Komposition
       in den Essays von Th. M. und Hugo von Hofmannsthal," *GQ,*
       30 (May 1957), 143-157.

818. †———. Der Essay als dichterische Kunstform: Stilistische und
       historische Probleme unter besonderer Berücksichtigung der
       Essayistik Th. M's, Heinrich Manns, Hugo von Hofmannsthals
       und Rudolf Borchardts. Ph. D. diss., University of Southern
       California, 1958.

819. ———. "Zur Essayistik Th. M's," *GRM,* N. F., 12 (January
       1962), [51]-78.

820. ———. "Some Reflections on a Th. M. Exhibit," *GQ,* 36
       (March 1963), 197-200.

821. ———. "Roman und Essay bei Th. M.," *Schweizer Monatshefte,*
       44 (June 1964), 243-258.

822. Eylau, Hans Ulrich. "Vollendung in Weimar: Zum 80.
       Geburtstag von Th. M.," *Sonntag,* Vol. 10, No. 23 (June 5,
       1955), p. 9. [80th birthday]

823. Eyssen, Jürgen. "Um die bürgerliche Welt: Th. M's
      'Bekenntnisse des Hochstaplers Felix Krull,' " *Deutsche
      Rundschau,* 80 (December 1954), 1305-1306.
824. Ezawa, Kennosuke. "Th. M. vor den 'Buddenbrooks,' "
      Geibun-Kenkyu, No. 2 (1953), pp. 87-118. [In German]
825. Fabian, Walter. "Gruss an Th. M.," *Luzerner Tagblatt,* No.
      128 (June 4, 1955). [80th birthday]
826. ————. "Wir feierten mit Th. M.," *Fränkische Presse,* June
      13, 1955. [80th birthday]
827. ————. "Ausklang einer Dichterfreundschaft," *Nürnberger
      Nachrichten,* November 18, 1960, p. 20. [Review of item
      #1,575]
828. Fadiman, Clifton. "Th. M.," in his *ed.* of *Fifty Years . . .
      Alfred and Blanche Knopf,* pp. 7-8, 717-718 et al. New York:
      Alfred A. Knopf, 1965.
829. Fähnrich, Hermann. "Tristan jenseits Wagners: Zum Gedenken
      an Th. M.," *Musica,* 9 (October 1955), 478-481.
830. Faesi, Robert. "Th. M's 'Bekenntnisse des Hochstaplers Felix
      Krull,' " *Neue Schweizer Rundschau,* N. F., 22 (November
      1954), 403-416.
831. *————. *"Th. M.: Ein Meister der Erzählkunst.* [Zurich]
      Atlantis [1955] 193 pp. Excerpts: [From pp. 5-12] "Aus
      einem Glückwunschbrief," *Luzerner Neueste Nachrichten,*
      Vol. 59, No. 128 (June 4, 1955), pp. 1, 3. — [From pp.
      171-194] "Grenzen und Gipfel von Th. M's Welt," *Neue
      Rundschau,* 66 (June 1955), 373-391. — [From pp. 191-194]
      "Th. M's Erscheinung," *National-Zeitung Basel,* June 5, 1955.
      Reviews: Jancke, #1,566 — Luft, #2,021 — J. Müller, #2,312
      —Schröder, #2,967 — Schwengeler, #2,996.
832. ————. "Erfüllung," *Aufbau* (New York), Vol. 21, No. 33
      (August 19, 1955), p. 2. [Obit.]
833. *————., [and] Th. M. *Briefwechsel.* [Zurich] **Atlantis** [1960]
      112 pp. Reviews: Anon., #120 — Baltzer, #173 — Bremser,
      #448 — Helbling, #1,268 — Hellmann, #1,301 —
      Helmerking, #1,319 — Jollos, #1,601 — Leibrich, #1,907 —
      Rychner, #2,809.

834. ———. "Th. M.," in his *Erlebnisse-Ergebnisse-Erinnerungen*, pp. 84-85 et al. [Zurich] Atlantis [1963]

835. Falk, Arthur F. "Die Idee von Th. M's Zauberberg in ihrem Verhältnis zur Psychologie der Lungensanatorien," *Nürnberg-Fürther-Morgenpresse*, July 12, 1926, Unterhaltungsblatt, p. 4.

836. Falqui, Enrico. "Mann e la felicità del lavoro," *Tempo*, January 16, 1961. Also in his *Novecento Letterario*, pp. [378]-383. [Firenze] Vallecchi [1963] [Review of Erika Mann, item #2,059]

837. ———. "Mann e la libertà di pensiero," *Tempo*, August 17, 1962. Also in item #836, pp. [373]-377. [Review of L. Mazzucchetti, item #2,210]

838. Fangen, Ronald. "Th. M.," in his *Tegn og gjaerninger*, pp. [101]-121. Oslo: Gyldendal, 1927.

839. Faye, Jean-Pierre. "Th. M. et Musil: Révolution du retour," *Critique*, 19 (February 1963), [111]-124. [Review of Th. M., *Gesammelte Werke in 12 Bänden*, S. Fischer, 1960; Bertram, item #1,575; Th. M., *Le Journal du Docteur Faustus;* Sontheimer, item #3,097; Deguy, item #649]

840. Fechter, Paul. "Th. M.," in his *Geschichte der deutschen Literatur*, pp. 504-523. Gütersloh: Bertelsmann, 1952.

841. ———. "Th. M's 'Fiorenza,' " in his *Das europäische Drama*, Vol. 2, pp. 369-372. Mannheim: Bibliographisches Institut, 1957.

842. *Feder, Ernst. *Th. M.* Rio de Janeiro: Jornal do Brasil, 1955. 14 pp. ["Gedenkrede auf der Feier der Botschaft der Bundesrepublik . . . 26. August 1955"]

843. Fedin, Konstantin. "Th. M.," *Inostrannaja literatura*, No. 1 (1955), pp. 165-169. German translation, "Würde, Sinn und Nutzen der Kunst: Th. M., der grosse deutsche Epiker," *Sonntag*, No. 34 (August 21, 1955), p. 8. Reprinted in G. Wenzel, item #3,453, pp. 65-72.

844. *Fedorov, A. A. *Tvorčestvo Tomasa Manna. Leksija.* Moskva: Izd. Mosk. univ., 1960. 44 pp.

845. Fehrman, Carl. "Th. M's Faustsaga," *Sydsvenska Dagbladet Snällposten*, January 4, 1949. [*Doktor Faustus*]

846. ————. "Tjugonde seklets Goethe," *Sydsvenska Dagbladet Snällposten*, August 14, 1955. [Obit.]

847. Fehse, Willy. "Anekdoten über Th. M.," in his *Blühender Lorbeer: Dichteranekdoten*, pp. 163-166 et al. Stuttgart: Reclam [1958]

848. ————. "Th. M.," in his *Von Goethe bis Grass*, pp. 77-103. Bielefeld: Gieseking [1963]

849. Feiler, Max Christian. "Th. M.: Dichter und Wanderprediger," *Münchner Merkur*, No. 146 (June 3-4, 1950), Feuilletonbeilage No. 59 'Die Propyläen.' [75th birthday]

850. Feith, Rudolf. "Th. M.: Rückkehr nach Europa," *Stimme des Friedens*, Vol. 4, No. (1953).

851. Fetscher, Iring. "Der andere Weg: Betrachtung zum 'Doktor Faustus,'" *Studentische Blätter*, Vol. 2, No. 5 (June 20, 1948), pp. 3-6.

852. ————. "Frankreich huldigt Th. M.," *Dokumente*, 11 (1955), 443-445. [Concerns item #1,493]

853. Feuchtwanger, Lion. "Das Erlebnis und das Drama," *Schaubühne*, 5 (1909), 185-188, 213-216. [Concerns *Bilse und ich*]

854. ————. "Mann Makes Sport of Congenial Scoundrel," *Los Angeles Daily News*, December 6, 1954. [Translated into English by Stanley Townsend] German original, "Felix Krull, ein bürgerlicher Schelm," *NDL*, 3 (February 1955), 141-142.

855. ————. "Th. M. zum 80. Geburtstag," *Aufbau* (Berlin), 11 (June 1955), [488]

856. ————. "Brief an Th. M.," *NDL*, Vol. 3, No. 6 (June 1955), p. 15. [facsim.] [80th birthday]

857. ————. "Kampf ohne Ende," *Aufbau* (New York), Vol. 21, No. 33 (August 19, 1955), p. 2. [Obit.]

858. ————. "Th. M. Rode Forth; the Cost of Greatness," *Nation* (New York), 181 (September 3, 1955), 192-194. [Obit.]

859. Feuerlicht, Ignace. "On Recent Editions of Th. M.," *GQ*, 33 (May 1960), 227-232.

860. ————. "Rolle, Dienst und Opfer bei Th. M.," *PMLA*, 77 (June 1962), 318-327. Also in #3,852, pp. 89-109.

861. ———. "Th. M's mythische Identifikation," *GQ,* 36 (March 1963), 141-151. [*Joseph Novels*] Also in #3,852, pp. 77-88.

862. †Fickert, Kurt J. "Hesse and Th. M.," Chapt. VII in his The Problem of the Artist and the Philistine in the Works of Hermann Hesse. Ph. D. diss., New York University, 1952.

863. Fiechtner, Helmut A. "Die Musik in Th. M's Doktor Faustus," *Badische Zeitung,* November 29, 1949. [Adds to I, item #2709]

864. ———. "Gewohnt im schiefen Licht zu stehen," *Furche,* June 9, 1962.

865. Fiedler, Kuno [pseud. F. Kauz] "Ein neues Th. M.-Buch," *Volksstimme,* Vol. 44, No. 180 (August 4, 1948). [*Neue Studien*]

866. ———. "Th. M., der Deutsche und Weltbürger," *Schweizer Familienkalender für das Jahr 1951,* 13 (1951), 28-29.

867. ———. "Th. M.: *Altes und Neues," Volksstimme,* May 20, 1953.

868. ———. "Th. M's Schiller-Rede," *Volksstimme,* July 29, 1955.

869. Field, G. Wallis. "Music and Morality in Th. M. and Hermann Hesse," *University of Toronto Quarterly,* 24 (January 1955), 175-190. [*Doktor Faustus — Das Glasperlenspiel*]

870. Fierz, Jürg. "Th. M.: Tonio Kröger," *Trivium,* 2 (1944), 235.

871. Fischer, Annie. "Th. M.: *Joseph in Aegypten," Cobden,* 1937, pp. 35-36.

872. Fischer, Ernst. "Anmut und Würde: Th. M. zum 80. Geburtstag," *Tagebuch,* Vol. 10, No. 12 (June 4, 1955), pp. 1-2.

873. ———. "Zu zwei Briefen von Th. M.," *Sinn und Form,* 11 (1959), 74-79. [*Der Zauberberg — Doktor Faustus*]

874. Fischer, Hedwig. "Aus den Erinnerungen: Erste Begegnung mit Th. M.," *Almanach: das 67. Jahr,* pp. 39-43. [Frankfurt a. M.] S. Fischer, 1953. [Cf. I, item #804]

875. Fischer, Heinrich. "German Writers of Today," *Horizon,* Vol. 15, No. 85 (1947), pp. 3-14. [*See* esp. pp. 8-11]

876. Fischer, Peter. "Roman eines Romans," *Frankfurter Rundschau,* May 14, 1949. [*Die Entstehung des Doktor Faustus*]

877. *Flämig, Walter. *Zum Konjunktiv in der deutschen Sprache der Gegenwart: Inhalts- und Gebrauchsweisen dargestellt auf Grund von Th. M's Romanen und Erzählungen.* Berlin: Akademie-Verlag, ²1962. [¹1959] 188 pp. [Ph. D. diss., University of Leipzig, 1959]

878. Flake, Otto. "Der Fall Th. M.," *Badener Tageblatt,* December 8, 1945. Also in Grosser, item #1,090, pp. 51-56. [Th. M. as an emigré]

879. *Fleischmann, Rudolf. "A proseci Fleischmann's Találkozás," *Ujság,* January 17, 1937, pp. 11-12. English version entitled *How Rudolf Fleischmann from Prosec met Th. M.,* Fulwood-Preston, 1957. [8 pp. — pamphlet concerning Th. M's Czech citizenship]

880. ―――. "The Man from Prosec," *Manchester Guardian,* January 15, 1966, p. 7.

881. Flesch, Hans. "Nachruf," in P.E.N., item #2,501.

882. ―――. "Address," in Wilkinson, item #3,494.

883. Flinker, Martin. "Th. M.," *Réforme,* Vol. 3, No. 96 (January 18, 1947), p. 4.

884. ―――. "Th. M. et le Problème de la Solitude," in item #1,493, pp. 155-165.

885. ―――. "Dernière Visite chez Th. M.," *Figaro Littéraire,* Vol. 10, No. 487 (August 20, 1955), p. 1.

886. ―――. "In memoriam Th. M.," *Almanac de la Librairie Flinker,* p. 5. [Paris, 1955]

887. *―――. *Th. M's politische Betrachtungen im Lichte der heutigen Zeit.* s-Gravenhage: Mouton, 1959. 172 pp. Reviews: Anon., #103 — Demetz, #656 — Gronicka, #1,087 — Hellmann, #1,290 — Loewy-Hattendorf, #1,998. *See also* #1,493.

888. Flood, Ethelbert. "Christian Language in Modern Literature," *Culture,* Vol. 22, No. 1 (1961), pp. [28]-42. [*See* esp. pp. 34-38 on *Joseph and His Brothers*]

889. Flora, Francesco. "Il Premio dell'Accademia dei Lincei a Th. M. nel 1952," *Letterature Moderne,* 6 (May-June 1956), 343-345.

890. Förster, Gisela. "Th. M. in seiner Zeit," *Spektrum,* Vol. 11, No. 5 (1965), pp. 157-169. [Biog.]

891. ————. "Hinweise auf Publikationen," *Spektrum,* Vol. 11, No. 5 (1965), pp. 218-219. [Bibliog.]

892. Förster, Wieland. "Versuch einer Ehrung," *Spektrum,* Vol. 11, No. 5 (1965), p. 177. [Concerns his statue of Th. M.]

893. Fontana, Oskar Maurus. "Die Brüder Mann," *Tag,* January 1, 1930. [*Die Forderung des Tages*]

894. ————. "Der Mann mit zuviel Eigenschaften," *Presse,* No. 1837 (November 7, 1954), p. 18. [*Felix Krull*]

895. ————. "Th. M's dichterischer Weg," *Presse,* No. 2010 (June 4, 1955), pp. 15-16. [80th birthday]

896. ————. "Gespräch mit Th. M.," in Willy Haas, item #1,132, pp. 49-51. [Cf. I, item #488]

897. ————. "Th. M. aus der Nähe gesehen," *Salzburger Nachrichten,* November 27, 1965, p. I. [Review of Bürgin-Mayer, item #504]

898. Ford, William J. "A Note on Hans Castorp," *News Letter . . . Literature and Psychology,* Vol. 2, No. 4 (September 1952), pp. 2-5. [*The Magic Mountain*]

899. Forst [de] Battaglia, Otto. "Th. M.," *Przegląd Wspólczesny,* No. 72 (1928), pp. 146-151.

900. ————. "Th. M. und der Nobelpreis," *Allgemeine Rundschau,* 26 (December 7, 1929), 959-960.

901. Forstetter, Michel. "Hommage à Th. M.," *Réforme,* August 27, 1955. [Obit.]

902. Fortini, Franco. "La selva ironica," *Il Contemporaneo,* Vol 2, No. 23 (June 4, 1955), p. 6.

903. Fougère, "Th. M.," *Verger,* Vol. 1, No. 2 (1947), pp. 4-11.

904. *————. *La Seduzione della Morte in Th. M.* Roma: Macchia, 1951. [Italian translation of I, item #1127]

905. *Fourrier, Georges. *Th. M.: Le Message d'un artiste-bourgeois, 1896-1924.* Paris: Les Belles Lettres, 1960. 424 pp. [Ph. D. diss., University of Paris, 1957] Excerpt in #906. Reviews: Leibrich, #1,897

906. ———. "Th. M's 'Fiorenza,' " in item #3,472, pp. 238-252.

907. Fowler, Alastair. "The Confidence Man," *Listener*, Vol. 65, No. 1675 (May 4, 1961), pp. 781-784. [*Felix Krull*]

908. †Fowler, J. R. Th. M's Humanism. An Examination of its Nature and Development. M. A. thesis, University of Wales, 1955.

909. Fradkin, Ilja. " 'Der Zauberberg' und die Geburt des modernen intellektuellen Romans," *Sinn und Form: Sonderheft Th. M.*, 1965, pp. 74-84. Transl. from the Russian by Gerhard Dick.

910. Fraiberg, Selma. "Two Modern Incest Heroes," *Partisan Review*, 28 (1961), 646-661. [*Invisible Man* — *The Holy Sinner*]

911. Frank, Bruno. "Auf einen lebenden Dichter," *NDL*, 3 (June 1955), 46. Reprinted from his *Der Schatten der Dinge: Gedichte*, p. 70. München: Langen [1912] Also in *Schaubühne*, June 10, 1915.

912. Frank, John G. "Letters by Th. M. to Julius Bab," *GR*, 36 (October 1961), [195]-204. *See also* H. Lehnert, #1,876.

913. Frank, Joseph. "Dedication to Th. M.," *Washington Square College Review*, Vol. 1, No. 7 (1937), p. 4.

914. ———. "Th. M.: The Artist as Individual," *Washington Square College Review*, Vol. 1, No. 7 (1937), pp. 5-6, 22-23.

915. ———. "Reaction as Progress: Th. M's 'Doctor Faustus,' " *Chicago Review*, Vol. 15, No. 2 (Autumn 1961), pp. 19-39. Also in his *The Widening Gyre: Crisis and Mastery in Modern Literature*, pp. [131]-161. New Brunswick, N. J.: Rutgers University Press [1963] [Part of this essay had been published before in I, item #2713]

916. Frankfurter, Felix. "Th. M.," in his *Of Law and Men: Papers and Addresses, 1939-1956*, pp. 346-351. New York: Harcourt, 1956. [Reprint of I, item #805]

917. Fränkl-Lundborg, Otto. "Th. M's 'Lotte in Weimar,' " in his *Geist und Ungeist: Literarische Betrachtungen, 1927-1959*, pp. 119-122. München: Die Rose [1960] [Cf. I, item #2587]

918. ———. "Th. M's 'Doktor Faustus,' " in item #917, pp. 197-199. [Cf. I, item #2712]

919. Franzel, Emil. "Roman des Untergangs," *Tagespost,* Vol. 2,
      No. 27 (March 5, 1949), p. 10. [*Doktor Faustus*]

920. ———. "Th. M.: Joseph der Ernährer," *Tagespost,* October
      26, 1949.

921. ———. "Th. M. und das 20. Jahrhundert," *Tagespost,* Vol.
      8, No. 100 (August 29, 1955), p. 8. [Obit.]

922. Fratzscher, A. "Eine Th. M.-Bibliographie," *Börsenblatt für
      den deutschen Buchhandel,* Frankfurter Ausgabe, Vol. 16,
      No. 29 (April 12, 1960), pp. 591-592. [Review of H. Bürgin,
      item #502]

923. Frederiksen, Emil. "Th. M. og det levende ord," *Berlingske
      Tidende,* June 6, 1955. [80th birthday]

924. ———. "Th. M. som taler," in *Adermanneskets ansvar,* item
      #2,431, pp. 142-148.

925. ———. "Th. M.: Lotte in Weimar," *Berlingske Tidende,*
      October 5, 1956.

926. Frenk, Mariana. "Th. M., Poeta y Pensador," *Novedades,* No.
      311 (March 6, 1955), pp. 1, 5.

927. Frenzel, Christian Otto. " 'Der Mann, den sein Gewissen
      trieb': Maurice Rostand, Ernest Hemingway, Th. M.
      appellieren an die Vernunft," *Westfälische Zeitung,* January
      27, 1931. [*Deutsche Ansprache*]

928. Frenzel, Herbert A., [and] Elisabeth Frenzel. "Th. M.," in
      their *Daten deutscher Dichtung,* pp. 294-297, 407-408. Köln:
      Kiepenheuer & Witsch, 1953. [²1959]

929. ———. "Gerhart Hauptmann e Th. M.: Il Problema di
      un'amicizia," *Convivium,* 23 (May-June, 1955), 297-310.

930. Freud, Sigmund. "Brief an Th. M. vom 6. 6. 1935," in
      Almanach: das 73. Jahr, pp. 34-35. [Frankfurt a. M.] S.
      Fischer, 1959.

931. ———. "Letter to Th. M. of November 29, 1936," in Ernest
      Jones, *Sigmund Freud; His Life and Works,* Vol. 3, pp. 492-
      494. New York: Basic Books [1957] *See also* pp. 199, 205-206,
      347. Both letters appear in Ernst L. Freud's edition of Sigmund
      Freud, *Briefe 1873-1939,* pp. 418-419, 424-427. [Frankfurt
      a. M.] S. Fischer [1960]

932. Freund, Michael. "Herr Permaneder," *Gegenwart,* 7 (December 20, 1952), 846-847. [*Die Buddenbrooks*]

933. ———. "Unabhängiges Gewissen," *Gegenwart,* 10 (June 4, 1955), 377-378. [80th birthday — *Betrachtungen eines Unpolitischen*]

934. Frey, Alexander M. "Vortragsabend Th. M's," *Die lit. Welt,* Vol. 3, No. 47 (1927), p. 10.

935. ———. "Begegnung Th. M.: Der unermüdliche Arbeiter," *Tages-Anzeiger,* Vol. 60, No. 231 (October 1, 1952), p. 2. [Personal Tributes — Premio Feltrinelli]

936. ———. "Altes und Neues von Th. M.," *St. Galler Tagblatt,* May 2, 1953.

•937. ———. "Th. M's neue Erzählung," *NZZ,* Vol. 174, No. 2266 (October 1, 1953), Bl. 1, pp. 1-2. [With postscript on facsimile edition by W. Weber]

938. ———. "Zum Tode von Th. M.: Der Mensch und der Dichter," *National-Zeitung Basel,* No. 373 (August 13/14, 1955), p. 2.

939. ———. "Kontakte mit Th. M.: Der Mensch und der Freund," *St. Galler Tagblatt,* Abendblatt No. 378 (August 15, 1955). [Obit.]

940. ———. "Th. M.: 'Der Tod in Venedig und andere Erzählungen,' " *Büchergilde,* No. 1 (1956), pp. 9-11.

941. †Frey, Erich. Amerika in den Werken Th. M's. Ph. D. diss., University of Southern California, 1963.

942. Friedemann, Fritz. "Th. M.," in his *Was ich erlebte,* Vol. 2, pp. 222-225. Berlin: A. Pulvermacher, 1909. [*Buddenbrooks*]

943. Friedenberg, Daniel M. "Mann's Obsession with the Circle of Duality," *Commonweal,* 74 (August 25, 1961), 476-477. [*The Story of a Novel: The Genesis of Doctor Faustus*]

944. Friedenthal, Richard. "Er hatte noch Recht in seinem Widerspruch: Vor zehn Jahren starb Th. M.," *Christ und Welt,* Vol. 18, No. 33 (August 13, 1965). [10th anniversary of M's death]

945. *Friedlaender, Otto. *Th. M. als Politiker*. Stockholm: Freier
Deutscher Kulturbund, 1945. 10 pp.
946. Friedlaender, Salomo. "Zauberbergpredigt eines ungläubigen
Thomas an Mannbare: Rezept zum Kitsch allerersten Ranges"
[von Mynona, pseud.] *Neue Bücherschau*, No. 4 (1926/27),
pp. 186-187.
947. Friedmann, Ernst. "Ein Besuch bei Th. M. im Jahre 1938,"
Edioth Hayon, June 28, 1957.
948. Friedrichs, Ernst. "Von den 'Buddenbrooks' zum 'Zauberberg,' "
Bremer Nachrichten, Vol. 183, No. 54 (June 5, 1925). [50th
birthday]
949. Frisé, Adolf. "Roman und Essay," in his anthology,
Definitionen: Essays zur Literatur, pp. 144-151. Frankfurt
a. M.: Klostermann, 1963.
950. Fritz, Walter Helmut. "Mathildenhöhe als Zauberberg: Th.
M.-Ausstellung in Darmstadt," *Christ und Welt*, Vol. 15,
No. 14 (April 6, 1962), p. 21.
951. Fromm, Hans. "Th. M.: Briefe 1889-1936," *Kranich*, 4
(1962), 133-136. [Review of item #2,062]
952. Fromm, Hans Rudolf. "Symphonia pathologica: Zum 80.
Geburtstag von Th. M.," *Pharmazeutische Zeitung*, Vol. 91-100,
No. 23 (June 9, 1955), pp. 597-599.
953. ———. "Usque ad hilaritatem: Zu Th. M's 90. Geburtstag,"
Deutsches Medizinisches Journal, 16 (October 20, 1965),
657-660.
954. Fuchs, Albert. "Th. M.: Les Buddenbrook," in his *Initiation
à l'Etude de la langue et littérature allemande modernes*,
pp. 182-193. Strasbourg: Faculté des Lettres de l'Université,
1939. [Paris: Les Belles Lettres ²1948, pp. 227-235]
955. ———. "Th. M.," in his *Deutsche Prosa seit der Vorklassik*,
pp. xxxv-xxxvi Paris: Les Belles Lettres, 1951.
956. Fürnberg, Louis. "Glückwunsch," in item #2,833.
957. ———. "Th. M.," in his *Das Jahr des vierblättrigen Klees*,
pp. 170-171 et al. Berlin: Dietz, 1959.
958. Fürst, Rudolf. "Dichter-Monographien," *Vossische Zeitung*,
November 7, 1913. [Review of Alberts, I, item #99]

959. Fürstenheim, E. G. "The Place of 'Der Erwählte' in the
      Work of Th. M.," *MLR*, 51 (January 1956), [55]-70.
960. Fueter, Eduard. "Jugenderinnerungen an Th. M.," *Du*, Vol. 16,
      No. 9 (September 1956), pp. 70, 73, 76. [Biog.]
961. *Fueter, Heinrich. *Im Spiegel. Th. M.: Sein Werk, seine Zeit*.
      Zurich: Condor-Film, 1963.
962. Furst, Lilian R. "Th. M's 'Tonio Kröger': A Critical
      Reconsideration," *Revue des Langues Vivantes — Levende
      Talen*, 27 (1961), 232-240.
963. Furstner, Hans. Review of K. W. Jonas, item #1,605, *Revue
      des Langues Vivantes — Levende Talen*, 23 (1957), 573-574.
964. Fussenegger, Gertrud. "Der Zauberer auf dem Olymp:
      Erinnerungen an Th. M.," *Saarbrücker Zeitung*, No. 182
      (August 7/8, 1965), Feuilleton, p. 1. [10th anniversary of
      M's death]
965. Gad, Carl. "Th. M's nye bog," *Berlingske Tidende*, December
      19, 1926. [*Der Zauberberg*]
966. Gading, Walter. "Der lange Satz bei Th. M.," *Muttersprache*,
      No. 6 (June 1955), pp. 207-212.
967. Gaertner, Johannes A. "Dialectic Thought in Th. M's *The
      Magic Mountain*," *GQ*, 38 (November 1965), 605-618.
968. Ganne, Gilbert. "Avant d'écrir 'Sang Réservé' Th. M. avait-il
      lu Elémir Bourges?," *Arts*, September 1955. [*Wälsungenblut —
      Le Crépuscule des Dieux*]
969. Gannet, Lewis. "The Holy Sinner," *NYHT*, September 10,
      1951. [*Der Erwählte*]
970. Gardiner, Harold C. "Two Novels That Distort the Past," in his
      In All Conscience: Reflections on Books and Culture, pp. 70-74.
      Garden City, New York: Hanover House [1959] [Cf. I,
      item #2885]
971. Garnier, Pierre. "Hommage à Th. M.," *Sinn und Form*, 7
      (1955), 350-354. [80th birthday]
972. Gasser, Manuel. "Th. M. mit achtzig Jahren," *Weltwoche*,
      Vol. 23, No. 1125 (June 3, 1955), p. 5. [80th birthday]
973. ———. "Th. M. — Ende und Beginn," *Weltwoche*, Vol. 23,
      No. 1136 (August 19, 1955), p. 5. [Obit.]

974. Gasser, Paul. "Ausstrahlung des Zauberberges," *Annalen,* 2 (1928), 555-558. [Concerns Willy Hellpach's lecture on 'Zauberbergkrankheit' #1,313]

975. Gast, E. E. "Die Geschichte Jaakobs," *Sammlung,* 1 (1945), 245-249.

976. Gaul, Gerhard. "Zur Lübecker Uraufführung des Filmes 'Tonio Kröger,' " *Lübeckische Blätter,* 124 (September 12, 1964), 229-231.

977. Geerdts, Hans Jürgen. "Klassisch-realistische Wiederholungen im Schaffen Th. M's," *Weimarer Beiträge,* 4 (1962), [711]-726.

978. ———. "Th. M's 'Tristan' in der literarischen Tradition," in G. Wenzel, item #3,472, pp. 190-206.

979. Gehlen, A. "Th. M's Goethe Betreffendes," *Wiener lit. Echo,* 2 (1949/50), 1-3.

980. Gehrke, M. M. "Der Zauberberg," *Pester Lloyd,* December 14, 1924, Morgenblatt, pp. 1-4.

981. †Gehrts, Barbara. Die Bedeutung der Frauengestalten im Romanwerk Th. M's. Ph. D. diss., University of Freiburg i. Br., 1958. 283 pp.

982. Geisenheyner, Max. "Adel des Geistes: Zum Tode Th. M's," *Allgemeine Zeitung Mainz,* No. 187 (August 15, 1955), Feuilleton, p. 6. [Obit.]

983. Geismar, Maxwell. "The Fulfillment of the Artist," *NYT Book Review,* September 18, 1955, pp. 1, 29. [*Felix Krull*]

984. Geissler, Ewald. "Paneuropa und Th. M.," *Deutsche Zeitung,* No. 141 (June 19, 1930), Beilage 'Kultur und Kunst.'

985. Geissler, Rolf. "Der Zauberberg Th. M's," in his *Dekadenz und Heroismus,* pp. 104-121. Stuttgart: DVA, 1964.

986. Genschmer, Fred. Review of R. A. Nicholls, item #2,407, *Monatshefte,* 47 (December 1954), 413-414.

987. George, Manfred. "Un allemand européen: Th. M.," *Revue Bleue,* 64 (1926), 330-331.

988. ———. "Th. M. zum 80. Geburtstag," *Aufbau* (New York), Vol. 21, No. 22 (June 3, 1955), p. 3.

989. ———. "Th. M's Erfolg in U.S.A.: Ein Gespräch mit seinem Verleger Alfred A. Knopf," *Aufbau* (New York), Vol. 21, No. 22 (June 3, 1955), pp. 4, 6. Also in *Tagesspiegel,* June 3, 1955, and *Merkur am Sonntag,* June 4-5, 1955.

990. ———. "Th. M. und der Aufbau," *Aufbau* (New York), Vol. 21, No. 33 (August 19, 1955), pp. 3-4.

991. ———. "Human Patriot," *Nation* (New York), 187 (September 20, 1958), 159. [Review of Erika Mann, item #2,059]

992. †Georgi, Hans. Die Gestalt des Deutschen bei Th. M. Ph. D. diss., University of Marburg, 1955.

993. Gerber, Hans Erhard. "Th. M.," in his *Nietzsche und Goethe: Studien zu einem Vergleich,* pp. 47-48 et al. Bern: P. Haupt [1954]

994. German, Kaspar. "Ermutigung," *Spektrum,* 11 (1965), 197-200.

995. Gerster, Georg. "Th. M. an der Arbeit," *Weltwoche,* Vol. 22, No. 1099 (December 3, 1954), p. 21.

996. Gide, André. "Préface à quelques écrits de Th. M.," *Marianne,* September 22, 1937. Also in Italian as "Prefazione all'edizione francese [di] *Attenzione Europa,*" in Th. M., *Moniti all'Europa,* pp. 59-62. [Milano] A. Mondadori [1947] [Cf. I, item #1,574]

997. Gierow, Karl Ragnar. "Th. M's övermänniska," *Svenska Dagbladet,* April 12, 1948. Reprinted in his *Mina utflykter,* pp. 275-281. Stockholm: Norstedt, 1950. [Cf. I, item #2,721 — *Doktor Faustus*]

998. ———. "Till Adrian Leverkühns förhistoria," *Svenska Dagbladet,* March 4, 1959. Reprinted in item #997, pp. 281-288.

999. ———. "Th. M. og Nietzsche," *Svenska Dagbladet,* March 11, 1949. Reprinted in item #997, pp. 288-294. [*Neue Studien*]

1,000. ———. "Berättelsens ande," *Svenska Dagbladet,* April 14, 1951. [*Der Erwählte*]

1,001. ———. "Th. M's helgon,"*Svenska Dagbladet,* April 16, 1951. [*Der Erwählte*]

1,002. ———. "Epoken Th. M.," *Svenska Dagbladet,* June 6, 1955. [80th birthday]

1,003. Giese, Richard. "Bürger zwischen zwei Welten," *Westdeutsche Allgemeine Zeitung,* June 5, 1950. [75th birthday]

1,004. Giesecke, Hans. "Stil und Geschichte in Th. M's Joseph-Roman," *Zeichen der Zeit,* Vol. 12, No. 5 (1958), [180]-183.

1,005. ———. "Th. M. und die Kunst der Zukunft: Zum 5. Todestag," *Neue Zeit,* No. 188 (August 12, 1960), p. 4.

1,006. Gigli, Lorenzo. "Th. M.," *Gazzetta del Popolo,* September 5, 1924. [*Tonio Kröger*]

1,007. Gill, Brendan. "Books: Last Performance," *New Yorker,* 31 (October 1, 1955), 136, 138. [*Felix Krull*]

1,008. Gillet, Louis. "Charlotte à Weimar ou la vieillesse de Goethe," *Revue des Deux Mondes,* October 15, 1941, pp. 494-505. [*Lotte in Weimar*]

1,009. Gilman, Milton. "Th. M." [poem] *Mutiny,* Vol. 2, No. 1 (Winter 1958), p. 18.

1,010. Gilman, Richard. "The Journey of Th. M.," *Commonweal,* 69 (October 24, 1958), 93-96. [Review of E. Heller, item #1,278]

1,011. ———. "Revelations of the Mind of Mann," *Commonweal,* 70 (March 6, 1959), 6-3. [*Last Essays*]

1,012. Girnus, Wilhelm. "Er lebt mit uns," *Literatur* (Berlin), No. 2 (February 2, 1965), ND-Beilage. [Politics]

1,013. ———. "Weltenwende im magischen Feuer: Dem Gedenken Th. M's zum 10. Todestag," *Neues Deutschland,* August 12, 1965, p. 4.

1,014. Gisselbrecht, André. "Th. M's Hinwendung vom Geist der Musikalität zur Bürgerpflicht," *Sinn und Form: Sonderheft Th. M.,* 1965, pp. 291-334. [Transl. from the French by Otto Distler]

1,015. Giusso, Lorenzo. "Th. M.," *L'Osservatore Politico Letterario,* Vol. 1, No. 6 (1955), pp. 39-47.

1,016. *Glanville-Hicks, Peggy. *The Transposed Heads.* New York: Assoc. Music Pub. [1948] 139 pp. [English libretto with German text by Moritz Bernhard]

1,017. Glass, E. "Th. M. on Life and Literature," *Sunday Referee,*
November 25, 1924. [Interview]

1,018 †Glebe, William V. The Relationship between Art and Disease
in the Works of Th. M. Ph. D. diss., University of Washington,
1960.

1,019. ———. "Selbstreferat," *Germanistik,* 1 (July 1960), 389-390.
[Review of item #1,018]

1,020. ———. "The 'Diseased' Artist Achieves a New 'Health': Th.
M's *Lotte in Weimar," MLQ,* 22 (March 1961), 55-62.

1,021. ———. "The Artist's 'Disease' in Some of Th. M's Earliest
Tales,"*Books Abroad,* 39 (Summer 1965), [261]-268.

1,022. Glinsky, Mattco. "Wagner visto da Th. M.," *Osservatore
Romano,* Vol. 91, No. 162 (1951), p. 3. [Concerns Th. M's
letter to Emil Preetorius from *La Revue Musicale Suisse*]

1,023. Godman, Stanley. "Zur Th. M.-Bibliographie," *Wandlung,* 4
(1949), 454-456. [Supplement to Bürgin, I, item #513]

1,024. Goebel, Heinrich. "Th. M.," in his *Neudeutsche Prosadich-
tungen,* Vol. 3, pp. [57]-61. Dresden: Ehlermann, 1926.

1,025. *Goedsche, C. R., [and] Walter E. Glaettli. *Th. M.* New York:
American Book Co. [1957] vi, 74 pp. [Textbook for
Beginners]

1,026. Gömöri, Jenö Tamás."An Th. M.," *Sinn und Form:
Sonderheft Th. M.,* 1965, p. 335. [German version of this
poem by B. K. Tragelehn]

1,027. Goes, Albrecht. "Lebensfreundlichkeit: Th. M. zum 80.
Geburtstag," *Neue Rundschau,* 66 (June 1955), 369-372.
Also in his *Ruf und Echo: Aufzeichnungen 1951-1955,* pp. 84-
[90] [Frankfurt a. M.] S. Fischer, 1956.

1,028. ———. "Huldigung und Bekenntnis," *Stuttgarter Zeitung,*
June 4, 1955, Beilage 'Die Brücke zur Welt.' [80th birthday]

1,029. ———. "Zu Th. M's 'Doktor Faustus,' " *Basler Nachrichten,*
Vol. 49, No. 22 (June 5, 1955), Sonntagsblatt, pp. 1-2.

1,030. ———. "In memoriam Th. M.," *Zeit,* Vol. 11, No. 32 (August
19, 1956), p. 5. [Obit.]

1,031. ———. "Zum Abschied von Th. M.," *Börsenblatt für den
Deutschen Buchhandel,* Frankfurter Ausgabe, 11 (August 26,

1955), 541-542. Translated into French by Freddy de Médicis as "Adieu à Th. M.," *Revue Générale,* (October 15, 1955), 2027-2031. [Obit.]

1,032. ———. "Lynkeus," in G. Wenzel, item #3,453, pp. 93-95. Also in A. Goes, *Die guten Gefährten,* pp. 161-162. Stuttgart: Cotta [1961]

1,033. ———. "Erinnerung an Th. M.: Schillerfeier, Stuttgart, 9. Mai 1955," in item #1,032, pp. 157-162.

1,034. ———. "In Naphtas Zimmer: Zum 10. Todestag von Th. M," *Stuttgarter Zeitung,* August 10, 1965.

1,035. Goetz, Bruno. "Anlässlich Th. M's 'Tod in Venedig,' " *Aktion,* 3 (1913), 559-560.

1,036. Goldbeck, Eduard. "Der Kampf mit dem Leben," *Leipziger Tageblatt,* Vol. 1, No. 10 (April 11, 1904), pp. 38-39, Beilage 'Mussestunden.' [*Buddenbrooks*]

1,037. Goldschmit, Rudolf. "Th. M. auf den Spuren Richard Wagners: Aufsätze, Betrachtungen, Briefe," *Stuttgarter Zeitung,* No. 147 (June 28, 1963), p. iv. [Review of E. Mann, item #2,065]

1,038. Goldschmit-Jentner, Rudolf K. "Vom Taugenichts zum Felix Krull," *Heidelberger Tageblatt,* November 23, 1945.

1,039. ———. "Das neue Werk von Th. M.: Der Erwählte," *Heidelberger Tageblatt,* April 3, 1951.

1,040. ———. "Th. M. und Heidelberg," *Heidelberger Tageblatt,* August 15, 1955. [Biog. — Obit.]

1,041. ———. "Zauberer hinter verschlossener Tür," *Süddeutsche Zeitung,* No. 193 (August 16, 1955), p. 3. [Obit.]

1,042. ———. "Der Europäer Th. M.," *Motor im Bild,* 12 (May 1958), 28-29.

1,043. Goldstein, Moritz. "Th. M.: Friedrich und die Grosse Koalition," *Berliner Börsen-Courier,* July 11, 1915.

1,044. Goldstein, Walter B. "Wassermann und Th. M.," in his *Jakob Wassermann,* pp. 9-11. Berlin: Künsterdank, 1933.

1,045. ———. "Th. M's Briefe von 1937 bis 1947," *MB,* Vol. 32, No. 27 (July 3, 1964), p. 5. [Review of item #2,066. Rejoinder by Erich Gottgetreu, item #1,050]

1,046. Golik, I. E. "Die Werke Th. M's in der UdSSR," *Neues Deutschland*, Vol. 16, No. 186 (July 8, 1961), Beilage 'Kunst und Literatur,' No. 27, p. 2.

1,047. ————. "Doktor Faustus," *Filologičeskie nauki*, 6 (1963), 108-109.

1,048. Goth, Ernst. "Königliche Hoheit," *Pester Lloyd*, Morgenblatt, October 17, 1909, pp. 23-24.

1,049. Gottgetreu, Erich. "Th. M. in seinen Briefen: Zum Erscheinen des ersten Bandes der neuen Auswahl," *MB*, Vol. 30, No. 5 (February 2, 1962), pp. 5-7. [Review of *Briefe I*, item #2,062]

1,050. ————. "Th. M's Haltung zum Judenproblem," *MB*, Vol. 32, No. 30 (July 24, 1964), pp. 9-10. [Sharp reply to W. B. Goldstein, #1,045]

1,051. Gozzi, Federico. "Il liberale Th. M.," *Il Mondo*, Vol. 7, No. 34 (August 23, 1955), pp. 1-2. [Politics]

1,052. Graf, Oskar Maria. "Kleiner Dank an Th. M.," *Aufbau* (New York), Vol. 21, No. 22 (June 3, 1955), pp. 5-6. Also in his *An manchen Tagen*, pp. 293-296. [Frankfurt a. M.] Nest [1961] [80th birthday]

1,053. ————. "Briefwechsel [mit Th. M.] anlässlich seines 70. Geburtstags," in his *An manchen Tagen*, item #1,052, pp. 289-292.

1,054. ————. "Widmung in einem Geburtstagsbrief 1955," [poem] in his *An manchen Tagen*, item #1,052, pp. 297-299.

1,055. ————. "In unfassbarem Schmerz," *Aufbau* (New York), Vol. 21, No. 33 (August 19, 1955), p. 1. Also in his *An manchen Tagen*, item #1,052, p. 300. [Obit.]

1,056. ————. "Th. M. als geistiges Erlebnis: Totenrede im Hunter College," in his *An manchen Tagen*, item #1,052, pp. 301-313. [Obit.]

1,057. ————. "Zwei Töchter sehen ihren Vater," in item #1,052, pp. 314-320. [Review of Erika Mann, item #2,059, and Monika Mann, item #2,100]

1,058. Grandi, Hans. Review of Žmegač, item #3,600, *DLZ*, 84 (September 1963), 730-732. *See also* item #660.

1,059.   Gray, Ronald. "Th. M.," in his *The German Tradition in Literature 1871-1945*, pp. 105-223. Cambridge: University Press, 1965. *See* Hatfield, #3,873.

1,060.   Grazzini, Giovanni. "Th. M.: Carlotta a Weimar — Confessioni del Cavaliere Felix Krull," *Ponte*, 12 (1956), 664-667.

1,061.   Gregor, Joseph. "Th. M's 'Fiorenza,' " in his *Der Schauspielführer*, Vol. 1, pp. 273-274. Stuttgart: Hiersemann, 1953.

1,062.   Gregor-Dellin, Martin. "Das jüngste Werk Th. M's," *Tägliche Rundschau*, August 26, 1954. [*Die Betrogene*]

1,063. *———. *Wagner und kein Ende: Richard Wagner im Spiegel von Th. M's Prosawerk*. Bayreuth: Musica [1958] 71 pp.

1,064.   ———. "Tristan: Faszination für einen Dichter," in *Tristan und Isolde-Programm*, pp. 45-48. Bayreuth: Verlag der Festspielleitung, 1958.

1,065.   ———. "Wagners 'Leitmotiv' bei Th. M.," *Festspiel-Nachrichten: Lohengrin* (Bayreuth), July 1959.

1,066.   ———. "Tristan und seine literarischen Folgen: Wagners 'alte ernste Weise' in der Sicht Th. M's," *Fränkische Presse*, Vol. 15, No. 170 (July 27, 1959). Also in *National-Zeitung Basel*, No. 466 (October 9, 1959), and enl. version in *Opernwelt*, No. 7-8 (1962).

1,067.   ———. "Zum Geleit," in item #510, p. [7]

1,068.   ———. "Gesittigt musizierende Gedankenprosa: Richard Wagner und die literarischen Folgen bei Th. M.," *Christ und Welt*, Vol. 15, No. 31 (August 3, 1962), p. 15.

1,069.   ———. "Balanceakt zwischen 'rechts und links,' " *Literarische Revue*, No. 3 (1962). [*Briefe I*, item #2,062]

1,070.   ———. "Richard Wagner und Th. M.: Gottestheaterspiel," *Christ und Welt*, Vol. 16, No. 21 (May 24, 1963), p. [17]

1,071.   ———. "Befestigung einer Zeit im Wort: Th. M's zweite Briefauswahl," *Deutsche Zeitung und Wirtschaftszeitung*, No. 21 (January 25, 1964), p. 18. Also in *Kritische Stimmen zur neuen deutschen Literatur*, No. 5 (1964). [*Briefe II*, item #2,066]

1,072. ———. "Die Wiederbegegnung mit Deutschland: Th. M's Autobiographie in Briefen," *Christ und Welt*, Vol. 18, No. 49 (December 3, 1965), p. 37. [*Briefe III*, item #2,071]

1,073. Greiner, Martin. "Th. M's Faustus-Roman: Versuch einer Struktur-Analyse," *Sammlung* (Göttingen), 9 (November 1954), 539-551.

1,074. ———. "Das artistische Element bei Th. M.," *Anstösse*, 5 (November 1957), 167-177.

1,075. Greinz, Hugo. "Th. M's Hochstapler-Roman," *Neues Wiener Tagblatt*, Vol. 57, No. 87 (March 30, 1923). [*Felix Krull*]

1,076. Grenzmann, Wilhelm. "Th. M s 'Bekenntnisse des Hochstaplers Felix Krull,' " *Wirkendes Wort*, 5 (July 1955), 280-285. Also in *Neuere deutsche Literatur*, Sammelband No. 3, pp. 428-433. Düsseldorf: Schwann, 1963.

1,077. ———. "Humanismus an der Schwelle: Deutsche Selbstbezeugung in den Briefen Th. M's," *Echo der Zeit*, No. 20 (May 17, 1964), p. 20. [Review of *Briefe I*, item #2,062]

1,078. ———. "Th. M.: Das Spätwerk. Leben und Geist," in his *Dichtung und Glaube*, pp. 36-81. Frankfurt a. M.: Athenäum [⁴1964]

1,079. ———. " 'Mystik der Gottesferne.' Aus Anlass eines Buches und im Gedanken an Th. M's Tod vor zehn Jahren," *Der christliche Sonntag*, Vol. 17, No. 33 (September 19, 1965), pp. 301-302. [Review of A. Hellersberg, item #1,285]

1,080. Gressel, Hans. "Ein Weg zu Th. M.," *Mindener Tageblatt*, Ausg. B, Vol. 48, No. 116 (May 21, 1955). [Biog.]

1,081. Grimm, Reinhold. Review of Amann, item #3,426, Bertram, item #1,575, Kerényi, item #1,700 c, and *Briefe I*, item #2,062, *GRM*, N. F., 12 (October 1962), 427-432.

1,082. Grözinger, Wolfgang. "Der Roman der Gegenwart," *Hochland*, 47 (December 1954), 167-178. [*See* esp. pp. 169-170 on *Felix Krull*]

1,083. Gronicka, André von. "In memoriam Th. M.," *MLF*, 41 (December 1956), 108-111.

1,084. ————. Review of F. Hirschbach, item #1,429, K. W. Jonas, item #1,605, and J. M. Lindsay, item #1,971, *GR*, 31 (April 1956), 154-157.

1,085. ————. "Myth plus Psychology: A Style Analysis of 'Death in Venice,' " *GR*, 31 (October 1956), 206-214. Also in H. Hatfield, item #1,229, pp. 46-61.

1,086. ————. Review of E. Heller, item #1,278, *GR*, 34 (December 1959), [298]-300.

1,087. ————. Review of Amann, item #3,426, Flinker, item #887, Diersen, item #677, and Venohr, item #3,350, *GR*, 36 (February 1961), 73-77.

1,088. ————. Review of K. Kerényi, item #1,700 c, and E. Bertram, item #1,575, *Monatshefte*, 53 (December 1961), [353]-355.

1,089. Grosse, Siegfried. "Die deutsche Satzperiode," *Deutschunterricht* (Stuttgart), 12 (1960), [66]-81. [Language — Style — *Felix Krull*]

1,090. *Grosser, J. F. G. *Die Grosse Kontroverse. Ein Schriftwechsel um Deutschland: Walter von Molo — Th. M.* Hamburg: Nagel [1963] 155 pp.
        Contributors: Anon., #76 — J. R. Becher, #219 — Flake, #878 — Hausenstein, #1,235 — Lestiboudois, #1,944 — Meyer-Benfey, #2,250 — Molo, #2,279 — Monecke, #2,281 — Preetorius, #2,598 — Redslob, #2,648 — Thiess, #3,269-3,270 — Zachäus, #3,568.
        Reviews: Biergann, #329 — Haiduk, #1,151 — Hellmann, #1,304.

1,091. Grossmann, Stefan. "Mario und der Zauberer," *Tagebuch*, 11 (1930), 874-875.

1,092. Grosz, Georg. "Deutsche Dichter und Denker," in his *Ein kleines Ja und ein grosses Nein*, pp. 263-268. Hamburg: Rowohlt [1955]

1,093. Grote, Adolf. "Th. M. und die Deutschen," in his *Unangenehme Geschichtstatsachen*, pp. 128-130. [Nürnberg] Glock & Lutz [1960]

1,094. Grubb, Frederick. "The Joseph-Saga of Th. M.," *Theology*, (April 1957), 151-155.

1,095. †Gruber, Renate. Der Humanismus bei Th. M. Ph. D. diss.,
        University of Vienna, 1958. 146 pp.

1,096. Gruenter, Rainer. "Th. M.: Versuch über Schiller," *Kritische
        Blätter*, No. 3 (1955), pp. 14-15. Also in *NDH*, No. 21
        (1955), p. 14.

1,097. *Grüters, Walter. *Der Einfluss der norwegischen Literatur auf
        Th. M's 'Buddenbrooks.'* [Düsseldorf: Triltsch] 1961. 105 pp.
        [Ph. D. diss., Bonn, 1961]

1,097a. Grützmacher, Richard. "Th. M., der Zeitgenosse,"
        Wilhelmstrasse, 1 (December 1925), 49-52.

1,097b. ————. "Gerhart Hauptmann et Th. M.," *Bibliothèque
        Universelle et Revue de Genève*, November 1927, pp. 614-616.
        [Excerpt from I, #936. Translated into French by Elise Moroy]

1,097c. Grupe, Walter. "Goethes Sekretär Ernst Carl John: Sein Bild
        in der Forschung und bei Th. M.," *Goethe*, 24 (1962),
        202-223. [*Lotte in Weimar*]

1,097d. Guéhenno, Jean. "La Montagne Magique," *Europe*, 27
        (November 15, 1931), 424-429.

1,097e. Günther, Alfred. "Th. M. — Moses," *Weltstimmen*, Vol. 17,
        No. 1 (1946), pp. 5-10. [*Das Gesetz*]

1,097f. Günther, Joachim. "Th. M.: Briefe 1889-1936," *NDH*, No. 87
        (May-June, 1962), pp. 151-156. [Review of #2,062]

1,097g. ————. "Der Briefautor Th. M.," *NDH*, No. 98 (March-April,
        1964), pp. 116-123. [Review of #2,066]

1,097h. ————. "Triumph der Bildung," *Tagesspiegel*, Vol. 21, No. 6,
        164 (December 19, 1965), p. 37. [*Reden und Aufsätze*]

1,097i. †Guenther, Margaret Beltz. Th. M. as a Critic of German
        Literature. [1900-1933] Ph. D. diss., Radcliffe College,
        Harvard University, 1958. 449 pp.

1,098. Guerard, Albert Joseph. "Th. M.," in his *André Gide*, pp.
        113-118. Cambridge, Mass.: Harvard University Press, 1951.
        [²New York: Dutton, 1963] [Concerns *Death in Venice* and
        Gide's *L'Immoraliste.*]

1,099. ————. "Pleasures in Life Itself," *VQR*, 32 (Spring, 1956),
        291-296. [*Felix Krull*]

1,100. Guérard, Albert Léon. "Th. M. and the Transcending of German Romanticism," in his *Fossils and Presences,* pp. 182-192. Stanford: Stanford University Press, 1957. [Cf. I, item #1301]

1,101. Guest, Carmel Haden. "Th. M. at Home," *John O'London's Weekly,* October 17, 1931, pp. 61, 66. [Biog. — Th. M. at Nidden]

1,102. Guillemin, Bernard. "Der neue Th. M.," *Nürnberger Zeitung,* No. 140 (June 18, 1930), p. 1. [*Mario und der Zauberer*]

1,103. Gumppenberg, Hanns von. "Fiorenza," *Münchner Neueste Nachrichten,* December 19, 1907.

1,104. Gurlitt, W. "Motive im Werk Th. M's. Zu seinem Tode am 12. August 1955," *Goetheanum,* 34 (August 28, 1955), 279-280.

1,105. Gustafsson, Lars F. "Det tyska ödet," *Expressen,* April 8, 1963. [Review of G. Bergsten, item #292]

1,106. Guthke, Karl S. "Th. M's Erzählungen," *Erasmus* (Darmstadt), 12 (June 25, 1959), 353-355.

1,107. ———. "Th. M. on his 'Zauberberg.' An Unpublished Letter to Hans M. Wolff, November 25, 1950," *Neophilologus,* 44 (April 1960), 120-121.

1,108. ———. "Th. M. on Heinrich von Kleist. An Unpublished Letter to Hans M. Wolff," *Neophilologus,* 44 (April 1960), 121-122.
See also #753.

1,109. Guthmann, Johannes. "Die Geburtsstunde des Mynheer Peeperkorn," in his *Goldene Frucht: Begegnungen mit Menschen, Gärten und Häusern,* pp. 411-418. Tübingen: R. Wunderlich [1955]

1,110. Guttmann, Bernhard. "Der Unpolitische nach vierzig Jahren," *Gegenwart,* 11 (November 17, 1956), 730-732. [*Betrachtungen eines Unpolitischen*]

1,111. Guttry, Aleksander. "Th. M.," *Tygodnisk Illustrowany,* No. 11 (March 12, 1927).

1,112. Gyllensten, .Lars. "Senilia: Tankar kring berättande och kring Th. M.," *BLM,* 24 (1955), 618-622.

1,113. Haack, Hanns Erich. "Das Teufelsbündnis: Betrachtungen zu
dem letzten Werk Th. M's," *Deutsche Rundschau*, 71 (1948),
218-220. [*Doktor Faustus*]

1,114. Haas, A. "Th. M. zum 60. Geburtstag," *Tages-Anzeiger*,
No. 123 (June 6, 1935).

1,115. Haas, Helmuth de. "Th. M's Künstlertum: Repräsentant der
Nation und Weltbürger," *Rheinische Post*, No. 128 (June 4,
1955). [80th birthday]

1,116. ————. "Die konservative Revolution der Prosa: Zu Th. M's
80. Geburtstag," in his *Das geteilte Atelier*, pp. 38-44.
[Düsseldorf] K. Rauch [1955]

1,117. Haas, Willy. "Bemerkungen zu einer Unterhaltungsbeilage,"
Die lit. Welt, Vol. 4, No. 14/15 (April 5, 1928). [Concerns I,
item #2282 — F. G. Jünger]

1,118. ————. "Zwei Zeitalter treffen sich," *Welt am Sonntag*, June
4, 1950. [75th birthday] [Concerns Eduard Mörike and Th. M.]

1,119. ————. "Rudolf Alexander Schröder und Th. M.," *Welt*,
March 28, 1953.

1,120. ————. "Th. M.: 'Hochstapler Krull,' " *Welt am Sonntag*,
September 26, 1954.

1,121. ————. "Th. M. wurde Ehrenbürger," *Welt*, May 21, 1955.
[Honorary citizen of Lübeck]

1,122. ————. "Th. M. und der englische Geist," *Englische
Rundschau*, No. 22 (June 1955), pp. 292-293.

1,123. ————. "Th. M.: Figuren und Episoden ohne Zahl — und alle
Bildnis der Zeit," *Welt*, No. 128 (June 4, 1955). [80th
birthday]

1,124. ————. "Trauer um Th. M.: Kilchberg am Zürichsee blieb die
letzte Adresse," *Welt*, No. 188 (August 15, 1955), p. 10.
[Obit.]

1,125. ————. "Ironisch-warmherzig: Das war Th. M. Erinnerungen
an den grossen Dichter," *Welt am Sonntag*, Vol. 8, No. 33
(August 15, 1955), p. 3. [Obit.]

1,126. ————. "Entscheidung mit Th. M.," *Kontrapunkte*, pp. 13-19.
Hamburg: Freie Akademie der Künste, 1956.

1,127. ————. "Wir stehen vor einem Skandal: Soll Briefwechsel der

Gebrüder Mann in alle Winde verstreut werden?" *Welt,*
No. 254 (October 31, 1958), p. 13.

1,128.   ———. "Briefe an jeden von uns," *Welt,* (October 19, 1961).
[*Briefe I,* item #2,062] •

1,129.   ———. "Späte Ehrung für den grossen Sohn," *Welt,* No. 20
(January 24, 1963), p. 9. [Ceremony in 'Schabbelhaus' in
Lübeck]

1,130.   ———. "Wagner nach dem Bilde Th. M's," *Welt,* June 1,
1963. [Review of item #2,065]

1,131.   ——— "Höhepunkt des Lebens — Höhepunkt auch des
Leidens," *Welt,* December 6, 1963. [Review of *Briefe II,*
item #2,066]

1,132.   ———. "Th. M.," in his *ed., Zeitgenössisches aus der
'Literarischen Welt' von 1925 bis 1932,* pp. [9]-13 et al.
Stuttgart: Cotta [1963]

1,133.   ———. "Ist Th. M. 'unsterblich'?" *Welt,* No. 129 (June 5,
1965). [90th birthday]

1,134.   Habe, Hans. "Brief nach Kilchberg: Zum 60. Geburtstag von
Erika Mann," *Aufbau* (New York) Vol. 31, No. 45
(November 5, 1965), p. 14.

1,135.   Hack, Bertold. "Th. M. und die Seinen," *Barke,* No. 4 (1965),
pp. 13-16. [Review of *Briefe III,* item #2,071; Bürgin-
Mayer, item #504; and books by Erika, Klaus and Monika
Mann]

1,136.   Hacker, Hermann. "Skandal um Th. M.: Störungsversuche
Jugendlicher im Beethovensaal: Arnolt Bronnen als
Zwischenrufer," *Deutsche Tageszeitung,* October 18, 1930.
[*See also* A. Bronnen, item #482. Concerns Th. M., *Deutsche
Ansprache*]

1,137.   Hacks, Peter. "Über den Stil in Th. M's 'Lotte in Weimar,' "
Sinn und Form: Sonderheft Th. M., 1965, pp. 240-254.

1,138.   Haerdter, Robert. "Momentaufnahme 1955," *Gegenwart,* 10
(June 4, 1955), [373]-376. [Concerns Schiller Celebration,
Stuttgart, May 8, 1955]

1,139.   Härtling, Peter. "Th. M. und 'Mass und Wert,' " *Welt der
Literatur,* No. 14 (July 8, 1965), p. 325.

1,140.   Haffner, Sebastian. "Th. M's 'Doktor Faustus,' " *Kronkret*, 5 (1964), 18-19.

1,141.   Hagberg, Knut. "Efterskrift," in Th. M., *Buddenbrooks*, Vol. 2, pp. 383-384. Stockholm: Natur och kultur, 1945.

1,142.   Hahne, Heinrich. "Th. M.: Meine Zeit," *Deutsche Universitätszeitung*, No. 6 (1951). [*Meine Zeit*]

1,143.   Haiduk, Manfred. "Th. M's Kampf gegen den Faschismus, dargestellt an seinen Reden, Aufsätzen und Tagebuchaufzeichnungen," *Wissenschaftliche Zeitschrift der Universität Rostock*, Vol. 3, No. 3 (1953/54), pp. 187-214.

1,144. †————. Wesen und Sprache der polemischen Schriften Th. M's. Ph. D. diss., University of Rostock, 1957.

1,145.   ————. "Der Gedanke des antifaschistischen Widerstandes bei Th. M.," *Wissenschaftliche Zeitschrift der Universität Rostock*, Sonderheft, 3 (1959/60), 53-59.

1,146.   ————. Review of I. Diersen, item #677, *Weimarer Beiträge*, 4 (1960), 835-841.

1,147.   ————. "Wesen und Sprache der polemischen Schriften Th. M's" [Autoreferat und Thesen zur Dissertation] *Wissenschaftliche Zeitschrift der Universität Rostock*, 10 (1961), 157-163.

1,148.   ————. "Die Bedeutung der polemischen Schriften im Schaffen Th. M's," in G. Wenzel, item #3,461, pp. 43-71.

1,149.   ————. "Bemerkungen zu Th. M's Novelle 'Wälsungenblut,' " in G. Wenzel, item #3,461, pp. 213-219.

1,150.   ————. "Der bürgerliche Schelm Felix Krull," in *Neue Texte 1965*, pp. 355-366 Berlin: Aufbau, 1965.

1,151.   ————. Review of Grosser, item #1,090, in G. Wenzel, item #3,472, pp. 443-446.

1,152.   ————. Review of Schröter, item #2,971, in G. Wenzel, item #3,472, pp. 458-461.

1,153.   Haile, Harry. "Th. M. und der 'Anglizismus,' " *Monatshefte*, 51 (October 1959), 263-269.

1,154.   ————. Review of P. Altenberg, item #34, *JEGP*, 61 (April 1962), 478-480.

1,155. Halász, Elöd. "As utolsó Faust," *Tiszatáj,* 2 (1948), [405]-425.

1,156. ———. "Th. M.," *Szegedi Egyetem,* Vol. 3, No. 12 (1955). [80th birthday]

1,157. ———. "Th. M. halálára," *Szegedi Egyetem,* Vol. 3, No. 15 (1955), p. 3. [Obit.]

1,158. ———. "Az idö funkciója a Varázshegyben," *Filológiai Közlöny,* 1959, pp. 13-20. Also in *Acta Universitatis Szegediensis: Sectio Litteraria,* 1959, pp. 47-54. [Concerns the function of time in *The Magic Mountain*]

1,159. *———. *Th. M.* Budapest: Gondolat, 1959. 103 pp.

1,160. *———. *Die Zeit als strukturbildendes Prinzip im 'Zauberberg.'* Budapest: Akadémiai Kiadó, 1962. 250 pp.

1,161. ———. Review and supplement to H. Bürgin, item #502, *Világirodalmi Figyelö,* 1962, pp. 273-278. [Addenda to Section V — Hungarian translations of M's writings]

1,162. Halding, John. "Ein Patrizier und Dichter aus Lübeck: Zum 5. Todestag," *Lübecker Nachrichten,* Vol. 15, No. 186 (August 11, 1960), p. 10.

1,163. Hall, James. "The Pedestal of Th. M.," *VQR,* 24 (Spring 1948), 303-306. [Concerns Neider, I, item #297]

1,164. Hallamore, Joyce. "Zur Siebenzahl in Th. M's 'Zauberberg,' " *GQ,* 35 (January 1962), 17-19.

1,165. *Hamakawa, S., ed. *Th. M's Briefe an Japaner.* Tokyo: Dogakusha, 1960. 29 pp. [In Japanese]

1,166. Hamberg, Lars. "Th. M's 'Leiden und Grösse Richard Wagners,' " *Horisont,* Vol. 10, No. 3 (1963), pp. 5-6.

1,167. Hamburger, Käte. "Th. M's Goethe," *Göteborgs Handels- och Sjöfarts-Tidning,* February 13, 1940. [*Lotte in Weimar*]

1,168. ———. "De ombytta huvudena," *Göteborgs Handels- och Sjöfarts-Tidning,* February 4, 1941. [*Die Vertauschten Köpfe*]

1,169. ———. "Th. M's Joseph-Roman," *Der Bund; der kleine Bund,* Vol. 24, No. 16 (November 14, 1943), pp. 361-364. Also in Swedish in *Göteborgs Handels- och Sjöfarts-Tidning,* November 18/19, 1943.

1,170. ———. "Th. M's Faustroman," *Göteborgs Handels- och Sjöfarts-Tidning,* November 27, 1947.

1,171. ———. "Th. M. och Goethe," *Göteborgs Handels- och Sjöfarts-Tidning,* May 21, 1949.

1,172. ———. "Gregorius på stenen," *Göteborgs Handels- och Sjöfarts-Tidning,* April 23, 1951. [*Der Erwählte*]

1,173. ———. "Vårens krokus och höstens tidlösa," *Göteborgs Tidningen,* May 24, 1954. [*Die Betrogene*]

1,174. ———. "En charmerande skojare," *Göteborgs Tidningen,* January 4, 1955. [*Felix Krull*]

1,175. ———. "Den store humanisten," in item #2,431, pp. 45-60.

1,176. ———. "Der Epiker Th. M.," *Orbis Litterarum,* 13 (1958), [7]-14.

1,177. ———. "Erzählformen des modernen Romans," *Deutschunterricht* (Stuttgart), Vol. 11, No. 4 (1959), pp. [5]-23. *See esp.* pp. 19-22.

1,178. ———. "Th. M.: Briefe an Paul Amann," *Stuttgarter Nachrichten,* November 25, 1959. [Concerns item #3,426]

1,179. ———. "Polarität von Leben und Geist," *Stuttgarter Zeitung,* Literaturblatt, July 30, 1960. [Review of E. Heller, item #1,278]

1,180. ———. "Doktor Faustus," *Buch und Leben,* No. 5 (May 1961), pp. 11-14.

1,181. ———. "Nachwort," in Th. M., *Meisternovellen,* pp. 476-488. Stuttgart: Europäischer Buchklub [1961]

1,182. ———. "Die Sehnsucht des Geistes nach dem Leben: Eine Betrachtung zu Th. M's Novellen," *Buch und Leben,* No. 4 (April 1962), pp. 1-4.

1,183. ———. "Th. M's Mose-Erzählung 'Das Gesetz' auf dem Hintergrund der Überlieferung und der religionswissenschaftlichen Forschung," in her *ed.* of Th. M., *Das Gesetz* [Vollständiger Text der Erzählung. Dokumentation] pp. [57]-112. [Frankfurt a. M.] Ullstein [1964] (Dichtung und Wirklichkeit, Vol. 17).
Reviews: E. Mater #2,142.

1,184.   ———. Review of G. Bergsten, item #292, *DLZ*, 85 (June
          1964), 515-520. Also in *Germanistik*, 5 (October 1964), 666-
          667. Reprinted in G. Wenzel, item #3,472, pp. 439-442.
1,185.   ———. "Th. M.," in H. Kunisch, *ed.*, *Handbuch der deutschen
          Gegenwartsliteratur*, pp. 415-421. München: Nymphenburg,
          1965.
1,186. *———. *Der Humor bei Th. M.: Zum Joseph-Roman*
          [München] Nymphenburg [1965] 240 pp. [Rev. and enlarged
          ed. of I, #2,450]
1,187.   Hamburger, Michael. "Address," in Wilkinson, item #3,494.
1,188.   ———. "Th. M.," in his *From Prophecy to Exorcism: The
          Premises of Modern German Literature*, pp. 75-93 et al. London:
          Longmans, Green, 1965.
1,189.   Hamburger, Paul. "Th. M's 'Dr. Faustus': A Contribution to
          the Philosophy of Music," *Music Survey*, Vol. 2, No. 1 (1949),
          pp. 20-24.
1,190.   Hamecher, Peter. "Der Dichter und die Modelle," *Deutscher
          Kurier*, November 13, 1913. [Concerns Friedrich Mann's attack
          upon his nephew Thomas's *Buddenbrooks*, see item #2,072]
1,191.   ———. "Th. M. und der Krieg," *Tägliche Rundschau*, June 24,
          1915, p. 525. [*Friedrich und die Grosse Koalition*]
1,192. †Hannemann, Helmut. Illusion und Desillusion in den
          Novellen Th. M's. Ph. D. diss., University of Hamburg, 1955.
1,193.   Harcourt, Robert d'. "Th. M., citoyen du monde," in #1,493,
          pp. 35-36.
1,194.   Hardegg, M. "Th.M.: Zum 6. Juni 1915," *Auslese*, Vol. 2,
          No. 90 (June 1915). [40th birthday]
1,195.   Hardt, Julius. "Literarische Rundschau," *Tag*, No. 75 (1904).
          [*Tonio Kröger*]
1,196.   Hardt, Reinhold. "Über Th. M's Sprachmeisterschaft im
          'Zauberberg,' " *Muttersprache*, 67 (November 1957), 426-428.
1,197.   Harlass, Gerald. "Das Kunstmittel des Leitmotivs: Bemerkungen
          zur motivischen Arbeit bei Th. M. und Hermann Broch," *Welt
          und Wort*, 15 (September 1960), 267-269.
1,198.   Harnisch, A. "Brief an den Herausgeber: Felix Krull literarisch
          minderwertig," *Welt*, September 13, 1957.

1,199. Harrie, Ivar. "Mann, trollkarl," *Expressen,* September 21, 1964. [Review of H. Levander, #1,958]

1,200. Hartl, Edwin. "Die Vertauschten Köpfe," *Wiener lit. Echo,* 1 (January-March, 1949), 56-57.

1,201. Hartung, Rudolf. "Th. M. und die Deutschen," *Fähre,* 2 (1946), 569-570.

1,202. ———. "Replik auf Fritz Rahn," *NDH,* No. 18 (September 1955), [475]-480. [Reply to Rahn's article, item #2,630]

1,203. Hartwig, Th. "Antitheologisches in dem Roman 'Doktor Faustus,' " *Befreiung,* 2 (1954), 57-59.

1,204. Harvesthus, Werner. "Friede, um Gottes willen Friede," *Westdeutsche Rundschau,* June 7, 1950. [75th birthday]

1,205. Harvey, W. J. "Th. M.," in his *Character and the Novel,* pp. 100-108 et al. Ithaca, N. Y.: Cornell University Press [1965] [*The Magic Mountain*]

1,206. Hasenclever, Walter. "Der Zauberberg in Massachusetts: Ein erfreuliches Erlebnis im Geiste," *Perspektiven,* No. 12 (Summer 1955), pp. 159-173.

1,207. Hass, Hans Egon. "Th. M.," *Bonner Universitätszeitung,* No. 15 (1947), pp. 6-8. [Concerns renewal of Th. M's honorary doctorate of Bonn University]

1,208. ———. "Das Goethebild bei Th. M.," *Welt am Sonntag,* July 17, 1949.

1,209. Hatfield, Henry C. Review of G. Lukács, I, item #2778, *GR,* 25 (December 1950), 307-308.

1,210. ———. "Realism in the German Novel," *CL,* 3 (Summer 1951), [234]-252. [*See esp.* pp. 250-251]

1,211. ———. "Th. M.: From *Joseph der Ernährer,*" in his *ed.* [with Jack M. Stein, co-editor] *Schnitzler. Kafka. Mann,* pp. 92-96. Boston: Houghton Mifflin [1953]

1,212. ———. "Castorp's Dream and Novalis," *History of Ideas Newsletter,* 1 (1954), 9-11. [*Der Zauberberg*]

1,213. ———. Review of P. P. Sagave, I, item #1367, *MLQ,* 15 (December 1954), 380-381.

1,214. ———. Review of J. M. Lindsay, item #1,971, *MLR,* 50 (July 1955), 361.

1,215.   ———. "Parody and Expressiveness: The Late Works of Th.
         M.," *University of Pennsylvania Bulletin*, Vol. 65, No. 3
         (1955), pp. 47-56.

1,216.   ———. Review of F. D. Hirschbach, item #1,429, *GQ*, 29
         (March 1956), 115-116.

1,217.   ———. Review of R. Nicholls, item #2,407, *MLQ*, 17
         (June 1956), 181-182.

1,218.   ———. "Can One Sell One's Soul? The Faust Legend," in
         Robert M. MacIver, *ed., Great Moral Dilemmas in Literature,
         Past and Present*, pp. 83-97. New York: Harper [1956. ²1964]
         [Concerns Marlowe, pp. 85-88 — Goethe, pp. 88-93 — Th. M.,
         pp. 93-97]

1,219.   ———. "Recent Studies of Th. M.," *MLR*, 51 (July 1956),
         [390]-403.

1,220.   ———. "The Achievement of Th. M.," *GR*, 31 (October
         1956), 206-214.

1,221.   ———. Review of K. W. Jonas, item #1,605, *Monatshefte*, 48
         (November 1956), 336.

1,222.   ———. Review of R. Hinton Thomas, item #3,273, *MLR*, 52
         (July 1957), 449-450.

1,223.   ———. "The Domestic Economy of a Genius," *Saturday
         Review*, Vol. 41, No. 33 (August 16, 1958), p. 14. [Review
         of Erika Mann, item #2,059]

1,224.   ———. "Timeless and Timely," *Saturday Review*, Vol. 41,
         No. 43 (October 25, 1958), p. 32. [Review of E. Heller, item
         #1,278]

1,225.   ———. "Death in the Late Works of Th. M.," *GR*, 34
         (December 1959), [284]-288.

1,226.   ———. "Der Zauberer und die Verzweiflung: Das Alterswerk
         Th. M's," *Wirkendes Wort*, 12 (1962), 91-102.

1,227. *———. *Th. M.: An Introduction to His Fiction*. Rev. ed.
         Norfolk, Conn.: New Directions, 1962. 196 pp. [Cf. I, item
         #199] *See also* review by F. W. Dupee, item #720.

1,228.   ———. "Drei Randglossen zu Th. M's 'Zauberberg,' "
         Euphorion, 56 (1962), [365]-372. *See also* his "Korrektur-
         note," *Euphorion*, 57 (1963), 226. [Concerns Walt Whitman

— Georg Lukács — Günther Herzfeld-Wüsthoff]

1,229. *————., ed. Th. M.: A Collection of Critical Essays. Englewood
Cliffs, N. J.: Prentice-Hall [1964] 172 pp. Contributors:
Blume, #372 — Gronicka, #1,085 — Hatfield, #1,230-1,231
— Heilman, #1,255 — E. Heller, # 1,278 c — H. E.
Holthusen, #1,486 — Kahler, #1,632 — Rilke, #2,729 —
Van Doren, #3,345 — H. Weigand, #3,431 — Wilkinson,
#3,495.
Reviews: Lange, #1,861 — Schiffer, #2,893.

1,230. ————. "Introduction," in item #1,229, pp. 1-6.

1,231. ————. "Th. M's 'Buddenbrooks': The World of the Father,"
in item #1,229, pp. 10-21. [Cf. I, item #2095]

1,232. ————. Review of R. Baumgart, #204, GQ, 38 (November
1965), 696-697.

1,233. ————. "Notizen zum 'Zauberberg,' " Sinn und Form:
Sonderheft Th. M., 1965, pp. 387-391.

1,234. Hatscher, Herbert. "Der grosse Puppenspieler," Frankfurter
Neue Presse, Vol. 5, No. 106 (May 9, 1950), p. 5. [Doktor
Faustus]

1,235. Hausenstein, Wilhelm. "Bücher — frei von Blut und Schande:
verehrter Herr Th. M.," in Grosser, item #1,090, pp. 62-75.
[Cf. I, item #1305]

1,236. Hausmann, Manfred. "Uns ist für gar nichts bange," Weser-
Kurier, March 29, 1947.

1,237. ————. "Manfred Hausmanns Antwort an Th. M.," Weser-
Kurier, July 11, 1947, p. 3.

1,238. ————. "Matter Ausklang," Weser-Kurier, September 13,
1949. [Joseph der Ernährer]

1,239. Hausmann, Wolf. "Der grosse alte Mann der deutschen
Literatur," Weser-Kurier, No. 127 (June 4, 1955), p. 15.
[80th birthday]

1,240. Haussmann, Walter. "Th. M. und die Jugend." Neue
Rundschau, 76 (Fall 1965), 535-539.

1,241. Havemann, W. "Die Grabower Verwandten der Schriftsteller
Heinrich und Th. M.," Land und Leute, 9 (1959), 244-251.

1,242. Havenith, E. "Bemerkungen zur Struktur des Goetheromans 'Lotte in Weimar,' " *Revue des Langues Vivantes — Levende Talen,* 27 (1961), 329-341.

1,243. Havenstein, Martin. "Th. M's 'Königliche Hoheit,' " in His *Vornehmheit und Tüchtigkeit,* pp. 35-50. Berlin: Mittler, ²1919.

1,244. Hayasaki, Yoshihisa. "Eine Studie über Th. M's Ironie," *Doitsu Bungaku — Die deutsche Literatur,* No. 13 (1954), pp. 38-41. [In German]

1,245. Hecht, Wolfgang. "Ich habe Th. M. gesehen," in G. Wenzel, item #3,453, pp. 99-102.

1,246. Heckmann, Herbert. "Naivität und ihre Folgen," *Welt der Literatur,* No. 13 (June 24, 1965), p. 316. [Review of K. Schröter, item #2,971. *See also* item #2,972]

1,247. Heer, Friedrich. "Ein Mann geht durch die Welt," *Österreichische Presse,* July 29, 1952. [Th. M's visit to Vienna]

1,248. Deleted.

1,249. Hegeler, Wilhelm. "Th. M. als Okkultist," *Hannoverscher Kurier,* December 16, 1923. [*Okkulte Erlebnisse*]

1,250. Heiberg, Hans. "Hilsen fra den Norske forfatterforening," in item #2,431, p. 163.

1,251. Heide, Heinrich. "Th. M., der Träger des Nobelpreises," *Staats-Zeitung und Herold,* December 8, 1929, Sonntagsblatt.

1,252. Heilborn, Ernst. "Th. M.: Unordnung und frühes Leid," *Literatur,* 29 (1926-27), 230-231.

1,253. ———. "Deutsche Würde," *Literatur,* 32 (1929-30), 186. [Nobel Prize]

1,254. ———. "Geistiges Bürgertum," *Literatur,* 33 (1930-31), 125. [*Deutsche Ansprache*]

1,255. Heilman, Robert B. "Variations on Picaresque (*Felix Krull*)," *Sewanee Review,* 66 (Autumn 1958), [547]-577. Also in Hatfield, item #1,229, pp. 133-154.

1,256. †Heim, Karl. Th. M. und die Musik. Ph. D. diss., University of Freiburg i. Br., 1952.

1,257. ———. "Th. M.," in Wolfgang Rehm [and] Joachim von Hecker, *eds., Die Musik in Geschichte und Gegenwart,* pp.

1587-1591. Kassel: Bärenreiter [1960]

1,258. ———. "Th. M.," in Hugo Riemann, *ed.*, *Musiklexikon*, Vol. 2, p. 142. Mainz: Schott, 1961.

1,259. Heimann, Bodo. "Th. M's 'Doktor Faustus' und die Musik- philosophie Adornos," *DVJS*, 38 (July 1964), [248]-266.

1,260. Heimann, Heidi. "A God in Three Disguises: A Tribute to Th. M's 75th Birthday," *World Review*, N. S., 16 (June 1950), 66-69.

1,261. ———. "Hermes kwam als schrijver op aarde," *Vrij Nederland*, June 4, 1955, p. 7. Also in German as "Hermes-Natur," *NZZ*, Vol. 176, Morgenausgabe No. 1498 (29), June 5, 1955, Bl. 4. Enlarged version, "Th. M's 'Hermesnatur,'" *PEGS*, N. S., 27 (1958), 45-72.

1,262. ———. "Zehn Schicksalsjahre im Spiegel von Th. M's Briefen," *AJR Information*, Vol. 19, No. 4 (April 1964), pp. 8-9. [Review of *Briefe II*, item #2,066]

1,263. ———. " 'Sub specie aeternitatis': Th. M's Briefe aus seinen letzten Lebensjahren," *AJR Information*, April 1966, pp. 6-8. [Review of *Briefe III*, item #2,071]

1,264. Heinitz, Werner. "Bemerkungen zu einem neuen Werk von Th. M.," *Heute und Morgen*, No. 5 (1954), pp. 291-293. [*Die Betrogene*]

1,265. Heiseler, Bernt von [and] Katja Mann. "Th. M. und die Deutschen," *Das Ganze Deutschland*, Vol. 7, No. 40 (1955), p. 5; also in *Tagesspiegel*, No. 3054 (September 25, 1955), p. 5.

1,266. Helbling, Carl. "Th. M.: Zum 60. Geburtstag," *NZZ*, Vol. 156, No. 958, 1. Sonntagsausgabe (June 2, 1935), Bl. 4.

1,267. ———. "Th. M.: Briefe 1889-1936," *NZZ*, Vol. 181 December 16, 1961 (Swiss ed.); also Fernausgabe No. 4863 (123), December 17, 1961, Bl. 4. [Review of *Briefe I*, item #2,062]

1,268. ———. "Der Briefwechsel Th. M. — Robert Faesi," *NZZ*, Vol. 183, November 8, 1962 (Swiss ed.); also Fernausgabe No. 4355, November 9, 1962. [Review of item #833]

1,269. ————. "Briefe Th. M's," *NZZ*, Vol. 184, Morgenausgabe
No. 5322, December 20, 1963, Bl. 6. [Review of *Briefe II*,
item #2,066]

1,270. Helger, Jørgen. "Omkring Th. M's 'Doktor Faustus,'"
Bogrevyen og Samleren, (1949), 100-108.

1,271. Hell, Heinz. "Th. M's Briefe 1889-1936," *Schwäbische
Donauzeitung*, March 17, 1962. [Review of #2,062]

1,272. Hellens, Franz. "Th. M.," *La Nouvelle Revue Française*,
October 1, 1955, pp. [775]-776. [Obit.]

1,273. Heller, Erich. "Von Hanno Buddenbrook zu Adrian Leverkühn:
Eine Geburtstagsrede über Kunst und Künstler im Werke Th.
M's," *Dokumente*, (1954), 245-279. [Cf. I, #1064]

1,274. ————. "Introduction," in Th. M., *Stories and Episodes*, pp.
v-xiv. London: J. M. Dent [1955]

1,275. ————. "Th. M's Place in German Literature," *Listener*, 53
(June 9, 1955), 1014-1016. [80th birthday]

1,276. ————. "The Story of an Artist," *TLS*, 54 (November 11,
1955), 665-666. Reprinted in G. Wenzel, #3,453, pp. 77-90.
Expanded German version entitled "Felix Krull oder die
Komödie des Künstlers: Zum Abschluss des Lebenswerkes von
Th. M.," *Wort und Wahrheit*, 11 (January 1956), 40-48.
Reprinted in G. Wenzel, #3,461, pp. 250-260.

1,277. ————. "Psychoanalyse und Literatur: Bemerkungen zum 10.
Todestag Sigmund Freuds," *Jahresring 56/57*, pp. 74-83. [*Der
Tod in Venedig — Der Zauberberg. See esp. pp. 75-76*]

1,278. *————. *The Ironic German: A Study of Th. M.* London:
Secker & Warburg; Boston: Little, Brown, 1958. 298 pp. —
Expanded edition with a more detailed discussion of *Felix
Krull:* Cleveland: World [²1961] 303 pp. — German edition:
Th. M. Der ironische Deutsche. Frankfurt a. M.: Suhrkamp,
1959. 363 pp.
Excerpts — English:

(a) "Parody, Tragic and Comic: Mann's 'Doctor Faustus' and
'Felix Krull,' " *Sewanee Review*, 66 (1958), [519]-546.

(b) "The Conservative Imagination: On Th. M's 'Non-Political' Meditations," *Encounter,* Vol. 10, No. 2 (February 1958), pp. 46-56.

(c) "Conversation on the Magic Mountain," in H. Hatfield, item #1,229, pp. 62-95.

Excerpts — German:

(d) "Die konservative Phantasie: Über Th. M's 'Betrachtungen eines Unpolitischen,' " *Jahresring 58/59,* pp. 17-31.

(e) "Des Teufels Romancier: "Über Th. M's 'Doktor Faustus,' " *Forum,* 6 (1959), 367-370.

(f) "Form als Mass und Übermass: Ein Gespräch über Th. M's 'Zauberberg,' " *Monat,* Vol. 11, No. 131 (1959), pp. 40-60; No. 132 (1959), pp. 60-67.

Reviews: Anon., #103 — Anon., #115 — H. Becher, #207 — Berendsohn, #268 — Bergmann, #290 — Brome, #481 — Brück, #487 — Butler, #523 — Dupee, #723 — Enright, #791 — Gilman, #1,010 — Gronicka, #1,086 — Hamburger, #1,179 — Hatfield, #1,224 — Hohoff, #1,462-1,463 — H. E. Holthusen, #1,485 — H. E. Jacob, #1,551 — Kazin, #1,691 — Konrad, #1,767 — Lamprecht, #1,839 — V. Lange, #1,857 — Lesser, #1,937 — Pryce-Jones, #2,614 — Rees, #2,651 — Rey, #2,696 — W. Rose, #2,764 — Shuster, #3,028 — Spender, #3,107 — E. E. Stein, #3,118 — Toynbee, #3,301 — Williams, #3,498.

1,279. ———— "Th. M. and the 'Domestic Perversity,' " *Encounter,* Vol. 12, No. 3 (March 1959), pp. 54-56. [Reply to G. Rees, #2,651]

1,280. ————. "Mann and His Brethren," *TLS,* No. 2954 (October 10, 1958), p. 577. [Letter to the Editor in reply to item #115, and answer of the Reviewer]

1,281. ————. "Th. M.," in Helmut Olles, *ed., Lexikon der Welt-literatur im 20. Jahrhundert,* Vol. 2, pp. 367-374. Freiburg i. Br.: Herder, 1961. Also in pocket book ed., pp. 228-231. [Freiburg i. Br.] Herder-Bücherei [1964]

1,282. †Heller, Peter. The Writer's Image of the Writer. A Study of the Ideologies of Six German Authors, 1918-1933. Th. M.,

Hermann Hesse, Ernst Toller, Bertolt Brecht, Hans Grimm, Ernst Jünger. Ph. D. diss., Columbia University, 1951.

1,283. ———. "Versuch über Th. M. an Hand von 'Versuch über Tschechow,' " *Forum,* 4 (May 1957), 185-188.

1,284. Hellersberg-Wendriner, Anna. "The Essence of Th. M.," *Commonweal,* 62 (September 16, 1955), 583-586. [Obit.]

1,285. *———. *Mystik der Gottesferne: Eine Interpretation Th. M's.* Bern: Francke [1960] 204 pp.
Reviews: Anstett, #123 — Basler, #195 — Becher, #207 — Grenzmann, #1,079 — Hellmann, #1,288 — Hirschbach, #1,432 — Hohoff, #1,463-4 — Jonas, #1,610 — Leibrich, #1,901 — Nicholls, #2,409 — Rosenstein, #2,769 — E. E. Stein, #3,120

1,286. Hellmann, Winfried. Review of I. Diersen, item #677, *Germanistik,* 1 (January 1960), 101-102.

1,287. ———. Review of Žmegač, item #3,600, *Germanistik,* 1 (April 1960), 253-254.

1,288. ———. Review of A. Hellersberg, #1,285, *Germanistik,* 1 (July 1960), 390-391.

1,289. ———. Review of L. Venohr, #3,350, *Germanistik,* 1 (July 1960), 312-313.

1,290. ———. Review of M. Flinker, #887, *Germanistik,* 1 (July 1960), 569-570.

1,291. ———. Review of P. Scherrer, #2,877, *Germanistik,* 1 (July 1960), 579.

1,292. ———. Review of A. Bauer, #200, *Germanistik,* 2 (January 1961), 121-122.

1,293. ———. Review of Bertram, #1,575, *Germanistik,* 2 (January 1961), 135-136.

1,294. ———. Review of Kerényi, #1,700 c, *Germanistik,* 2 (January 1961), 136-137.

1,295. ———. Review of I. Metzler, #2,239, *Germanistik,* 2 (July 1961), 447-448.

1,296. ———. Review of B. Richter, #2,709, *Germanistik,* 2 (October 1961), 616-617.

1,297. ———. Review of Th. M., *Ges. Werke in 12 Bänden,* *Germanistik,* 3 (January 1962), 172-174. [12 vol. *ed.* of S. Fischer Verlag]

1,298. ———. Review of P. Altenberg, item #34, *Germanistik,* 3 (April 1962), 281-282.

1,299. ———. Review of *Briefe I,* #2,062, *Germanistik,* 3 (July 1962), 454-455.

1,300. ———. Review of K. Sontheimer, item #3,097, *Germanistik,* 3 (July 1962), 464-465.

1,301. ———. Review of Th. M. — E. Faesi, item #833, *Germanistik,* 4 (April 1963), 359-360.

1,302. ——— Review of H. Koopmann, item #1,769, *Germanistik,* 4 (July 1963), 528-529.

1,303. ———. Review of G. Wenzel, item #3,461, *Germanistik,* 4 (October 1963), 746-747.

1,304. ———. Review of Grosser, item #1,090, *Germanistik,* 5 (January 1964), 157-158.

1,305. ———. Review of R. D. Miller, item #2,260, *Germanistik,* 5 (April 1964), 373-374.

1,306. ———. Review of E. Mann, item #2,065, *Germanistik,* 5 (July 1964), 514.

1,307. ———. Review of H. Stresau, item #3,181, *Germanistik,* 5 (July 1964), 521.

1,308. ———. Review of K. Schröter, item #2,971, *Germanistik,* 5 (October 1964), 694.

1,309. ———. Review of E. Mann, item #2,066, *Germanistik,* 6 (January 1965), 159.

1,310. ———. Review of Pütz, item #2,620, *Germanistik,* 6 (April 1965), 364-365.

1,311. ———. Review of Kerényi, item #1,071, *Germanistik,* 6 (April 1965), 243-244.

1,312. Hellpach, Willy. "Das preussische 'Gespenst'; ein paar Anmerkungen zu Th. M's 'Friedrich,' " *Berliner Tageblatt,* No. 41 (January 23, 1916). [*Friedrich und die Grosse Koalition*]

1,313. ———. "Die 'Zauberberg'-Krankheit," *Medizinische Welt,*
        1 (1927), 1465-1466. [Continuation of I, item #2270]
        [Cf. P. Gasser, #974]

1,314. ———. "Die Heilskräfte der geistigen Arbeit: Die Lehren des
        'Zauberbergs,' " *Schweizer Medizinische Wochenschrift,* 60
        (1930), 573.

1,315. Helwig, Werner. "Th. M's letzte Reden," *Rheinische Post,*
        No. 64 (March 16, 1957). [*Nachlese*]

1,316. ———. "Bürgerliebe zum Menschlichen," *Rheinische Post,*
        June 22, 1963. [*Sämtliche Erzählungen*]

1,317. ———. "Th. M., Richard Wagner und unsere Zeit," *Rheinische
        Post,* September 28, 1963. [Review of #2,065]

1,318. ———. "Erinnerung an Klaus Mann," *Merkur,* 19 (August
        1965), 795-797.

1,319. Helmerking, Heinz. "Zum Briefwechsel Th. M.-Robert Faesi,"
        Tat, Vol. 27, No. 291 (October 27, 1962), p. 33. [Review
        of item #833]

1,320. Hempel, Wido. "Th. M.," in his *Giovanni Vergas Roman 'I
        Malavoglia' und die Wiederholung als erzählerisches
        Kunstmittel,* pp. 90-92 et al. Köln: Böhlau, 1959.

1,321. Hennecke, Hans. "Nachlese und Erinnerungen," *NDH,* (June
        1957), pp. 273-275. [Concerns E. Mann, item #2,059, and M.
        Mann, item #2,100]

1,322. ———. "Der vollkommen gemeisterte Satz: Th. M.," in his
        Kritik: Gesammelte Essays zur modernen Literatur, pp. 150-
        159. [Gütersloh] Bertelsmann, 1958.

1,323. Henning, Hans. "Th. M.," in his *Faust in fünf Jahrhunderten,*
        pp. 105-114. Halle: Sprache und Literatur, 1963. [*Doktor
        Faustus*]

1,324. Hennings, Elsa. *Unsterblicher Faust: Eine Genealogie von
        Simon Magnus bis zum 'Faust'-Roman Th. M's.* Hamburg,
        1953. 25 pp. (Universitätsgesellschaft, No. 5).

1,325. Henriksen, Aage. "Th. M's amor fati," in item #2,431,
        pp. 77-94.

1,326. Henschel, Peter. Review of K. Kerényi, item #1,700 c,

Lübeckische Blätter, Vol. 120, No. 20 (November 26, 1960), p. 262.

1,327. ———. "Pro domo," *Lübeckische Blätter,* Vol. 121, No. 1 (January 7, 1961), pp. 3-4.

1,328. ———. Review of K. Sontheimer, item #3,097, *Lübeckische Blätter,* Vol. 122, No. 8 (April 14, 1962), pp. 107-109.

1,329. ———. "Th. M. zum 90. Geburtstag," *Lübeckische Blätter,* Vol. 125, No. 12 (June 5, 1965), p. 177.

1,330. Hensel, Georg. "Gang durch ein Dichterleben," *Welt,* March 28, 1962. [Th. M. — Exhibition in Darmstadt]

1,331. Henze, Eberhard. "Die Rolle des fiktiven Erzählers bei Th. M.," *Neue Rundschau,* 76 (Summer 1965), 189-[201] [*Der Zauberberg — Joseph und seine Brüder — Doktor Faustus* — Style — Technique]

1,332. †Hepworth, James B. The Dionysian Element in the Works of Th. M. Ph. D. diss., University of Utah, 1957.

1,333. ———. "Tadzio-Sabazios: Notes on *Death in Venice,*" *Western Humanities Review,* 17 (1963), 172-175.

1,334. Herbig, Franz. "Neue Romane," *Hochland,* 7 (November 1909), 222-225. [*Königliche Hoheit, see* pp. 224-225]

1,335. Herchenröder, Jan. "Eröffnung des Th. M.-Archivs," *Lübecker Nachrichten,* Vol. 16, No. 49 (February 26, 1961), p. 9 [Zurich Archive]

1,336. ———. "Leben und Schaffen Th. M's: Zu der Ausstellung in des Dichters Heimatstadt Lübeck," *Mannheimer Morgen,* June 25, 1962, p. 30. [Th. M. Exhibition]

1,337. ———. "Ein Schriftsteller litt an Deutschland," *Lübecker Nachrichten,* December 15, 1963. [Review of *Briefe II,* item #2,066]

1,338. Hering, Gerhard F. "Felix Krull und die verlorene Freiheit," *Deutsche Zeitung und Wirtschaftszeitung,* No. 95 (December 27, 1954), Feuilleton, p. 22.

1,339. Hermand, Jost. "Peter Spinell," *MLN,* 79 (October 1964), 439-447. [*Tristan*]

1,340. Hermlin, Stefan. "Th. M.," *Sonntag,* June 5, 1955. [80th birthday]

1,341. ———. "Glückwunsch," in item #2,833.
1,342. ———. "Pozegnanie z Tomaszen Mannem," *Twórczość*. No. 8 (1956).
1,343. Herrle, Stephan. "Th. M's Altersstil," *Flensburger Tageblatt*, June 13, 1951.
1,344. Herting, Helga. "Entwicklungsgang in Briefen," *Weimarer Beiträge*, No. 3 (1965), pp. 441-457. Shorter version, entitled "Bekenntnis einer Wandlung," in *Neues Deutschland*, No. 8 (August 5, 1965). [Review of items #2,062 and 2,066]
1,345. Herz, Gerhard. "The Music in Mann's 'Doctor Faustus,'" *Perspectives*, Vol. 3, No. 1 (1948), pp. 48-64.
1,346. Herz, Ida. "Th. M's Bekenntnis zu Platen," *Nürnberg-Fürther Morgenpresse*, No. 258 (October 10, 1930), p. 4.
1,347. ———. "Erinnerungen an Th. M., 1925-1955," *GLL*, N. S., 9 (July 1956), 281-290.
1,348. ———. "Th. M. und der deutsche Antisemitismus," *AJR Information*, Vol. 15, No. 2 (February 1960), p. 7.
1,349. ———. "Das Th. M.-Archiv in Zürich," *AJR Information*, Vol. 16, No. 5 (May 1961), p. 6.
1,350. ———. "Zum 80. Geburtstag von Katia Mann," *AJR Information*, Vol. 18, No. 8 (August 1963).
1,351. ———. "Lin Roman wandert aus: Zum Erscheinen von 'Die Geschichten Jaakobs,'" *GQ*, 38 (November 1965), 630-639.
1,352. Herz, S. T. "Manche dieser Seiten sind schön," *Allgemeine Zeitung der Juden in Deutschland*, Vol. 3, No. 3 (April 20, 1956), p. 11. [*Betrachtungen eines Unpolitischen*]
1,353. Herzog, Bernt. "Th. M.," *Schweizer Rundschau*, N. F., 55 (September 1955), 289.
1,354. Herzog, Friedrich. "Th. M. zum 75. Geburtstag," *Tag*, June 6, 1950.
1,355. Herzog, Wilhelm. "Die Überschätzung der Kunst: Gegen 'Gedanken im Krieg,'" *Forum*, 1 (1914), 445-448.
1,356. ———. "Th. M.," in his *Menschen, denen ich begegnete*, pp. 268-318. Bern: Francke [1959] [With two facsim. letters from Th. M.]

1,357. Hesse, Hermann. "Bekenntnis und Glückwunsch," *Neue Rundschau,* 66 (June 1955), 256-257. [80th birthday]
1,358. ――――. "Lieber Th. M.," *NZZ,* Vol. 175, Sonntagsausgabe No. 1497 (28), June 5, 1955, Bl. 3. [80th birthday]
1,359. ――――. "Th. M.," *Morgenblatt für Freunde der Literatur,* No. 10 (1957). [*Doktor Faustus*]
1,360. ――――. "Abschiedsgruss an Th. M.," *NZZ,* Vol. 175, Abendausgabe No. 2138 (August 15, 1955), Bl. 8. Under the title "Letzter Gruss" in *Aufbau* (New York), Vol. 21, No. 34 (August 26, 1955), p. 4. Also in G. Wenzel, item #3,453, p. 64. [Obit.]
1,361. . "Neun Briefe an Th. M.," in his *Betrachtungen und Briefe,* pp. 48-49 et al. [Frankfurt a. M.] Suhrkamp [1959] [*Ges. Schriften,* Vol. 7. Cf. I, item #940]
1,362. ――――. "Neunzehn Briefe an Th. M., 1932-1955," in his *Briefe. Erw. Ausgabe,* pp. 47-49 et al. [Frankfurt a. M.] Suhrkamp [1964]
1,363. ――――. "Leiden und Grösse der Meister," in Bernhard Zeller, ed., *Neue deutsche Bücher: Literaturberichte für Bonniers Litterära Magasin 1935-36,* pp. 24-25. Marbach: Schiller-Nationalmuseum, 1965. [This review of Th. M's *Leiden und Grösse der Meister* first appeared in Hesse's article "Nya Tyska Böcker," *BLM,* Vol. 4, No. 7 (September 1935), pp. 50-57.]
1,364. †Hesse, Walter G. Das Bild der modernen Welt in Th. M's Roman 'Der Zauberberg.' M. A. thesis, University of Cape Town, 1945. 224 pp.
1,365. ――――. "Doktor Faustus van Th. M.," *Standpunte,* Vol. 14, No. 4 (April 1949), pp. 45-52. [In Afrikaans]
1,366. †Heumann, F. S. Major Hebrew Sources of Th. M's Joseph Novels. M. A. thesis, Columbia University, 1951.
1,367. Heuss, Theodor. "Th. M.: Zum 60. Geburtstag am 6. Juni 1935," *Hilfe,* 41 (1935), 262-263. [*Leiden und Grösse der Meister*]
1,368. ――――. "Mann gegen Mann," *Hilfe,* 25 (May 22, 1919), 261-263. Also in his *Vor der Bücherwand,* pp. 284-291.

Tübingen: Wunderlich [1961] [Heinrich and Th. M.]

1,369. ———. "Worte zur Th.M.-Feier in München, 1955," *Neue Rundschau,* 67 (Autumn 1956), 519-520. Also in item #1,368, pp. 292-294.

1,370. Hewett-Thayer, Harvey Waterman. "Th. M.," in his *The Modern German Novel,* pp. 13-16 et al. Boston: M. Jones, 1924. [*Buddenbrooks — Königliche Hoheit — Herr und Hund*]

1,371. Hewitt, Douglas. "New Novels: The Black Swan," *Manchester Guardian,* October 19, 1954, p. 4. [*Die Betrogene*]

1,372. ———. "Last Word," *Manchester Guardian,* November 1, 1955, p. 4. [*Felix Krull*]

1,373. Heym, Stefan. "Sprecher der Menschheit: Aus der Rede zu Ehren des 80. Geburtstags von Th. M.," *Berliner Zeitung,* June 14, 1955. [80th birthday]

1,374. ———. "Th. M. im 'Deutschen Volksecho,' " *Sinn und Form; Sonderheft Th. M.,* 1965, pp. 336-346.

1,375. Hicks, Granville. "Mann's New Novel: Spring in November," *New York Post,* June 6, 1954, p. M 12. [*Die Betrogene*]

1,376. ———. "Th. M.: A Summing Up," *New York Post,* October 9, 1955, p M 10. [*Felix Krull*]

1,377. ———. "Last Testament," *Saturday Review,* Vol. 12, No. 7 (February 14, 1959), p. 22. [*Last Essays*]

1,378. Hiehle, Kurt. "Zur angeblichen Ablehnung der eingeleiteten Rechtschreibungsreform durch Th. M.," *Papier und Druck,* Vol. 4, No. 12 (1955).

1,379. Hildebrandt, Dieter. "Zwei Briefbände von Th. M.," *Neue Rundschau,* 74 (1964), 142-146. [Review of items #2,062 and #2,066]

1,380. Hildebrandt, Wolfgang. "Zauberberg und Kriegsgefangene: Offener Brief an Th. M.," *Der Ruf,* No. 14 (October 1, 1945), p. 4. [Cf. I, item #1307 — *Der Zauberberg*]

1,381. ———. "Offener Brief: Kampfgruppe rügt Th. M.," *Neue Zeitung,* No. 172 (1949).

1,382. Hildenbrandt, Fred. "Der Leseabend von Th. M.," in his *Kleine Chronik,* pp. 121-122. Potsdam: Kiepenheuer, 1926.

1,383. Hill, Claude. "Germany's Contribution to Modern World Literature," *Universitas*, 2 (1958), 141-155. [On Th. M., pp. 154-155]

1,384. ———. Review of F. Kaufmann, item #1,683, *GQ*, 33 (January 1960), 85-86.

1,385. ———. "Th. M.," in his *Zweihundert Jahre deutscher Kultur*, pp. 352-353 et al. New York: Harper & Row [1966)

1,386. Hill, Roland. "Novelist of Decline: The Mind of Th. M.," *Tablet*, August 20, 1955, p. 178. [Obit.]

1,387. *Hillard-Steinbömer, Gustav. *Th. M.; ein Vortrag*. Cassel: Gebr. Gotthelft, 1911. 15 pp.

1,388. ———. "Parodistische Legende," *Merkur*, 5 (1951), 1090-1093. [*Der Erwählte*] [Cf. #3,890]

1,389. ———. "Th. M.," in his *Herren und Narren der Welt*, pp. 273-274 et al. München: List [1954]

1,390. ———. "Die Parabel vom Hochstapler: Zu den 'Bekenntnissen des Felix Krull,'" *Merkur*, 9 (March 1955), 285-288. Also in his *Wert der Dauer: Essays, Reden, Gedenkworte*. pp. 84-90. Hamburg: Hoffmann und Campe [1961]

1,391. ———. "Th. M's Mythenspiel: Zum Joseph-Roman," *Merkur*, 10 (February 1956), [112]-123. Also in his *Wert der Dauer*, item #1,390, pp. 71-84.

1,392. ———. "Th. M. im Blick seiner Töchter," *Merkur*, 10 (October 1956), 1024-1026. [Review of E. Mann, item #2,059, and M. Mann, item #2,100]

1,393. ———. "Th. M.," *Jahresring 56/57*, pp. 289-298. Stuttgart: DVA [1956] Under the title "Späte Begegnung mit Th. M.," in *Der Wagen*, pp. 146-152. [Lübeck, Westphal, 1957] Also in his *Wert der Dauer*, item #1,390, pp. 139-149.

1,394. ———. "Die Zürcher Gedenkstätten an Th. M.," *Lübecker Nachrichten*, No. 249 (October 25, 1959), p. 41. Slightly expanded version in *NDH*, No. 65 (December 1959), pp. 839-841. [Th. M. Archive in Zurich] [Cf. #3,892]

1,395. ———. "Tief ist der Brunnen der Vergangenheit: Zum 10. Todestag von Th. M.," *Lübecker Nachrichten*, August 10, 1965, p. 14 [Cf. #3,891]

1,396.   Hiller, Kurt. "Der Dichterfürst als Kulturphilosoph," *Geist und Tat,* 8 (1953).

1,397.   †Hilscher, Eberhard. Th. M's Goetheroman 'Lotte in Weimar.' Staatsexamensarbeit, Humboldt University, Berlin, 1951, 107 pp.

1,398.   † ————. Die Neugestaltung von Hartmanns Gregoriuslegende durch Th. M. Ergänzungs-Staatsexamen, Humboldt University, Berlin, 1952. 98 pp. [*Der Erwählte*]

1,399.   ————. "Bemerkungen zu den Joseph-Romanen Th. M's," *Aufbau* (Berlin), 10 (July 1954), 656-661.

1,400.   ————. "Th. M's politische Essays," *Aufbau* (Berlin), 10 (December 1954), 1090-1094.

1,401.   ————. "Th. M. und Schiller," *Aufbau* (Berlin), 11 (March 1955), 225-228.

1,402.   ————. "Ein Künstler als Abenteurer," *NDL,* 3 (May 1955), 131-142. [*Felix Krull*]

1,403.   ————. "Th. M. in unserer Zeit," *Berliner Zeitung,* June 4, 1955. [80th birthday]

1,404.   ————. "Th. M's Religiosität," *Sammlung* (Gëttingen), 10 (June 1955), 285-290.

1,405.   ————. "Th. M. als Sprachkünstler," *NDL,* 3 (August 1955), 56-71.

1,406.   ————. "Th. M's Lebenswerk," *Berliner Zeitung,* August 14, 1955. [Review of 12-vol. ed. of Mann's works by Aufbau-Verlag, Berlin]

1,407.   ————. "Th. M. und Goethe," *Aufbau* (Berlin), 11 (August 1955), 733-736.

1,408.   ————. "Begegnung mit Th. M.," *Aufbau* (Berlin), 11 (September 1955), 798-799.

1,409.   ————. "Th. M. und die Sowjetunion," *Neues Deutschland,* June 3, 1956.

1,410.   ————. "Der biblische Joseph in orientalischen Literaturwerken," *Mitteilungen des Instituts für Orientforschung,* 4 (1956), 81-108.

1,411.   ————. "Schiller in deutscher Dichtung," *Weimarer Beiträge,* 3 (1956), 343-364. [Th. M.: pp. 354-355]

1,412. ———. "Ein hohes Vermächtnis," *Neues Deutschland*, Vol. 15, No. 154 (June 5, 1960), p. 4. [85th birthday]

1,413. ———. "Heinrich und Th. M.," *Lehrgang Deutsche Sprache und Literatur*, 37 (1961), 9-15. [*Der Zauberberg — Mario und der Zauberer*]

1,414. ———. "Die Geschichte vom guten Sünder," in G. Wenzel, item #3,461, pp. 220-232. [*Der Erwählte*]

1,415. ———. Review of Koopmann, item #1,769, *Sonntag*, No. 44 (October 18, 1962).

1,416. ———. Review of G. Wenzel, item #3,461, *Sonntag*, April 28, 1963.

1,417. ———. "Th. M's Auseinandersetzung mit dem Faschismus," *Greifenalmanach*, pp. 296-[311]. Rudolstadt: Greifenverlag [1963]

1,418. ———. "Aufrechter Bekennermut," *Sonntag*, No. 23 (June 6, 1965), p. 15. [90th birthday]

1,419. ———. "Ironie, Parodie und Humor bei Th. M.," *Tagebuch* (Wien), Vol. 20, No. 6 (June 1965), p. 7. [Excerpt from item #1,420]

1,420. *———. *Th. M.: Leben und Werk*. Berlin: Volk und Wissen, 1965. 220 pp. Reviews: items #664, 3,971 and 4,002.

1,421. ———. "Th. M. und Gerhart Hauptmann, *"Sinn und Form: Sonderheft Th. M.*, 1965, 278-290.

1,422. Himmel, Adolf. "Th. M. in britischer Sicht: Zum 80. Geburtstag des Dichters," *Englische Rundschau*, No. 12 (1955), 162.

1,423. Himmel, Helmuth. "Th. M.," in his *Geschichte der deutschen Novelle*, pp. 371-373 et al. Bern: Francke [1963]

1,424. Hîncu, Dumitru. "Die Sendung eines grossen Künstlers unserer Zeit," *Gazeta Literară*, No. 25 (June 23, 1925), p. 5. [In Rumanian]

1,425. Hindus, Milton. "The Duels in Mann and Turgenev," *CL*, 11 (Fall 1959), 308-312.

1,426. Hines, Jack. "Story of Bashan, a Priceless Companion," *NYT Book Review*, February 4, 1923.

1,427. Hirsch, Felix E. "Th. M. and Germany," *NYHT*, June 2, 1955. [80th birthday]

1,428. Hirsch, Karl Jakob [pseud. Joe Gassner] "Der neue Roman von Th. M.: 'Lotte in Weimar,' " *Neue Volkszeitung,* April 13, 1940.

1,429. *Hirschbach, Frank Donald. *The Arrow and the Lyre: A Study of the Role of Love in the Works of Th. M.* The Hague: M. Nijhoff, 1955. ix, 195 pp. [Revised version of I, item #1033] Reviews: Gronicka, #1,084 — Hatfield, #1,216 — Kohut, #1,763 — Schultz, #2,979.

1,430. ————. Review of H. M. Wolff, item #3,532, *JEGP,* 57 (October 1958), 790-792.

1,431. ————. "Götterlieblinge und Hochstapler," *GQ,* 32 (January 1959), 22-33. [*Joseph und seine Brüder* — Goethe — *Felix Krull*]

1,432. ————. Review of A. Hellersberg, #1,285, *Monatshefte,* 53 (January 1961), pp. 41-43.

1,433. ————. "Th. M.," in John Gearey and Willy Schumann, *eds., Einführung in die deutsche Literatur,* pp. 381-400. New York: Holt, Rinehart, Winston [1964]

1,434. Hiss, Walter. "Zurück zur Ursprungsstätte: Gespräch mit Th. M.," *Abendzeitung,* September 9, 1952.

1,435. Hocke, Gustav René. "Ernte der Standhaftigkeit," *Ruf,* No. 14 (October 1, 1945), p. 4.

1,436. ————. "Th. M. bei Pius XII.," *Frankfurter Neue Presse,* Vol. 8, No. 112 (May 16, 1953), p. 20.

1,437. Hølmebakk, Gordon. "Th. M's noveller," *Vinduet,* Vol. 17, No. 3 (1963), pp. 211-214.

1,438. Hoentzsch, Alfred. "Ritter zwischen Tod und Teufel: Zu Hesses 'Glasperlenspiel' und Manns 'Dr. Faustus,' " *Allgäuer,* July 16, 1949.

1,439. Hof, Walter. "Realistischer Humanismus: Th. M's Alterswerke," in Städtisches Realgymnasium Königstein. *Eine kleine Festschrift zum zehnjährigen Bestehen,* pp. 5-21. Königstein/ Taunus, 1956.

1,440. ————. "Ironie und Humanität bei Th. M.," *Wirkendes Wort,* 13 (June 1963), 147-155.

1,441. Hoffman, Frederick John. "Th. M.," in his *Freudianism and the Literary Mind,* pp. 207-228. Baton Rouge: Louisiana State University Press, ²1957. [Cf. I, item #943]

1,442. †Hoffmann, Fernand. Kunst und Krankheit bei Th. M. Ph. D. diss., University of Luxembourg, 1955. 200 pp.

1,443. ———. "Das Problem der 'Paradis artificiels' bei Th. M.," *Academia,* No. 2-3 (Summer-Autumn, 1955), pp. 105-124. [*Doktor Faustus*]

1,444. *———. *Th. M. als politischer und europäischer Dichter.* [n.p., n.d.] 8 pp.

1,445. ———. "Die Beziehungen zwischen Kunst und Krankheit im Werke Th. M's," *Academia: Nouvelle Revue Luxembourgeoise,* No. 3 (1965), pp. 253-285.

1,446. Hoffmann, Gerd. "Die Musik im Werke Th. M's," *Aufbau* (Berlin), 11 (June 1955), 561-572.

1,447. ———. "Bildungseinflüsse auf Hans Castorp im 'Zauberberg,' " in G. Wenzel, item #3,453, pp. 134-148.

1,448. Hoffmann, Paul. "Kleine Novelle von Th. M.: Die Betrogene," *Hellweger Anzeiger,* February 12, 1954.

1,449. *Hoffmeister, Werner G. *Studien zur erlebten Rede bei Th. M. und Robert Musil.* The Hague: Mouton, 1965. 173 pp. [Ph. D. diss., Brown University, 1962. — *DA,* 23 (1963), 2526-2527]
Reviews: Schumann, #2,988 — Swales, #3,227.

1,450. *Hofman, Alois. *Th. M. a Rusko: Literárni studie.* Prague, 1959. 182 pp. [With thirty letters from Th. M. to A. S. Eliasberg, written between 1914 and 1924]
Reviews: Venohr, #3,351.

1,451. ———. "Th. M. und Russland: Eine ungelöste Frage der vergleichenden Literaturwissenschaft," *Zeitschrift für Slawistik,* 7 (1962), 415-421.

1,452. ———. "Th. M. und sein Verhältnis zur literarischen Rezeption," *Philologica Pragensia,* 7 (1964), 120-128. [In Czech, with German resumé]

1,453. ———. " 'Doktor Faustus' und die 'Brüder Karamasoff,'"
        Philologica Pragensia, 7 (1964), 374-388. [In Czech, with
        German resumé]

1,454. ———. "Th. M." in *I. S. Turgenev und Deutschland,*
        Vol. 1, pp. [330-350]. Berlin: Akademie-Verlag, 1965.

1,455. ———. "Tolstois und Turgenjews humanistischer Realismus
        in den 'Buddenbrooks,' " *Sinn und Form: Sonderheft Th. M.,*
        1965, pp. 186-203.

1,456. ———. "Dostojewski und Th. M's erste Novellensammlung,"
        in G. Wenzel, item #3,472, pp. 169-189.

1,457. Hofmiller, Josef. "Th. M's 'Tod in Venedig,' " *Merkur,* 9
        (June 1955), [505]-520. [Cf. I, item #1948 and II, #3,894]

1,458. Hogestraat, Erich. "Rückkehr zur alten Erde," *Freie Presse
        Bielefeld,* June 16, 1953. [Biog.]

1,459. *Hohmeyer, Jürgen. *Th. M's Roman 'Joseph und seine Brüder.'*
        Marburg/Lahn: N. G. Elwert, 1965. 140 pp.

1,460. Hohoff, Curt. "Über neue Romane," *Hochland,* 44 (1951/52),
        169-174. [*Der Erwählte*]

1,461. ———. "Epilog zum Schillerjahr: Zu Th. M's 'Versuch' und
        einem Sammelband mit Schillerreden," *Rheinischer Merkur,*
        April 27, 1956, Literaturblatt.

1,462. ———. "Der ironische Deutsche," *Christ und Welt,* Vol. 13,
        No. 11 (March 10, 1960), p. 18. [Review of E. Heller, item
        #1,278]

1,463. ———. "Neue Th. M.-Literatur," *NZZ,* Vol. 181, Morgenaus-
        gabe No. 1716 (May 19, 1960), Bl. 1. [Review of E. Heller,
        item #1,278, and A. Hellersberg, item #1,285]

1,464. ———. "Th. M. — theologisch betrachtet," *Christ und Welt,*
        Vol. 13, No. 31 (July 28, 1960), p. 16. [Review of A.
        Hellersberg, item #1,285]

1,465. ———. "Th. M.," in Albert Soergel [and] Curt Hohoff,
        Dichtung und Dichter der Zeit, Vol. 2, pp. 850-880.
        Düsseldorf: Bagel [1961]

1,466. ———. "Th. M's religiöse Erfahrung,' in his *Schnittpunkte,*
        pp. 284-[298] Stuttgart: DVA, 1963.

1,467. ———. "Briefschreiber Th. M.: Blindheit für das Elementare," *Rheinischer Merkur,* Vol. 19, Literaturblatt No. 31 (July 31, 1964), p. 15. [*Briefe I, #2,062, and Briefe II, #2,066*]
1,468. Hollander, Jürgen von. "Bürger und Künstler: Eine Stunde mit Th. M.," *Film und Frau,* Vol. 14, No. 23 (1962), pp. 70-79. [Biog.]
1,469. Holmberg, Olle. "Esteten och borgaren: Till Th. M's femtiårsdag den 6. juni," *Dagens Nyheter,* June 6, 1925. [Review of Eloesser, I, #619]
1,470. ———. "Nej, herr Törngren!" *Dagens Nyheter,* February 20, 1946. [Reply to P. H. Törngren, #3,292]
1,471. ———. "Faust och djävulen," *Dagens Nyheter,* November 18, 1947. [*Doktor Faustus*]
1,472. ———. "Den utvalde," *Dagens Nyheter,* April 14, 1951. [*Der Erwählte*]
1,473. ———. "Den vise och skälmen," *Dagens Nyheter,* January 3, 1955. [*Felix Krull*]
1,474. ———. "Frågetecken vid en skälmroman," in item #2,431, pp. 137-141. [*Felix Krull*]
1,475. ———. "Familjen Friedemann," *Dagens Nyheter,* December 17, 1958. [Short stories]
1,476. ———. "Th. M's brev," *Dagens Nyheter,* September 17, 1962. [*Briefe I, #2,062*]
1,477. ———. "Th. M's landsflykt," *Dagens Nyheter,* September 14, 1964. [*Briefe II, #2,066*]
1,478. ———. "Allvar, ironi och parodi," *Dagens Nyheter,* December 14, 1964, p. 4. [Review of H. Levander, #1,958]
1,479. Holmqvist, Bengt. "Th. M. — pajas och häxmästare," *OBS,* Vol. 6, No. 22 (1949), pp. 11-16.
1,480. ———. "Trollkarlens avsked," *BLM,* 24 (December 1955), 843-844. Also in *Dagens Nyheter,* June 11, 1956. [*Betrachtungen eines Unpolitischen, #2,058* — E. Mann, #2,059]
1,481. ———. "Th. M. parodikern," *Röster i radio,* Vol. 23, No. 23, (1956), pp. 11, 24.
1,482. ———. "Th. M.," in Th. M.," *Sjöresa med Don Quichote och andra Essayer,* pp. 7-14. Stockholm: Tidens Förlag, 1964.

1,483. Holthusen, Hans Egon. "Th. M.," in his *Der unbehauste Mensch,* pp. 264-266. München: Piper [³1955]

1,484. ———. "Crossing the Zero Point: German Literature since World War II," in *French and German Letters Today,* pp. 39.53. Washington: Library of Congress, 1960. [*See* pp. 44-47 on *Doktor Faustus*]

1,485. ———. "Kritik und Einbildungskraft: Zu Erich Hellers Th. M.-Monographie," *Merkur,* 14 (August 1960), [774]-788. Also in his *Kritisches Verstehen: Neue Aufsätze zur Literatur,* pp. 173-196. München: Piper [1961] [Review of #1,278]

1,486. ———. "The World Without Transcendence," in H. Hatfield, item #1,229, pp. 123-132. [Excerpt from I, item #2746 — *Doktor Faustus*]

1,487. Holthusen, Wilhelm [and] Adalbert Taubner. "Dürers 'Philipp Melanchthon' und 'Bildnis einer jungen Frau' als visuelle Vorbilder für die Eltern von Adrian Leverkühn in Th. M's 'Doktor Faustus.' " *Die Waage,* Vol. 3, No. 2 (1963), pp. 67-69.

1,488. Holz, Hans Heinz. "Die Repräsentanz deutschen Geistes," *Deutsche Woche,* Vol. 5, No. 34 (August 24, 1955), p. 15. [Obit.]

1,489. ———. "Die Repräsentanz deutschen Geistes," *Tat,* Vol. 25, No. 339 (December 10, 1960), p. 17. [Concerns 12-vol. ed. of M's works, S. Fischer Verlag, in part identical with previous item]

1,490. ———. "Ein Ort literarischer Tradition," *Frankfurter Allgemeine Zeitung,* No. 43 (February 20, 1961), p. 14 [Zurich Archive]

1,491. ———. "Misstrauensvotum letzter Hand: Eröffnung des Th. M.-Archivs in Zürich," [by] Michael Hess [pseud.] *Deutsche Woche,* Vol. 11, No. 9 (March 1, 1961), p. 17. [Th. M. Archive Zurich]

1,492. ———. "Th. M. und Kleist," in his *Macht und Ohnmacht der Sprache: Untersuchungen zum Sprachverständnis und Stil Heinrich von Kleists,* pp. 20-23. Frankfurt a. M.: Athenäum, 1962.

1,493. *Hommage de la France à Th. M. Paris Editions Flinker, 1955.
169 pp. Contributors: Blanchot, #345 — Boucher, #415 —
Boulez, #417 — Breitbach, #444 — Brion, #462 — Cocteau,
#593 — Duhamel, #719 — Flinker, #884 — Harcourt,
#1,193 — Leibrich, #1,889 — Marcel, #2,108 — Mauriac,
#2,165 — Maurois, #2,166 — Romains, #2,758 —
Sagave, #2,823 — Schlappner, #2,902 — Schlumberger,
#2,909 — M. Schneider, #2,924 — Schuman, #2,986 —
Schweitzer, #2,991 — Servicen, #3,017 — Vallentin, #3,343
— Vermeil, #3,355 — Yourcenar, #3,566.
Reviews: Dinaux, #686 — Fetscher, #852 — Jancke, #1,566
— Laborde, #1,832 — Wintzen, #3,508.

1,494. Hommel, Friedrich. "Posthumes Dichterheim," Stuttgarter
Zeitung, February 16, 1961. [Th. M. Archive Zurich]

1,495. ———. "Bodmers Erben," Stuttgarter Zeitung, July 31, 1961.
[See also G. Mann, #2,077, and F. Martini, #2,132]

1,496. Honorary Degrees [of the] University of Cambridge. 4 June
1953. Cambridge, 1953. 12 pp. brochure. [Address of the
orator on Th. M., p. 8]

1,497. Honsza, Norbert. "Poglady polityczne i dzialalność
publicystyczna Tomasza Manna," Przegląd Zachoani, No. 6
(1963), pp. [227]-252. [Politics]

1,498. ———. "Problematyka ostatnich nowel Tomasza Manna,"
Przeglad Humanistyczny, No. 3 (1965), pp. [63]-76.

1,499. Hoppe, Manfred. "Europa im Exil: Th. M's Briefe 1937-1947,"
Du, Vol. 23, No. 274 (December 1963), pp. 118, 120, 122.

1,500. Horst, Karl August. "Zu Th. M's Moses-Biographie,"
Rheinischer Merkur, July 23, 1949. [Das Gesetz]

1,501. ———. "Krankheit und Tod im Zauberberg," in his Die
deutsche Literatur der Gegenwart, pp. 39-41 et al. [München]
Nymphenburg [1957]

1,502. ———. "Mythos und Humanität," Frankfurter Allgemeine
Zeitung, No. 170 (July 23, 1960). [Review of K. Kerényi,
item #1,700 c]

1,503. ———. "Die traurige Geschichte Friedrichs des Grossen,"
Merkur, 16 (1962), [697]-700. [Heinrich and Th. M.]

1,504. ————. "Th. M.," in his *Strukturen und Strömungen,* pp. 88-
91. [München] Nymphenburg [1963]

1,505. ————. "Th. M.," in his *Das Abenteuer der deutschen
Literatur im 20. Jahrhundert,* pp. 88-91 et al. München:
Nymphenburg [1964]

1,506. Høst, Gerd. "Hilsen fra en oversetter," in item #2,431,
pp. 149-153.

1,507. Hotes, Leander. "Th. M.," in his *Das Leitmotiv in der
neueren deutschen Romandichtung,* pp. 97-150. [Bückeburg:
H. Prinz] 1931. [Ph. D. diss., University of Frankfurt a. M.]
Concerns: *Buddenbrooks — Tonio Kröger — Königliche
Hoheit — Der Tod in Venedig — Der Zauberberg*]

1,508. Howard, Brian. "Th. M.," *New Statesman and Nation,*
January 27, 1934. [Review of Cleugh, I, item #148]

1,509. Huddleston, Sibley. "German Author Expresses Views as to
Causes of War," *Christian Science Monitor,* April 1, 1926.
[Th. M's speech in Paris — Politics]

1,510. Hübinger, Paul Egon. "Th. M. und die Juden: Eine
unveröffentlichte Äusserung des Dichters aus dem Jahre 1921,"
Frankfurter Allgemeine Zeitung, No. 12 (January 15, 1966).

1,511. Huebner, Friedrich Markus. "Der Fall Bernd Isemann,"
Sturm, 4 (1913/14), 87. [Concerns I, item #1949]

1,512. ————. "Th. M. und Professor Willy Hellpach," *Wiecker
Bote,* Vol. 1, No. 6 (1913/14), pp. 15-16.

1,513. Hübner, Fritz. "Der Tod in Venedig, Novelle von Th. M.,"
Bücherwurm, 3 (1913), 213-214.

1,514. Hübner, Paul. "Th. M. und die Blutschande: Zu Rolf Thiels
Film 'Wälsungenblut,' " *Rheinische Post,* February 13, 1965.

1,515. Hübscher, Arthur. "Die überarbeiteten 'Betrachtungen eines
Unpolitischen,' " *Gewissen,* Vol. 9, No. 25 (June 20, 1927).
[Cf. I, item #1548]

1,516. ————. "Vier Jahrzehnte in ironischer Distanz; Th. M's
Münchener Zeit in seinen Briefen," *Welt und Wort,* 17 (April
1962), 169-171. Also in *Unser Bayern; Bayer. Staatszeitung,*
Vol. 11, No. 6 (1962), pp. 44-45. [*Briefe 1889-1936,*
#2,062]

1,517. Hühnerfeld, Paul. "Zu Th. M's neuer Erzählung," *Zeit*, Vol. 8, No. 43 (October 22, 1953), p. 5. [*Die Betrogene*]

1,518. ———. "Das Phänomen der Familie Mann," *Zeit*, Vol. 11, No. 34 (August 23, 1956), p. 4. [Klaus Mann: *Mephisto*. — Monika Mann, item #2,100]

1,519. Hülsen, Hans von. "Das Gesicht hinter der Maske," *Blätter des Deutschen Theaters*, 2 (1912), 394-399.

1,520. ———. "Die Brüder Mann," *Kultur der Gegenwart*, No. 46 (1914), pp. 1199-1201.

1,521. ———. "Der deutsche Geist," *Vossische Zeitung*, No. 332 (July ?, 1915), 3. Beilage. [*Friedrich und die Grosse Koalition*]

1,522. ———. "Th. M.," in his *Zwillings-Seele*, Vol. 2, pp. 64-65. München: Bernhard Funck [1947]

1,523. ———. "Kleine Adresse — später grosse; Jugendjahre zweier grosser Dichter in Rom," *Schweizer Monatshefte*, 39 (October 1959), 637-640. [Gerhart Hauptmann — Th. M.]

1,524. Hülsmeyer, Ernst. "Th. M. und die Politik," *Heidelberger Student*, Vol. 67, No. 2 (November 28, 1930), pp. 12-13. [*Deutsche Ansprache*. — Cf. Golo Mann, item #2,073]

1,525. Hughes, William M. "Th. M. and the Platonic Adulterer," *Monatshefte*, 51 (February 1959), [75]-80.

1,526. Hunt, Joel A. "The Stylistics of a Foreign Language: Th. M's Use of French," *GR*, 32 (February 1957), 19-34.

1,527. ———. "The *Walpurgisnacht* Chapter: Th. M's First Conclusion," *MLN*,76 (December 1961), 826-829.

1,528. ———. "Mann and Whitman: Humaniores Litterae," *CL*, 14 (Summer 1962), 266-271.

1,529. Hupka, Herbert. Review of F. Lion, item #1,979, *Welt und Wort*, 2 (October 1947). [Cf. I, #263]

1,530. Huppert, Hugo. "Th. M's Entscheidung," *Internationale Literatur — Deutsche Blätter*, Vol. 7, No. 5 (May 1937), pp. [109]-111.

1,531. ———. "Nachgeholte Beiordnungen," *Sinn und Form: Sonderheft Th. M.*, 1965, pp. 112-122.

1,532. Hussong, Friedrich. "Saulus Mann," *Tag*, October 15, 1922. [*Von Deutscher Republik*]

1,533.   ———. "Geister und kein Geist," *Tag*, December 16, 1923.
          [*Okkulte Erlebnisse*]

1,534.   Hutchens, John K. "As Th. M. Arrives at Eighty," *NYT Book
          Review*, June 5, 1955.

1,535.   ———. "Confessions of Felix Krull," *NYT*, September 19,
          1955.

1,536.   Ianosi, Ion. "Der Künstler und der Zauberer," *Gazeta Literară*,
          No. 47 (November 9, 1964), pp. 1, 8. [In Rumanian]

1,537.   ———. "Einheit und Metamorphose," *Luceafarul*, No. 24
          (November 21, 1964), p. 11. [In Rumanian]

1,537a.   ———. "Muntele vrăjit de Th. M.," *Viata-românească*, No. 4
          (April 1965), pp. 107-122.

1,538. * ———. *Th. M.* Bucharest: Editura Pentru Literatura
          Universala Bucuresti, 1965. 323 pp.

1,539.   Iglesias-Laguna, Antonio. "Th. M. descubre a 'Don Quijote,' "
          Cuadernos hispano-americanos, 59 (1962), 38-50.

1,540.   Ihlenfeld, Kurt. "In memoriam Th. M.," in his *Zeitgesicht:
          Erlebnisse eines Lesers*, pp. 451-455. Witten: Eckart, 1961.
          [Obit.]

1,541.   ———. "Th. M's Briefe 1889-1936," *Eckart-Jahrbuch*,
          1961-62, pp. 256-264. [Review of item #2,062]

1,542.   ———. "Th. M's Josefsroman," in his *Stadtmitte: Kritische
          Gänge in Berlin*, pp. 219-220. Witten: Eckart, 1964.

1,543.   ———. "Bin die Verschwendung — bin die Poesie: Th. M's
          Briefe 1937-1947," *Sonntagsblatt*, No. 11 (March 15, 1964).
          Also in item #1,542, pp. 344-346. [Review of item #2,066]

1,544.   Isaac, Henry D. "Th. M., Goethe und die Juden: Letter to
          the Editor," *Aufbau* (New York), Vol. 27, No. 20 (May 19,
          1961), p. 26.

1,545.   Isolani, Gertrud. "Zurück zur alten Erde: Besuch bei Th. M.
          in Erlenbach," *Genossenschaft*, No. 33 (August 15, 1953),
          [Biog.]

1,546.   ———. "Th. M. privat," *Bund*, Vol. 106, Morgenausgabe
          No. 381 (August 17, 1955), pp. 3-4. [Obit. — Biog.]

1,547.   ———. "Eine vorbildliche Dichtergattin: Zum 80. Geburtstag
          von Katja Mann am 24. Juli," *Tat*, Vol. 28, No. 195 (July 18,

1963), p. 5. Also in *Aufbau* (New York), Vol. 29, No. 32 (August 9, 1963), p. 22.

1,547a. Itoh, Tsutomu. "Goethe und Th. M.," *Bulletin, Nagoya Technische Hochschule*, 1962. [36 pp.]

1,548. Itschert, Hans. Review of R. A. Nicholls, item #2,407, *Die Neueren Sprachen*, N. F., No. 2 (February 1957), pp. 103-104.

1,549. Izquierdo, Julián. "Th. M.: Los temas capitales de su obra," *Indice de Artes y Letras*, Vol. 10, No. 86-87 (November-December, 1955), p. 25.

1,550. †Jackson-Berger, Margret. Studien zum Präteritalsystem des Deutschen. [Mit Beispielen aus Th. M's 'Zauberberg.'] Ph. D. diss., University of Münster, 1959. 80 pp.

1,551. Jacob, Heinrich Eduard. "Th. M. — Ironie und Engagement," *Süddeutsche Zeitung*, March 12, 1960. [Review of E. Heller, item #1,278.]

1,552. Jacob, P. Walter. "Th. M.: Ich erneuere die Bekanntschaft," in his *Rampenlicht; Köpfe der Literatur und des Theaters*, pp. 7-13. Buenos Aires: Editorial Cosmopolita, 1945.

1,553. Jacobson, Anna. "Zum 6. Juni 1945," *Neue Rundschau*, Sondernummer, 6. Juni 1945, pp. 161-162. [70th birthday]

1,554. ———. "Th. M's amerikanisches Erbe: Der Einfluss E. A. Poes und Walt Whitmans," *Aufbau* (New York), Vol. 21, No. 22 (June 3, 1955), pp. 5-6. [80th birthday]

1,555. ———. Review of K. W. Jonas, item #1,605, *JEGP*, 55 (July 1956), 484-485.

1,556. Jaensson, Knut. "De ombytta huvudena," *BLM*, 10 (November 1941), 749-751. [*Die Vertauschten Köpfe*]

1,557. Järv, Harry. "Politikern Th. M.," *Arbetaren*, December 12, 1952.

1,558. Jaesrich, Hellmut. "Das verlängerte Fragment: Zu den 'Bekenntnissen des Hochstaplers Felix Krull,' " *Monat*, 7 (December 1954), 268-271.

1,559. ———. "Der Tod des Zauberers: In memoriam Th. M.," *Monat*, 7 (September 1955), 506-508. [Obit.]

1,560. Jahnke, Walter. "In memoriam Th. M.: Die Kraft seines Werkes," *Sonntag*, August 21, 1955. [Obit.]

1,561.   Jahnn, Hans Henny. "Gruss an Th. M.," *Sinn und Form,* 7
         (1955), 346-348.

1,562.   Jaloux, Edmond. "Th. M. in französischer Beleuchtung,"
         Berliner Börsen-Courier, No. 245 (May 30, 1926). [Th. M.
         in Paris]

1,563.   ———. "Les possibilités de rapprochement franco-allemand
         d'après M. Th. M.," *Tribune de Genève,* June 18, 1926.

1,564.   Jancke, Oskar. "Th. M.," in his *Kunst und Reichtum deutscher
         Prosa,* pp. 521-546. München: Piper [²1954]

1,565.   ———. "Zum Tode Th. M's," *Christ und Welt,* Vol. 8,
         No. 33 (August 18, 1955), p. 2. [Obit.]

1,566.   ———. "Drei Werke über Th. M.," *Kritische Blätter,* No. 1
         (October 1955), pp. 12-13. [Review of F. Lion, item #1,979,
         R. Faesi, item #831, and item #1,493]

1,567.   ———. "Totengespräch mit Th. M., Gottfried Benn und
         Bertolt Brecht," *NDH,* No. 35 (1957), pp. 225-232.

1,568.   Jansen, Elmar. "Die Memoiren Felix Krulls als zeichnerische
         Burlesken: Der Th. M.-Zyklus des Hallenser Malers Karl
         Erich Müller," *Marginalien,* No. 13 (March 1963),
         pp. 22-24.

1,569.   Janssen, Albrecht. "Th. M. und die Freimaurer," *Bruderschaft,*
         3 (June 1961), 209-215.

1,570.   Jansson, Sven-Bertil. Review of G. Bergsten, item #292,
         Upsala Nya Tidning, April 15, 1963.

1,571.   Jaspers, Karl. "Künder unserer Zeit," *Aufbau* (New York),
         Vol. 21, No. 33 (August 19, 1955), p. 1. [Obit.]

1,572.   Jaspersen, Ursula. " 'Lotte in Weimar' von Th. M.,"
         Hamburger Akademische Rundschau, 1 (September 1946),
         107-110.

1,573.   Jastrun, Mieczyslaw. "Th. M. oder von der Berufung des
         Künstlers," *Aufbau* (Berlin), 12 (August 1956), 704-710.
         [Translated from Polish by Wolfgang Grycz]

1,574.   Jauss, Hans Robert. "Die Ausprägung des Zeit-Romans in
         Th. M's 'Zauberberg' und James Joyce 'Ulysses,' " in his *Zeit
         und Erinnerung in Marcel Prousts 'A la recherche du temps
         perdu,'* pp. 35-53. Heidelberg: C. Winter, 1955.

1,575. *Jens, Inge. "Nachwort," in her *ed.* of *Th. M. und Ernst Bertram: Briefe aus den Jahren 1919-1955,* pp. 293-307. [Pfullingen] Neske, [1960] Reviews: H. Becher, #208 — Blöcker, #363 — Boehlich, #385 — Brües, #493 — Buchner, #498 — Dannecker, #638 — Fabian #827 — Faye, #839 — Grimm, #1,081 — Gronicka, #1,088 — Hellmann, #1,293 — I. Jens, #1,576 — Mennemeier, #2,225 — Reuter, #2,691 — Rychner, #2,806-2,807 — K. L. Schneider, #2,922 — Sieburg, #3,052 — Ter-Nedden, #3,254 — Weber, #3,419 — Wolffheim, #3,535 — Wuthenow, #3,542.

1,576. ―――. "Der Poet und sein Minister," *Gehört-gelesen,* Vol. 17, No. 10 (October 1960). [Concerns #1,575]

1,577. ―――. "Von fin de siècle zum amerikanischen Exil," *Zeit,* Vol. 17, No. 4 (January 26, 1962), p. 14. Also in G. Wenzel, item *#3,472, pp. 461-465. [Review of *Briefe I,* item #2,062]

1,578. ―――. "Dichters Lehrjahre: Th. M. im Spiegel seiner Biographie," *Christ und Welt,* Vol. 17, No. 42 (October 16, 1964), p. 28. [Review of K. Schröter, #2,971]

1,579. Jens, Walter. "Joseph der Ernährer," *Württembergische Abendzeitung,* November 29, 1949.

1,580. ―――. "Th. M. zu seinem 75. Geburtstag," *Württembergische Abendzeitung,* June 3, 1950.

1,581. ―――. "Th. M. — problematisch," *Welt am Sonntag,* October 4, 1953. [*Die Betrogene*]

1,582. ―――. "Der Gott der Diebe und sein Dichter: Ein Versuch über Th. M's Verhältnis zur Antike," *Antike und Abendland,* 5 (1956), 139-153. Under the title "Th. M. und die Welt der Antike," in his *Statt einer Literaturgeschichte,* pp. 87-107. [Pfullingen] Neske [1957]

1,583. ―――. "Der 26-Jährige hat seinen Stil gefunden: Eine Betrachtung über die Buddenbrooks," *Lübecker Morgen,* October 8, 1960.

1,584. ―――. "Nachwort," in Th. M., *Buddenbrooks,* pp. 518-520. Frankfurt a. M.: S. Fischer, 1962.

1,585.   ————. "Wachsam, hellsichtig und ohne Illusion: Th. M's Briefe aus den Jahren der Emigration und des Krieges," *Zeit*, No. 30 (July 1964), p. 11. Also in Wenzel, item #3,472, pp. 465-473. [Review of *Briefe II*, item #2,066]

1,586.   ————. "Th. M. und die Rhetorik," *Süddeutsche Zeitung*, No. 188 (August 7-8, 1965). [Rhetoric — Language]

1,587.   ————. "Die Maske des gelassenen Zelebrierers: Der dritte und letzte Band der Briefe Th. M's," *Zeit*, No. 6 (February 4, 1966), p. 17. [Review of *Briefe III*, item #2,071]

1,588.   Jensen, Fritz. "An Th. M. scheiden sich die Geister," *Österreichisches Tagebuch*, June 12, 1952.

1,589.   Jentgens, Alfred. "Th. M.: 'Betrachtungen eines Unpolitischen,' " *Rheinische Hefte*, May 1957, p. 8.

1,590.   Jerosch, Ernst. "Eine Stunde Vornehmheit: Offener Brief an Th. M.," *Ostpreussische Zeitung*, No. 245 (September 4, 1931).

1,591.   Joelsohn, Hermann. "Vom Künstler und vom Bürger. Anlässlich Th. M's Novelle 'Der Tod in Venedig,' " *Wiecker Bote*, Vol. 1, No. 1 (1913), pp. 6-10.

1,592.   Johann, Ernst. "Th. M. als Novellist," *Frankfurter Allgemeine Zeitung*, Vol. 10, No. 253 (October 31, 1958). [*Erzählungen*]

1,593.   ————. "Das Th. M.-Denkmal," *Frankfurter Allgemeine Zeitung*, Vol. 11, No. 2 (November 28, 1959). [Review of H. Bürgin, item #502]

1,594.   ————. "Der Roman der 'Betrachtungen,' " *Frankfurter Allgemeine Zeitung*, Vol. 12, No. 113 (May 14, 1960). [Review of Amann, item #3,426]

1,595.   ————. "Die Stimmigkeiten eines Lebens," *Frankfurter Allgemeine Zeitung*, Vol. 17, No. 284 (December 7, 1965), Literaturblatt, p. 2. [Review of Bürgin-Mayer, item #504, and Th. M., *Reden und Aufsätze*, I and II]

1,596.   ————. "Manifeste," *Frankfurter Allgemeine Zeitung*, March 15, 1966, Literaturblatt. [Review of Berendsohn, item #284]

•1,597.   Johnson, Eyvind. "Th. M. attio år," in item #2,431, p. 161. [80th birthday]

1,598. Joho, Wolfgang. "Th. M. ist für den Frieden," *Sonntag*, Vol. 5, No. 21 (May 21, 1950), p. 1. [Politics — Controversy over Stockholm Peace Prize]

1,599. ———. "Die Sympathie mit dem Menschlichen," *Sonntag*, Vol. 10, No. 23 (June 5, 1955), p. 8. [*Joseph und seine Brüder*]

1,600. ———. "In memoriam Th. M.: Bewahrer, Vollender, Überwinder," *Sonntag*, Vol. 10, No. 34 (August 21, 1955), p. 7. [Obit.]

1,601. Jollos, Nadja [pseud. Maria Nils] "Th. M's ältester Schweizer Freund," *Tages-Anzeiger*, No. 283 (December 1, 1962), p. 7. [Review of item #833]

1,602. ———. "Gefährtin eines grossen Dichters: Zum 80. Geburtstag von Katja Mann," *Tages-Anzeiger*, (July 24, 1963), p. 15.

1,603. ———. "Dichter zwischen Norden und Süden: Gedächtnisfeier für Th. M. im Schauspielhaus," *Tages-Anzeiger*, No. 137 (June 15, 1965), p. 15. [90th birthday]

1,604. Jonas, Ilsedore B. "Ein Leben für die deutsche Literatur: Zum Gedenken an Lavinia Mazzucchetti," *NZZ*, Vol. 186, Morgenausgabe No. 3009 (July 16, 1965), Bl. 5, Feuilleton. — "In memoriam Lavinia Mazzucchetti," *Basler Nachrichten*, No. 330 (August 8, 1965). — "Th. M. und Italien," *Luzerner Neueste Nachrichten*, No. 183 (August 10, 1965). — Also in Italian, "Una vita per la letteratura tedesca: ricordo di Lavinia Mazzucchetti," *Duemila*, Vol. 1, No. 3 (1965), pp. 85-86.

1,605. *Jonas, Klaus W. *Fifty Years of Th. M. Studies: A Bibliography of Criticism*. Minneapolis: University of Minnesota Press, 1955. xxi, 217 pp. [With a Preface by Th. M., "Ein Wort hierzu," pp. xii-xv]
Reviews: Babler, #159 — Berendsohn, #271 — Browning, #485 — Drexl, #715 — Eppelsheimer, #795 — Furstner, #963 — Gronicka, #1,084 — Hatfield, #1,221 — Jacobson, #1,555 — Krueger, #1,809 — Leibrich, #1,892 — Reichart,

#2,655 — Thieberger, #3,266 — A. Werner, #3,476 — Willoughby, #3,501.

1,606. ———. "Als Schriftsteller bin ich deutsch . . .," *Lübecker Nachrichten,* No. 116 (May 19, 1955), p. 11. Under the title "Wie Amerika den grossen europäischen Dichter feiert," *Luzerner Neueste Nachrichten,* Vol. 59, No. 128 (June 4, 1955). Also published in English as "A Note by Th. M's Bibliographer," *YULG,* 30 (July 1955), 10-15.

1,607. ———. "Th. M. Collections," *Monatshefte,* 50 (April-May, 1958), [145]-156. Expanded German version entitled "Th. M's Manuskripte in europäischen und amerikanischen Sammlungen," *Jahrbuch für Amerikastudien,* 4 (1959), [236]-248.

1,608. ———. Review of H. Bürgin, item #502, *PBSA,* 55 (Second Quarter, 1961), 160-162. Expanded version, with supplement and corrections, in *Monatshefte,* 52 (December 1960), [353]-360; German version in *DLZ,* 82 (April 1961), 315-320.

1,609. ———. "Das Th. M.-Archiv in Zürich," *Börsenblatt für den deutschen Buchhandel,* Frankfurter Ausgabe, 17 (November 28, 1961), Aus dem Antiquariat, 2047-2050. Also in *Duitse Kroniek,* 15 (1963), 7-13. English version in *GQ,* 35 (January 1962), 10-16.

1,610. ———. Review of A. Hellersberg, item #1,285, *GQ,* 35 (May 1962), 373-374.

1,611. ———. "Th. M. in englischer Übersetzung: Erinnerungen an H. T. Lowe-Porter," *NZZ,* Vol. 184, Sonntagsausgabe No. 2361 (60), June 9, 1963, Bl. 5. Also in English, entitled "In memoriam Helen T. Porter Lowe, 1876-1963," *Monatshefte,* 55 (November 1963), [322]-324.

1,612. ———. "Th. M. und Amerika," *Börsenblatt für den deutschen Buchhandel,* Frankfurter Ausgabe, 20 (June 5, 1964), Aus dem Antiquariat, 1100-1102.

1,613. ———. "Th. M's Manuskripte," *Philobiblon,* 9 (September 1965), 153-174.

1,614. ———. "Ein unbekanntes Klaus Mann-Archiv," *Börsenblatt für den deutschen Buchhandel,* Frankfurter Ausgabe, 21

(October 19, 1965), Aus dem Antiquariat, 2229-2231.

1,615. ———. "Th. M. in America," *Stechert-Hafner Book News,* Vol. 280, No. 2 (October 1965), pp. 17-20.

1,616. ———. "Die Hochschulschriften des In- und Auslandes über Th. M.," in G. Wenzel, #3,472, pp. 511-531. Enlarged version in *Börsenblatt für den deutschen Buchhandel,* Frankfurter Ausgabe, 22 (July 12, 1966), Aus dem Antiquariat, 1397-1406.

1,617. ———. "Th. M. in Germany and Switzerland," *Stechert-Hafner Book News,* Vol. 20, No. 9 (May 1966), pp. 121-124.

1,618. Jost, Dominik. "Th. M.," in his *Ludwig Derleth: Gestalt und Leistung,* pp. 52-53 et al. Stuttgart: Kohlhammer, 1965.

1,619. József, Attila. "Th. M. üdvëzlése," *Szép Szép,* 4 (1937), 47-48; also in his *Osszes versei,* pp. 468-469. [Budapest] 1956. German translation by Zoltán Franyo, "Gruss an Th. M.," in *Szép Szó,* 6 (1938), 413. [Cf. I, item #723] Both the original Hungarian text and a German translation by Stephan Hermlin appeared in *Internationale Buchkunstausstellung* [Leipzig, 1952, 4 pp.] This German translation was reprinted as "Th. M. zum Gruss," *Sinn und Form,* Vol. 6, No. 2 (1954), pp. 217-218. English translation by Vernon Watkins, "Welcome to Th. M.," *TLS,* No. 2,991 (June 26, 1959), p. 389. Also in Italian, #3,228.

1,620. Judrin, Roger. "Th. M.: Les Confessions du chevalier d'industrie Felix Krull," *Nouvelle Revue Française,* 4 (1956), 153-154.

1,621. Jung, Fritz. "Gedenken an Th. M.: Aus einer Ansprache bei der Feierstunde des Katharineums," *Katharineum,* Vol. 7, No. 21 (September 1955), pp. [1]-2.

1,622. Jung, Victor. "Nobelpreis 1929: Th. M.," in his *Die Nobelpreisträger,* pp. 254-256. Wien: Winkler, 1930.

1,623. Kaarz, Vera. "Überlieferungsbewusst und zukunftswillig.' Politische Bekenntnisse Th. M's," *Spektrum,* Vol. 11, No. 5 (1965), pp. 170-174.

1,624. Kästner, Erhart. "Th. M. und 'Die Vertauschten Köpfe,' " *Allgemeine Zeitung Mainz,* November 26, 1948.

1,625. ———. "Th. M's Schiller-Essay," *Schwäbische Landeszeitung,* Vol. 11, No. 205 (September 7, 1955), p. 8.

1,626. Kästner, Erich. "Betrachtungen eines Unpolitischen," in his *Gesammelte Schriften: Vermischte Beiträge,* Vol. 5, pp. 342-345. Köln: Kiepenheuer & Witsch, 1959. [Cf. I, item #1530 — Politics — "Innere Emigration"]

1,627. Kafka, Hans. "Ein Brief an Th. M.," *Die lit. Welt,* Vol. 2, No. 48 (November 26, 1926). [*Unordnung und frühes Leid*]

1,628. *Kafka, Vladimir. *Th. M. 1875-1955.* Prague, 1956. 23 pp. [Bibliography]

1,629. Kahler, Erich. "Th. M.," *Almanach: das 65. Jahr,* pp. 97-100. Frankfurt a. M.: S. Fischer, 1951. [Excerpt from I, item #813]

1,630. ———. "Die Erwählten," *Neue Rundschau,* 66 (1955), 298-311. [*Der Erwählte — Felix Krull*]

1,631. ———. "Gedenkrede auf Th. M.," *Neue Rundschau,* 67 (1956), 535-548.

1,632. ———. "The Devil Secularized: Th. M's Faust," in Hatfield, item #1,229, pp. 109-122. [Reprint of I, item #2753]

1,633. Kahn, Ludwig. "Th. M.," in his *Literatur und Glaubenskrise,* pp. 143-146 et al. Stuttgart: W. Kohlhammer [1964]

1,634. Kaiser, Joachim. "Nichts als dunkle Hoffnung," *Texte und Zeichen,* 3 (1957), 422-426.

1,635. ———. "Im Bergwerk des Zauberers," *Süddeutsche Zeitung,* February 21, 1961. [Zurich Archive]

1,636. ———. "Th. M's Masken und die Welt: Die Ausstellung eines Dichters, Kulturexport und Theodor W. Adorno," *Süddeutsche Zeitung,* March 27, 1962. [With excerpts from Theodor W. Adorno's introduction]

1,637. Kalenter, Ossip. "Wie der Dichter starb: Die letzten Tage," *Aufbau* (New York), Vol. 21, No. 33 (August 19, 1955), pp. 1-2.

1,638. ———. "Th. M., lyrisch-dramatischer Dichter; das Th. M.-Archiv in seinem neuen Zürcher Heim 'Zum oberen Schönenberg,'" *Mannheimer Morgen,* No. 47 (February 25, 1961).

1,639. Kamenetsky, Christa. "Th. M's Concept of the 'Bürger,' "
College Language Association Journal, 5 (1962), 184-194.

1,640. Kamnitzer, Heinz. "Buddenbrooks: Bemerkungen zu Zeit und
Roman," Aufbau (Berlin), 14 (May-June 1958),
[582]-596.

1,641. Kang, In Tsek. "Über Th. M's Werke," Sung Kyun Kwan —
Zeitschrift für Germanistik, 2 (1964), 100-106. [In
Korean]

1,642. Kanters, R. "Th. M.: Doktor Faustus," Age Nouveau, No. 51
(1950), pp. 104-106.

1,643. Kantorowicz, Alfred. "Glossarium: Th. M's 'Appell an die
Vernunft,' " Die lit. Welt, Vol. 6, No. 44 (October 31, 1930).
[Deutsche Ansprache]

1,644. ———. "Glossarium: Die 'Commission des Lettres et des
Arts': Th. M. über die geistige Zusammenarbeit," Die lit. Welt,
Vol. 7, No. 34 (August 21, 1931).

1,645. ———. "Th. M. spricht zu den Deutschen," The German-
American, December 1942.

1,646. ———. "Th. M. im Spiegel seiner Essays," Tägliche Rundschau,
June 6, 1949.

1,647. ———. "Th. M. in Spiegel seiner politischen Essays; eine
Kompilation," in his Deutsche Schicksale, pp. 39-94. Berlin:
A. Kantorowicz, 1949. [Reprint of I, item #1317]

1,648. ———. "Th. M's Weg zur Demokratie," Tägliche Rundschau,
June 6, 1950. [75th birthday]

1,649. ———. "Der Weg des Bürgers Th. M.," Forum, No. 5
(1950), p. 4.

1,650. ———. "Th. M., Demokrat und Humanist," Neues Deutschland, May 12, 1952.

1,651. ———. "Der Zola-Essay als Brennpunkt der weltanschaulichen
Beziehungen zwischen Heinrich und Th. M.," Wissenschaftliche
Zeitschrift der Humboldt Universität zu Berlin, 3 (1953),
127-138. Also in NDL, Vol. 3, No. 4 (April 1955), pp. 42-55.

1,652. ———. "Mahner seines Volkes: Zum 80. Geburtstag Th. M's,"
Tägliche Rundschau, June 5, 1955.

1,653.   ———. "Th. M.: Briefe an Heinrich Mann, 1900-1927,"
          Aufbau (Berlin), 11 (June 1955), 525-560.

1,654.   ———. "Th. M's Botschaft an Deutschland: Der Briefwechsel
          Walter von Molo — Th. M.," *NDL*, Vol. 3, No. 10 (October
          1955), pp. 34-53. [Contains letters of Th. M. and W. von Molo
          and commentary by Kantorowicz]

1,655. *———*Heinrich und Th. M.: Die persönlichen, literarischen
          und weltanschaulichen Beziehungen der Brüder.* Berlin: Aufbau,
          1956. 135 pp.
          Reviews: Leibrich, #1891-1893 — Ude, #3,323.

1,656.   ———. "Th. und Heinrich Mann," *Geist und Zeit,* Vol. 1,
          No. 3 (1956), pp. 27-36.

1,657.   ———. "Th. M.," in his *Deutsches Tagebuch: I. und II. Teil.*
          [München] Kindler [1959-61]

1,658.   ———. "Th. M's Brief an Deutschland," *Das Schönste,*
          Vol. 6, No. 8 (August 1960), pp. 62-65. [Concerns Th. M's
          letter to W. von Molo: 'Warum ich nicht nach Deutschland
          zurückgehe']

1,659.   ———. "Th. M. und die Deutschen," *Das Schönste,* Vol. 8,
          No. 7 (July 1962), pp. 52-54. [Based on K. Sontheimer,
          item #3,097]

1,660.   ———. " 'Nur wer Gnade übt, wird Gnade finden.' Ein
          unbekannter Brief Th. M's an Walter Ulbricht," [July 1951]
          Welt, No. 137 (June 15, 1963). Also in French as "Lettre
          à Walter Ulbricht," *Preuves,* No. 151 (1963), pp. 31-33.

1,661.   ———. "Buchenwald commence . . .," *Preuves,* No. 151
          (1963), pp. 30-31. [Concerns Th. M's visits to East Germany
          in August 1949 and May 1955]

1,662.   ———. "Beim Wiedersehen mit Deutschland," *Stuttgarter
          Zeitung,* No. 129 (June 5, 1965), p. 14. [90th birthday]

1,663.   ———. "Th. M.: Der unbequeme Dichter. Zu seinem 10.
          Todestag," *Spandauer Volksblatt,* Vol. 20, No. 5, 835 (August
          12, 1965), p. 7. [Politics]

1,664.   Karger-Decker, Bernt. "Th. M.," *Berliner Modenblatt,* Vol. 16,
          No. 8 (August 1960), pp. 4-5, 22. [Biog.]

1,665. Karsch, Walther. "Literaturgeschichte als Roman," *Tagespost,* January 26, 1947. [*Lotte in Weimar*]

1,666. ————. "Die Musik ist immer verdächtig gewesen," *Tagesspiegel,* May 8, 1949. [*Doktor Faustus*]

1,667. ————. "Ein Dichter, zwei Kündigungen und keine Stellungnahme," *Tagesspiegel,* June 5, 1958. [Controversy Manfred Hausmann — Ernst Schnabel — Deutsche Akademie Darmstadt]

1,668. Karsh, Yousuf. "Th. M.," in his *Portraits of Greatness,* p. 122. [London, New York: T. Nelson, 1960] Text and photo.

1,669. Karst, Roman. "Gruss an Th. M.," *Sinn und Form,* 7 (1955), 354-357. [80th birthday]

1,670. ————. "Th. M. in Warschau," *Monatsschrift Polen,* No. 3 (1964), pp. 17, 20. [Also in English, French, German, Polish, and Spanish editions]

1,671. Kasack, Hermann. "Gedenkwort für Th. M.," in his *Mosaiksteine: Beiträge zu Literatur und Kunst,* pp. [335]-337. [Frankfurt a. M.] Suhrkamp, 1956. Also in Deutsche Akademie für Sprache und Dichtung, Darmstadt. *Jahrbuch* 1955, pp. 127-128. [Heidelberg] L. Schneider, 1956.

1,672. Kasamatsu, Kazuo. "Zu Th. M's 'Doktor Faustus' — im Zusammenhang mit Georg Lukács, 'Die Tragödie der modernen Kunst,' " *Wissenschaftliche Berichte der Präfektur-Universität Osaka,* 6 (1958), 91-100. [In Japanese]

1,673. ————. "Zu Th. M's 'Doktor Faustus' — das Pathologische und das Biologische," *Wissenschaftliche Berichte der Präfektur-Universität Osaka,* 7 (1959), 147-158. [In Japanese]

1,674. Kashiwabara, Hyozo. "Über Th. M's 'Zauberberg,' " *Keisei,* No. 19 (1962), pp. 2-17.

1,675. Kassner, Rudolf. "Zu Th. M's 'Zauberberg,' " in his *Geistige Welten,* pp. 85-90. [Frankfurt a. M.] Ullstein [1958] [Cf. I, item #2284] Also in H. Saueressig, item #2,844, pp. 63-67.

1,676. Katayama, Ryöten. "Th. M. und Gottfried Benn: Die frühen Werke der Dichter," *Quelle,* No. 12 (1963), pp. 2-24. [In Japanese]

Katzenellenbogen, Konrad, *see* Kellen

1,677. Katzin, Winifred. "Ein literarisches Kuriosum," *Die Horen,* 5 (December 1928), 268-273. [Criticism of "Romane der Welt," edited by Th. M. and George H. Scheffauer — with a letter from Th. M. of October 27, 1928, on pp. 273-275]

1,678. Kaufmann, Alfred. "Gedanken zu Th. M's Roman 'Doktor Faustus' aus medizinischer Perspektive," in G. Wenzel, item #3,453, pp. 149-164.

1,679. Kaufmann, Edward. "Th. M's Sunday Child," *Chicago Review,* 10 (Spring 1956), 117-123. [*Felix Krull*]

1,680. Kaufmann, Fritz. "Universale Repräsentation bei Th. M.," in J. Alan Pfeffer, *ed., Essays on German Language and Literature in Honor of Theodore B. Hewett, University of Buffalo Studies,* 20 (May 1952), 9-20. Also in his *Das Reich des Schönen,* pp. [312]-322. Stuttgart: Kohlhammer [1960]

1,681. ———. "Imitatio Goethe: Th. M. and his French Confreres," *Monatshefte,* 48 (October 1956), 245-259. [Goethe — Barrès — Gide]

1,682. ———. "Th. M's Weg durch die Ewigkeit in die Zeit," *Neue Rundschau,* 67 (Autumn 1956), 564-581.

1,683. *———. *Th. M.: The World as Will and Representation.* Boston: Beacon Press [1957] 322 pp.
Reviews: Anon., #115 — Hill, #1,384 — Lesser, #1,937 — Seidlin, #3,013 — Weigand, #3,430.

1,684. ———. "Dr. Fausti Weheklag," in his *Das Reich des Schönen,* item #1,680, pp. [362]-385. [Cf. I, item #2,755]

1,685. Kawahigashi, Shoji. "Über Ironie bei Th. M.," *Bulletin, University of Naniwa,* No. 1 (1953), pp. 161-175. [In Japanese]

1,686. Kaye, Julian Bertram. "Conrad's 'Under Western Eyes' and Mann's 'Doktor Faustus,' " *CL,* 9 (Winter 1957), [60]-65.

1,687. Kayser, Rudolf. "Th. M.," *Universal Jewish Encyclopedia,* pp. 326-327. New York, 1942.

1,688. ———. "Das Lebenswerk des Dichters," *Aufbau* (New York), Vol. 21, No. 22 (June 3, 1955), pp. 3-4. [80th birthday]

1,689. ————. "Aus Th. M's amerikanischen Jahren: Zum
         Geburtstag des Dichters," *Tat,* Vol. 26, No. 149 (June 3,
         1961), p. 18.
1,690. Kayser, Wolfgang. "Th. M.," in his *Das Groteske,* pp. 169-173.
         [Oldenburg] Stalling, 1957. Also in English translation by
         Ulrich Weisstein in *The Grotesque in Art and Literature,*
         pp. 157-161. Bloomington: Indiana University Press [1963]
         [*Doktor Faustus*]
1,691. Kazin, Alfred. "The German and the Novelist," *Reporter,*
         Vol. 18, No. 1 (January 8, 1959), pp. 38-40. [Review of
         E. Heller, item #1,278] Under the title "Th. M.: or the
         German as Novelist," in his *Contemporaries,* pp. 278-283.
         Boston: Little, Brown [1962]
1,692. Keim, H. W. "Neue Essaybücher," *Literatur,* 26 (1923-24),
         468-471. [*Goethe und Tolstoi*]
1,693. Kejzlarová, Inge. "Th. M's Erkenntnis und Warnung: Zu
         seiner Novelle 'Mario und der Zauberer,' " *Philologica
         Pragensis,* 44 (1962), 193-198. [In Czech]
1,694. Kellen, Konrad. "Als Sekretar bei Th. M.," *NDH,* No. 81
         (May-June 1961), pp. 37-46. Also in *Lübeckische Blätter,*
         Vol. 122, No. 1 (January 6, 1962), pp. 1-5. Excerpted in
         Tagesspiegel, June 17, 1961. Also in English, "Reminiscences
         of Th. M.," *Yale Review,* 54 (March 1965), [383]-391.
1,695. Keller, Ernst. "Th. M. and Democracy," *AUMLA,* 8th Congress
         (1963), p. 39.
1,696* ————. *Der unpolitische Deutsche: Eine Studie zu den 'Betrach-
         tungen eines Unpolitischen' von Th. M.* Bern: Francke [1965]
         191 pp. Reviews: Baltzer, #174.
1,697. Kellerson, Germaine. "A Nidden chez Th. M.," *L'Eveil des
         Peuples,* Vol. 1, No. 1 (November 6, 1932), pp. 1, 3. [Biog.]
1,698. Kelsch, Wolfgang. "Settembrini und Naphta," *Bruderschaft,* 2
         (April 15, 1960), 116-118.
1,699. Kerényi, Karl. "Geistiger Weg Europas," *NZZ,* Vol. 175,
         No. 2,976 (54), November 28, 1954, Bl. 4. Expanded version
         in his *Geistiger Weg Europas,* pp. 9-23. Zurich: Rhein-Verlag
         [1955]

1,700. ———. "Der Erzschelm und der Himmelsstürmer: Ein Kapitel aus der Heroenmythologie der Griechen," *Neue Rundschau,* 66 (June 1955), 312-323.

1,700a. ———. "Marginalien zu den 'Vertauschten Köpfen,' " *NZZ,* Vol. 176, Sonntagsausgabe No. 1,498 (29), June 5, 1955, Bl. 4.

1,700b. ———. "Die goldene Parodie: Randbemerkungen zu den 'Vertauschten Köpfen,' " *Neue Rundschau,* 67 (1956), 549-556.

1,700c.* ———. *Th. M. — Karl Kerényi: Gespräch in Briefen.* Zurich: Rhein-Verlag [1960] Contents: "Vorbetrachtungen," pp. 9-33. Teil I: *Romandichtung und Mythologie* [Cf. I, #1,247] — Teil II: *Humanismus — schweres Glück: 1945-1955.* — Both parts translated into Italian by Ervino Pocar: *Romanzo e Mitologia. Felicità difficile.* Milano: Il Saggiatore [1960]
Excerpt in Rychner, #2,789.
Reviews: Bertaux, #309 — Blöcker, #358, 363 — Emig, #769 — Grimm, #1,081 — Gronicka, #1,088 — Hellmann, #1,294 — Henschel, #1,326 — Horst, #1,502 — Levander, #1,954 — Mühlberger, #2,308 — Nitsche, #2,423 — Reuter, #2,690 — Robin, #2,740 — Rychner, #2,805 — Sörensen, #3,084 — E. E. Stein, #3,120 — Ter-Nedden, #3,254 — Weber, #3,418 — Wolffheim, #3,534.

1,700d. ———. "Th. M. — Naphta — Lukács György," *Uj Láthéhatár,* Vol. 5, No. 1 (1962), pp. 30-38. German version, "Th. M. und der Marxist," *NZZ,* Vol. 184, Sonntagsausgabe No. 2361 (60), June 9, 1963, Bl. 5. Expanded version, entitled "Zauberbergfiguren: Ein biographischer Versuch," in his *Tessiner Schreibtisch,* pp. 125-141. Stuttgart: Steingrüben [1963] [*See also* H. Neumeister, #2,398]

1,701. ———. "Th. M. und der Teufel in Palestrina," *NZZ,* Vol. 182, Sonntagsausgabe No. 3 (1), January 1, 1961, Bl. 3. Expanded version in *Neue Rundschau,* 73 (1962), 328-346. Also in his *Tessiner Schreibtisch,* pp. 86-109. Stuttgart: Steingrüben [1963]. *See* comments by Hellmann, #1,311.

1,702. ————. "Th. M. zwischen Norden und Süden: Rede gehalten an der Gedenkfeier im Schauspielhaus Zürich," *NZZ,* Vol. 186, Fernausgabe No. 180 (July 3, 1965), Bl. 19. ["Gladius Dei" — *Fiorenza*]

1,703. ————. "Th. M., der Alchemist," *Tat,* Vol. 30, No. 190 (August 13, 1965), p. 29. [Biog.]

1,704. Kern, Alfred. "Hommage à Th. M.," *Cahiers des Saisons,* No. 2 (October 1955), pp. 81-83. [80th birthday]

1,705. Kern, Irmgard. " '. . . was zu entlarven.' Eine Identifikation der Eltern des Adrian Leverkühn," *Frankfurter Allgemeine Zeitung,* No. 95 (April 24, 1959), p. 11.

1,706. Kerpel, Eugen. "Weltchor der Selbstkritik," *Pester Lloyd,* November 1, 1930, Morgenblatt, pp. 4-6. [*Deutsche Ansprache*]

1,707. Kersten, Kurt. "Der Ewigkeit entgegen," *Aufbau* (New York), Vol. 21, No. 33 (August 19, 1955), p. 1. [Obit.]

1,708. Kessler, Harry Graf. "Th. M.," in his *Tagebücher 1918-1937,* pp. 763-764 et al. Wiesbaden: Insel, 1961.

1,709. Kesten, Hermann. "Der Hochstapler Felix Krull," *Neue Zeitung,* No. 246 (October 18/19, 1952), pp. 17-18.

1,710. ————. "Für Th. M.," *Der Bund; der kleine Bund,* Vol. 106, No. 246 (June 3, 1955), p. 7. [80th birthday]

1,711. ————. "Heinrich und Th. M.," *Monat,* 11 (February 1959), [59]-69. Also in his *Der Geist der Unruhe,* pp. 310-329. Köln: Kiepenheuer & Witsch [1959] [*See* reply by W. Liersch, item #1,966]

1,712. ————. "Th. M.: Der gedichtete Goethe," in his *Lauter Literaten,* pp. 295-307. München: Desch [1963] [*Lotte in Weimar*]

1,713. ————. "Briefe von Th. M.," in Hermann Kesten, *ed., Deutsche Literatur im Exil,* pp. 221-222 et al. München: Desch [1964]

1,714. Keyssner, G. "Belletristisches," *Münchner Neueste Nachrichten,* Vol. 56, No. 360 (October 5, 1903). [*Buddenbrooks* — *Tristan*]

1,715. Kiaulehn, Walther. "Die Heimkehr des Proteus," *Münchner Merkur,* August 16, 1955. [Obit.]

1,716. Kiewert, Walter. "Th. M's Radiobotschaften," *Berliner Hefte,* No. 12 (1947), pp. 941-944. [*Deutsche Hörer*]

1,717. Kihlmann, Erik. "Mynheer Peeperkorn och Baron Lackau," ın his *Nordiska Profiler,* pp. [432]-438. Helsingfors: Söderström [1935] [Concerns *The Magic Mountain* and Baron Samuel Cornelius Lackau]

1,718. Kim, Dschae-Min. "Ironie, Tod und Krankheit bei Th. M.," *Zeitschrift für Germanistik* (Seoul, Korea), No. 3 (1961), pp. 119-133. [In Korean]

1,719. Kirchberger, Lida. "Th. M's 'Tristan,' " *GR,* 36 (December 1961), [282]-297. [Comparison with E. T. A. Hoffmann's *Rat Krespel*]

1,720. ———. Review of Karl S. Weimar, item #3,435, *Monatshefte,* 53 (December 1961), 363-364.

1,721. †Kiremidjian, Garabed D. A Study of Parody: James Joyce's *Ulysses* and Th. M's *Doktor Faustus.* Ph. D. diss., Yale University, 1964.

1,722. Kirn, Richard. "Die Lust zu fabulieren," *Frankfurter Neue Presse,* Vol. 9, No. 247 (October 23, 1954), p. 27. [*Felix Krull*]

1,723. Kirsch, Edgar. "Serenus Zeitblom: Beitrag zur Analyse des 'Doktor Faustus,' " *Wissenschaftliche Zeitschrift der Universität Halle,* 7 (September 1958), [1103]-1107. Under the title "Die Verungleichung des Gleichen; ein Beitrag zur Analyse des Identitätsproblems im 'Doktor Faustus,' " in G. Wenzel, item #3,461, pp. 204-212.

1,724. Klapheck, Anna. "Th. M. in zweitausend Bänden: Die Sammlung eines Düsseldorfer Buchhändlers," *Rheinische Post,* No. 186 (August 12, 1965). [Collection of Hans-Otto Mayer]

1,725. Klatt-Krieser, Charlotte. "Alte Legende liefert den Stoff," *Neue Ruhr-Zeitung,* June 3, 1951. [*Der Erwählte*]

1,726. Klausing, Helmut. "Ein deutscher Weltbürger: Zum 80. Geburtstag Th. M's," *Wege zueinander,* June 1955, p. 4.

1,727. Klein, Johannes. "Th. M.," in his *Geschichte der deutschen Novelle von Goethe bis zur Gegenwart,* pp. 416-427. Wiesbaden: Steiner, ³1956.

1,728. ———. "Th. M.," *Hessische Blätter für Volksbildung,* 9 (1959), 95-110.

1,729. Kleine, Don W. "Felix Krull as Fairy Tale Hero," *Accent,* 19 (Summer 1959), 131-141.

1,730. Klemm, Reinhold. "Der Dichter und die Zeitwende: In memoriam Th. M.," *Wort in der Zeit,* 1 (August 1955), 62-63. [Obit.]

1,731. Klemperer, Felix. "Th. M's 'Zauberberg' im ärztlichen Urteil," *New Yorker Volkszeitung,* August 1, 1926, Sonntagsblatt, pp. 7-8. [Cf. I, item #2,288]

1,732. Klemperer, Klemens von. "Th. M.," in his *Germany's New Conservatism,* pp. 51-55. Princeton: Princeton University Press, 1957. [*Betrachtungen eines Unpolitischen*]

1,733. Klessmann, Eckart. "Briefe Th. M's: Um die 'Betrachtungen eines Unpolitischen,' " *Christ und Welt,* Vol. 13, No. 10 (March 3, 1960), p. 19. [Cf. Amann, item #3,426]

1,734. Klöckner, Albert. "Th. M's 'Deutsche Ansprache,' " *Ostdeutsche Blätter,* 4 (1930), 105-110, 115-116. [*Appell an die Vernunft*]

1,735. Klose, G. Johanna. "Die Entstehung des Doktor Faustus," *Rhein-Echo,* April 23, 1949.

1,736. Kluft, Ernst. "Th. M. und die russische Kultur," *Neue Zeit,* November 25, 1951.

1,737. ———. "Das jüngste Werk von Th. M.: *Die Betrogene,*" *Neue Zeit,* February 28, 1954.

1,738. Klugkist, Kurt. "Der Hochstapler und die Schauspielkunst," *Lübecker Nachrichten,* November 28, 1954. [*Felix Krull*]

1,739. ———. "Das Menschliche bei Th. M.," *Lübecker Nachrichten,* No. 129 (June 5, 1955), p. 25. [80th birthday]

1,740. ———. "Th. M's literarisches Werk," *Lübecker Nachrichten,* August 14, 1955. [Obit.]

1,741. ———. "Th. M. in Lübeck," *Flensburger Tageblatt,* September 19, 1959. [Biog.]

1,742. Knaus, Albrecht. "Die vertauschbaren Köpfe: Zu Th. M's
        'Doktor Faustus,' " *Thema*, No. 5 (1949), pp. 44-46.

1,743. ———. "Th. M's letzte Tage," in P.E.N., *Tribute Meeting*,
        #2,501.

1,744. ———. "Nachwort" in Th. M., *Das Eisenbahnunglück*,
        pp. 63-69. München: Piper, 1955.

1,745. Knipowitsch, J. "Das historische Gefühl: Th. M. in der
        sowjetischen Kritik," *Kunst und Literatur*, 10 (July 1962),
        703-713.

1,746. Knoertzer, C. "Th. M., peint par lui-même," *L'Alsace Française*,
        11 (1931), 404-407. [*Lebensabriss*]

1,747. Knopf, Alfred A. "Report on Th. M's 80th birthday," *Borzoi
        Books*, No. 2 (1955), pp. 6-8.

1,748. ———. "Farewell," *Aufbau* (New York), Vol. 21, No. 33
        (August 19, 1955), p. 2. [Obit.]

1,749. Koch, Thilo. "Vollkommenheit," *Texte und Zeichen*, 1 (1955),
        133-135. [*Felix Krull*]

1,750. ———. "Grosser Chronist der Dekadenz," *Zeit*, November
        29, 1956. [Review of #2,058]

1,751. ———. "Die List der Vernunft," in his *Berliner Luftballon*,
        pp. 37-40. München: Langen [1958] [Politics]

1,752. Koeppen, Wolfgang. "Glückwunsch an Th. M.," *Sonntag*,
        Vol. 10, No. 23 (June 5, 1955), p. 7. Also in item #2,833.

1,753. Köttelwesch, Clemens. "Th. M.," in H. W. Eppelsheimer and
        his *Bibliographie der deutschen Literaturwissenschaft*, Vol. 2,
        1954-1956, pp. 262-270. Frankfurt a. M.: Klostermann
        [1958]

1,754. ———. "Th. M.," in H. W. Eppelsheimer and his *Biblio-
        graphie der deutschen Literaturwissenschaft*, Vol. 3, 1957-
        1958, pp. 173-176. Frankfurt a. M.: Klostermann [1960]

1,755. ———. "Th. M.," in H. W. Eppelsheimer and his *Biblio-
        graphie der deutschen Literaturwissenschaft*, Vol. 4, 1959-
        1960, pp. 216-221. Frankfurt a. M.: Klostermann [1961]

1,756. ———. "Th. M.," in H. W. Eppelsheimer and his *Biblio-
        graphie der deutschen Literaturwissenschaft*, Vol. 5, 1961-1962,
        pp. 243-249. Frankfurt a. M.: Klostermann [1963]

1,757. Kogon, Eugen. "Eugen Kogon fordert Th. M., in Weimar 'öffentlich' zu schweigen," *Neue Zeitung,* No. 103 (July 30, 1949), pp. 1-2. [Open letter to Th. M., dated July 28, 1949. Cf. I, item #1467]

1,758. Kohler, Marlyse. "Über die Eigenart von Th. M's 'Erwähltem,' " *Revue des Langues Vivantes — Levende Talen,* 26 (1960), 437-443.

1,759. Kohlschmidt, Werner. "Musikalität, Reformation und Deutschtum; eine kritische Studie zu Th. M's 'Doktor Faustus,' " in his *Die entzweite Welt,* pp. 98-112. Gladbeck: Freizeiten-Verlag [1953] [Cf. I, item #2,763]

1,760. Kohn, Hans. "The Politics of Th. M.," *New Leader,* 39 (February 13, 1956), 28-29.

1,761. ———. "Th. M.," in his *The Mind of Germany,* pp. 252-258 et al. London, New York: Macmillan, 1961. Also in German, translated by Wilhelm and Modeste Pferdekamp, in his *Wege und Irrwege,* pp. 267-273 et al. Düsseldorf: Droste [1962] [*Betrachtungen eines Unpolitischen — Der Zauberberg*]

1,762. Kohut, Heinz. " 'Death in Venice' by Th. M.: A Story about the Disintegration of Artistic Sublimation," *Psychoanalytic Quarterly,* 26 (1957), 206-228. Also in Hendrik M. Ruitenbeek, *ed., Psychoanalysis and Literature,* pp. 282-302. New York: E. P. Dutton, 1964.

1,763. ———. Review of F. D. Hirschbach, #1,429, *Psychoanalytic Quarterly,* 26 (1957), 273-275.

1,764. Kolb, Annette. "Th. M.," in her *Glückliche Reise,* pp. 138-146. Stockholm: Bermann-Fischer, 1940.

1,765. ———. "Th. M.," in her *1907-1964: Zeitbilder,* pp. 148-155. [Frankfurt a. M.] S. Fischer [1964]

1,765a. Komor, Ilona. "Ein unveröffentlichter Brief Th. M's an József Turóczi-Trostler," *Acta litteraria,* 6 (1964), 165-167. [Letter of February 21, 1955]

1,766. Konelev, A. "La Jeunesse de Th. M.," in his *Le coeur est toujours à gauche,* 120-146. Moscow, 1960. [In Russian]

1,767. Konrad, Gustav. "Bemühungen um Th. M.," *Welt und Wort,*
17 (April 1962), 106-107. [Review of E. Heller, #1,278,
and P. Altenberg, #34]

1,768. Koopmann, Helmut. "Die Kategorie des Hermetischen in Th.
M's Roman 'Der Zauberberg,' " *ZDP,* 80 (1961), 404-422.

1,769.* ———. *Die Entwicklung des 'intellektualen' Romans bei
Th. M.* Bonn: H. Bouvier, 1962. 174 pp. [Ph. D. diss., Bonn,
1960] [Concerns *Buddenbrooks — Königliche Hoheit — Der
Zauberberg*]
Reviews: Anon, #119 — Bänsch, #166 — Hellmann, #1,302
— Hermsdorf, #3,885 — Hilscher, #1,415 — Reiss, #2,681
— Schiffer, #2,890.

1,770. ———. Review of P. Altenberg, #34, *ZDP,* 81 (1962),
380-383.

1,771. ———. "Th. M.," in Benno von Wiese, *ed., Deutsche Dichter
der Moderne,* pp. 68-91. Berlin: E. Schmidt, 1965.

1,772. Korn, Karl. "Rechtfertigung durch die Kunst: Zum Tode
Th. M's," *Frankfurter Allgemeine Zeitung,* No. 187 (August
15, 1955), p. 8. [Obit.]

1,773. ———. "Th. M.: 1875-1955," in his *Die Grossen Deutschen,*
Vol. 4, pp. 548-563. Berlin: Propyläen, 1957.

1,774. Korrodi, Eduard. "Braun, nicht blau!" *NZZ,* Vol. 146, No.
1017 (June 28, 1925), Bl. 7. [Concerns R. Geck's letter to
Th. M., about *Unordnung und frühes Leid*]

1,775. ———. "Th. M. über Theodor Storm," *NZZ,* Vol. 151,
Morgenausgabe No. 2,338 (December 2, 1930), Bl. 2.

1,776. ———. "Joseph in Ägypten," *NZZ,* Vol. 157, No. 1815
(October 22, 1936), Bl. 1.

1,777. ———. "Lotte in Weimar. Th. M's neuer Roman. II.," *NZZ,*
Vol. 160, No. 2068 December 6, 1939), Bl. 6, pp. 1-2. [Adds
to I, item #2,602]

1,778. ———. "Eine Studie über Th. M.," *NZZ,* January 23, 1947.
Review of F. Lion, I, item #263. *See also* #1,979.]

1,779. ———. " 'Neue Studien' von Th. M.," *NZZ,* Vol. 169,
No. 1,287 (June 16, 1948), Bl. 8.

1,780. Kortüm, Albrecht. "Buddenbrooks — Verfall einer Familie," *Nation* (Berlin), 6 (July 1956), 518-525.

1,781. Kracauer, Siegfried. "Th. M. geleitet: Zu der Serie 'Romane der Welt,'" *Frankfurter Zeitung*, May 22, 1927, Literaturblatt.

1,782. Krämer-Bodoni, Rudolf. "Dr. Faustus auf ausgefahrenen Wegen," *Sonntagsblatt*, June 12, 1949.

1,783. Kraft, Irma. "Th. M. Longs for Olden Days," *American Hebrew*, September 19, 1930, pp. 464, 490, 498.

1,784. Krammer, Jenö. Review of H. Bürgin, item #502, *Acta Litteraria*, 4 (1961), 379-383.

1,785. Krammer, Marie. "Manns biblisches Epos," *Telegraf*, December 15, 1950. [*Joseph und seine Brüder*]

1,786. Kranz, Gilbert. "Th. M.," *Kirche in der Welt*, 8 (1955), 103-106.

1,787. Kratz, Henry. "A Methodological Critique of W. R. Maurer's 'Names from *The Magic Mountain*,'" *Names*, Vol. 11, No. 1 (March 1963), pp. 20-25. [Concerns #2,163]

1,788. Kraul, Fritz. "Die 'Buddenbrooks' als Gesellschaftsroman," *Deutschunterricht*, (Stuttgart), 11 (1959), [88]-103.

1,789. Kraus, Fritz. "Th. M., der Mythenerzähler," *Badische Zeitung*, February 23, 1950.

1,790. ———. "Th. M.: Dichter und Deuter," *Deutsche Rundschau*, 81 (June 1955), 592-598. [80th birthday]

1,791. Kraus, Karl. "Ich bin oft in Verlegenheit um ein Adjektiv," *Fackel*, Vol. 15, No. 372/373 (1913/14), p. 45. [Language-Style]

1,792. Kraus, René. "Th. M. ganz privat; ernsthaftes Feriengespräch mit dem Dichter," *Neue Freie Presse*, No. 23 679 (August 15, 1930), p. 14. [Interview in Nidden]

1,793. †Kreft, Jürgen. Hamlet (Georg Britting) — Don Juan (Hermann Broch) — Faustus (Th. M.) [Vaterflucht — Mutterbindung — Disintegration]. Interpretationen dreier moderner Romane; zugleich Versuch eines Beitrags zum Problem des modernen Romans. Ph. D. diss., University of Bonn, 1955.

1,794. Krekeler, Heinz L. "Kämpfer für die Freiheit," *Aufbau* (New York), Vol. 21, No. 33 (August 19, 1955), p. 1. [Obit.]

1,795. Krell, Max. "Der Unpolitische," in Horst Stobbe, *ed.*, *Almanach der Bücherstube*, pp. 42-45. München, 1918. [*Betrachtungen eines Unpolitischen*]

1,796. ————. "Über neue erzählende Prosa," *Neue Rundschau*, 31 (1920), 1190-1199. [*Herr und Hund*]

1,797. ————. "Er gewann das Ohr der Völker," *Vorwärts*, June 3, 1955. [80th birthday]

1,798. ————. "Th. M.," in his *Das alles gab es einmal*, pp. 48-54 et al. Frankfurt a. M.: Scheffler [1961]

1,799. Kreuzer, Helmut. "Th. M. und Gabriele Reuter: Zu einer Entlehnung für den 'Dr. Faustus,' " *NDH*, Vol. 10, No. 96 (November-December 1963), pp. 108-119.

1,800. Krey, Johannes. "Die gesellschaftliche Bedeutung der Musik im Werk von Th. M.," *Wissenschaftliche Zeitschrift der Friedrich Schiller-Universität Jena*, 3 (1954), [301]-332.

1,801. Kristensen, Tom. "Th. M. fylder tres," *Politiken*, June 6, 1935, pp. 13-14. [60th birthday]

1,802. ————. "Th. M's Josefslegende," *Politiken*, May 28, 1949. Reprinted in his *Til dags dato*, pp. 213-215. Copenhagen; Gyldendal, 1953. Also in item #2,431, pp. 127-136.

1,803. ————. "Humoristen Th. M.," *Politiken*, June 6, 1955, pp. 14-15. [80th birthday]

1,804. ————. "Ved Th. M's død," *Politiken*, August 14, 1955, p. 40. [Obit.]

1,805. *Kroepfle, Hans Herbert. *Die Struktur des Erzählschlusses bei Th. M.* Münster i. W.: Kramer, 1962. 169 pp. [Ph. D. diss., University of Munster, 1961]

1,806. Krüger, Heinz. "Bürgertum und Künstlertum — zur Problematik Th. M's," in his *Zwischen Dekadenz und Erneuerung*, pp. 115-122. Frankfurt a. M.: J. Knecht [1953]

1,807. ————. "Die Fragwürdigkeit des Künstlers," in item #1,806, pp. 129-134.

1,808. ————. "Vorkämpfer des sozialen Humanismus; ein Wort zum 80. Geburtstag Th. M's," *Gesamtdeutsche Rundschau,*

Vol. 3, No. 26/27 (June 24, 1955), p. 6. [80th birthday]

1,809. Krueger, Joachim. "Dichter-Bibliographien," *Marginalien*, No. 8 (1960), pp. 57-59. [Review of H. Bürgin, item #502, and K. W. Jonas, item #1,605]

1,810. Kudszus, Hans. "Zwischen Stuttgart und Weimar: Kritisches Nachwort zur Schillerrede Th. M's," *Das ganze Deutschland*, Vol. 7, No. 21 (1955), p. 5.

1,811. Kühn, Karl Herbert. "Eine Stunde bei Th. M.," *Königsberger Tageblatt*, No. 220 (August 10, 1930), p. 13. [Interview in Nidden]

1,812. Küntzel, Hans. "Th. M.: årets Nobelpristagare i litteratur," *Bibliotekshladet*, 14 (December 1929), 285-290.

1,813. Küsel, Herbert. "'Königliche Hoheit': Besuch im Filmtheater von Göttingen," *Gegenwart*, 8 (1953), 830, 839-841.

1,814. ———. "Aussenaufnahmen: Auf Erkundungsfahrt bei den Filmleuten in Göttingen," *Gegenwart*, Vol. 9, No. 199 (January 16, 1954), pp. 46-49. [*Königliche Hoheit*]

1,815. Kufner, Herbert L. "Sprachbemerkungen zu Th. M's 'Zauberberg,'" *Muttersprache*, 68 (December 1958), 353-362.

1,816. Kuhn, Friedrich. "Die Forderung des Tages," *Sonntags-Zeitung*, April 6, 1930.

1,817. Kuhn, Hugo. "Der gute Sünder — der Erwählte," in Hartmann von Aue, *Gregorius*, pp. 255-271. [Ebenhausen] Langenwiesche-Brandt, 1959. Also in Karl Rüdiger, *ed.*, *Hüter der Sprache*, pp. 63-73. München: Bayer. Schulbuch-Verlag, 1959.

1,818. Kunert, Günter. "Verzauberung," *Sinn und Form: Sonderheft Th. M.*, 1965, pp. 377-378.

1,819. Kunz, Josef. "Genialität und Bildung: Die Motivkreise im Werke Th. M's," *Christ und Welt*, Vol. 8, No. 22 (June 2, 1955), p. 12. [80th birthday]

1,820. ———. "Th. M.," *Eckart*, 25 (October-December 1955), 54-57. [Obit.]

1,821. ———. "Th. M.," in H. Friedmann [and] Otto Mann, *eds.*, *Deutsche Literatur im 20. Jahrhundert*, Vol. 2, pp. 101-122. Heidelberg: Rothe [⁴1961] [Cf. I, item #437]

1,822. Kunz, Ludwig. "Th. M.," *Kroniek van kunst en kultuur,*
        15 (1955), 114-116.

1,823. Kurella, Alfred. "Th. M. und die Gegenwart," *Das Wort,*
        Vol. 2, No. 6 (June 1937), pp. 88-92. Also in his *Zwischen-*
        durch. Verstreute Essays, 1934-1940, pp. 126-132. Berlin:
        Aufbau, 1961. [*Freud und die Zukunft*]

1,824. Kurzweil, Baruch. "Th. M.," in his *Masseket ha-Roman,*
        pp. 316-355. Tel Aviv: Schocken, 1953. [*Joseph und seine*
        Brüder — Doktor Faustus — Der Erwählte]

1,825. Kutscher, Arthur. "Th. M. als Dramatiker," *Hannoversches*
        Unterhaltungsblatt, No. 6 (January 19, 1908). [*Fiorenza*]

1,826. *Kyyrö, Kauko. *Th. M.* Turku: Turun Yliopiston Kunstantama,
        1956. 70 pp. [In Finnish]

1,827. Laaths, Erwin. "Die Mythologie des Genius," *Rheinische Post,*
        September 13, 1947. [*Lotte in Weimar*]

1,828. ———. "Der Faustusroman," *Rheinische Post,* December 18,
        1948.

1,829. ———. "Zwiespältige Legende: Th. M's Roman 'Der
        Erwählte,' " *Rheinische Post,* July 4, 1951.

1,830. ———. "Schweres Geschütz gegen Th. M.," *Mittag,*
        November 15, 1953. [Concerns item #2,349, W. Muschg's
        attack on Th. M. in his *Tragische Literaturgeschichte*]

1,831. ———. "Th. M.: Ein feierliches Wort zu seinem 80.
        Geburtstag," *Mittag,* June 4-5, 1955.

1,832. Laborde, Jean. "Toute sa vie Th. M. est resté l'Elu de
        l'Allemagne et le témoin de l'Europe," *Jeune Europe,* No. 54
        (September 1, 1955), p. 11. [Obit. — Review of item #1,493]

1,833. Lämmert, Eberhard. "Th. M. und Theodor Fontane," in his
        Bauformen des Erzählens, pp. 226-233. Stuttgart: Metzler,
        1955.

1,834. ———. "Th. M.: Moralist im Bannkreis der Sprache,"
        Parlament, No. 23 (June 8, 1955), p. 8 [80th birthday]

1,835. ———. "Th. M.: 'Buddenbrooks,' " in B. von Wiese, *ed.,*
        Der deutsche Roman vom Barock bis zur Gegenwart, Vol. 2,
        pp. [190]-233. Düsseldorf: Bagel [1963]

1,836. Lamm, Hans. "Ein gütiges Herz: Th. M's 'Briefe,' "

Allgemeine Wochenzeitung der Juden, Vol. 18, No. 36 (December 6, 1963), p. 23. [Review of *Briefe II,* item #2,066]

1,837. Lamprecht, Helmut. "Der Erzähler und das Lyrische, angedeutet am Beispiel Th. M's," *NDH,* No. 37 (August 1957), pp. 449-454.

1,838. ———. "Christlichkeit und Parodie: Ein Versuch über Th. M's 'Erwählten,' " *Diskurs: Frankfurter Studentenzeitung,* Vol. 8, No. 1 (January 1958), pp. i-v.

1,839. ———. "Ästhetische Selbstbehauptung," *Frankfurter Hefte,* 16 (February 1961), 137-138. [Review of E. Heller, item #1,278]

1,840. Landau, E. M. "Werkstatt des Weltbürgers," *Kölnische Rundschau,* February 25, 1961. [Th. M. Archive Zurich]

1,841. Landquist, John. "Dubiös Th. M.-roman," *Aftonbladet,* October 25, 1955. [*Felix Krull*]

1,842. ———. "Th. M. och nazismen," *Aftonbladet,* November 25, 1963. [Reply to V. Svanberg item #3,225] *See also* H. Levander, #1,956]

1,843. Landry, Harald. "Th. M.: Die Forderung des Tages," *Die lit. Welt,* Vol. 5, No. 51/52 (December 19, 1929), p. 9.

1,844. Landsträsser, Ludwig. "Th. M.-Nachlese," *Westermanns Monatshefte,* Vol. 98, No. 12 (1957), pp. 94, 96. [Concerns Th. M., *Nachlese,* and H. M. Wolff, item #3,532]

1,845. Lang, Hans Joachim. "Neue Studien über Th. M.," *Hamburger Akademische Rundschau,* 2 (May-June 1948), 626. [Review of Bauer, I, item #113; Hamburger, I, item #2,450; Lion, I, item #263] *See also* item #1,979

1,846 †Lange, Gerhard. Der Goethe-Roman Th. M's im Vergleich zu den Quellen. Ph. D. diss., University of Bonn, 1954. 329 pp. [*See* critical comment by Herman Meyer, item #2,246]

1,847. Lange, I. M. "Th. M's 'Lotte in Weimar,' " *Deutschunterricht* (Berlin), 5 (1952), 565-567.

1,848. *———. "Th. M.," in *Th. M.: Hilfsmittel für den Literaturunterricht an den Ober- und Fachschulen,* pp. 5-38. Berlin: Volk und Wissen, 1954.

1,849.   ———. "Zu Th. M's Schillerstudie 'Schwere Stunde,' "
          Deutschunterricht (Berlin), 8 (January 1955), 310-312.

1,850.   ———. "Mythos und Humanität: Zu Th. M's 'Joseph und seine
          Brüder,' " *NDL*, 3 (June 1955), 37-46.

1,851.   Lange, Sven. "Th. M.," *Politiken*, December 12, 1929, pp.
          11-12. [Nobel Prize]

1,852.   Lange, Victor. "Mann's Literary Essays," *Yale Review*, 37
          (September, 1947), 166-168. [*Essays of Three Decades*]

1,853.   ———. "Th. M.: 1875-1955," *SRL*, Vol. 38, No. 38
          (September 17, 1955), p. 26. [Obit.]

1,854.   ———. "Th. M.: The Somber and the Satiric," *New Republic*,
          Vol. 133, No. 14 (October 3, 1955), pp. 19-21. [*Felix Krull*]

1,855.   ———. "Betrachtungen zur Thematik von 'Felix Krull,' "
          GR, 31 (October 1956), [215]-224.

1,856.   ———. "Th. M. in Old Age," *New Republic*, Vol. 140, No. 7
          (February 16, 1959), pp. 18-19. [*Last Essays*]

1,857.   ———. "The Janus Voice," *Yale Review*, 48 (March 1959),
          447-451. [Review of E. Heller, item #1,278]

1,858.   ———. "Ausdruck und Erkenntnis. Zur politischen
          Problematik der deutschen Literatur seit dem Expressionismus,"
          Neue Rundschau, 74 (1963), 93-108.

1,859.   ———. "Th. M. Commemoration," *Princeton University
          Library Chronicle*, 26 (Winter 1965), 110-112. [Text of
          his remarks at a ceremony on October 24, 1964, consisting of
          the unveiling of a tablet at 65, Stockton Street, Th. M's former
          Princeton residence] Also published in item #3,276,
          pp. 9-[12]

1,860.   ———. "Th. M.: Politics and Art," in *Wert und Wort:
          Festschrift für Else M. Fleissner*, pp. 69-[75] Aurora, New
          York: Wells College, 1965.

1,861.   ———. Review of H. Hatfield, item #1,229, *GQ*, 38
          (November 1965), 697-698.

1,862.   Lasso de la Vega, José S. "Unanimismo y mito clásico en la
          obra de Th. M.," *Filología Moderna*, Vol. 3, No. 7-8 (1962),
          pp. 35-64.

1,863. Lauret, René. "A propos de Th. M.," *Revue Rhénane —
Rheinische Blätter,* 2 (1922), 232-234. [Politics — Franco-
German relations]

1,864. Lauschus, Leo. "Th. M.: 'Der Weg zum Friedhof,' "
Deutschunterricht (Stuttgart), 10 (1958), 66-81.

1,865. Lawrence, D. H. "Th. M.," in Anthony Beal, *ed.,* D. H.
Lawrence, *Selected Literary Criticism,* pp. 260-265. London:
W. Heinemann [1960] [Cf. I, item #2,112]

1,866. Lean, Tangye. "I Accuse," *News Chronicle,* September 29,
1938. [*The Coming Victory of Democracy*]

1,867. Leber, Hugo. "Th. M. als Briefschreiber," *Tages-Anzeiger,*
No. 241 (October 13, 1962), p. 20. [Review of *Briefe I,*
item #2,062]

1,868. Lederer, Joe. "Im Flug über die moderne Literatur: Besuch
bei Th. M.," *Welt am Sonntag,* May 22, 1949.

1,869. Leemans, Paul. "Inleiding tot Th. M.," *Standaard der letteren,*
March 3, 1962. [Review article, in Flemish, based on Eichner,
item #750]

1,870. Lehnert, Herbert. "Hans Castorps Vision: Eine Studie zum
Aufbau von Th. M's Roman 'Der Zauberberg,' " *Rice Institute
Pamphlet,* Vol. 47, No. 1 (April 1960), pp. 1-37.

1,871. ———. "Th. M. und Schiller," *Rice Institute Pamphlet,* Vol.
47, No. 1 (April 1960), pp. 99-118.

1,872. ———. "Th. M. in Exile, 1933-1938," *GR,* 33 (November
1963), [277]-294.

1,873. ———. "Th. M's Vorstudien zur Josephs-Tetralogie,"
Jahrbuch der Deutschen Schiller-Gesellschaft, 7 (1963),
458-520.

1,874. ———., [and] Wulf Segebrecht. "Th. M. im Münchner
Zensurbeirat (1912-1913): Ein Beitrag zum Verhältnis
Th. M's zu Frank Wedekind," *Jahrbuch der Deutschen
Schiller-Gesellschaft,* 7 (1963), 190-200.

1,875. ———. "Th. M. in Princeton," *GR,* 34 (January 1964),
[15]-32. [Contains on pp. 22-27 first publication of German
text of Mann's speech in Princeton, May 18, 1938]

1,876. ———., [and] John G. Frank. "Letters by Th. M. to Julius
        Bab. Some New Readings," GR, 34 (January 1964), [33]-36.
        [Cf. item #912]

1,877. ———. "Heine, Schiller, Nietzsche und der junge Th. M.,"
        Neophilologus, 48 (February 1964), 51-56.

1,878. ———. "Th. M's Early Interest in Myth and Erwin Rohde's
        Psyche," PMLA, 79 (June 1964), 297-304. [Der Tod in
        Venedig] Also in German in item #1,882, pp. 109-118.

1,879. ———. "Anmerkungen zur Entstehungsgeschichte von Th.
        M's 'Bekenntnissen des Hochstaplers Felix Krull,' 'Der
        Zauberberg,' und 'Betrachtungen eines Unpolitischen,' "
        DVJS, 38 (1964), 267-272.

1,880. ———. "Th. M's Own Interpretations of 'Der Tod in
        Venedig' and their Reliability," Rice University Studies, Vol.
        50, No. 4 (Fall 1964), pp. 41-60. Also in German in item
        #1,882, pp. 120-139.

1,881. ———. "Note on Mann's 'Der Tod in Venedig' and 'The
        Odyssey,' " PMLA, 80 (June 1965), 306-307. Also in German
        in item #1,882, pp. 118-120.

1,882. *———. Th. M.: Fiktion, Mythos, Religion. Stuttgart:
        Kohlhammer, 1965. 272 pp.

1,883. ———. "Th. M's Lutherbild," in G. Wenzel, item #3,472,
        pp. 269-381. [Rev. version in #1,882]

1,884. †Leibholz, R. N. P. An Analysis of the Construction of the
        Modern German Short Story with Reference to Th. M. and
        Hermann Hesse. Ph. D. diss., Oxford University, 1948.
        [Cf. I, item #2,984]

1,885. Leibrich, Louis. Review of J. Fougère, I, item #1127, EG, 2
        (1947), 478.

1,886. ———. "Th. M.: Felix Krull, 1. Teil," Allemagne
        d'Aujourd'hui, No. 7 (November 1954), pp. 720-721.

1,887. ———. Review of H. Eichner, I, item #159, EG, 10
        (January-March, 1955), 80-81. [Cf. #750]

1,888. ———. "Th. M.: Felix Krull, 1. Teil," EG, 10 (1955),
        353-355.

1,889. ———. "La spiritualité de Th. M.," in item #1,493,
pp. 149-152.

1,890. ———. "Th. M.: 1875-1955," *L'Esprit des Lettres,* No. 5
(1956), pp. 10-21. [Obit.]

1,891. ———. "Publications récentes de la famille Mann," *Allemagne
d'Aujourd'hui,* No. 5 (1956), pp. 66-67. [Review of
Betrachtungen eines Unpolitischen, item #2,058; A.
Kantorowicz, item #1,655; Erika Mann, item #2,059;
Monika Mann, item #2,100]

1,892. ———. "L'Année Th. M.," *EG,* 11 (January-March, 1956),
63-67. [Bibliographical survey of recent Th. M. criticism —
includes review of K. W. Jonas, item #1,605]

1,893. ———. "Confirmation de Th. M.," *Critique,* 13 (November-
December, 1957), [915]-927, [1040]-1051. [Review of R.
Hinton Thomas, item #3,273; A. Kantorowicz, item #1,655;
Betrachtungen eines Unpolitischen, item #2,058; *Nachlese*]

1,894. *———. *Th. M.* Paris: Editions Universitaires [1957] 140 pp.
[2nd, rev. ed. Cf. I, item #251. — Preface by M. Brion, item
#465]

1,895. ———. "Th. M.," *Dictionnaire Biographique des Auteurs,*
Vol. 2, pp. 164-166. Paris: Laffont-Bompiani, 1957.

1,896. ———. Review of H. Bürgin, item #502, *EG,* 15 (April-
June, 1960), 199-201.

1,897. ———. Review of G. Fourrier, item #905, *EG,* 15 (October-
December, 1960), 397-398.

1,898. ———. Review of P. Scherrer, item #2,877, *EG,* 15 (October-
December, 1960), 398-399.

1,899. ———. Review of I. Diersen, item #677, *EG,* 16 (January-
March, 1961), 71-72.

1,900. ———. Review of V. Žmegač, item #3,600, *EG,* 16 (July-
September, 1961), 298.

1,901. ———. Review of A. Hellersberg, item #1,285, *EG,* 17
(April-June, 1962), 219-220.

1,902. ———. Review of P. Altenberg, item #34, *EG,* 17 (October-
December, 1962), 490-491.

1,903.   ————. Review of Deguy, item #649, *Germanistik*, 4
          (January 1963), 143.
1,904.   ————. "Etat actuel de la recherche sur Th. M.," *EG*, 18
          (October-December, 1963), 457-463.
1,905.   ————. "Französische Wirklichkeit im Werke Th.
          M's," in
          Deutschland/Frankreich: Ludwigsburger Beiträge, Vol. 3,
          pp. [168]-186. Stuttgart: DVA, 1963.
1,906.   ————. "Th. M. et Nietzsche," *RLM*, Nos. 76-77 (1963),
          pp. 63-72. [Reprint of I, item #1,674]
1,907.   ————. Review of Th. M. — E. Faesi, item #833, *EG*, 19
          (April-June, 1964), 224.
1,908.   Leip, Hans. "Grüsse Hamburger Dichter an Th. M.,"
          Hamburger Anzeiger, No. 129 (June 6, 1925). [50th birthday]
1,909.   Lem, Stanislaw. "Über das Modellieren der Wirklichkeit im
          Werk von Th. M.," *Sinn und Form: Sonderheft Th. M.*, 1965,
          pp. 157-177. [Translated from Polish by Erich Doberstein]
1,910.   Lemke, Karl. "Th. M's "Appell an die Vernunft,'" *Neue Zeit*,
          No. 289 (October 19, 1930). [*Deutsche Ansprache*]
1,911.   Lennartz, Franz. "Th. M.," in his *Dichter und Schriftsteller
          unserer Zeit*, pp. 482-494. Stuttgart: Kröner, 1959. [Rev.,
          enl. *ed.* of I, item #656]
1,912.   Lennert, Rudolf. "Brüderlichkeit des Geistes: Erinnerung an
          Th. M.," *Sammlung*, 10 (November 1955), 539-543.
1,913.   Lenz, Renate. "Wiedersehen mit Nidden, Th. M's Sommer-
          haus," *Königsberger Hartungsche Zeitung*, No. 333 (July 19,
          1930). [Biog.]
1,914.   Leonhardt, Wilhelm. "Die Bergedorfer 'Buddenbrooks,'"
          Lübeckische Blätter, Vol. 129, No. 16 (1961), pp. 211-213.
          [Th. M's relatives in Hamburg]
1,915.   Leopold, Keith. "Point of View in the Novels of Th. M.,"
          AUMLA, No. 8 (May 1958), pp. 29-36.
1,916.   ————. "The Time Levels in Th. M's 'Joseph the Provider,'"
          University of Queensland Papers, Faculty of Arts, Vol. 1,
          No. 1 (October 1958), pp. 3-13. [*Joseph and his Brothers*]
1,917.   Leopoldi, Hans Heinrich. " 'Tief ist der Brunnen der
          Vergangenheit'; über die niederdeutsche Herkunft von

Heinrich und Th. M.," *Kiek in de Welt,* Vol. 10, No. 112 (1961), pp. 3-15.

1,918. Lepel, Hermann. "Ein deutscher Rektor über Th. M.," *National-Zeitung Basel,* March 3, 1938. [Defends Th. M. against attacks leveled against him by Ernst Krieck, "Nazi Rektor" of Heidelberg University]

1,919. Lepman, Jella. "Th. M., so wie viele ihn nicht kennen," *Heim und Leben,* September 23, 1961, pp. 20-21, 38.

1,920. ————. "Die Gefährtin des Dichters: Katja Mann," *Heim und Leben,* September 23, 1961, pp. 22-23, 38.

1,921. Leppert, Günter Fred. "Ehrenbürger seiner Vaterstadt," *Vaterstädtische Blätter,* Vol. 6, No. 3 (March 1955), pp. [2-3] [With facsim. of a letter from Th. M.]

1,922. Leppmann, Franz. "Ein neuer Th. M.: Das Wunderkind," *Vossische Zeitung,* No. 629 (December 11, 1914), 3. Beilage.

1,923. ————. "Th. M. über Friedrich den Grossen," *Berliner Tageblatt,* Beilage 'Literarische Rundschau,' June 21, 1915. [*Friedrich und die Grosse Koalition*]

1,924. Leppmann, Wolfgang. Review of R. A. Nicholls, item #2,407, *CL,* 17 (Fall 1955), 366-367.

1,925. ————. "Th. M.," in his *The German Image of Goethe,* pp. 159-166. Oxford: Clarendon Press, 1961. Also in German, *Goethe und die Deutschen,* pp. 213-219. Stuttgart: Kohlhammer, 1962.

1,926. ————. "Der Amerikaner im Werke Th. M's," *GQ,* 38 (November 1965), 619-629.

1,927. Lernet-Holenia, Alexander. "Auf den Tod Th. M's," *Forum,* 2 (September 1955), 315.

1,928. Lervik, Kaare. "Th. M. og det tyske problem," *Svertrykk: Minerva's Kvartalschrift,* No. 2 (1960), pp. 1-4.

1,929. Leschnitzer, Franz. "Ja aus Nein," *Sinn und Form: Sonderheft Th. M.,* 1965, pp. 391-394.

1,930. Lesser, Jonas. "Th. M's biblischer Roman 'Joseph und seine Brüder,' " *Glocke,* Vol. 3, No. 40/41 (March 1, 1937), pp. 3-14.

1,931.   ———. "Einige Bemerkungen über Th. M's Verhältnis zur
          Philosophie und Religion," *Neue Rundschau,* 66 (June 1955),
          518-523.

1,932.   ———. "Th. M. zu Ehren," *Deutsche Rundschau,* 81
          (September 1955), 890-893. [Bibliographical survey of
          recent Th. M. criticism]

1,933.   ———. "In memoriam Th. M.," *AJR Information,* Vol. 10
          (September 1955), pp. 4-5. [Obit.]

1,934.   ———. "Th. M's Joseph-Trilogie," in Ernst Niekisch, *ed.,*
          Der Gesichtskreis: Joseph Drexel zum 60. Geburtstag, pp. 128-
          141. [München: Beck, 1956]

1,935.   ———. "Th. M.," *Contemporary Review,* 189 (March 1956),
          169-172. [Th. M. as a novelist]

1,936.   ———. "Noch einmal: Zu Th. M's 'Doktor Faustus,' "
          *Blätter der Knittlinger Faust-Gedenkstätten und des Faust-
          Museums,* No. 4 (1957), pp. 66-67.

1,937.   ———. "Neue Bücher über Th. M.," *Deutsche Rundschau,* 85
          (January 1959), 84-86. [Review of E. Heller, #1,278, and
          F. Kaufmann, #1,683]

1,938.   ———. "Th. M. und Wilhelm Raabe: Einiges über
          Deutschlands Sündenweg," *Deutsche Rundschau,* 85 (1959),
          518-523.

1,939.   ———. "Th. M. und Golo Mann," *Deutsche Rundschau,* 88
          (February 1962), 180-182.

1,939a.   ———. "Th. M. und der Rationalismus des Westens,"
          Begegnung, 18 (1963), 289-291.

1,940.   ———. "Th. M.," in his *Germany: The Symbol and the Deed,*
          pp. 108 ff., 292 ff., 555 ff. New York: T. Yoseloff [1965]

1,941.   ———. "Th. M. und das Ende des bürgerlichen Romans,"
          in G. Wenzel, #3,472, pp. 131-142.

1,942.   Lessing, Theodor. "Antwort," in his *Samuel zieht die Bilanz
          und Toni melkt die Moralkuh,* pp. 43-46. Hannover: Verlag des
          'Antirüpel,' 1910. [Reply to Th. M., "Der Doktor Lessing,"
          ibid., pp. 28-33. Adds to I, item #657]

1,943.   ———. "Chaos und Ordnung," *Das Stachelschwein,* No. 1
          (1926), pp. 8-12. [Concerns Th. M., "Die Ehe im Übergang"]

1,944. Lestiboudois, Herbert. "Lieber Frank Thiess," *Neue West-fälische Zeitung,* January 22, 1946. Also in Grosser, item #1,090, pp. 92-94. [Th. M. as an emigré]

1,945. Leutner, Karl. "Th. M.," in his *Deutsche, auf die wir stolz sind,* Vol. 2, pp. 368-372. [Berlin] Verlag der Nation [1958]

1,946. Leuzinger, Peter. "Th. M. fête aujourd'hui son quatre-vingtième anniversaire," *Tribune de Genève,* June 6, 1955, p. 13. [80th birthday]

1,947. Levander, Hans. "Bergstagen efter trettio år," *Morgon-Tidningen,* September 18, 1954. [*Der Zauberberg*]

1,948. ———. "Naphtas två ansikten," *Morgon-Tidningen,* September 24, 1954. [*Der Zauberberg*]

1,949. ———. "Th. M's skälmroman," *Morgon-Tidningen,* November 7, 1954. [*Felix Krull*]

1,950. ———. "Th. M. — mittens diktare," *Morgon-Tidningen,* June 6, 1955. [80th birthday]

1,951. ———. "Th. M.," *Studiekamraten,* 37 (1955), 161-164.

1,952. ———. "Th. M: och naturalism," in his *Studier tillägnade Henry Olsson,* pp. [52]-59. Stockholm: Norstedt [1956]

1,953. ———. "Inledning," in Th. M's *Noveller,* pp. [5-8] [Stockholm] Bonnier [1958]

1,954. ———. "Den hermetiske Th. M.," *Svenska Dagbladet,* November 21, 1960. [Review of Kerényi, item #1,700 c]

1,955. ———. "Brev från Th. M.," *Stockholms-Tidningen,* February 10, 1962. [*Briefe I,* item #2,062]

1,956. ———. "Mann och 'Broder Hitler,' " *Stockholms-Tidningen,* October 23, 1963. [Reply to V. Svanberg, item #3,225. *See also* John Landquist, item #1,842]

1,957. ———. Review of G. Bergsten, item #292, *BLM,* 32 (1963), 411-414.

1,958. *———. *Th. M.: Silhuetten och verket.* Stockholm: Bonnier [1964] 317 pp.
Reviews: Aspelin, #143 — Bergsten, #293 — Carlsson, #544 — Harrie, #1,199 — Holmberg, #1,478 — Schoolfield, #2,951 — Svanberg, #3,226.

1,959. Levin, Harry. "Th. M.," in his *James Joyce,* pp. 212-213 et al. Norfolk, Conn.: New Directions [1941]

1,960. Levinsson, André. "Avant-propos," in Th. M., *Les Budden-brooks,* pp. [7]-11. Paris: Fayard [1932]

1,961. Levy, Margarete. "Bemerkungen zum 'Zauberberg' von Th. M.," *Deutsche Medizinische Wochenschrift,* Vol. 51, No. 28 (July 10, 1925), p. 1166. Also in H. Saueressig, item #2,844, pp. 56-57.

1,962. Lewalter, Christian E. " 'Du kommst in so fragwürdiger Gestalt' . . . Der Chronist und sein Ruhm," *Zeit,* No. 22 (June 2, 1955). [80th birthday]

1,963. Lezama Lima, José. "Mann y el fin de la grandeza," in his *Tratados en la Habana,* pp. 107-110. [La Habana] Universidad Central de las Villas, 1958.

1,964. Lichtenberger, Henri. "Th. M. à Paris," *Revue de l'Enseigne-ment des Langues Vivantes,* 43 (January 1926), 120-121.

1,965. Liepmann, Heinz. "Begegnung mit Th. M.," *Neues Wiener Journal,* November 14, 1926.

1,966. Liersch, Werner. "Aufgabe der Werte," *NDH,* 7 (1959), 114-119. [Reply to H. Kesten, item #1,711, concerning Heinrich and Th. M.]

1,967. Lindblom, J. "Möten med Th. M.," *Sydsvenska Dagbladet Snällposten,* August 12, 1960.

1,968. Lindemann, Reinhold. "Genius der Mitte: Zu Th. M's Briefen aus der Zeit von 1889 bis 1936," *Rheinische Post,* Vol. 17, No. 61 (March 13, 1962). [Review of *Briefe I,* item #2,062]

1,969. ———. "Genie der Sachlichkeit und Humanität," *Rheinische Post,* Vol. 20, No. 282, Ausgabe A (December 4, 1965). [Review of Bürgin-Mayer, item #504]

1,970. Lindhardt, Stephan. "Zwischen Dämon und Wirklichkeit: Zum 85. Geburtstag von Th. M.," *Osnabrücker Volksblatt,* June 4, 1960.

1,971. *Lindsay, J. M. *Th. M.* Oxford: B. Blackwell, 1954. v, 137 pp. [Cf. I, item #2,985a] Reviews: Gronicka, item #1,084 — Hatfield, #1,214 —

McClain, #2,352 — Nicholls, #2,408 — Nicolson, #2,412 —
Parry, #2,485 — Rie, #2,714.

1,972. ———. Review of P. Altenberg, item #34, *GLL*, N. S., 16
(1962), 73-74.

1,973. ———. "Der Zeitbegriff im 'Zauberberg,' " *Sinn und Form:
Sonderheft Th. M.*, 1965, pp. 144-156. [Transl. from English
by Elga Abramowitz]

1,974. Lindt, Peter. "Dr. Th. M.," in his *Schriftsteller im Exil*,
pp. 55-57. New York: Willard, 1944.

1,975. Lindtke, Gustav. *Die Stadt der Buddenbrooks: Lübecker
Bürgerkultur im 19. Jahrhundert.* Lübeck: Max Schmidt-
Römhild [1965] 132 pp.

1,976. Linn, Rolf N. "Conversation with Th. M.," *GQ*, 33 (May
1960), 224-226.

1,977. Lion, Ferdinand. "Gewebe in Th. M's 'Buddenbrooks,' " in
his *Geheimnisse des Kunstwerks*, pp. 55-61. Stuttgart: DVA,
1932.

1,978. ———. "Zwischen Leben und Tod," *NZZ*, Vol. 156, No. 958,
1. Sonntagsausgabe (June 2, 1935), Bl. 4, pp. 1-2. [60th
birthday]

1,979. *———. *Th. M.: Leben und Werk.* Zurich: Oprecht [1955]
209 pp. [2nd, enl. ed — Cf. I, item #263]
Reviews: Bianquis, #322 — Hupka, #1,529 — Jancke, #1,566
— Korrodi, #1,778 — Luft, #2,021 — Schröder, #2,966.

1,980. ———. "Th. M. come filosofo," *Aut aut*, No. 29 (September
1955), pp. 376-383.

1,981. ———. "Le Laboratoire de Th. M.," *Preuves*, No. 56 (October
1955), pp. 37-40.

1,982. ———. "Th. M's Geheimstes, Geheimstes," *Deutsche Zeitung*,
July 30/31, 1960.

1,983. ———. "Halb der Zukunft zugewandt, halb dem Vergessenen,"
Deutsche Zeitung, August 5, 1961. [*Mass und Wert*, 1937-
1940]

1,984. ———. "Mass und Wert," *Akzente*, No. 1 (February 1963),
pp. 36-40.

1,985. Lipsky, E. "The Lawgiver," *New Palestine,* November 14,
        1945. [*Das Gesetz*]
1,986. Lissner, Erich. "Gruss an Th. M.," *Frankfurter Rundschau,*
        Vol. 8, No. 260 (November 8/9, 1952), p. 2. [On the
        occasion of M's lecture on Gerhart Hauptmann in Frankfurt]
1,987. Litzmann, Grete. "Th. M.: Rede und Antwort," *Hannoverscher
        Kurier,* January 13, 1922.
1,988. †Ljungerud, Ivar. Bemerkungen zur modernen deutschen
        Dichtersprache unter besonderer Berücksichtigung der Sprache
        Th. M's, Hermann Hesses und Hans Carossas. Ph. D. diss.,
        University of Lund, 1948. Also rev. version in his *Zur
        Nominalflexion in der deutschen Literatursprache nach 1900.*
        Lund: Gleerup; Copenhagen: Munksgaard, 1955.
1,989. Lockemann, Fritz. "Die Ordnungsmacht der Illusion: Th. M.,"
        in his *Gestalt und Wandlungen der deutschen Novelle,*
        pp. 329-341. München: Hueber, 1957.
1,990. Loder, Dietrich. "Der Gast," *Arminius,* April 19, 1926.
        [With Th. M's letter to 'Redaktion' der *Münchner Neuesten
        Nachrichten,* replying to attack by Hanns Johst. Concerns
        Th. M. in Paris]
1,991. Löb, László. "Gondeln und Särge," *Du,* Vol. 18, No. 4
        (April 1958), pp. 72, 74, 76. [*Der Tod in Venedig*]
1,992. Lönnroth, Erik. "Historiska middagar hos Th. M.," *Dagens
        Nyheter,* July 29, 1954.
1,993. Loerke, Oskar. "Akademierede auf Th. M. anlässlich der
        Verleihung des Nobelpreises 1929," in his *Reden und kleinere
        Aufsätze,* pp. 43-44. Wiesbaden: F. Steiner, 1956.
1,994. ———. "Th. M.," in his *Tagebücher, 1903-1939,* pp. 107-108
        et al. Heidelberg: L. Schneider, 1956.
1,995. Loetscher, Hugo. "Humanismus und Widerspruch," *Zürcher
        Woche,* Vol. 7, No. 22 (June 3, 1955), p. 2. [80th birthday]
1,996. Loewy-Hattendorf, Erwin. "Ärztliche Probleme in der
        modernen Dichtkunst," *Zeitschrift für Ärztliche Fortbildung,*
        22 (1925), 603-606. [*Der Zauberberg*]
1,997. ———. "Oedipus, Oestron und Th. M.," *Ars Medici,* 44
        (1954), 481-482.

1,998. ———. "De Gaulle weiss es selbst kaum . . .," *Frankfurter Hefte*, 17 (March 1962), 210-211. [Review of Flinker, item #887]

1,999. Lohner, Edgar. Review of R. H. Thomas, item #3,273, *MLN*, 73 (December 1958), 635-637.

2,000. †Lohnes, Walter F. W. Der Unpolitische und die Politik: Th. M., 1900-1918. Ph. D. diss., Harvard University, 1961. 284 pp.

2,001. Loose, Gerhard. "Glocken über Rom," *MLN*, 74 (November 1959), 633-636. [*Betrachtungen eines Unpolitischen* — Palestrina — *Der Erwählte*]

2,002. ———. Review of H. M. Wolff, item #3,532, *MLN*, 75 (January 1960), 92-93.

2,003. Lorson, Pierre. "Les lettres à l'étranger," *Etudes*, (1948), 87-93. [*Doktor Faustus*]

2,004. Lothar, Ernst. "Die Sendung der Ironie: Ein neues Werk von Th. M.," *Neue Freie Presse*, Morgenblatt, December 11, 1925. [*Bemühungen*]

2,005. Loup, Kurt. "Th. M.," in *Schönheit und Freiheit: Friedrich Schiller und das Düsseldorfer Schauspielhaus, pp.* 10-14 et al. Düsseldorf: Ophoff, 1959.

2,006. ———., [and] Hans-Otto Mayer. "Struktur und Wandlung einer Stadt," *Lions*, No. 1 (January 1962), pp. 27-38. [Th. M. in Düsseldorf]

2,007. ———. "Kontraste und Paradoxe: Das kulturelle Klima Düsseldorfs in den zwanziger Jahren," *Düsseldorfer Hefte*, Vol. 8, No. 22 (November 16-30, 1963), pp. 1062-1067. [*Die Betrogene*]

2,008. Lowe-Porter, Helen T. "Translating Th. M.," *Symposium*, 9 (Fall 1955), 260-272. [With a note on Mrs. Lowe by E. M. Fleissner] Also in *Wells College Alumnae News*, Vol. 22, No. 2 (January 1957), pp. 4-11, and in #3,916.

2,009. Lowenthal, E. G. "Von den Gesetzen der moralischen Welt. Th. M.: Ein Jahr nach seinem Tode," *Allgemeine Wochenzeitung der Juden in Deutschland*, Vol. 11, No. 19 (August 10, 1956), p. 6.

2,010. Lowry, Thomas. "The Way Mann Worked," *Saturday Review*, Vol. 40, No. 16 (April 20, 1957), p. 17. [Review of R. H. Thomas, item #3,273]

2,011. Lublinsky, Samuel. "Th. M.," in his *Die Bilanz der Moderne*, pp. 224-228. Berlin: Cronbach, 1904. [*Buddenbrooks*]

2,012. Lucas, Guy. "Die Darstellung der Gesellschaft in Th. M's 'Buddenbrooks,' " *Revue des Langues Vivantes — Levende Talen*, 30 (1964), 195-200.

2,013. Luciana, Fernando. "Orientamenti attuali della letteratura tedesca: l'esempio di Th. M.," *Idea*, 15 (November 1959), 772-774. [*Tonio Kröger*]

2,014. Luckow, Marion. "Th. M.: Der Tod in Venedig," in her *Die Homosexualität in der literarischen Tradition: Studien zu den Romanen von Jean Genêt*, pp. 58-63. Stuttgart: Enke, 1962. [Ph. D. diss., University of Hamburg]

2,014a. Ludovic, D. "Corespondența lui Th. M.," *Viața-românească*, No. 1 (January 1965), pp. 199-200.

2,015. Ludwig, Emil. "Tommy in Weimar; frei nach Faust II. Teil, 2. Akt," *Moscia*, No. 5 (1939). [15 pp.] [Parody of Th. M. after the appearance of his *Lotte in Weimar*]

2,016. Lüdecke, Heinz. "Erwähltheit und Bewährung," in his *Auf dem Weg*, pp. 50-55. Berlin: Henschel, 1954. [*Der Erwählte*. Cf. I, item #2,906]

2,017. ———. "Der beste Bürger und seine Entscheidung," in item #2,016, pp. 109-118.

2,018. Lüth, Erich. "Th. M. kommt nach Lübeck," *Lübecker Nachrichten*, June 10, 1953. Expanded version, "Th. M's Heimkehr über Hamburg," in his *Neues Hamburg*, pp. 97-100. Hamburg: Hammerich & Lesser, 1959. Also in *Antworten: Jahrbuch der Freien Akademie der Künste*, pp. 211-[222] Hamburg, 1963.

2,019. Luetzeler, Heinrich. "Neue Romane: Th. M's 'Die Geschichten Jaakobs,' " *Hochland*, 31 (1933/34), 81-85.

2,020. Luft, Friedrich. "Gelesen — wiedergelesen: Th. M's 'Altes und Neues,' " *Neue Zeitung*, April 5, 1953.

2,021. ————. "Ein milder Zauberer," *Welt am Sonntag,* No. 23 (June 5, 1955), p. 9. [Review of E. Faesi, item #831, and F. Lion, item #1,979]

2,022. ————. "Felix Krull gibt keine Ruhe," *Welt,* May 16, 1957. [Concerns law suit against Th. M. for alleged plagiarism brought by Hans Kafka, author of *Welt und Kaffeehaus* (first published in 1930 in *Münchner Illustrierte*)].

2,023. Lukács, György. "Th. M. uj regénye," *Nyugat,* 2 (1909), 486-491. Also in his books *Modern Könyvtár,* pp. 201-203. Budapest: Athenaeum, 1909, and *Esztétikai Kultura,* pp. 72-81. Budapest: Athenaeum, 1913. — German version, "Th. M. und sein neuer Roman," in Festschrift *Georg Lukács zum siebzigsten Geburtstag,* pp. 213-224. Berlin: Aufbau [1955]. Also in Italian translation in his *Th. M.* [Milano, 1956], item #2,031, pp. 171-180. [*Königliche Hoheit*]

2,024. ————. Italian version of I, item #1,767, concerning *Leiden und Grösse der Meister,* item #2,031, pp. 153-169.

2,025. ————. "Op Zoek naar de burger," *Kroniek van kunst en kultuur,* July-August, 1948, pp. 197-221. [Dutch translation of I, #1,104]

2,026. ————. "Das Spielerische und seine Hintergründe," *Aufbau* (Berlin), 11 (June 1955), 501-524. Also in #2,031, pp. 113-151, and #2,033, pp. 583-617. [*Felix Krull*]

2,027. ————. "Th. M. und das heutige öffentliche Leben," *Ungarische Revue,* No. 7 (July 1955), pp. 16-17. [Also in English and French]

2,028. ————. "Th. M's Gegensatz zur Dekadenz der Gegenwart," *Heute und Morgen,* No. 6 (1955), pp. 331-339.

2,029. ————. "L'anima borghese di Th. M.," *Il Contemporaneo,* Vol. 2, No. 23 (June 4, 1955), pp 3-4. [80th birthday]

2,030. ————. "Der letzte grosse Vertreter des kritischen Realismus," *Sinn und Form,* 7 (1955), 665-668. Also in item #2,032, pp. 192-195.

2,031. *————. *Th. M. e la tragedia dell'arte moderna.* Milano: Feltrinelli [1956] 180 pp. [Cf. I, item #2,778. Translated from German by Giorgio Dolfini, containing as additional items #2,026, #2,023, and I, item #1,767] Reviews: Barilli, #181 — Dolfini, #703.

2,032. *————. *Th. M.* Berlin: Aufbau, 1957. 201 pp. [Fifth ed., Cf. I, #2,778] *See also* English and Italian translations, items #2,035 and #2,031.

2,033. ————. "Th. M.," in his *Deutsche Literatur in zwei Jahrhunderten,* pp. 501-618. [Neuwied] Luchterhand [1963] Contains I, item #1,104; I, item #2,778; and #2,026.

2,034. ————. "Th. M.," in his *Skizze einer Geschichte der neueren deutschen Literatur,* pp. 188-190 et al. [Neuwied a. Rh.] Luchterhand [1964]

2,035. *————. *Essays on Th. M.* London: Merlin Press; New York: Grosset & Dunlap [1964] 169 pp. Translated from the German by Stanley Mitchell. Reviews: Potoker, #2,595 — Toynbee, #3,302.

2,036. Lundgren, Gustaf. " 'Der Zauberberg' som psykoanalytisk roman," in item #2,431, pp. 113-126.

2,037. Lundkvist, Artur. "Josef och hans bröder: Den Unge Josef," *BLM,* Vol. 4, No. 10 (December 1935), pp. 47-49. [*Der Junge Joseph*]

2,038. ————. "Josef i Egypten," *BLM,* 8 (October 1939), 644-645. [*Joseph in Ägypten*]

2,039. ————. "Josefromanen fullbordad," *BLM,* 14 (January 1945), 46-48. [*Joseph und seine Brüder*]

2,040. ————. "Pakten med djävulen," *BLM,* 17 (December 1948), 771-773. [*Doktor Faustus*]

2,041. Lyon, James K. "Words and Music: Th. M's Tone Poem," *Western Humanities Review,* 13 (1959), 99-102. [*Doctor Faustus*]

2,042. Mach, Helga. "Th. M.," in Johannes Beer, *ed., Reclams Romanführer,* Vol. 1, pp. 572-575, 577. Stuttgart: Reclam [1962] [*Unordnung und frühes Leid. Joseph und seine Brüder. Lotte in Weimar. Der Erwählte*]

2,043. Magon, Leopold [and] Gerhard Steiner. "Arbeitsbesprechung im Th. M.-Archiv," *Mitteilungsblatt,* Vol. 6, No. 2 (1959), pp. 41-42. [Concerns projected critical edition of M's works]

2,043a. Mainka, Jürgen. "Ein Polemikum: Th. M's Wagnerbild," *Beiträge zur Musikwissenschaft,* 5 (1963), 231-234.

2,044. Maione, Italo. "Il 'Felix Krull' di Th. M.," *Il Mattino,* July 9, 1964.

2,045. †Maitre, H. Joachim. Aspekte der Kulturkritik Th. M's in seiner Essayistik. Ph. D. diss., McGill University, 1965.

2,046. ———. "Ein respektloser Grenzgänger: Plädoyer für Th. M's essayistisches Werk," *Welt,* July 31, 1965.

2,047. Malmberg, Bertil. "Mångrammatik," *BLM,* Vol. 4, No. 3 March 1935), pp. 58-60. Reprinted in his *Värderingar: Uppsatser,* pp. 161-167. [Stockholm] Bonnier [1937]

2,048. ———. "Th. M. — litteraten," *Dagens Nyheter,* February 8, 1954. Reprinted in his *Förklädda memoarer,* pp. 85-89. [Stockholm] Bonnier [1956] [Concerns W. Muschg's criticism, item #2,349]

2,049. Mandel, Siegfried. "Twentieth Century Knave," *Saturday Review,* Vol. 38, No. 38 (September 17, 1955), pp. 26-27. [*Felix Krull*]

2,050. Mandelkow, Karl Robert. "Th. M's 'Lotte in Weimar,' " in his *Der proteische Dichter,* pp. 3-6, 13. Groningen: Wolters, 1962.

2,051. ———. "Der proteische Dichter: Ein Leitmotiv in der Geschichte der Deutung und Wirkung Goethes," *Neophilologus,* 46 (1962), 19-31. [*Lotte in Weimar*]

2,052. Manghi, Alda. "Chiosa marginale a Th. M.," *RLMC,* 10 (1957), 290-291.

2,053. Manierre, Virginia. "How Long is a Minute?" *NMQ,* 26 (Autumn 1956), 238-248. [Concerns M's notion of time]
Mann, Elisabeth. *See* Borgese, Elisabeth Mann.

2,054. Mann, Erika. "Professor Zauberer," *Münchner Illustrierte,* No. 40 (October 2, 1954).

2,055. ———. "Der Vater," *Du,* Vol. 15, No. 6 (June 1955), pp. 4-14. Excerpted in *Welt der Arbeit,* No. 33 (August 19, 1955).

2,056.   ———. "Der Zauberer," *Münchner Illustrierte,* No. 35
(August 27, 1955). *See also* #2,069.

2,057.   ———. "Th. M.," *Times,* November 8, 1955. [Letter to
the Editor clarifying relationship between Th. M. Archives in
Berlin and Zurich]

2,058.*   ———. "Einleitung" in her *ed.* of Th. M., *Betrachtungen
eines Unpolitischen,* pp. ix-xxiv. [Frankfurt a. M.] S. Fischer,
1956.
Reviews: E. Brock, #478 — Holmqvist, #1,480 — Koch,
#1,750 — Leibrich, #1,891, #1,893 — Schröder, #2,968.

2,059.*   ———. *Das letzte Jahr: Bericht über meinen Vater.* [Frankfurt
a. M.] S. Fischer, 1956. 74 pp.
Excerpt: "Die letzten Stunden Th. M's," in *Almanach: das 70.
Jahr,* pp. 166-169. [Frankfurt a. M.] S. Fischer, 1956.
Reviews: Anon., #102 — Bernardelli, #301 — Enright, #791
— Falqui, #836 — George, #991 — Graf, #1,057 —
Hatfield, #1,223 — Hennecke, #1,321 — Hillard, #1,392 —
Holmqvist, #1,480 — Leibrich, #1,891 — Muir, #2,326 —
Rychner, #2,803 — Weber, #3,415.
Translations:
(a) Dutch: *Het laatste jaar van Th. M.,* transl. by C. J. E. Dinaux.
Amsterdam: Querido, 1956. 91 pp.
(b) English: *The Last Year: A Memoir of My Father,* transl. by
Richard Graves. [London] Secker & Warburg [1958] 92 pp.;
New York: Farrar, Strauss, 1958. 119 pp.
(c) Italian: *L'Ultimo anno: Resoconto su mio Padre,* transl. by
Roberto Margotta. Milano: Mondadori, 1960. 211 pp.
(d) Polish: *Ostatni rok; opowieść o moim ojcu,* transl. by Irena
Naganowska. [Poznań] Wydawnictwo Poznańskie â1961]
(e) Spanish: *El ultimo año; informe sobre mi padre,* transl. by
Jorge Oscar Piekenhayn. Buenos Aires: Ed. Sudamericana
[1958]

2,060.   ———. "Th. M. — eine Antwort," *Welt am Sonntag,* No. 33
(August 17, 1958), p. 4. [Reply to Curt Riess, items #2,720-
2,721. *See also* item #2,722]

2,061. ———. "Mit eigener Feder," *Das Schönste,* Vol. 7, No. 7
(July 1961), pp. 32-33. [Concerns Robert Neumann's novel
Olympia]

2,062.* ———. "Einleitung" in her *ed.* of Th. M., *Briefe 1889-1936,*
pp. v-[xii] Frankfurt a. M.: S. Fischer, 1961. [*Briefe I*]
Reviews: Anon., #104 — Anon., #118 — H. Becher, #208
— Blöcker, #364 — Blomster, #370 — Blume, #373 —
Boehlich, #386 — Brion, #467 — Busch, #520 —Chiarini,
#573 — Dach, #625 — Engler, #787 — Gottgetreu, #1,049
— Gregor-Dellin, #1,069 — Grenzmann, #1,077 — Grimm,
#1,081 — Günther, #1,097 f — Haas, #1,128 — Helbling,
#1,267 — Hell, #1,271 — Hellmann, #1,299 — Herting,
#1,344 — D. Hildebrandt, #1,379 — Hohoff, #1,467 —
Holmberg, #1,476 — Hübscher, #1,516 — I. Jens, #1 577 —
Leber, #1,867 — Levander, #1,955 — Lindemann, #1,968
— Motylowa, #2,298 — Remak, #2,685 — Rychner, #2,808
—Schöffler, #2,937 — Sieburg, #3,053 — Siedler, #3,058 —
Süskind, #3,214 — Suter, #3,221 — Ter-Nedden, #3,255.

2,063. ———. "Brief-Wahl," *Spiegel,* Vol. 16, No. 20 (May 30,
1962), p. 81. [Concerns *Briefe I,* item #2,062]

2,064. ———. "Die letzten Jahre Th. M's," *Duitse Kroniek,* 15
(1963), 2-6. [Biog.]

2,065.* ———. ed., *Th. M., Wagner und unsere Zeit.* [Frankfurt a.
M.] S. Fischer, 1963. 185 pp. [*See* Preface by W. Schuh,
#2,976]
Reviews: Goldschmit, #1,037 — Haas, #1,130 — Hellmann,
#1,306 — Helwig, #1,317.

2,066. *———. "Einleitung" in her *ed.* of Th. M., *Briefe 1937-1947,*
pp. 5-[6] [Frankfurt a. M.] S. Fischer, 1963. [*Briefe II*]
Reviews: Basler, #196 — Blöcker, #365 — Blomster, #370 —
Blume, #374 — Bo, #379 — Boehlich, #387 — Chiarini,
#573 — Goldstein, #1,045 — Gottgetreu, #1,050 —
Gregor-Dellin, #1,071 — Günther, #1,097g — Haas, #1,131
— Heimann, #1,262 — Helbling, #1,269 — Hellmann,
#1,309 — Herchenröder, #1,337 — Herting, #1,344 —
D. Hildebrandt, #1,379 — Hohoff, #1,467 — Holmberg,

#1,477 — Hoppe, #1,499 — Ihlenfeld, #1,543 — W. Jens, #1,585 — Lamm, #1,836 — Munteanu, #2,331 — Österling, 2, 453 — Orabuena, #2,461 — Rychner, #2,810 — Sieburg, #3,055 — Spiel, #3,109 — Süskind, #3,217 — Wassermann, #3,402 — Wien, #3,487. *See also* #120.

2,067. ———. "Hans Reisiger: Zum 80. Geburtstag (21. Oktober)," *NZZ*, Vol. 185, Morgenausgabe No. 4445 (October 21, 1964), Bl. 6. [With a letter from Th. M. of November 1, 1952]

2,068. ———. "Th. M.: Die letzte Adresse," *Schöner Wohnen*, No. 4 (August 1965), pp. 82-91. [Biog.]

2,069. ———. "Der Zauberer," *Spektrum*, 11 (1965), 143. [Cf. #2,056]

2,070. ———. "Th. M.," *Sinn und Form: Sonderheft Th. M.*, 1965, pp. 5-9.

2,071. *———. "Einleitung" in her *ed.* of Th. M., *Briefe 1948-1955 und Nachlese*, pp. 5-[7] [Frankfurt a. M.] S. Fischer, 1965. [*Briefe III*]
Reviews: Blöcker, #366 — Gregor-Dellin, #1,072 —Hack, #1,135 — Heimann, #1,263 — W. Jens, #1,587 — Saueressig, #2,848. *See also* #106.

2,072. Mann, Friedrich. "Buddenbrooks," *Lübeckische Blätter*, Vol. 121, No. 16 (1961), p. 213. [Sharp attack upon his nephew Th. M., first published as a paid announcement in *Lübeckische Anzeigen*, October 1913. *See* comments by Hamecher, #1,190]

2,073. Mann, Golo. "Th. M. und die Politik: Eine Erwiderung," *Heidelberger Student*, Vol. 67, No. 3 (December 17, 1930), p. 21. [Reply to Hülsmeyer, #1,524]

2,074. ———. "Recollections of My Father," *Claremont Quarterly*, Vol. 5, No. 3 (Spring 1958), pp. 5-15. Also in German, "Ein Stück Erinnerung," *Du*, 20 (December 1960), pp. 72-76. — *Erinnerungen an meinen Vater*. Bonn: Inter Nationes, 1965. Excerpt: "Mann-Marginalien," *GQ*, 38 (November 1965), 716-718. [Cf. #2,933]

2,075. ———. "Die Intellektuellen," in his *Deutsche Geschichte des 19. und 20. Jahrhunderts*, pp. 700-718. [Frankfurt a.M.]

S. Fischer [1960] *See* esp. pp. 702-705.

2,076. ———. "Th. M.," in his *Deutsche Geschichte 1919-1945*, pp. 44-46. [Frankfurt a. M.] Fischer-Bücherei [1961]

2,077. ———. "Zuviel Publizität: Ein Brief in Sachen Th. M.-Archiv," *Stuttgarter Zeitung*, August 21, 1961. [*See also* Hommel, #1,495, and F. Martini, #2,132]

2,078. ———. "Schlusswort," in *Reden zur Eröffnung des Th. M.-Archivs*, item #2,644, pp. 24-26. Also in *Blätter der Th. M.-Gesellschaft Zürich*, No. 3 (1962), pp. 23-25.

2,079. Mann, Heinrich. "Th. M.," *Berliner Tageblatt*, November 13, 1929. Under the title "Der Nobelpreis" in his *Essays*, Vol. 1, pp. 434-437. Berlin: Aufbau, 1954. [Speech given on November 12, 1929, in 'Berliner Rundfunk']

2,080. ———. "Th. M.," in his *Das öffentliche Leben*, pp. 126-130. Berlin: Zsolnay, 1932.

2,081. ———. "Mein Bruder," in his *Ein Zeitalter wird besichtigt*, pp. 231--243. Berlin: Aufbau, 1947. [Cf. I, item #662 and #826]

2,082. ———. "Fünf Briefe an Th. M.," *Sinn und Form*, 13 (1961), 845-851.

2,083. ———. "Th. M.," in his *Briefe an Karl Lemke und Klaus Pinkus*, pp. 89, 103 et al. [Hamburg] Claassen [1963] *See also* A. Kantorowicz, item #1,655.

2,084. Mann, Julia. *Aus Dodos Kindheit: Erinnerungen*. Konstanz: Rosgarten, 1958. 79 pp. [Childhood recollections of Th. M's mother, written in 1903]

2,085. ———. "Tante Elisabeth," *Sinn und Form*, 15 (Summer 1963), 482-496. [Letter to Th. M. about Elisabeth Haug-Mann, "Tony Buddenbrook." Cf. Baukloh, item #202, and Dietzel, #679]

2,086. Mann, Katja. "Letter to Alfred A. Knopf," *Chicago Natural History Museum Bulletin*, Vol. 29, No. 5 (May 1958), pp. 4-5. [Concerns Th. M's visits to the museum and his *Felix Krull*]
———. *See also* B. von Heiseler, item #1,265.

2,087. Mann, Klaus. "Th. M.: Exile. My Father's Political Develop-
        ment," *Common Sense*, Vol. 6, No. 2 (February 1937),
        pp. 8-10.

2,088. ———. "Feierlich bewegt," *Der Ruf*, No. 14 (October 1,
 ✸   1945), p. 5. [Cf. I, item #827 — 70th birthday]

2,089. ———. "Unser Vater," *Süddeutsche Zeitung*, Vol. 11, No. 119
        (August 20/21, 1955), p. 30.

2,090. ———. *La svolta*. Milano: Il Saggiatore [1962] [Italian
        translation of I, item #664, *Der Wendepunkt*, by Barbara
        Allison]

2,091. Mann, Michael. "The Musical Symbolism in Th. M's 'Doctor
        Faustus,' " *Music Review*, 17 (November 1956), 314-322.
        Also in *Music Library Association News*, Ser. II, Vol. 14,
        No. 1 (December 1956), pp. 33-42.

2,092. ———. "Adrian Leverkühn — Repräsentant oder Antipode?"
        Neue Rundschau, 76 (Summer 1965), 202-[206] [*Doktor
        Faustus*]

2,093. ———. "Eine unbekannte 'Quelle' zu Th. M's 'Zauberberg,' "
        GRM, N. F., 15 (October 1965), 409-413.

2,094.* ———. "Vorrede," in his *Das Th. M.-Buch: Eine innere
        Biographie in Selbstzeugnissen*, pp. 9-16. Frankfurt a. M.: S.
        Fischer, 1965.

2,095. ———. "Allegorie und Parodie in Th. M's Idyll 'Herr und
        Hund,' " *Monatshefte*, 57 (December 1965-March 1966),
        [336]-342.

2,096. Mann, Monika. "Goldene Hochzeit," *Südkurier*, February
        19, 1955.

2,097. ———. "Gespräch mit einem Kind: Meinem Vater zum 80.
        Geburtstag," *Aufbau* (New York), Vol. 21, No. 22 (June 3,
        1955), pp. 35-36.

2,098. ———. "Eighty Years of Th. M.," *Saturday Review*, Vol. 38,
        No. 9 (June 4, 1955), pp. 38-40.

2,099. ———. "Porträt meines Vaters," *Frankfurter Allgemeine
        Zeitung*, Vol. 7, No. 129 (June 6, 1955), p. 8. [80th birthday]

2,100. ———. *Vergangenes und Gegenwärtiges: Erinnerungen*.
        München: Kindler [1956] 166 pp. Also in English, *Past and*

Present, transl. by Frances E. Reid and Ruth Hein. New York:
St. Martin's Press, 1960. 175 pp.
Reviews: Anon., #102 — Graf, #1,057 — Hennecke, #1,321
— Hillard, #1,392 — Hühnerfeld, #1,518 — Leibrich,
#1,891 — Morton, #2,291 — Redman, #2,647 — Weber,
#3,415.

2,101.   ———. "Th. M. in Rom," Konkret, No. 1 (January 1964),
p. 19. [About M's visit in Rome with Pope Pius XII in 1953]

2,102.   ———. "So war mein Vater wirklich," Stuttgarter Zeitung,
Vol. 18, No. 290 (December 15, 1962), p. 51.

2,103.   ———. "Streichholzlichter: Erinnerungen an den Vater,"
NDH, No. 92 (March-April, 1963), pp. 58-59.

2,104.   Mann, Otto. "Th. M.," in his Deutsche Literaturgeschichte,
pp. 504-511. [Gütersloh] Bertelsmann [1964]

2,105.* Mann, Viktor. Wir waren Fünf. Edited by Theo Plana. Berlin:
Der Morgen, 1962. 428 pp. [Gekürzte Lizenzausgabe of I,
#666]

2,106. *———. Wir waren Fünf: Bildnis der Familie Mann. Konstanz:
[Südverlag, ²1964] 618 pp. [Cf. I, #666. See #3,881]
Reviews: Attorps, #145 — Berendsohn, #260.

2,107.   Manz, Gustav. "Das schwebende Taschentuch: Th. M's
'Okkulte Erlebnisse,' " Zeit (Berlin), Morgen-Ausgabe,
December 15, 1923.

2,108.   Marcel, Gabriel. "Th. M. et Nietzsche," in item #1,493,
pp. 41-47.

2,109.   Marck, Siegfried. "Die deutsche und europäische Krise im
Spiegel des Lebenswerkes von Th. M.," in his Grosse Menschen
unserer Zeit, pp. 87-118. Meisenheim a. G.: Hain, 1954.

2,110.   ———. "Th. M.: Dichter, Denker, politischer Mensch. Zu
seinem 80. Geburtstag," Die andere Zeitung, No. 4 (June 2,
1955), p. 14.

2,111.   ———. "Th. M. als Denker," Kant-Studien, 47 (1956),
225-233. Also in English, "Th. M. as a Thinker," Ethics, 67
(October 1956), 53-57.

2,112.   Marcus, Carl David. "Nytt av Th. M.," Nya Dagligt
Allehanda, October 28, 1926. [Pariser Rechenschaft — Lübeck

als geistige Lebensform — Unordnung und frühes Leid]

2,113. Marcus, Erich. "Th. M's 'Okkulte Erlebnisse,' " *National-Zeitung Berlin,* December 13, 1923. Also *Frankfurter Zeitung,* December 17, 1923, and *Neues Wiener Journal,* December 18, 1923.

2,114. Marcus, Kersti. "Th. M.," *Tidskrift for bogvenner,* No. 1 (1956), pp. 7-9.

2,115. Marcuse, Ludwig. "Tristan: Vierter Akt; Versuch einer Huldigung," *Aufbau* (New York), Vol. 21, No. 22 (June 3, 1955), pp. 3-4. [80th birthday]

2,116. ————. "Der letzte Besuch," *Aufbau* (New York), Vol. 21, No. 33 (August 19, 1955), p. 2. [Obit.]

2,117. ————. "Th. M.," in his *Mein 20. Jahrhundert,* pp. 286-288. München: List [1960] [With a letter from Th. M., March 27, 1942]

2,118. ————. "Th. M.," in his *Aus den Papieren eines bejahrten Philosophie-Studenten,* pp. 183, 201 et al. [München] List [1964]

2,119. ————. "Th. M.," in his *Obszön: Geschichte einer Entrüstung,* pp. 51, 238 et al. München: P. List [1962]

2,120. ————. "Die graziöse Amazone: Erika Mann wird am neunten November sechzig Jahre alt," *Zeit,* No. 45 (November 9, 1965), p. 11.

2,121. Margul-Sperber, Alfred. "Prefaţa," in Th. M., *Mario si vrăjitorul.* Bucharest: Espla, 1955. [*Mario und der Zauberer*]

2,122. Marietti, Angèle. "Th. M., Gide, Rilke et Nietzsche," *RLM,* 3 (1956), 209-224; 285-462; 513-560; 737-767.

2,123. Marsman, Hendrik. "Th. M.," in his *Critische Proza,* pp. 156-163. Amsterdam: Querido, 1938. [60th birthday]

2,124. ————. "Th. M. over Europa's toekomst," *Critisch Bulletin,* 18 (November 1938), 1,295-1,297. [*Vom Zukünftigen Sieg der Demokratie*]

2,125. Martens, Kurt. "Der Tod in Venedig," *Zwiebelfisch,* Vol. 5, No. 1 (1913), pp. 62-63.

2,126. ———. "Literarischer Fall für einen Sherlock Holmes," *Stachelschwein*, No. 17 (September 1925), pp. 23-25.

2,127. ———. "Begegnung mit Th. M.," *Hamburger Fremdenblatt,* Abendausgabe No. 341 (December 9, 1929).

2,128. Martin, John S. "Circean Seduction in Three Works by Th. M.," *MLN*, 78 (1963), 346-352.

2,129. Martini, Fritz. "Th. M.," in Hans Schwerte and Wilhelm Spengler, *eds., Denker und Deuter im heutigen Europa,* pp. 113-118. Oldenburg: Stalling [1954]

2,130. ———. "Europäische Humanität aus deutscher Kultur," *Stuttgarter Nachrichten*, No. 127 (June 4, 1955), Beilage 'Querschnitt.' Also in G. Wenzel, item #3,453, pp. 56-60.

2,131. ———. "Th. M.: Der Tod in Venedig," in his *Das Wagnis der Sprache,* pp. 178-224. Stuttgart: Klee [⁴1961]

2,132. ———. "Brief an das Feuilleton: Zu 'Bodmers Erben,' " *Stuttgarter Zeitung*, August 4, 1961. [Concerns F. Hommel, item #1,495. *See also* G. Mann, item #2,077. Th. M. Archive Zurich]

2,133. ———. "Nachwort," in his *ed., Klassische Deutsche Dichtung: Wegbereiter der modernen Prosa,* pp. 600-612. Freiburg i. B.: Herder, 1965. [Concerns *Der Tod in Venedig* and *Mario und der Zauberer*]

2,134. Maruko, Shuhei. "Zwei Dritte Reiche," *Doitsu Bungaku — Die deutsche Literatur*, No. 24 (1960), pp. 8-14. [Japanese text with resumé in German. — Concerns Th. M's relations to Germany]

2,134a. ———. "Th. M.: Felix Krull," *Doitsu Bungaku — Die deutsche Literatur*, No. 30 (1963), pp. 85-95.

2,135. Marx, Erich. "Unterhaltung mit Th. M.," *Israelitisches Wochenblatt für die Schweiz*, Vol. 37, No. 11 (1937), p. 4.

2,136. Mason, Eudo C. "Th. M.," *Europa*, No. 3 (1931), pp. 9-10.

2,137. ———. "Th. M. und Rilke," *Orbis Litterarum*, Vol. 13, No. 1-2 (1958), pp. [15]-26. Also in his *Exzentrische Bahnen*, pp. 250-264. Göttingen: Vandenhoeck & Ruprecht, 1963.

2,138. Matenko, Percy. "The Prototype of Cipolla in 'Mario und der Zauberer,' " *Italica*, 31 (September 1954), 133-135.

2,139. †Mater, Erich. Th. M's Erzählung 'Das Gesetz.' Untersuchung über poetische Ausdrucksmittel. Ph. D. diss., Humboldt University, 1959. Resumé ["Autorreferat"] in *Wissenschaftliche Zeitschrift der Humboldt Universität Berlin,* 10 (1961), 121.

2,140. ————. "Zur Wortbildung und Wortbedeutung bei Th. M.," in G. Wenzel, item #3,461, pp. 141-148.

2,141. ————. "Möglichkeiten und Grenzen einer historisch-kritischen Th. M.-Ausgabe," in G. Wenzel, item #3,472, pp. 382-418.

2,142. ————. Review of K. Hamburger's *ed.* of Th. M., *Das Gesetz,* item #1,183, in G. Wenzel, item #3,472, pp. 456-458.

2,143. †Matlochóva, Lucy. Politische Kundgebungen Th. M's in Wort und Schrift. Ph. D. diss., Karls-Universität, Prague, 1957. 119 pp.

2,144. ————. "Th. M. a Leonhard Frank," *Časopis pro moderní filologii,* 40 (1958), 124-125.

2,145. ————. "Dienst an Deutschland: 'Deutsche Hörer,' " in G. Wenzel, item #3,461, 130-137.

2,146. Matsumoto, Michisuke. "Das Spielerische bei Th. M.," *Doitsu Bungaku — Die deutsche Literatur,* No. 27 (1961), pp. 79-84. [Japanese text with German resumé]

2,147. Matsuura, Kensaku. " 'Der Erwählte,' " *Doitsu Bungaku — Die deutsche Literatur,* No. 24 (1960), pp. 35-42. [Japanese text with German resumé]

2,148. ————. "Th. M's 'Doktor Faustus,' " *Doitsu Bungaku — Die deutsche Literatur,* No. 27 (1961), pp. 85-92. [Japanese text with German resumé]

2,149. ————. "Bemerkungen zu einem Satz aus Th. M's 'Joseph und seine Brüder,' " *Keisei,* No. 19 (1963), pp. 23-32. [Japanese text with German resumé]

2,150. Matter, Harry. "Mario und der Zauberer: Die Bedeutung der Novelle im Schaffen Th. M's," *Weimarer Beiträge,* 6 (1960), [579]-596.

2,151. ————. "Verzeichnis des im Gebiet der Deutschen Demokra-

tischen Republik erschienenen Schrifttums von Th. M. (1945-
1960)," in G. Wenzel, item #3,461, pp. [283]-309.

2,152. ———. "Th. M. und die Deutschen," *Weimarer Beiträge*, 4
(1963), 807-812. [Review of K. Sontheimer, item #3,097]

2,153. ———. "Das Schrifttum über Th. M. in der Deutschen
Demokratischen Republik (1960-1964)," in G. Wenzel,
item #3,472, pp. 532-627.

2,154. Matthias, Klaus. "Zu Th. M's 'Die Begegnung," *Lübeckische
Blätter*, Vol. 90, No. 2 (January 24, 1954), pp. 18-19. [*Felix
Krull*]

2,155. ———. "Th. M's Bekenntnisse des Hochstaplers Felix Krull,"
Lübeckische Blätter, Vol. 90, No. 20 (November 28, 1954),
p. 251.

2,156. †———. Die Musik bei Th. M. und Hermann Hesse: Eine
Studie über die Auffassung der Musik in der modernen
Literatur. Ph. D. diss., University of Kiel, 1956. 352 pp.

2,157. ———. "Besuch in Kilchberg: Tagebuchblätter von einem
Aufenthalt im Hause Th. M's," *Lübeckische Blätter*, Vol. 116,
No. 13 (September 2, 1956), pp. 163-165.

2,158. ———. Review of P. Scherrer, item #2,877, *Lübeckische
Blätter*, Vol. 120, No. 6 (March 19, 1960), p. 72.

2,159. ———. "Prof. Dr. Karl Kerényi über Th. M. als
Briefschreiber," *Lübeckische Blätter*, Vol. 123, No. 12 (June
8, 1963), pp. 177-178.

2,160. ———. "Aufgaben einer Th. M.-Gesellschaft in Lübeck,"
Lübeckische Blätter, Vol. 125, No. 12 (June 5, 1965),
pp. 178-180. [Concerns projected Th. M. Society in Lübeck]

2,161. ———. "Zur Erzählweise in den 'Buddenbrooks,' "
Lübeckische Blätter, Vol. 125, No. 14 (August 21, 1965),
pp. 209-217; No. 15 (September 4, 1965), pp. 240-244.

2,162. Mauner, Friederike. "Th. M.," in her *Lesen — aber was?*,
pp. 300-304. Frankfurt a. M.: Forum [1955]

2,163. Maurer, Warren R. "Names from 'The Magic Mountain,' "
Names, Vol. 9, No. 4 (December 1961), pp. 248-259.

2,164. ———. "Another View of Literary Onomastics," *Names*,

Vol. 11, No. 2 (June 1963), pp. 106-114. [Reply to
criticism by H. Kratz, item #1,787]

2,165. Mauriac, François. "Th. M. a maintenu," in item #1,493,
p. 21. [facsim.] Also in *Almanac de la Librairie Flinker,* p. 6.
[Paris, 1955]

2,166. Maurois, André. "Hommage" in item #1,493, p. 65.

2,167. Mautner, Franz H. "Th. M. über 'Tod in Venedig,' "
Monatshefte, 50 (October 1958), [256]-257. [Adds to I,
#1,962]

2,168. Mayer, Hans. "Th. M. als bürgerlicher Schriftsteller," in his
Literatur der Übergangszeit: Essays, pp. 156-163. [Berlin]
Volk und Welt [1949]

2,169. ————. "Th. M's Roman 'Doktor Faustus,' " in item #2,168,
pp. 164-176. [Cf. I, item #2790]

2,170. ————. "Echnatons Wirtschaftsminister,' *Rhein-Neckar-
Zeitung,* December 10, 1949. [*Joseph und seine Brüder*]

2,171. ————. "Th. M's Roman 'Der Zauberberg,' " *Neues Deutschland,* Vol. 8, No. 213 (September 9, 1953), p. 4.

2,172. *————. *Th. M.* [Torino] Einaudi, 1955. 356 pp. [Rev. and
enlarged *ed.* of I, item #278, transl. into Italian by Clara
Bovero]
Reviews: Bianquis, #324 — Paci, #2,476.

2,173. ————. "Leiden und Grösse Th. M's; eine Rede zum 6.
Juni 1955," *Sinn und Form,* 7 (1955), 369-386. Also in K.
Saller, item #2,833, pp. 10-22, and in Hans Mayer, *Deutsche
Literatur und Weltliteratur,* pp. 114-132. Berlin: Rütten &
Loening [1957]. Also reprinted in item #2,174.

2,174. *————. *Leiden und Grösse Th. M's; zwei Reden.* Berlin:
Aufbau, 1956. 51 pp. [Contents: Zum 80. Geburtstag. Rede
gehalten auf der Th. M.-Feier des Deutschen Kulturtages in
München. — In memoriam Th. M.: Rede gehalten auf der
Gedenkfeier der Friedrich Schiller-Universität Jena am 27.
Oktober 1955]

2,175. ————. "Th. M's 'Doktor Faustus': Roman einer Endzeit
oder Endzeit eines Romans," in his *Von Lessing bis Th. M.,*
pp. 383-403. [Pfullingen] Neske [1959]

2,176. ————. "Nachwort," in Th. M., *Mario und der Zauberer,*
pp. 75-82. Leipzig: Reclam, 1959.

2,177. ————. "Leiden und Grösse Th. M's," *Stuttgarter Zeitung,*
No. 129 (June 5, 1965). [90th birthday]

2,178. ————. " 'Verzweiflung ist mein Lebensend' . . . Zum 90.
Geburtstag Th. M's," *Tagesspiegel,* Vol. 21, No. 5,999,
(June 6, 1965) p. 4.

2,179. ————. "Th. M. nach zehn Jahren," *Hannoversche Allgemeine
Zeitung,* December 24/25, 1965, p. ix.

2,180. Mayer, Hans-Otto. "Th. M. und Max Niderlechner,"
Börsenblatt für den deutschen Buchhandel, Frankfurter
Ausgabe, 20 (June 5, 1964), 1,098-1,099.

2,181. ————. "Sammlerglück in München," *Der Junge Buchhandel,*
17 (August 14, 1964), 115-116. [Collections — Bibl.]

2,182. ————. Review of Th. M., *Reden und Aufsätze, Bücherkommentare,* 14 (November 15, 1965), 149.
See also item #504 and #2,006.

2,183. Mazzucchetti, Lavinia Jollos. "Germania, le grandi novelle,"
I Libri del Giorno, February 1927, pp. 106-108. [*Unordnung
und frühes Leid*]

2,184. ————. "Verità e poesia in 'Carlotta in Weimar' di Th. M.,"
Svizzera Italiana, No. 69 (June 1948), pp. 219-222. [*Lotte
in Weimar*]

2,185. ————. "Introduzione," in her *ed.* of Th. M., *Doctor Faustus,*
pp. [xv]-xxxvi. [Milano] Mondadori [1949]

2,186. ————. "Th. M. e il teatro," *Studi Teatrali,* No. 5 (1953),
pp. 60-68.

2,187. ————. "Introduzione," in her *ed.* of Th. M., *Novelle e
Racconti,* pp. [539]-543. [Milano] Mondadori [1953]
[*Fiorenza*]

2,188. ————. "Introduzione," in item #2,187, pp. [753]-738.
[*Königliche Hoheit*]

2,189. ————. "Perduta," in item #2,187, pp. [1,234-1,235]
["Gefallen"]

2,190. ————. "Perduta," *Nuova Antologia,* 19 (June 1955), 195-
196. ["Gefallen" — *see also* #2,189]

2,191. ———. "Introduzione," in her *ed.* of Th. M., *Carlotta a Weimar. Le Confessioni del cavaliere d'industria Felix Krull,* pp. [xv]-xxiii. [Milano] Mondadori [1955]

2,192. ———. "Ricordo di Th. M.," *Aut aut,* No. 29 (September 1955), pp. 400-401. Also in her *Novecento in Germania,* pp. 304-306. [Milano] Mondadori [1959]

2,193. ———. "Th. M. e Goethe," in her *ed.* of Th. M., *Dialogo con Goethe,* pp. xvii-xxxv. [Milano] Mondadori [1955]

2,194. ———. "L'uomo Th. M.," *Il Ponte,* 11 (June 1955), 895-898. Also in her *Novecento,* item #2,192, pp. 297-303. [80th birthday]

2,195. ———. "Per Th. M.," *Svizzera Italiana,* Vol. 15, No. 112-113 (June-August, 1955), pp. 5-6.

2,196. ———. "Th. M.," *Il Ponte,* 11 (August-September, 1955), 1,449-1,452. [Obit.]

2,197. ———. "Th. M., i medici e la medicina," *La Serpe,* 4 (December 1955), 193-200.

2,198. ———. Review of Devescovi, item #661, *Ponte,* 12 (1956), 282-284.

2,199. ———. "L'ultima messe di Th. M.," *Svizzera Italiana,* Vol. 16, No. 12 (December 1956), pp. 12-16.

2,200. ———. "Introduzione," in her *ed.* of Th. M., *Scritti Politici,* pp. [13]-14. [Milano] Mondadori [1957]

2,201. ———. "Introduzione: *Von Deutscher Republik,*" in item #2,200, p. [114]

2,202. ———. "Introduzione: *Pariser Rechenschaft,*" in item #2,200, p. [160]

2,203. ———. "Il romanziere della rivoluzione tedesca e suo fratello," in her *Novecento,* item #2,192, pp. 64-69. [Cf. I, item #967]

2,204. ———. "Incontri con Th. M.," in her *Novecento,* item #2,192, pp. 273-276.

2,205. ———. "La conversione di Th. M.: Omaggio nel suo settantesimo compleanno," in her *Novecento,* item #2,192, pp. 277-282. [Cf. I, item #1,338]

2,206.   ————. "Auguri a Th. M.," in her *Novecento,* item #2,192,
          pp. 284-287. [Cf. I, item #731]

2,207.   ————. "Il 'Doktor Faustus' di Th. M.," in her *Novecento,*
          item #2,192, pp. 288-296. [Cf. I, item #2,792-2,794]

2,208.   ————. "Der dunkle Weg, ueber den sich nicht denken
          laesst . . .," *Aut aut,* Vol. 7, No. 38 (March 1957), pp. 143-
          147. Also in her *Novecento,* item #2,192, pp. 307-315.

2,209.   ————. "Grenzgängerin zwischen Italien und Deutschland:
          Ein Leben im Dienste der deutschen Literatur," *Zeit,* No. 8
          (February 23, 1962), pp. 9-10.

2,210. *————. "Introduzione e Commentato," in her *ed.* of Th. M.,
          Lettere a italiani, pp. 9-14. [Milano] Il Saggiatore [1962?]
          See also Falqui, #837, Santarcangeli, #2,838.

2,211.   ————. "La Mostra Th. M. in Italia," *Lo Smeraldo,* Vol. 17,
          No. 1 (January 30, 1963), pp. 18-21.

2,212.   ————. "Th. M. al Forte dei Marmi," *La Provincia di Lucca,*
          Vol. 4, No. 2 (April-June, 1964), pp. 48-54.

2,213.   ————. "Geschmuggelte Freundschaften," in her *Die andere
          Achse: Italienische Resistenza und geistiges Deutschland,* pp.
          9-21. Hamburg: Claassen [1964]

2,214.   ————. "Th. M. und der Zauberer: Der deutsche Dichter war
          kein Feind Italiens," *Zeit,* No. 32 (August 6, 1965), pp. 11-12.
          [Concerns *Mario und der Zauberer.* Cf. I, item #2050,
          translated into German by Dora Mitzky]

2,215.   ————. "Th. M. und das Theater," *Sinn und Form: Sonderheft
          Th. M.,* 1965, pp. 268-277.

2,216.   Meder, Toni. "Th. M.," in *Dichter der Gegenwart,* Vol. 4,
          pp. 55-63. Bamberg: Bayer. Verlagsanstalt [1955; ²1960]

2,217.   Meidinger-Geise, Inge. "Th. M.," in her *Welterlebnis in
          deutscher Gegenwartsdichtung,* Vol. 1, pp. 104-105 et al.
          Nürnberg: Glock & Lutz, 1956. [*Doktor Faustus*]

2,218.   Meisel, James A. "A Letter from Princeton: Defence of the
          'Reflections of a Non-Political Man,' " *Partisan Review,* 6
          (February 1939), 124-125. [Letter of December 19, 1938,
          about *Betrachtungen eines Unpolitischen*]

2,219. Melchinger, Siegfried. "Th. M. postumus: *Altes und Neues*,"
        Wort und Wahrheit, 8 (October 1953), 771-773. [*Altes und
        Neues*]

2,220. ———. "Th. M's Hochstaplerroman," *Bücherkommentare*,
        Vol. 3, No. 3 (1954). Also in *Wort und Wahrheit*, Vol. 10,
        No. 1 (January 1955), pp. 62-63. [*Felix Krull*]

2,221. Menck, Clara. "Th. M's 'Doktor Faustus,' " *Schwäbische Post*,
        September 15, 1948.

2,222. ———. "Die Entstehung des Doktor Faustus," *Schwäbische
        Post*, July 13, 1949.

2,223. Mendelssohn, Peter de. "Grosses Jahr deutscher Prosa," *Sie*,
        January 25, 1948. [*Doktor Faustus*]

2,224. ———. "Tagebuch des Zauberers," *Neue Rundschau*, 66 (June
        1955), 511-517.

2,225. Mennemeier, Franz Norbert. "Glanz und Elend einer deutschen
        Freundschaft: Zu dem Briefband Th. M. an Ernst Bertram,"
        Neues Rheinland, Vol. 18 (1961), p. 47. [Review of #1,575]

2,226. Menzel, Richard. "Ein unerfüllt gebliebener Wunsch: Zur
        Erinnerung an Th. M.," *Scripta manent*, Vol. 1, No. 2 (1957),
        pp. 15-18. [With three letters from Th. M.]

2,227. Mercanton, Jacques. "Th. M.," *Suisse Contemporaine*, No. 7
        (July 1944), pp. 595-609. [Cf. I, item #1,199]

2,228. ———. "Les tables de la loi," *Labyrinthe*, November 15, 1944.
        [Cf. I, item #1,199, concerning Th. M's *Das Gesetz*]

2,229. ———. "Charlotte à Weimar," *Lettres*, Vol. 4, No. 1
        (January 1946), pp. 83-89. [Cf. I, item #1,199, concerning
        Th. M's *Lotte in Weimar*]

2,230. ———. "A propos de Th. M.," *Journal de Genève*, No. 279
        (November 29, 1953.).

2,231. ———. "Le Frédéric-le-Grand de Th. M.," *Gazette Littéraire:
        Gazette de Lausanne*, August 22, 1954.

2,232. ———. "Th. M.," *Gazette Littéraire: Gazette de Lausanne*,
        June 4, 1955. [80th birthday]

2,233. ———. "Préface," in Th. M., *La Montagne Magique*, pp.
        vii-xiii. Lausanne: Guilde du Livre [1956]

2,234.   ———. "Th. M.," *La Nouvelle Nouvelle Revue Française*, 4 (February 1, 1956), [308]-314. Also in G. Wenzel, item #3,453, pp. 73-78. German translation by Elise Schaulz in G. Wenzel, item #3,461, pp. 36-40.

2,235.   ———. "Th. M. in seinen Briefen," *Sinn und Form: Sonderheft Th. M.*, 1965, pp. 379-387. [Translated from French by Christel Gersch]

2,236.   Merian-Genast, Ernst. "Th. M. als Meister des Stils," *Du*, Vol. 15, No. 6 (June 1955), pp. 60, 64.

2,237.   Mertens, Gerard M. "Hemingway's 'Old Man and the Sea' and Mann's 'The Black Swan,' " *Literature and Psychology*, Vol. 6, No. 3 (August 1956), pp. 96-99. [*Die Betrogene*]

2,238.   Messer, Max. "Th. M's 'Tristan,' " *Zeit* (Berlin), No. 446 (April 18, 1903).

2,239.   *Metzler, Ilse. *Dämonie und Humanismus: Funktion und Bedeutung der Zeitblomgestalt in Th. M's Doktor Faustus.* Essen: Rohden, 1960. 99 pp. [Ph. D. diss., Munich] Reviews: Hellmann, item #1,295.

2,240.   Meyer, Agnes E. "He helped us to find our way," *Aufbau* (New York), Vol. 21, No. 33 (August 19, 1955), p. 2. [Obit.]

2,241.   ———. "Mann and His Heritage," *Washington Post*, February 15, 1959, p. E 7. [*Last Essays*]

2,242.   †Meyer, Gerhard. Untersuchungen zur Darstellung und Deutung des Todes im Frühwerk Th. M's. Ph. D. diss., University of Tuebingen, 1957.

2,243.   Meyer, Helge. "Hos Th. M.," *Nationaltidende*, November 16, 1921. [Biog.]

2,244.   Meyer, Herman. "Th. M's 'Buddenbrooks,' " in his *Der Typus des Sonderlings in der deutschen Literatur*, pp. 224-226. Amsterdam: H. J. Paris, 1943. Also in his *Der Sonderling in der deutschen Literatur*, pp. 292-294. München: Hanser [1963]

2,245.   ———. "Integrative Zitierkunst in 'Lotte in Weimar,' " in Curt von Faber du Faur et al., ed., *Wächter und Hüter: Festschrift für Hermann J. Weigand*, pp. 133-146. New Haven: Yale University, 1957.

2,246.   ———. "Th. M's 'Der Zauberberg' und 'Lotte in Weimar,' "
         in his *Das Zitat in der Erzählkunst,* pp. 207-245 et al. Stuttgart:
         Metzler [1961] [With comments on G. Lange, #1,846]

2,247.   ———. "Zum Problem der epischen Integration," in his
         Zarte Empirie, pp. 12-32. Stuttgart: Metzler, 1963, [*See* esp.
         pp. 21-32 on *Der Zauberberg.* Cf. I, item #2,308]

2,248.   Meyer, Oscar. "Antwort an Max Barth: Der Angriff auf
         Th. M. war zu scharf," *Neue Volkszeitung,* Vol. 15, No. 39
         (September 1945), p. 6. [Concerns item #184 — Th. M.
         as an emigré]

2,249.   Meyer-Benfey, Heinrich. "Th. M.," in his *Welt der Dichtung,*
         pp. 356-365. Hamburg: Deutscher Literatur-Verlag [1962]
         [Cf. I, item #283]

2,250.   ———. "Th. M. und das Künstlerproblem," in item #2,249,
         pp. 366-373. Also in Grosser, item #1,090, pp. 110-120.
         [Cf. I, item #1,069, review of W. Alberts, I, #99]

2,251.   ———. "Th. M. als Idyllendichter," in item #2,249, pp.
         374-378. [Cf. I, item #1,989 — *Herr und Hund — Gesang
         vom Kindchen*]

2,252.   Michael, Friedrich. "Th. M's Idyllen," *Berliner Tageblatt,*
         December 12, 1919. [*Herr und Hund — Gesang vom
         Kindchen*]

2,253.   ———. "Th. M's Othello," *Berliner Tageblatt,* December 6,
         1921. ["Versuch über das Theater"]

2,254.   Michael, Wolfgang. "Stoff und Idee im 'Tod in Venedig,' "
         DVJS, 33 (April 1959), [13]-19.

2,255.   ———. "Th. M. und Rilke," *Archiv,* 202 (August 1965),
         112-114.

2,256.   Milch, Werner. "Th. M's Doktor Faustus," *Neue Schau,* 1948,
         pp. 52-53. Also expanded version in his *Kleine Schriften zur
         Literatur- und Geistesgeschichte,* pp. [229]-240. Heidelberg:
         L. Schneider, 1957. [Cf. I, item #2,798]

2,257.   Mileck, Joseph. "A Comparative Study of 'Die Betrogene' and
         'Der Tod in Venedig,' " *MLF,* 42 (December 1957), 124-129.

2,258. Mille, Pierre. "Un romancier allemand contre la démocratie," *Courrier des Etats Unis,* June 5, 1920. [Concerns *Betrachtungen eines Unpolitischen.* Cf. I, item #1,536]

2,259. Miller, Edwin H. "A Tribute to Th. M.: 1875-1955," *Simmons Review,* 38 (Fall 1955), 9-12. [Obit.]

2,260.* Miller, Raymond D. *The Two Faces of Hermes: A Study of Th. M's Novel The Magic Mountain.* Harrogate: Duchy Press, 1962. 124 pp.
Reviews: Hellmann, #1,305.

2,261. Minskers, Irene. Review of K. Hamburger, I, item #2,450, *MLR,* 42 (1947), 533-535.

2,262. ———. Review of H. A. Maier, I, item #963, *MLR,* 44 (1949), 137-141.

2,263. Minssen, Friedrich. "Th. M. als Politiker," *Frankfurter Rundschau,* Vol. 6, No. 22 (January 26, 1950), p. 5. [Concerns radio lecture by Alfred Andersch]

2,264. ———. "Th. M.," *Frankfurter Hefte,* 2 (September 1957), 953-957. [Politics]

2,265. Missenharter, Hermann. "Die Frau von 50 Jahren," *Stuttgarter Nachrichten,* November 28, 1953. [*Die Betrogene*]

2,266. ———. "Ein Hochstapler namens Krull," *Stuttgarter Nachrichten,* No. 242 (October 16, 1954), p. 16. [*Felix Krull*]

2,267. ———. "Ein wahrer Deutscher und grosser Europäer: Zu Th. M's Tod," *Stuttgarter Nachrichten,* August 15, 1955. [Obit.]

2,268. Mittenzwei, Johannes. "Die Beziehungen zwischen Musik und bürgerlicher Dekadenz in den Werken Th. M's," in his *Das Musikalische in der Literatur,* pp. 314-[367] Halle/Saale: Verlag Sprache und Literatur, 1962.

2,269. Mittner, Ladislao. "L'ottica doppia di Th. M. e la doppia condanna del mondo di ieri," in his *La Letteratura tedesca del novecento e altri saggi,* pp. 168-176. [Torino] Einaudi, 1960.

2,270. ———. "Th. M., decadente longevo," in item #2,269, pp. 210-221.

2,271. Moe, Ole Henrik. "Det musikalske i Th. M's verk," in item #2,431, pp. 26-44.

2,272. Möck, Helmut. "Th. M's Schülerzeitschrift," *Eulenspiegel: Zeitschrift des Gymnasiums Gernsheim/Rhein,* Vol. 10, No. 40 (October 1962), pp. 94-102.

2,273. Moeller, Charles. "Un grand disparu: Th. M.," *Revue Nouvelle,* No. 15 (1955), pp. 353-357. [Obit.]

2,274. Möller, Hanns. "Nationalsozialismus," *Hamburgischer Correspondent,* November 9, 1930. [*Deutsche Ansprache*]

2,275. Møller, Kai Fritz. "Th. M's store tema," in item #2,431, pp. 154-160.

2,276. Mönch, Walter. "Th. M.," in his *Deutsche Kultur von den Anfängen bis zur Gegenwart,* pp. 338-341 et al. München: Hueber, 1962. [Th. M. and Richard Wagner]

2,277. Moering, Ernst. "Th. M.: Mensch und Werk," *Anstösse,* 1957, pp. 163-166.

2,278. Molander, Michael. "Th. M. und die kleine Koalition," *Wochenpost Stuttgart,* March 9, 1947.

2,279. Molo, Walter von. "Offener Brief an Th. M.," *Hessische Post,* August 4, 1945, also *Münchner Zeitung,* August 13, 1945, and *NDL,* Vol. 3, No. 10 (October 1955), pp. 45-46. Reprinted in his *Zwischen Tag und Traum,* pp. 329-333. Berlin: E. Schmidt, 1950. Also in Grosser, item #1,090, pp. 18-21. The complete correspondence also appears under the title "Briefwechsel mit Th. M. über innere und äussere Emigration" in his *So wunderbar ist das Leben,* pp. 404-420. Stuttgart: Deutsche Volksbücherei [1957] [Cf. I, item #1,439 — Th. M. as an emigré]

2,280. Mondadori, Alberto. "Addio Tommy," *Epoca,* August 21, 1955. [Obit.]

2,281. Monecke, Wolfgang. "Brief an Frank Thiess vom 7. Januar 1946," in Grosser, item #1,090, pp. 88-91.

2,282. Montanelli, Indro. "Mann fa a se uno scherzo di cattivo genere," *Corriere della Sera,* Vol. 78, No. 273 (November 20, 1948), p. 3. [*Betrachtungen eines Unpolitischen*]

2,283. Morikawa, Toshio. "Über den Parallelismus im 'Doktor Faustus,' " *Fundo,* No. 1 (1953), pp. 34-40. [In Japanese]

2,284.   ————. "Über 'Doktor Faustus' und den Begriff der
Errettung," *Doitsu Bungaku — Die deutsche Literatur*, No. 12
(1954), pp. 37-41. [In Japanese]

2,285.   Morita, Hiroshi. "Eine Perspektive über Th. M.," *Doitsu
Bungaku — Die deutsche Literatur*, No. 24 (1960), pp. 3-8.
[Japanese text with German resumé]

2,286.   Morse, J. Mitchell. "The Artist as Savior," *MFS*, 5 (Summer
1959), 103-107. [Concerns portraits of artists by Joyce, Proust,
Mann and Kafka]

2,287.   ————. "Joyce and the Early Th. M.," *RLC*, 36 (July-
September 1962), [377]-385.

2,288.   Morton, Frederic. "A Talk with Th. M. at Eighty," *NYT Book
Review*, June 5, 1955, pp. 6, 32. [80th birthday]

2,289.   ————. "Th. M. at Eighty: Still the Adventurer," *Nation* (New
York), 180 (June 11, 1955), 504-505.

2,290.   ————. "Th. M's Farewell," *Atlantic Monthly*, Vol. 196,
No. 4 (October 1955), pp. 76-78. [*Felix Krull*]

2,291.   ————. "The Story of an Artist in Society," *NYT Book
Review*, October 2, 1960, p. 10. [Review of *A Sketch of my
Life*, Th. M, *Letters to Paul Amann*, item #3,426, and Monika
Mann, item #2,100]

2,292.   ————. "Behind the Scenes with Doctor Mann and 'Doctor
Faustus,' " *NYT Book Review*, August 27, 1961, p. 6. [*The
Story of a Novel — Die Entstehung des Doktor Faustus*]

2,293.   Moschner, Manfred. "Der füllig gewordene Hochstapler,"
Tag, October 10, 1954. [*Felix Krull*]

2,294.   Moschytz, Norbert J. "Hofrat Behrens," in H. Saueressig,
item #2,844, pp. 57-63. [Cf. I, item #2,310]

2,295.   Moseley, Edwin M. "Th. M.," in his *Pseudonyms of Christ in
the Modern Novel*, pp. 82-83 et al. Pittsburgh: University of
Pittsburgh Press [1962]

2,296.   Motylowa, Tamara. "Leo Tolstoi und die deutsche Literatur,"
Kunst und Literatur, 8 (November 1960), 1,108-1,115.

2,297.   ————. "Th. M.," *Novyi Mir*, No. 2 (1962), pp. 227-242.

2,298.   ————. "Th. M.," *Novyi Mir*, No. 7 (July 1963). German
translation, "Neues über Th. M.," by Antja Winkler, *Kunst*

und Literatur, 11 (December 1963), 1,308-1,315. [Review
of *Briefe I,* item# 2,062]

2,299. ———. "Th. M. und die Erneuerung des Realismus," *Sinn und
Form: Sonderheft Th. M.,* 1965, pp. 123-133. Translated
from Russian by Gudrun Düwel.

2,300. Muckermann, Friedrich. "Trau, schau, wem . . .," *Gral,* 21
(July 1927), [603]-607. [Concerns Th. M. and H. G.
Scheffauer, 'Romane der Welt']

2,300a. Mühlberger, Josef. "Th. M's 'Doktor Faustus,' " *Welt und
Wort,* No. 5-6 (May-June 1949), pp. 177-178.

2,301. ———. "Spiegel unserer Epoche," *Neue Württembergische
Zeitung,* September 17, 1949. [*Doktor Faustus*]

2,302. ———. "Th. M. in der Sackgasse," *Rhein-Neckar-Zeitung,*
May 20, 1951. [*Der Erwählte*]

2,303. ———. "Westlich-östliches Welttheater," *Neue Württembergische Zeitung,* November 21, 1952. Also *Neue liter. Welt,*
Vol. 4, No. 53 (1953), p. 6. [*Joseph und seine Brüder*]

2,304. ———. "Summe eines halben Jahrhunderts," *Schwäbische
Donauzeitung,* April 22, 1953. [*Altes und Neues*]

2,305. ———. "Absurde Verzauberung," *Neue Württembergische
Zeitung,* September 17, 1953. [*Die Betrogene*]

2,306. ———. "Th. M's Joseph-Romane," *Welt und Wort,* 10
(June 1955), 181-182.

2,307. ———. "Th. M. über Schiller," *Neue Württembergische
Zeitung,* June 30, 1955. Also in *Welt und Wort,* 10 (1955),
269. [*Versuch über Schiller*]

2,308. ———. "Das Mythische im modernen Roman. Ein Briefwechsel
zwischen Th. M. und K. Kerényi," *Rhein-Neckar-Zeitung,*
August 26, 1960. [Review of item #1,700c]

2,309. *Müller, Fred. Th. M's literarhistorische Essays. Ph. D. diss.,
University of Hamburg, 1963. [Published "im Selbstverlag" in
1964]

2,310. Müller, Herbert. "Humanism of Th. M.," *SAQ,* 36 (1937),
302-313.

2,311. Müller, Joachim. "Laudatio für Th. M.," *Greifenalmanach
1958,* pp. 275-[285] [Jena, 1958] [Tribute to Th. M. —

"Ehrenpromotion," University of Jena, May 15, 1955]

2,312. ————. Reviews of R. Faesi, item #831, and R. Hinton Thomas, item #3,273, *DLZ*, 79 (1958), 222-230.

2,313. ————. "Th. M's 'Doktor Faustus': Grundthematik und Motivgefüge," *Euphorion*, N. F., Vol. 54, No. 3 (1960), [262]-280.

2,314. ————. "Glücksspiel und Göttermythe: Zu Th. M's 'Krull,' " *Sinn und Form*, 12 (1960), 463-478. Reprinted in G. Wenzel, item #3,461, pp. 233-249.

2,315. ————. "Faust und Faustus — Th. M's Roman und Goethes Tragödie," *Universitas*, 16 (July 1961), 731-743.

2,316. ————. "Th. M. über Adalbert Stifter," in *Adalbert-Stifter-Institut des Landes Oberösterreich*, Vol. 12, No. 1-2 (1963), pp. 60-63.

2,317. ————. "Th. M's Sinfonia Domestica," *ZDP*, 83 (1964) 142-170. [*Herr und Hund — Gesang vom Kindchen — Unordnung und frühes Leid*]

2,318. ————. "Hermann Hesse und Th. M.: Ihr Lebenswerk, ihre Begegnung und ihre Verwandtschaft," *Universitas*, 19 (November 1964), 1,157-1,168.

2,319. Müller, Robert. "Th. M.," in his *Europäische Wege: Im Kampf um den Typus*, pp. [22]-39. Berlin: S. Fischer, 1917. [*Der Tod in Venedig*]

2,320. Müller-Blattau, Joseph. "Richard Wagner in unserer Zeit," *Universitas*, 18 (March 1963), 281-291. [*See* esp. pp. 282-283]

2,321. ————. "Die Musik in Th. M's 'Doktor Faustus' und Hermann Hesses 'Glasperlenspiel,' " in his *Von der Vielfalt der Musik*, pp. 337-350. Freiburg i. Br.: Rombach, 1966. [Cf. I, item #1,157]

2,322. Müller-Freienfels, Richard. "Th. M.," in his *Die Vögel der deutschen Dichter* [by Sebastian Segelfalter, pseud.] pp. 88-90. Berlin: Herbig [1947]

2,323. Müller-Graefe, Rudolf. "Ich porträtierte Th. M.," *Hamburger Abendblatt*, No. 110 (May 12, 1955), p. 7.

2,324. Müller-Seidel, Walter. Review of R. Baumgart, item #204, *Germanistik*, 6 (April 1965), 343-344.

2,325.   Muir, Edwin. "The Last Laugh: Confessions of Felix Krull,
         Confidence Man," *Observer*, October 30, 1955.

2,326.   ———. "Bourgeois and Artist," *New Statesman*, 55 (April
         26, 1958), 536-537. [Concerns *Buddenbrooks* and Erika
         Mann, #2,059]

2,327.   Mulisch, Harry. "Über gesunden Menschenverstand, Christen
         und Th. M.," in his *Strafsache 40/61: Eine Reportage*, pp. 153-
         160. Köln: DuMont Schauberg [1963]

2,328.   Mundt, Carlo G. "Im Namen von Th. M.: Pankows kulturelle
         und wirtschaftliche Aktivität in Italien," *Rheinischer Merkur*,
         No. 18 (April 29, 1960). [Concerns East German 'Centro
         Th. M.' in Rome]

2,329.   ———. "Th. M. als roter Sturmbock: Kulturkampf Bonn-
         Pankow auf italienischem Boden," *Stuttgarter Nachrichten*,
         No. 145 (June 28, 1961), p. 8. ['Centro Th. M.' in Rome]

2,330.   Munk Nielsen, C. A. "Eyvind Johnson und Th. M.," *Orbis
         Litterarum*, Vol. 13, No. 1-2 (1958), pp. 27-43.

2,331.   Munteanu, R. "Corespondenţa lui Th. M.," *Gazeta Literară*,
         No. 8 (February 21, 1963), p. 8. [Review of *Briefe II*, item
         #2,066]

2,332.   Munz, Peter. "Th. M.," *Landfall*, Vol. 10, No. 37 (March
         1956), pp. 23-32.

2,333.   Murata, Tsunekazu. "Th. M's Wille zur Harmonie,"
         *Forschungsbericht der Philosophischen Fakultät der Gakushuin
         Universität*, No. 4 (1957), pp. 251-344. [In Japanese]

2,334.   ———. "Das Problem der Schönheit beim frühen Th. M.,"
         Japanische Gesellschaft für Germanistik, Bericht 1955/56,
         (1957), pp. 32-34. [In Japanese]

2,335.   ———. "Th. M. und Storm," *Monatsbericht für die
         ausgewählten Werke Storms*, No. 6 (1959), pp. 1-2.
         [In Japanese]

2,336.   ———. "Eine neue Seite des frühen Th. M.: 'Gefallen' und
         'Wälsungenblut,' " *Forschungsbericht der Gesellschaft für
         Germanistik in der Städtischen Universität Tokio*, No. 2
         (1959), pp. 11-18. [In Japanese]

2,337. ———. "Th. M. contra Italien," *Studi Italici* (Kyoto), No. 8 (1959), pp. 47-57. [In Japanese]

2,338. ———. "Th. M. in Japan; eine bibliographische Studie," *Doitsu Bungaku — Die deutsche Literatur*, No. 24 (1960), pp. 48-56. [In German]

2,339. ———. "Unordnung und frühes Leid," in Japanese *ed.* of Th. M., *Unordnung und frühes Leid*, pp. 59-86. Tokyo: Ikbundo-Verlag, 1960. [In Japanese]

2,340. ———, [and] Keiji Ihara. "Erläuterung zu 'Wälsungenblut,' " in Japanese *ed.* of Th. M., *Wälsungenblut*, pp. 51-65. Tokyo: Sanshusha-Verlag, 1961. [In Japanese]

2,341. ———. "Verzeichnis der Literatur über Th. M. und Übersetzungen seiner Werke in Japan," *Forschungsbericht der Philosophischen Fakultät der Gakushuin Universität*, No. 7 (1961), pp. 169-193; No. 8 (1962), pp. 343-369; No. 9 (1963), pp. 121-158. [In Japanese — Bibliog.]

2,342. Muret, Maurice. "Les 'Buddenbrooks' par M. Th. M.," *Journal des Débats*, March 24, 1908. Also in his *La littérature allemande d'aujourd'hui*, pp. [213]-219. Lausanne: Payot, 1909.

2,343. ———. "Altesse Royale," *Journal des Débats*, May 7, 1910.

2,344. ———. "M. Th. M., auteur de nouvelles," *Journal des Débats*, December 3, 1913.

2,345. ———. "Ecrivain en exil: Les variations de M. Th. M.," *L'Allemagne Contemporaine*, March 20, 1937.

2,346. ———. "Le témoignage allemand de M. Th. M.," *Revue des Deux Mondes*, No. 21 (1950), pp. 137-152.

2,347. Murphy, James, [and] Th. M. "The Cultural Mission of the Middle Class: A Tea Table Dialogue at the Home of Th. M. in Munich," *International Forum*, Vol. 1, No. 2 (February 15, 1956), pp. 5-8.

2,348. Musa, Gilda. "Il cavaliere d'industria," *La Fiera Letteraria*, Vol. 19, No. 4 (January 26, 1964), pp. 4, 6. [*Felix Krull*]

2,349. Muschg, Walter. "Th. M.," in his *Tragische Literaturgeschichte*, pp. 425-426 et al. Bern: Francke [²1953] [In third rev. ed., 1957, pp. 402-404 et al.] Excerpted under the title "Th. M.

oder der Sieg des Literaten," *Domino,* No. 1 (November 1953), pp. 14-15. [Cf. I, item #449]. *See also* Laaths, item #1,830, and Malmberg, item #2,048.

2,350. Musil, Robert. "Brief an Klaus Pinkus vom 14. September 1934," in his *Prosa, Dramen, Späte Briefe,* pp. 737-738. Hamburg: Rowohlt [1957]

2,351. Muster, Wilhelm. "Th. M.," *Arbor,* 33 (1956), [382]-397. [Spanish translation of German original by Francisco de A. Caballero]

2,352. McClain, William H. Review of J. M. Lindsay, item #1,971, *MLN,* 71 (March 1956), 236-238.

2,353. ————. "Penetrating Essays by Th. M.," *Baltimore Sunday Sun,* February 22, 1959. [*Last Essays*]

2,354. ————. "Ein unveröffentlichter Th. M.-Brief über den 'Erwählten,' " *Monatshefte,* 54 (January 1962), 9-10.

2,355. ————. "Wagnerian Overtones in 'Der Tod in Venedig,' " *MLN,* 79 (December 1964), 481-495.

2,356. McLean, Helen V. "Freud and Literature," *Saturday Review of Literature,* Vol. 18, No. 19 (September 3, 1938), pp. 18-19. [Review of *The Basic Writings of Sigmund Freud,* deals in part with Th. M's *Death in Venice* and *The Magic Mountain*]

2,357. McNamara, Eugene. " 'Death in Venice': The Disguised Self," *College English,* 24 (1962), 233-234.

2,358. †McWilliams, James R. Th. M's Heroes: Their Guilt and its Significance. Ph. D. diss., University of California, Berkeley, 1964.

2,359. Nadler, Käte. "Musik als Symbol der Menschenliebe oder der Menschenverachtung," in her *Hermann Hesse: Naturliebe, Menschenliebe, Gottesliebe,* pp. 109-136. Leipzig: Koehler & Amelang, 1956. [Concerns *Der Steppenwolf* and *Doktor Faustus*]

2,360. Nádor, György. "A Goethe-imitáció szerepe Th. M. életmüvében," *Világirodalmi Figyelö,* 1960, pp. 14-44. [Concerns "Die Rolle der Goethe-Imitation im Lebenswerk Th. M's."]

2,361. Nagahashi, Fumiko. "Die 'Leistungs'-Ethik bei Th. M.,"
Doitsu Bungaku — Die deutsche Literatur, No. 15 (1955),
pp. 45-50. [In Japanese]

2,362. Nagano, Fujio. "Th. M's Humanismus," *Seiki,* No. 39 (1952),
pp. 32-36. [In Japanese]

2,363. Nagel, Ivan. "Th. M.: Zum 80. Geburtstag eines grossen
Deutschen," *Tages-Anzeiger,* No. 128 (June 4, 1955), p. 5.

2,364. Nakada, Hoshiki. "Th. M. zum Gedächtnis," *Doitsu Bungaku
— Die deutsche Literatur,* No. 15 (1955). [Obit.]

2,365. Nalkowska, Zofja. "Szczęście," *Wiadomósci Literackie,* No. 11
(March 13, 1927).

2,366. Natonek, Hans. "Dichter an der Propagandafront: Offener
Brief an Th. M.," *Neue Leipziger Zeitung,* October 27, 1929.

2,367. Naumann, Heinrich. "Kolbenheyer und Th. M.," *Bauhütten-
brief,* Vol. 5, No. 13 (1959), pp. 14-15.

2,368. Nebel, Gerhard. "Th. M. zu seinem 75. Geburtstag," *Frankfurter Allgemeine Zeitung,* June 6, 1950.

2,369. Necco, Giovanni. "L'ultimo Th. M.," *Mondo Occidentale,*
1950, pp. 54-60.

2,370. ———. "Th. M. ci confessa," *Il Messaggero,* May, 1953, p. 3.
[Interv.]

2,371. ———. "Gli ottant'anni di Th. M.," *Il Messaggero,* June 6,
1955, p. 3. [80th birthday]

2,372. ———. "Th. M. in italiano," *Gazzetta del Mezzogiorno,*
Vol. 69, No. 76 (March 16, 1956), p. 4. [*Le Opere di Th. M.,*
Vols. 4 and 5]

2,373. Neckels, Conrad. "Th. M's Geburtstagsfeier in seiner
Vaterstadt," *Vaterstädtische Blätter,* No. 20 (June 20, 1926),
p. 81 [51st birthday]

2,374. ———. "Th. M. und Lübeck," *Vaterstädtische Blätter,* No. 19
(June 7, 1925), p. [73]

2,375. ———. "Tony Buddenbrook und ihr Grossvater," *Lübecker
Nachrichten,* Vol. 4, No. 56 (May 14, 1949), p. 9. [Biog. —
Johann Heinrich Marty]

2,376. ———. "Das Buddenbrookhaus ersteht wieder," *Lübecker
Nachrichten,* Vol. 12, No. 122 (May 26, 1957), p. 17.

2,377. Neider, Charles. "Speaking of Books: Th. M. Recalled," *New York Times Book Review,* August 8, 1965, p. 2. [Biog. — 10th anniversary of death]

2,378. Nelke, Jorge. "A la sombra de 'La Montaña Encantada,' " *Nosotros,* 1930, pp. [400]-403.

2,379. Nemerov, Howard. "Th. M's Faust Novel," *Graduate Journal,* 3 (Fall 1960), 205-217. Also in his *Poetry and Fiction: Essays,* pp. 303-315. New Brunswick, N. J.: Rutgers University Press [1963] [*Doktor Faustus*]

2,380. ————. "Themes and Methods: The Early Stories of Th. M.," *Carleton Miscellany,* Vol. 2, No. 1 (Winter 1961), pp. 3-20. Also in his *Poetry and Fiction,* item #2,379, pp. 288-302.

2,381. Nemo, Koribian. "Th. M. achtzig Jahre alt," *Weltbühne,* 10 (June 8, 1955), 719-723.

2,382. ————. "Nachruf für Th. M.," *Weltbühne,* 10 (August 24, 1955), 1,068-1,071. [Obit.]

2,383. Nerman, Ture. "Hilsen fra Sveriges författareförening; til Th. M. på 80 årsdagen," in item #2,431, p. 164 [80th birthday]

2,384. Nette, Herbert. "Th. M. — Emil Barth: Ein stilkritischer Vergleich," *Du,* Vol. 21, No. 8 (August 1961), pp. 53-54. Also in *NDH,* No. 87 (May-June 1962), pp. 98-105. [Comparison of some pages in *Die Betrogene* and Barth's autobiographical novel *Der Wandelstern*]

2,385. Neumann, Alfred. "Ein Brief . . . an Th. M. über 'Doktor Faustus,' " *Schweizer Bücher-Zeitung,* Vol. 13, No. 9 (September 1955), pp. 110-111.

2,386. Neumann, Erich. "Die Entstehung des Th. M.-Archivs der Deutschen Akademie der Wissenschaften zu Berlin," *Wissenschaftliche Annalen,* 5 (September 1956), 695-701. [With Th. M's letters to Erich Neumann]

2,387. ————, [and] Georg Wenzel. "Lebenszeugnisse Th. M's: Zur Übernahme der Scheyer-Stiftung ins Th. M.-Archiv," *Spektrum,* 7 (1961), 266-270.

2,388. ————. " 'Zufallserzeugnisse': Ein Überblick über Th. M's Beteiligung an Zeitungs-Umfragen und ähnlichen Veranstaltungen," *Spektrum,* Vol. 11, No. 5 (1965), pp. 178-186.

2,389.   ————, Hans Bürgin, [and] Walter A. Reichart. "Das Werk Th. M's" (1957-1964), in item #3,472, pp. 491-510.

2,390.   Neumann, Felix. "Eine Jugenderinnerung: Mit Th. M. auf der Schulbank," *Der Bund; der kleine Bund,* Vol. 106, No. 266 (June 10, 1955), p. 7. [Cf. I, item #675]

2,391.   Neumann, Gerty. "Th. M.: Die Sehnsucht nach Deutschland ist die Sehnsucht nach der Vergangenheit," *Neues Politisches Volksblatt,* January 29, 1935, p. 4. [Interview]

2,392.   ————. "Am 61. Geburtstag in Budapest," *Neues Politisches Volksblatt,* June 9, 1936, p. 5. [Interview]

2,393.   Neumann, Robert. "Der Sturz: Nach Th. M.," in his *Mit fremden Federn,* pp. 16-17. Stuttgart: J. Engelhorn, 1928. Also in his *Die Parodien,* p. 27. Wien: Desch [1962]

2,394.   ————. "Der neue Hamlet: Nach Th. M.," in his *Mit fremden Federn,* item #2,393, pp. 22-23. Also in his *Die Parodien,* item #2,393, pp. 31-32.

2,395.   ————. "Die Entstehung: Nach Th. M.," in his *Die Parodien,* item #2,393, pp. 326-327.

2,396.   ————. "Goethe hat ihn gelobt: Nach Dr. Jonas Lesser. Nach Dr. Paul Fechter. Nach Dr. Th. M.," in his *Die Parodien,* item #2,393, pp. 365-[370]

2,397.   ————. "Th. M.," in his *Ein leichtes Leben,* pp. 57, 65 et al. München: Desch, 1963.

2,398.   Neumeister, Heddy. "Die Spur des Dichters Th. M. im Werke K. Kerényis," *Frankfurter Allgemeine Zeitung,* Vol. 16, No. 39 (February 15, 1964). [Concerns Kerényi's *Tessiner Schreibtisch,* item #1700d]

2,399.   †Neumeyer, Peter F. The Modern German Novel in England: With Special Emphasis on the Work of Franz Kafka and Th. M. Ph. D. diss., University of California, Berkeley, 1963. 441 pp.

2,400.   Newman, Ernest. "Doktor Faustus," *Sunday Times,* May 15, 1949. [Part II, adds to I, item #2,804]

2,401.   ————. "A Schönberg Comedy," *Sunday Times,* June 12, 1949.

2,402.   Newton, Caroline. "Foreword," in item #3,275, pp. [4]-5.

2,403. ———. "Introductory Remarks," in item #3,275, pp. 8-11.
2,404. ———. "The Th. M. I Know," *Bryn Mawr Alumnae Bulletin,* Vol. 27, No. 1 (Fall 1956), p. 5.
2,405. ———. "Th. M. and Sigmund Freud," *Princeton University Library Chronicle,* 24 (Winter 1963), 135-139.
2,406. ———. "Th. M. and the Mann Commemorations," in item #3,276, pp. 34-[37]
2,407. *Nicholls, Roger Archibald. *Nietzsche in the Early Works of Th. M.* Berkeley: University of California Press, 1955. 119 pp. [Ph. D. diss., Cf. I, item #2,994] Reviews: Genschmer, #986 — Hatfield, #1,217 — Itschert, #1,548 — Leppmann, #1,924 — Politzer, #2,578.
2,408. ———. Review of J. M. Lindsay, item #1,971, *Modern Philology,* 54 (November 1956), 143-144.
2,409. ———. Review of A. Hellersberg, item #1,285, *Modern Philology,* 58 (February 1961), 224-225.
2,410. Nicolson, Harold. "Th. M. and the Nazis," *Daily Telegraph,* November 17, 1933. [Review of Cleugh, I, item #148]
2,411. ———. "Tribute to Th. M.," *Listener,* 43 (June 15, 1950), 1,025-1,026. [75th birthday]
2,412. ———. "Tonio Kröger," *Observer,* December 19, 1954, p. 11. [Review of J. M. Lindsay, item #1,971]
2,413. ———. "Th. M.," *Neue Rundschau,* 66 (June 1955), 508-510. [80th birthday]
2,413a. Niderlechner, Max. Review of Bürgin-Mayer, #504, *Börsenblatt für den Deutschen Buchhandel,* Vol. 22, No. 33 (April 26, 1966), Aus dem Antiquariat, pp. 845-846.
2,414. Niekisch, Ernst. "Th. M.," in his *Das Reich der niederen Dämonen,* pp. 60-63. Hamburg: Rowohlt [1953] [Politics]
2,415. Nielsen, Harald. "Th. M.," in his *Moderna litteratur; kritiske skitser,* Vol. 2, pp. [70]-108. Copenhagen: H. Aschenhoug, 1923.
2,416. Nielsen, Marion L. "Th. M.," *Intermountain Review,* Vol. 2, No. 3 (1938).
2,417. Niemöller, Martin. "Th. M. und die Deutschen," *Aufbau* (New York), Vol. 21, No. 33 (August 19, 1955), p. 2.

[Obit.]

Nils, Maria, *see* Nadja Jollos.

2,418. Nilsen, Jan Andrew. "Europa i marionettens lignelse," *Samtid och Framtid,* 18 (1961), 240-246.

2,419. Nimtz, H. "Ein verlassenes Haus: Erinnerungen an Th. M.," *Ostdeutsche Monatshefte,* 24 (1958), 697.

2,420. Nishi, Yoshiyuki. "Ein Goethebild bei Th. M.," *University of Kenazawa Bulletin,* No. 1 (1953), pp. 65-74. [In Japanese]

2,421. Nitsche, Roland. "Th. M. und der Fall Nietzsche," *Presse,* June 14, 1947.

2,422. ————. "Der missverstandene Goethe," *Forum,* 5 (June 1958), 223-225.

2,423. ————. "Ein humanistischer Briefwechsel: Th. M., Karl Kerényi und der Geist des Mythos," *Forum,* 7 (December 1960), 445-447. [Concerns Kerényi, item #1,700c]

2,424. Nivelle, Armand. "La Structure des 'Buddenbrooks,' " *Revue des Langues Vivantes — Levende Talen,* 24 (1958), 329-339.

2,425. Nobel, Alphons. "Der Teufel des Th. M.," *Ruhr-Nachrichten,* May 7, 1949. [*Doktor Faustus*]

2,426. ————. "Nachruf auf Th. M.," *La Tribune de Genève,* August 26, 1955. [Obit.]

2,427. Noguchi, Hiroshi. " 'Die Betrogene' Th. M's und das Problem der Natur," *Kage,* No. 4 (1962), pp. 14-29. [In Japanese]

2,428. Nolte, Erich. "Th. M.," *Aussaat,* 1 (1947), 45-46.

2,429. Nordmeyer, Henry W., ed. "Th. M.," *PMLA,* 71 (April 1956), 232-233. [Bibl.]

2,430. Norman, Arthur M. Z. "Seven Symbolism in 'The Magic Mountain,' " *Monatshefte,* 47 (November 1955), 360.

2,431. *Norske Studentersamfund, Oslo. *Åndsmenneskets ansvar: Nordiske akademikeres festskrift til Th. M. på 80 årsdagen.* Redaktor: Kaare Lervik. Oslo: Studentersamfunds Kultur-utvalg, 1955. 166 pp.
Contributors: Berendsohn, #264 — Carlsson, #538 — Dal, #631, — Frederiksen, #924 — Hamburger, #1,175 — Heiberg, #1,250 — Henriksen, #1,325 — Høst, #1,506 — Holmberg, #1,474 — Johnson, #1,597 — Kristensen, #1,802

— Lundgren #2,036 — Moe, #2,271 —Møller, #2,275 —
Nerman, #2,383 — Rohde, #2,752 — Tau, #3,243.

2,432. Noth, Ernst Erich. "Farewell to Th. M.," *Books Abroad,* 29
(Summer 1955), 296. [Obit.]

2,433. Nozzoli, Guido. "Nostra intervista con Th. M.," *L'Unità
del Lunedì,* May 3, 1954. Also in German, "Besuch bei Th.
M.," *Heute und Morgen,* No. 8 (1954), pp. 589-594.

2,434. *Nündel, Ernst. *Th. M's Kunstanschauungen in seinen Essays,
Reden und Miszellen.* Ph. D. diss., University of Münster
i. W., 1960. [Köln] 1960 [Fuchs] 254 pp.

2,435. †O'Bear, Elizabeth. The Significance of France in the Writings
of Th. M. Ph. D. diss., Ohio State University, 1953.

2,436. Obenauer, Karl Justus. "Th. M.," *Zeitschrift für deutsche
Bildung,* 13 (1937), 422. [Reply to item #74. *See also* K. G.
Conrady, item #598]

2,437. Oberholzer, Otto. "Th. M.: Zum 80. Geburtstag am 6. Juni
1955," *Neues Winterthurer Tageblatt,* Vol. 78, No. 127
(June 4, 1955), Wochenbeilage. [80th birthday]

2,438. *Odeman, Robert T. *Der kleine Zauberberg: Ein klinisch-
epigonaler Roman in Versen — eine Th. M.-Parodie.* Berlin:
Der Neue Geist, 1948. [Parody]

2,439. Oehlmann, Werner. "Th. M. und die deutsche Musik,"
Tagesspiegel, Vol. 4, No. 42 (712) (February 19, 1948),
Beiblatt.

2,440. Oehme, Walter. "Ein Archiv und seine Nutzanwendung,"
NDL, 11 (February 1963), 171-175. [Th. M. Archive in
Berlin]

2,441. Österling, Anders. "En satir av Th. M.," *Svenska Dagbladet,*
August 21, 1921. [*Wälsungenblut*]

2,442. ———. "Th. M. och mästarna," *Svenska Dagbladet,* June 15,
1935. [*Leiden und Grösse der Meister*]

2,443. ———. "Th. M's skälmroman," *Stockholms-Tidningen,*
September 21, 1939. [*Joseph in Ägypten*]

2,444. ———. "Lotte i Weimar," *Stockholms-Tidningen,* January 30,
1940.

2,445. ————. "Th. M. och Tyskland," *Stockholms-Tidningen*,
November 3, 1947. [*Deutschland und die Deutschen*]

2,446. ————. "Th. M's nya roman,"*Stockholms-Tidningen*,
January 12, 1948. [*Doktor Faustus*]

2,447. ————. "Th. M's nya roman," *Stockholms-Tidningen*, March
30, 1951. [*Der Erwählte*]

2,448. ————. "Inledning," in Th. M., *Fem berättelser*, pp. 5-6.
Stockholm: Bonnier, 1952.

2,449. ————. "Th. M's nya bok," *Stockholms-Tidningen*,
September 28, 1953. [*Die Betrogene*]

2,450. ————. "Th. M's skälsroman," *Stockholms-Tidningen*,
September 28, 1954. [*Felix Krull*]

2,451. ————. "Th. M's efterskörd," *Stockholms-Tidningen*, October
28, 1956. [*Nachlese*]

2,452. ————. "Th. M. och Nobelpriset," *Stockholms-Tidningen*,
January 28, 1962. [Nobel Prize]

2,453. ————. "Th. M. i exil," *Stockholms-Tidningen*, December 9,
1963. [Review of *Briefe II*, item #2,066]

2,454. Ohtani, Shigehiko. "Th. M's Novelle 'Schwere Stunde,' "
Doitsu Bungaku, No. 31 (1963), 88-105. [In German]

2,455. Olberg, Paul. "Th. M.: Tyskland föres mot avgrunden,"
Socialdemokraten, January 23, 1937. [*Ein Briefwechsel*]

2,456. ————. "Th. M. om Europas kardinalproblem," *Socialdemokraten*, October 21, 1938. [*Vom Zukünftigen Sieg der
Demokratie*]

2,457. Oliver, Kenneth. "Two Unpublished Letters of Th. M.,"
Monatshefte, 51 (December 1959), [325]-327.

2,458. Olofsson, Christer. "Th. M. och det tyska problemet," *Lunds
Veckoblad*, June 14-19, 1963. [Review of G. Bergsten, item
#292]

2,459. †Olschewski, Hans. 'Doktor Faustus' von Th. M.: Struktur und
Problematik eines modernen Romans. Ph. D. diss., University
of Göttingen, 1954. [For a critical discussion *see* Prinzing,
item #2,610]

2,460. Oppenheim, Max. "Th. M.," in his *Menschen finden ihren
Maler*, pp. 46-48. Zurich: Oprecht, 1938.

2,461. Orabuena, José. "Th. M.-Briefe," *Atlantis,* Vol. 36, No. 4
        (April 1964). [Review of item #2,066]

2,462. Ormos, Ladislaus. "Th. M. plaudert . . .," *Pester Lloyd,*
        Morgenblatt, December 18, 1929, pp. 1-2. [Interview]

2,463. Orthbrand, Eberhard. "Der alte Th. M.," *Stuttgarter Nach-
        richten,* No. 77 (May 13, 1948), p. 5. [*Die Entstehung des
        Doktor Faustus*]

2,464. ———. "Th. M.," in *Cottas deutsche Chronik des Jahres
        1956,* pp. 92-95. Stuttgart: Cotta, 1957.

2,465. Ottevaere, Edmond. "Th. M.: Deutschland und die Deutschen,"
        Dietsche Warande en Belfort, No. 1 (January 1959), pp. 49-56.

2,466. Otto, Werner. "Mann über Bord: Zu Th. M's Vortrag 'Von
        Deutscher Republik,' " *Gewissen für den Ring,* Vol. 4, No. 35
        (October 23, 1922).

2,467. Ottwalt, Ernst. "Der Turm zu Babel," *Neue deutsche Blätter,*
        1 (December 15, 1933), 253-258. [*Die Geschichten Jaakobs*]

2,468. Ozarki, Jun. "Versuch über 'Tonio Kröger' von Th. M.,"
        Doitsu Bungaku — Die deutsche Literatur, No. 28 (1962),
        pp. 100-110. [In German]

2,469. Pabst, Walter. "Satan und die alten Götter Venedigs: Entwick-
        lung einer literarhistorischen Konstante," *Euphorion,* 49
        (Fall 1955), [325]-359. [*Der Tod in Venedig*]

2,470. Paci, Enzo. "Th. M. e la filosofia," *Studi Filosofici,* 3 (1946),
        pp. Also in his *Esistenza e immagine,* pp. 49-87. Milano: A.
        Tarantola, 1947. [Cf. #3,944]

2,471. ———. "Th. M. e la musica," *Rivista Musicale Italiana,* 1
        (1946). [Cf. I, item #1,161, and II, #3,943]

2,472. ———. "Introduzione a Th. M.," *Bollettino di Letterature
        Moderne,* Vol. 1, No. 1-2 (January-February 1947), pp. 5-12.

2,473. ———. "Th. M.: Nobiltà dello Spirito," *Aut aut,* No. 16
        (July 1953), pp. 362-363. [*Adel des Geistes*]

2,474. ———. "L'ironia di Th. M.," *Aut aut,* No. 29 (September
        1955), pp. 363-375. [Cf. #3,946]

2,475. ———. "Due momenti fondamentali nell'opera di Th. M.,"
        Aut aut, No. 29 (September 1955), 423-439. [Cf. #3,945]

2,476. ———. "Note e segnalazioni," *Aut aut,* No. 29 (September 1955), pp. 485-463. [Review of H. Mayer, item #2,172, and C. Cases, item #552]

2,477. ———. "L'esistenza diabolica in Th. M.," in his *Ancora sull'-esistenzialismo,* pp. 131-144. Torino: Radio Italiana, 1956.

2,478. ———. "Memoria e presenza dei 'Buddenbrook,' " *Aut aut,* No. 78 (1963), pp. 7-27. [Cf. #3,948]

2,479. Painter, George D. "New Novels," *Listener,* 54 (November 25, 1954), 927. [*Die Betrogene*]

2,480. Pallmann, Hans. "Begrüssung durch den Präsidenten des Schweizerischen Schulrates," in item #2,644, pp. 7-9.

2,481. Paneth, Ludwig. "Anders als die andern," *National-Zeitung. Basel,* Vol. 26, No. 248 (June 3, 1945).

2,482. Paoli, Rodolfo. "Th. M. e Cecov," *La Nazione Italiana,* June 23, 1956.

2,483. ———. "Lettere di Th. M.," *L'Approdo Letterario,* Vol. 10, No. 26 (April-June 1960), pp. 117-119. [Briefe an P. Amann, item #3,426]

2,484. *Pareja Diézcanseco, Alfredo. *Th. M. y el Nuevo Humanismo.* Quito: Ed. Casa de la Cultura Ecuatoriana, 1956. 262 pp.

2,484a. *———. *Actualidad y Presencia en 'La Montaña Mágica.'* Guayaquil, Ecuador: Sociedad de Artistos y Escritores, 1942. [*Der Zauberberg*]

2,485. Parry, Idris. Review of J. M. Lindsay, item #1,971, *GLL,* N. S., 8 (April 1955), 225-226.

2,486. ———. "Th. M's Latest Phase," *GLL,* N. S., 8 (July 1955), 241-251. [*Die Betrogene — Felix Krull*]

2,487. ———. "Th. M.: 1875-1955," *GLL,* N. S., 9 (October 1955), 15-19. [Obit.]

2,488. ———. "Revolutionary in Spats," *Listener,* 56 (October 11, 1956), 575. [Review of R. H. Thomas, item #3,273]

2,489. ———. "A Hero of Our Time: The Genesis of a Novel by Th. M.," *Listener,* 66 (October 26, 1961), 669. [*Die Entstehung des Doktor Faustus*]

2,490. Pascal, Roy. "Th. M.: The Magic Mountain," in his *The German Novel,* pp. 76-98. [Manchester] Manchester University

Press [1956]

2,491. ———. "Th. M.: 1875-1955," in his *The German Novel*,
pp. 258-296. [Manchester] University of Manchester Press
[1956]

2,492. ———. "Fortklang und Nachklang des Realismus im Roman,"
in Werner Kohlschmidt, *ed.*, *Spätzeiten und Spätzeitlichkeit*,
pp. 136-137. Bern: Francke [1962]

2,493. Passage, Charles E. "Hans Castorp's Musical Incantation," *GR*,
38 (May 1963), [238]-256. [*Der Zauberberg*]

2,494. Pastior, Oskar. "Simbolul social in romanul 'Muntele Vrajit'
al lui Th. M.," *Revista de Filologia Romanica si Germanica*, 5
(1961), [303]-319. [Concerns social symbolism in *The Magic
Mountain*. In Rumanian, with resumé in German and Russian]

2,495. *Peacock, Ronald. *Much is Comic in Th. M.* London: University
of London, Bedford College, 1964. 21 pp. [Cf. #3,949]

2,496. Pearson, Gabriel. "The Heroism of Th. M.," in John Wain, *ed.*,
International Literary Annual, 1 (1959), 122-130.

2,497. Pechel, Rudolf. "Th. M.: 1875-1955," *Deutsche Rundschau*,
81 (September 1955), 889. [Obit.]

2,498. Peckham, H. H. Review of H. Hatfield, I, item #199, *GQ*, 25
(January 1952), 57-58.

2,499. Pedzinsky, Zbiginiew. "L'audience de Th. M. en Pologne,"
Cahiers Pologne-Allemagne, Vol. 16, No. 1 (January-March,
1963), [106]-109.

2,500. Peibst, H. "Experimente aus Th. M's 'Doktor Faustus,' "
Wissenschaft und Fortschritt, 8 (1958), 113.

2,501. *P.E.N. Zentrum deutscher Autoren im Ausland. *Tribute
Meeting: Th. M., 1875-1955.* [12 pp. pamphlet] Contributions
by Hans Flesch, item #881, Wilhelm Unger, item #3,332a,
and Albrecht Knaus, item #1,743.

2,502. Penchenier, Georges. "Th. M., le 'dernier Européen,' " *Le
Monde*, Vol. 12, No. 3283 (August 5, 1955), pp. 1-2. [Obit.]

2,503. Perez, Hertha. "Lupta între progres și reacțiune in romanul
lui Th. M. *Zauberberg*," *Analele Știinţifice,*, 2 (1956), [231]-
244. ["Der Kampf zwischen Fortschritt und Reaktion in Th.
M's 'Zauberberg' "]

2,504. ————. "Personencharakteristiken in den Novellen Th. M's,"
        Analele Ştiinţifice, 3 (1957), 275-287.
2,505. ————. "Th. M. si Goethe," *Flacăra Iaşului*, 1957, pp. 33-80.
2,506. ————. "Insemnari despre eroii nuvelelor lui Th. M.," *Iaşul
        literar*, No. 5 (1958), pp. 78-82. ["Aufzeichnungen über die
        Helden der Novellen Th. M's"]
2,507. ————. "Th. M. 'Casa Buddenbrook,' " *Iaşul literar*, No. 4
        (1958), pp. 94-96.
2,508. ————. "Wiederholung, Aufzählung, Satzkonstruktion in den
        Novellen Th. M's," *Analele Ştiinţifice*, 5 (1959), [153]-160.
2,509. ————. "Th. M. despre Friedrich Schiller," *Studii şi cercetări
        Ştiinţifice*, 1 (1960), 100-106. [Th. M. über Friedrich
        Schiller"]
2,510. †————. Th. M. als Novellist. Ph. D. diss., University of
        Bucharest, 1961. [Autorreferat: *Nuvelistica lui Th. M.*
        University of Bucharest, 1961. 19 pp. In Rumanian]
2,511. ————. "Conflictual între artă si realitatea burgheză in proza
        lui Th. M.," *Studii de literatură universală*, 3 (1961), [207]-
        226. ["Der Konflikt zwischen Kunst und bürgerlicher
        Wirklichkeit in der Prosa Th. M's"]
2,512. ————. "Locul nuvelei in opera lui Th. M.," *Revista de
        Filologia Romanică şi Germanică*, 5 (1961), [285]-302.
        ["Die Stellung der Novelle im Gesamtwerk Th. M's"—In
        Rumanian, with resumé in Russian and German]
2,513. ————. "Inceputurile literare ale lui Th. M.," *Analele
        Stiintifice*, 8 (1962), [129]-141. ["Die literarischen Anfänge
        Th. M's"]
2,514. ————. "Contribuţia lui Th. M. la lupta impotriva fascismului,"
        Orizont, No. 1 (1964), pp. 84-90.
2,515. Perfall, K. V. "Th. M's neuestes Werk," *Kölnische Zeitung*,
        December 9, 1923. [*Felix Krull*]
2,516. Perinetti, Ludovico Aotis. "Crisi di una cultura nel 'Faustus'
        di Th. M.," *Aut aut*, No. 16 (July 1953), pp. 350-361.
2,517. Peters, Arno. "Freunde des Sozialismus: Th. M.," *Periodikum
        für wissenschaftlichen Sozialismus*, No. 5 (March 1959),
        pp. 51-60.

2,518. Peters, Willi. "Th. M.," *Düsseldorfer Hefte,* 7 (March 15, 1952), 197-199.

2,519. Peterson, Virgilia. "A Nocturne in Mann's Mirror," *NYHT,* June 6, 1954. [*Die Betrogene — The Black Swan*]

2,520. Petitpierre, Max. "Bundespräsident Petitpierre über Th. M.," *NZZ,* Morgenausgabe No. 1536 (June 9, 1955), Bl. 1. [Address delivered on June 4, 1955, on the occasion of M's 80th birthday]

2,521. Petriconi, Helmuth. "Th. M. liest," *Flöte,* 4 (1921/22), 54-59.

2,522. ————. " 'La Mort de Venise' und 'Der Tod in Venedig,' " *Romanistisches Jahrbuch,* 6 (1956), 133-151. Also in his *Das Reich des Untergangs,* pp. 67-95. Hamburg: Hoffmann & Campe [1958] [Comparison between Maurice Barrès and Th. M. — *See* comments by E. E. Stein, #3,118]

2,523. ————. "Verfall einer Familie und Höllensturz eines Reichs," in his *Das Reich des Untergangs,* item #2,522, pp. [151]-184. [*Buddenbrooks — Doktor Faustus*]

2,524. †Pezzei, Meinhard. La France dans l'oeuvre littéraire de Th. M. Ph. D. diss., University of Innsbruck, 1949. 229 pp.

2,525. Pfeifer, Martin. "Hermann Hesse und Th. M.," *Union,* August 25, 1955.

2,526. ————. "Hermann Hesse und Th. M.: Eine bibliographische Studie," *Börsenblatt für den deutschen Buchhandel,* Frankfurter Ausgabe, 18 (November 2, 1962), Aus dem Antiquariat, 1922-1926.

2,527. Pfeiffer, Herbert. "Das Zentralproblem bei Th. M.," *Pädagogische Blätter,* Vol. 6, No. 11-12 (1955).

2,528. Pfeiffer, Johannes. "Th. M.: Tristan," in his *Wege zur Erzählkunst,* pp. [97]-105. Hamburg: Wittig [1953]

2,529. ————. "Über Th. M's Erzählung 'Die Betrogene,' " *Wirkendes Wort,* 8 (November 1957), 30-33. Reprinted in "Dichterische Wirklichkeit und 'weltanschauliche' Wahrheit, erläutert an Novellen von Hans Grimm, Th. M. und Franz Kafka," in his *Die dichterische Wirklichkeit,* pp. [94]-113.

Hamburg: Meiner [1962] [*See* esp. pp. 102-106 on *Die Betrogene*]

2,530. Pfeiffer-Belli, Erich. "Unterhaltung mit Th. M.," *Königsberger Hartungsche Zeitung,* Abendausgabe No. 390 (August 21, 1931).

2,531. ———. "Th. M's 'Doktor Faustus,' " *Deutsche Beiträge,* 2 (1948), 88-93. [Adds to I, item #2,811]

2,532. ———. "Festliche Tage in München," *Tagesspiegel,* July 30, 1949. [Biog.]

2,533. ———. "Jene kriminelle Abart des Künstlers," *Münchner Merkur,* August 18, 1951. [*Felix Krull*]

2,534. ———. "Mit Th. M. in einem alten Salzburger Garten," *Münchner Merkur,* August 16, 1952. [Biog.]

2,535. ———. "In Kilchberg bei Th. M.," *Münchner Merkur,* July 23, 1954. [Biog.] [Cf. I, item #681]

2,536. ———. "Th. M. wird Montag 80 Jahre," *Hessische Nachrichten,* June 4, 1955. [80th birthday]

2,537. ———. "Th. M. beigesetzt: Sein Werk und sein Andenken leben weiter über unseren verworrenen Zeiten," *Welt,* Feuilleton No. 190 (August 17, 1955), p. 6. [Obit.]

2,538. ———. "Beinahe eine Dichtung," *Süddeutsche Zeitung,* June 23, 1956.

2,539. Pfeiffer-Belli, Wolfgang. "Th. M's Alterswerk," *Begegnung,* 10 (December 15, 1955), 372. [*Felix Krull*]

2,540. Pfeiler, William K. Review of Brennan, I, item #140, *GR,* 19 (December 1944), 313-314. [Cf. #450]

2,541. ———. "Th. M.," in his *German Literature in Exile,* pp. 19-20 et al. Lincoln: University of Nebraska Press [1957]

2,542. Pfemfert, Franz "Der Tod in Venedig," *Aktion,* 3 (May 28, 1913), 599-600.

2,543. Pflug, Karl. "Offener Brief an Th. M.," *Kreuz-Zeitung,* October 16, 1922. [*Von Deutscher Republik*]

2,544. Philippson, Ernst August. "Über zwei 'Erfindungen' in Th. M's 'Der Erwählte,' " in Hugo Kuhn and Kurt Schier, *eds., Märchen, Mythos, Dichtung. Festschrift zum 90. Geburtstag*

von Friedrich von der Leyen, pp. 487-489. München: Beck
[1963]

2,545. Pfund, Harry W. "Zurich's Literary Shrines: The Th. M.
Archives," *AGR,* Vol. 24, No. 3 (February-March, 1963),
pp. 14-17.

2,546. Pick, Robert. "Th. M.," *Book-of-the-Month Club News,*
August 1951, pp. 6-7.

2,547. †Pietsch, Eva-Maria. Die russische Literatur als Bildungserlebnis
Th. M's. Staatsexamensarbeit, University of Leipzig, 1954.
70 pp.

2,548. †————. Th. M. und F. M. Dostojewski. Ph. D. diss.,
University of Leipzig, 1957.

2,549. ————. "Th. M's Verhältnis zur russischen Literatur," *Geist
und Zeit,* No. 4 (1960), pp. 127-134. Also in *Deutschunterricht*
(Berlin), 13 (1960), 437-441.

2,550. ————. Review of Admoni, #8, *DLZ,* 83 (July-August 1962),
655-657.

2,551. ————. "Notizen über den Hochstapler Felix Krull," in G.
Wenzel, #3,461, pp. 261-272.

2,552. ————. "Gogol in der Publizistik Th. M's," *Spektrum,* 11
(1965), 187-191.

2,553. ————. Review of H. Stresau, #3,181, in G. Wenzel, #3,472,
pp. 446-450.

2,554. Piontek, Heinz. "Th. M's Nachlese," *Welt und Wort,* 11
(November 1956), 360-361.

2,555. Piroué, Georges. "Th. M. et la tentation du parfait," *La Table
Ronde,* (October 1955), [151]-153.

2,556. Plant, Richard. "Warm Regards from a Fellow-Artist," *NYT
Book Review,* March 8, 1959. [*Last Essays*]

2,557. *Plard, Henri. *Th. M. und Ernst Bertram. Vortrag.* [Remscheid:
Schlagmann] 1962. 34 pp.

2,558. Platzer, Martin. "Von und über Th. M.," *Eisenacher Tagespost,*
Beilage 'Wartburgland,' No. 39-44 (January 24-February 28,
1924), pp. 162-183. [Review of Helbling, I, item #1063;
Brüll, I, item #145; and Th. M., *Felix Krull — Goethe und
Tolstoi — Von Deutscher Republik*]

2,559. ————. "Bekenntnisse des Hochstaplers Felix Krull," *National-Zeitung Basel*, Vol. 5, No. 10 (March 9, 1924).

2,560. ————. "Th. M. und der Okkultismus," *Eisenacher Tagespost*, Beilage 'Wartburgland," No. 47 (March 20, 1924), p. 194. [*Okkulte Erlebnisse*]

2,561. ————. "Mario und der Zauberer," *National-Zeitung Basel*, Morgenblatt, May 25, 1930.

2,562. ————. "Zu Th. M's 60. Geburtstag am 6. Juni 1935," *National-Zeitung Basel*, Sonntags-Beilage, Vol. 16, No. 248 (June 2, 1935), pp. 1-2.

2,563. Plesner, Knud Frederick. "Kaldets digter," in his *Kulturbaerere: Tidskritiske studier*, pp. [27]-66. Copenhagen: Aschehoug, 1938.

2,564. *————. *Th. M. to foredrag*. Copenhagen, 1955. 45 pp. [*Doktor Faustus*. — 80th birthday] [150 copies]

2,565. Plesske, Hans-Martin. "Th. M. 80 Jahre," *Musica*, 9 (June 1955), 284. [80th birthday]

2,566. Plessner, Monika. "Identifikation und Utopie: Versuch über Heinrich und Th. M. als politische Schriftsteller," *Frankfurter Hefte*, 16 (December 1961), 812-826.

2,567. †Plöger, Jürgen. Das Hermesmotiv in der Dichtung Th. M's. Ph. D. diss., University of Kiel, 1960. 194 pp. [*Der Zauberberg — Joseph und seine Brüder — Felix Krull*]

2,568. Plumien, Eo. "Th. M's Welt und Werk: Eine Ausstellung auf der Darmstädter Mathildenhöhe," *Mannheimer Morgen*, March 30, 1962, p. 36. [Th. M. Exhibit]

2,569. Pobé, Marcel. "Eine Pariser Erinnerung an Th. M.," *Neue Zürcher Nachrichten*, Vol. 51, No. 188 (August 16, 1955), pp. 1-2.

2,570. Pocar, Ervino. "Introduzione," in Th. M., *I Buddenbrook*, pp. [xv]-xx. [Milano] A. Mondadori [1965]

2,571. ————. "Un uomo libero," *Epoca*, August 21, 1955. [Obit.]

2,572. ————. "Introduzione," in Th. M., *La Montagna Incantata*, pp. xv-xx. [Milano] A. Mondadori [1965]

2,573. Poggiolo, Renato. "Aschenbach, Kröger & Ci.," *Solaria*, No. 7-8 (1931). Also in *Antologia Solaria* [Milano: Lerici, 1958]

2,574. Pokorná, Lydie. "Felix Krull," *Časopis pro moderní filologii,* 42 (1960), 62-63.

2,575. Politis, Ath. "Au cercle 'al Diafa': Une réception en honneur du célèbre écrivain allemand Th. M.," *La Semaine Egyptienne,* Vol. 4, No. 15-16 (1930), pp. 4-6. [Address in honor of Th. M's visit to Egypt]

2,576. Politzer, Heinz. "Joseph in His Glory," *Forum* (Jerusalem), Vol. 7, No. 49 (November 24, 1944), p. 4. [*Joseph und seine Brüder*]

2,577. ———. "Der neue Faust," *Turm,* Vol. 3, No. 1 (1948), pp. 41-43. [*Doktor Faustus*]

2,578. ———. Review of R. A. Nicholls, item #2,407, *JEGP,* 55 (April 1956), 339-341.

2,579. ———. "Of Time and Doctor Faustus," *Monatshefte,* 51 (April-May, 1959), [145]-155. [Faust theme in literature: Marlowe — Lessing — Goethe — Th. M.]

2,580. ———. "The 'Break-Through': Th. M. and the Deeper Meaning of Disease," *Ciba-Symposium,* Vol. 9, No. 11 (1961), pp. 36-43. [Also in German, Dutch, French, Italian, and Spanish]

2,581. ———. "Th. M.," in his *Franz Kafka: Parable and Paradox,* pp. 39-41 et al. Ithaca: Cornell University Press [1962] [*Tonio Kröger — The Magic Mountain*] Also in German *ed.,* *Franz Kafka der Künstler.* [Frankfurt a. M.] S. Fischer, 1965.

2,582. ———. "Th. M. — der Dichter und die Mächte," *NDH,* No. 106 (July-August, 1965), pp. 5-30.

2,583. Pollak, Hans. "Kleine Beiträge zur Beurteilung von Th. M.," *GRM,* N. F., 7 (1957), 394-396.

2,584. Polzer, Viktor. "Th. M. in Wien: Gespräch mit dem Dichter," *Neues Wiener Tagblatt,* No. 26 (January 25, 1935).

2,585. ———. "Th. M. über seinen heutigen Vortrag," *Echo,* May 8, 1936. [Sigmund Freud]

2,586. ———. "Gespräch mit Th. M.," *Neues Wiener Tagblatt,* No. 16 (January 16, 1937).

2,587. Ponce, Juan Garcia. "Quién es Adrián Leverkühn," *La Palabra y el Hombe*, No. 26 (April-June, 1963), pp. 269-286. [*Doktor Faustus*]

2,588. Pongs, Hermann. "Exkurs: Th. M's Alterskunst," in his *Im Umbruch der Zeit: Das Romanschaffen der Gegenwart*, pp. 214-217, 231-234. [Tübingen] Verlag der Deutschen Hochschullehrer-Zeitung [³1958]

2,589. Ponten, Josef. "An Th. M.," in his *Der Jüngling in Masken*, pp. 7-10. Potsdam: Kiepenheuer, 1922.

2,590. ———. "Antwort an den Herausgeber," *Vorhof*, 3 (1925), 102-103. [*See also* Karl Rauch #2,638]

2,591. Popkin, Henry. "Th. M's Latest Novel," *Commonweal*, 63 (October 7, 1955), 21-22. [*Felix Krull*]

2,592. Porena, Boris. "Th. M. e la musica contemporanea," *Musica d'oggi*, 1 (February 1958), 91-95. [*Betrachtungen eines Unpolitischen — Doktor Faustus*]

2,593. ———. "Musica e morale nell'opera di Th. M.," *Letteratura*, Vol. 6, No. 31-32 (January-April, 1958), pp. 42-53.

2,593a. Poschmann, Henri. Review of Altenberg, #34, *Weimarer Beiträge*, 9 (1963), 387-391.

2,594. Poser, Hans. "Th. M.: 'Doktor Faustus,' " in Rolf Geissler, ed., *Möglichkeiten des modernen deutschen Romans*, pp. 5-44. Frankfurt a. M.: Diesterweg [1962]

2,595. Potoker, Edward M. "Conscience of a Culture," *Saturday Review*, Vol. 48, No. 45 (November 6, 1965), pp. 39-40, 70. [Review of G. Lukács, item #2,035]

2,596. Praz, Mario. "Th. M.: 'Wälsungenblut,' " in his *La carne, la morte, il diavolo nella letteratura romantica*, p. 433. Firenze: Sansoni [³1948] Also in English, translated by Angus Davidson as *The Romantic Agony*, pp. 467-468. Oxford: Oxford University Press, ²1957. Translated into German by Lisa Rüdiger as *Liebe, Tod und Teufel: Die Schwarze Romantik*, pp. 443-444. [München] Hanser [1963]

2,597. Preetorius, Emil. "Glückwunsch an Th. M. zu seinem 60. Geburtstag," in Rudolf Adolph, *Emil Preetorius*, p. 112. Aschaffenburg: Pattloch [1960]

2,598. ———. "Verehrter Th. M.," in Grosser, item #1,090, pp. 57-61. [Concerns Th. M. as an emigré]

2,599. ———. "Aus dem Briefwechsel Th. M.-Emil Preetorius," *Blätter der Th. M.-Gesellschaft Zürich,* No. 4 (December 1963), pp. 9-24. [*See also* H. Wysling, item #3,548, Cf. #3,421].

2,600. ———. "Th. M. und Glucks Iphigenie: Der Dichter macht mich zum Bühnenbildner. Erinnerungen," *Blätter der Th. M.-Gesellschaft Zürich,* No. 4 (December 1963), pp. 4-7.

2,601. ———. "Th. M.," in his *Über die Kunst und ihre Schicksale in dieser Zeit: Münchener Erinnerungen,* pp. 56-69. Düsseldorf: H. Küpper, 1953.

2,602. ———. "Th. M.," in his *Geheimnisse des Sichtbaren: Gesammelte Aufsätze zur Kunst,* pp. 183-197. München: R. Piper, 1963.

2,603. Prescott, Orville. "Th. M.: *The Black Swan,*" *NYT,* June 7, 1954.

2,604. ———. "Confessions of Felix Krull, Confidence Man," *NYT,* September 19, 1955.

2,605. Priestley, John B. "Th. M.: The Magic Mountain," in his *Literature and Western Man,* pp. 420-423 et al. New York: Harper [1960] Also translated into German by Paul Baudisch, *Der Europäer und seine Literatur,* pp. 458-460. Wien: Desch [1960]
Pringsheim, Hans Erik. *See* R. Takahashi.

2,606. Pringsheim, Heinz. "Th. M. und die Musik," *Schweizerische Musikzeitung,* 95 (1955), 286-290.

2,607. Pringsheim, Klaus. "Ein Nachtrag zu 'Wälsungenblut,'" *NZZ,* Vol. 182, Sonntagsausgabe No. 4,863 (December 17, 1961), Bl. 4. Also in G. Wenzel, item #3,472, pp. 253-268.

2,608. ———. "Die Zwillinge in der Arcisstrasse: Ein Protest und unsere Antwort," *Süddeutsche Zeitung,* No. 190 (August 9, 1963), p. 10. [Concerns *Wälsungenblut.* Cf. Süskind, #3,215. *See also* #105]

2,609. Pringsheim, Klaus H. "Th. M. in America," *AGR,* Vol. 30, No. 3 (February-March, 1964), pp. 24-34.

2,610. *Prinzing, Walter. *Stil der Schwebe im 'Doktor Faustus.'* Ph. D. diss., Technische Hochschule Stuttgart, 1956. [Contains critical comments of Olschewski, item #2,459]

2,611. Prölss, Erich R. "Die Rückversicherung in Werken der Weltliteratur," *Versicherungswissenschaftliches Archiv,* No. 1 (1959), pp. 1-2. [Concerns *Buddenbrooks* and Galsworthy's *Forsyte Saga*]

2,612. Pross, Harry. "Zeitschriften-Rundschau," *Deutsche Rundschau,* 83 (July 1957), 723-725. [Survey of recent Th. M. criticism]

2,613. Prüssian, Alexander. "Der Zauberberg," *Münchener Medizinische Wochenschrift,* Vol. 72, No. 17 (April 24, 1925), pp. 696-697. Also in H. Saueressig, item #2,844, pp. 46-51.

2,614. Pryce-Jones, Alan. "The 'Two Faces' of Th. M.," *Listener,* 60 (November 20, 1958), 828-830. [Review of E. Heller, #1,278]

2,615. Psaar, Werner. "Th. M's 'Bekenntnisse des Hochstaplers Felix Krull' — Gesellschaftsburleske oder Selbstparodie," *Wissenschaftliche Zeitschrift der Pädagogischen Hochschule Potsdam,* Vol. 2, No. 2 (July 1956), pp. 115-128.

2,616. Puccini, Mario. "Ritratto di Tonio Kröger," *Gazzetta del Popolo,* June 11, 1924. [*Tonio Kröger — Tristan — Der Tod in Venedig*]

2,617. ———. "La morte a Venezia," *L'Ambrosiana,* 6 (November 13, 1927).

2,618. ———. "Tommaso Mann Premio Nobel," *Giornale di Genova,* 8 (November 19, 1929). Also in *Giornale di Sicilia,* November 21, 1929.

2,619. ———. "Pensieri su Mann minore," *Gazzetta del Mezzogiorno,* October 19, 1955.

2,619a. ———. "Th. M.," *Paese,* December 22, 1956.

2,620. *Pütz, Heinz Peter. *Kunst und Künstlerexistenz bei Nietzsche und Th. M.* Bonn: Bouvier, 1963. 156 pp. [Ph. D. diss., Bonn]
Reviews: Anon., #119 — Hellmann, #1,310.

2,621. ———. "Die teuflische Kunst des 'Doktor Faustus' bei Th. M.," *ZDP,* 82 (1963), 500-515.

2,622. Puppo, Mario. "L'Umanesimo di Th. M.," *Studium*, 51 (October 1955), 647-653.

2,623. Pyritz, Hans. "An Th. M.," in Ilse Pyritz, *ed.*, Hans Pyritz, *Schriften zur deutschen Literaturgeschichte*, pp. 97-98. Köln: Böhlau, 1962.

2,624. Quattrocchi, Luigi. "Un vincolo tenue ma autentico fra Th. M. e Roma," *Capitolium*, 38 (November 1963), 562-564.

2,625. Rabenius, O. "Introduction," in Th. M., *Huset Buddenbrook*, pp. 5-8. Stockholm: Saxon & Lindström, 1934.

2,626. Rabinowitz, Jesaiah. "Th. M.," in his *ha-Sifrut be-mashbber ha-Dor*, pp. 27-54. New York: Obel, 1947. [Th. M's Humanism]

2,627. ———. "Th. M.," in his *Yezer we-yezirah*, pp. 102-126. Jerusalem: Mosad Bialik, 1952.

2,628. Rad, Gerhard von. "Biblische Joseph-Erzählung und Joseph-Roman," *Neue Rundschau*, 76 (1965), 546-[559]

2,629. Radovici, E. "Noi mărturii despre Th. M.," *Steana*, No. 11 (November 1958), p. 106. [Concerns new editions of M's writings]

2,630. Rahn, Fritz. "Das Spätwerk Th. M's und die Frage der künstlerischen Sittlichkeit," *NDH*, No. 15 (June 1955), pp. 174-194. [*See* reply by Hartung, item #1,202]

2,631. Rahv, Philip. "The Triumph of Decay," *Commentary*, 18 (July 1954), 82-84. [*The Black Swan*]

2,632. Rainalter, Erwin H. "Th. M.," *Pester Lloyd*, Morgenblatt, April 4, 1923, pp. 1-2.

2,633. ———. "Th. M.," *Salzburger Volksblatt*, March 26, 1925.

2,634. Randall, A. W. G. "Th. M.: 'Bemühungen,' " *New Criterion*, 4 (1926), 616-617.

2,635. ———. Review of J. Cleugh, I, #148, *Spectator*, 515 (1933), 943.

2,635a. Rasch, Wolfdietrich. "Th. M's Erzählung 'Tristan,' " in *Festschrift für Jost Trier*, pp. 430-465. Köln: Böhlau, 1964.

2,636. Ratsprechers, Martin [pseud.] "Die Figur Josephs in den Werken von J. Rainis [pseud.] und Th. M.," *Daugava*, No. 10 (October 1938), pp. 952-962; No. 11 (November 1938), pp. 1055-1070. [In Latvian, concerns Latvian writer Jānis Pliekšāns]

2,637. ———. "Th. M's dichterische Sendung," *Abend,* August 17, 1955. [Obit.]

2,638. Rauch, Karl. "Die Jungen mit Josef Ponten gegen Th. M.," *Vorhof: Ein Führer zum guten Buch,* Vol. 3, No. 3 (1925), pp. 54-56. [*See also* J. Ponten, #2,590]

2,639. Raupach, Richard K. "Des grossen Hannes Zeitfrömmigkeit: Besuch im Th. M.-Archiv Zürich," *Deutsche Woche,* April 22, 1959.

2,640. ———. "Th. M. und das Ende des Dritten Reiches: Unveröffentlichte Briefe des Dichters," *Tat,* Vol. 28, No. 114 (April 27, 1963), p. 29.

2,641. Rauscher, Ulrich. "Fiorenza," *Schaubühne,* 9 (1913), 82-83.

2,642. Rebing, Günther O. "Th. M's Letters to Agnes E. Meyer," *YULG,* 39 (July 1964), 9-29.

2,643. Rebelsky, Freda Gould. "Coming of Age in Davos: An Analysis of the Maturation of Hans Castorp in Th. M's 'The Magic Mountain,' " *American Imago,* 18 (1961), 413-421.

2,644. **Reden zur Eröffnung des Th. M.-Archivs.* Zurich: Eidgenössische Technische Hochschule, 1961. 26 pp.
Contributors: G. Mann, #2,078 — H. Pallmann, #2,480 — P. Scherrer, #2,882 — R. Schweizer, #2,995.

2,645. Redlich, Lukas. "Hans Castorp und seine Brüder: Ein Versuch über den Deutschen Th. M.," *Journal,* Vol. 1, No. 4 (1948), pp. 29-38. [Politics]

2,646. Redman, Ben Ray. "That Old, Roving Eye," *Saturday Review,* Vol. 37, No. 23 (June 5, 1954), pp. 15, 32. [*The Black Swan*]

2,647. ———. "Fighter for Freedom of the Self," *Saturday Review,* Vol. 43, No. 36 (September 3, 1960), pp. 23-24. [Concerns Th. M., *A Sketch of My Life* — Letters to Paul Amann, item #3,426 — Monika Mann, item #2,100]

2,648. Redslob, Erwin. "Th. M.," *Tagesspiegel,* October 23, 1945. Also in Grosser, item #1,090, pp. 37-39. [Th. M. as an emigré]

2,649. Reed, T. J. "Th. M., Heine, Schiller: The Mechanics of Self-Interpretation," *Neophilologus*, 47 (1963), [41]-50.

2,650. ————. "Mann and Turgenev — a First Love," *GLL*, N. S., 17 (July 1964), 313-318.

2,651. Rees, Goronwy. "Th. M.," *Encounter*, 12 (January 1959), 81-84. [Review of E. Heller, item #1,278 Cf. #1,279]

2,652. Rehm, Walther. "Th. M. und Dürer," in *Die Wissenschaft von deutscher Sprache und Dichtung: Festschrift für Friedrich Maurer*, pp. 487-497. Stuttgart: Klett [1963] Also in his *Späte Studien*, pp. 344-358. Bern: Francke [1964]

2,653. Reich-Renicki, Marcel. "Th. M.," in his *Z dziejów literatury niemieckjej: 1871-1954*, pp. 37-49 et al. Warsaw: Wiedza Powszechna, 1955.

2,654. ————. "Th. M.," in his *Literatur und Leben in Deutschland*, pp. 265-267 et al. München: Piper [1965]

2,655. Reichart, Walter A. Review of K. W. Jonas, item #1,605, *MLQ*, 17 (September 1956), 278-279.

2,656. ————. "Th. M.," *PMLA*, 72 (April 1957), 374-375. [Bibl.]

2,657. ————. "Th. M.," *PMLA*, 73 (April 1958), 329-339. [Bibl.]

2,658. ————. "Th. M.," *PMLA*, 74 (May 1959), 304. [Bibl.]

2,659. ————. "Th. M.," *PMLA*, 75 (May 1960), 383-384. [Bibl.]

2,660. ————. "Th. M.," *PMLA*, 76 (May 1961), 327-328. [Bibl.]

2,661. ————. "Th. M.," *PMLA*, 77 (May 1962), 352-353. [Bibl.]

2,662. ————. "Th. M.," *PMLA*, 78 (May 1963), 314-315. [Bibl.]

2,663. ————. "Th. M.," *PMLA*, 79 (May 1964), 328-329. [Bibl.]

2,664. ————. "Th. M.," *PMLA*, 80 (May 1965), 289-290. [Bibl.]
        See also Bürgin, item #502, and E. Neumann, item #2,389.

2,665. Reifenberg, Benno. "Vollmacht der Vernunft," *Gegenwart*, 10 (June 4, 1955), 376-377. [80th birthday — *Lebensabriss*]

2,666. ————. "Instanz des Geistes: In memoriam Th. M.," *Gegenwart*, 10 (August 27, 1955), 562-563. [Obit.]

2,667. Reifferscheidt, Friedrich M. "Hermann Hesse und Th. M.," *Deutsche Woche*, Vol. 2, No. 28 (1952), p. 13.

2,668. ————. "Ironie als epischer Ausdrucksstil, dargestellt am Werke Th. M's," *Eckart*, 23 (April-June, 1954), [214]-220.

2,669. ———. "Th. M's Hochstapler-Roman," *Eckart*, 24 (January-March, 1955), 172-174. [*Felix Krull*]

2,670. ———. "12. August 1955. 8 Uhr 10. Zum Todestag Th. M's," *Weltbühne*, 11 (1956), 1063-1064.

2,671. Reiners, Ludwig. "Ironie: Th. M.," in his *Stilkunst*, pp. 554-562 et al. München: Beck [1943]

2,672. Reinhardt, Karl. "Th. M.," in his *Die Krise des Helden*, pp. 108-109. [München] DTV [1962] [*Der Zauberberg*]

2,673. Reinhardt, Rudolf. "Th. M.: Dichter, Schriftsteller und Publizist," *Neue deutsche Presse*, Vol. 9, No. 9 (1955), pp. 1-3.

2,674. ———. "Dichter des ganzen Deutschlands," *Neues Deutschland*, Vol. 10, No. 189 (August 14, 1955), p. 4. [Obit.]

2,675. Reinhold, Kurt. "Rede und Antwort," *Tagebuch*, 11 (October 25, 1930), 1731-1732.

2,676. ———. "Wälsungenblut," *Tagebuch*, 12 (August 15, 1931), 1299-1301.

2,677. †Reisener, Charlotte. Th. M's 'Buddenbrooks' und Theodor Fontanes Romankunst. Staatsexamensarbeit, University of Göttingen, 1959. 95 pp.

2,678. Reisiger, Hans. "Th. M. und die Sternenaugen; ein Gruss zu seinem 80. Geburtstag am 6. Juni," *Stuttgarter Zeitung*, Vol. 11 (June 4, 1955), Beilage 'Die Brücke zur Welt,' p. 33. [80th birthday]

2,679. Reiss, Hans Siegfried. "Zum Stil und zur Komposition in der deutschen Prosaerzählung der Gegenwart," *Studium Generale*, 8 (1955), [19]-31. [Style — Parody]

2,680. ———. Review of P. P. Sagave, I, item #1,367, *GLL*, N. S., 9 (October 1955), 74-75.

2,681. ———. Review of H. Koopmann, item #1,769, *GLL*, N. S., 17 (October 1963), 169-170.

2,682. Remak, Henry H. H. Review of P. P. Sagave, I, item #1,367, *JEGP*, 55 (January 1956), 192-194.

2,683. ———. Review of H. M. Wolff, item #3,532, *Monatshefte*, 50 (December 1958), [367]-370.

2,684. ———. Review of P. Altenberg, item #34, *Monatshefte*, 57 (March 1965), 136-138.

2,685. ———. Review of Th. M., *Briefe I*, item #2,062, *JEGP*, 64 (April 1965), 384-389.

2,686. Reuter, Generalleutnant a. D. "Zurücknahme des gegen Th. M. erhobenen Vorwurfs der Verunglimpfung der Kriegsopfer," *Allgemeine Zeitung*, No. 471 (November 20, 1924). [The general had meant to attack Ernst Mann, author of *Die Moral der Kraft*]

2,687. Reuter, Ernst. "An Th. M.: Aus einem Briefwechsel," *Colloquium*, Vol. 9, No. 9 (September 1955), pp. 8-10. Also in Walter Heymen, *ed.*, *Das Buch deutscher Briefe*, pp. 913-919. [Wiesbaden] Insel, 1957.

2,688. Reuter, Gabriele. "A Book on German Writers by Th. M.," *NYT Book Review*, July 7, 1935. [*Leiden und Grösse der Meister*]

2,689. Reuter, Hans Heinrich. "Th. M.: Briefe an Paul Amann 1914-1952," *Weimarer Beiträge*, No. 3 (1960), pp. 662-668. [Review of item #3,426]

2,690. ———. Review of Th. M.-K. Kerényi, item #1,700c, *Weimarer Beiträge*, No. 4 (1962), pp. 795-800.

2,691. ———. Review of Th. M.-E. Bertram, item #1,575, *Weimarer Beiträge*, No. 4 (1962), pp. 800-806.

2,692. Reuter, Jasmin. "El 'Doktor Faustus' de Th. M.," in her *Fausto, el Hombre*, pp. 72-[94] México: Teatro de la Universidad de México [1965]

2,693. Reutimann, Hans. "Das ist gewiss der Grösste . . . Dem Gedächtnis Th. M's," *Landbote*, No. 188 (August 15, 1955), Bl. 3. [Obit.]

2,694. *———. *Th. M. Verantwortung im Wort*. Braunschweig, 1955. 23 pp.

2,695. Rey, William H. "Tragic Aspects of the Artist in Th. M's Work," *MLQ*, 19 (September 1958), 195-203. [*Death in Venice*]

2,696. ———. "A Tragic View of Th. M.," *MLQ*, 20 (June 1959), 167-172. [Concerns E. Heller, item #1,278]

2,697. ————. "Return to Health?— 'Disease' in Mann's *Doctor Faustus," PMLA*, 65 (March 1960), 21-26.

2,698. ————. "Selbstopferung des Geistes: Fluch und Verheissung in Hofmannsthals 'Der Turm' und Th. M's 'Doktor Faustus,' " *Monatshefte*, 52 (April-May 1960), [145]-157.

2,699. ————. "Rechtfertigung der Liebe in Th. M's Erzählung 'Die Betrogene,' " *DVJS*, 34 (November 1960), 428-448.

2,700. Réz, Pál. "Th. M. és a legenda," *A Könyvtáros*, (1958), 292-294. [*Der Erwählte*]

2,701. ————. "Th. M. és Kosztolányi Dezsö," *Világirodalmi Figyelö*, No. 3-4 (1959), pp. 390-403. [With M's hitherto unpublished letters to Kosztolányi in German and in Hungarian]

2,702. ————. "Th. M. kiadatlan Gömöri Jenöhöz," *Nagyivilág*, 6 (February 1961), [279]-282. [Concerns M's relations with Gömöri and includes Hungarian translation of four hitherto unpublished Th. M. letters]

2,703. ————. "Th. M. and Hungary: His Correspondence with Hungarian Friends," *New Hungarian Quarterly*, 2 (July-September 1961), [84]-99.

2,704. ————. "Une lettre de Th. M. sur la traduction," *The Hungarian P.E.N., Le P.E.N. hongrois*, No. 2 (1961), pp. 18-21. [Includes Th. M's letter of November 15, 1951, to Jenö Gömöri]

2,705. Richardson, Maurice. "The Black Swan," *New Statesman and Nation*, 48 (October 16, 1954), 480-482.

2,706. ————. "Confessions of Felix Krull," *New Statesman and Nation*, 50 (November 5, 1955), 590-592.

2,707. Richter, Bernt. "Wie nötig wäre unserer Zeit die gütige Grösse . . .," *Colloquium*, Vol. 9, No. 9 (1955), p. 7. [Obit.]

2,708. ————. "Nachwort," in Th. M., *Sorge um Deutschland, sechs Essays*, pp. 130-133. Frankfurt a. M.: S. Fischer, 1957.

2,709. ————. Th. M's Stellung zu Deutschlands Weg in die Katastrophe: Ein Beitrag zum politischen Denken des Dichters. Ph. D. diss., Free University of Berlin, 1960. xxviii, 678 pp. *Partially published as *Trennung von Deutschland*. Berlin:

Ernst Reuter-Gesellschaft, 1960. 83 pp. [Cf. I, item #3,000]
Reviews: Hellmann, #1,296.

2,710. ———. "Der Mythos-Begriff Th. M's und das Menschenbild
der Joseph-Romane," *Euphorion,* 54 (1960), [411]-433.

2,711. ———. "Psychologische Betrachtungen zu Th. M's Novelle
'Mario und der Zauberer,' "in G. Wenzel," 3,461, pp. 106-
117.

2,712. ———. Review of R. Baumgart, #204, in G. Wenzel, #3,472,
pp. 450-456.

2,713. Richter, Hans Martin. "Königliche Hoheit," *Münchner
Neueste Nachrichten,* Vol. 62, No. 505 (October 28, 1909).

2,714. Rie, Robert. Review of J. M. Lindsay, #1,971, *Wirkendes
Wort,* 6 (June-July, 1956), 312-313.

2,715. Riedel, Herbert. "Th. M.," in his *Musik und Musikerlebnis in
der erzählenden deutschen Dichtung,* pp. 686-689. Bonn:
Bouvier, 1959. [Ph. D. diss., Bonn, 1959]

2,716. Rieder, Heinz. "Die säkularisierte Kunst: Zum Weltbild Th.
M's," *Zeit im Buch,* 14 (February 1960), 1-4.

2,717. Riemstad, Christian. "Nobelpristageren Th. M.," *Politiken,*
November 13, 1929, p. 10.

2,718. Riesenfeld, Paul. "Schreibt Th. M. gutes Deutsch? Eine
Stilprüfung," *Muttersprache,* No. 6 (1955), pp. 212-219.

2,719. Riess, Curt. "Interview with Th. M.," *Direction,* Vol. 2, No. 8
(December 1939), pp. 4-5.

2,720. ———. "Th. M. auf Menschenjagd" [by C. R. Martin, pseud.]
Welt am Sonntag, No. 22 (June 1, 1958), p. 8. [*Buddenbrooks*]

2,721. ———. "Buddenbrooks verklagen Th. M." [by C. R. Martin,
pseud.] *Welt am Sonntag,* No. 23 (June 8, 1958). [Cf.
#2,723]

2,722. ———. "Eine Antwort an Erika Mann" [by C. R. Martin,
pseud.] *Welt am Sonntag,* No. 30 (August 24, 1958). [Reply
to E. Mann, #2,060]

2,723. ———. "Th. M. schreibt 'Buddenbrooks,' " in his *Bestseller:
Bücher, die Millionen lesen,* pp. 75-92. [Hamburg] Wagner
[1960] [Based on items #2,720-2,721]

2,724.   ———. "Th. M.," in his *Gustaf Gründgens: Eine Biographie*,
         pp. 59-60 et al. Hamburg: Hoffmann & Campe, 1965.
2,725.   †Riley, Anthony W. Die Erzählkunst im Alterswerk von Th. M.
         mit besonderer Berücksichtigung der 'Bekenntnisse des
         Hochstaplers Felix Krull.' Ph. D. diss., University of Tübingen,
         1958. 308 pp.
2,726.   ———. "Notes on Th. M. and English and American
         Literature," *CL*, 17 (Winter 1965), 57-72.
2,727.   ———. "Three Cryptic Quotations in Th. M's 'Felix Krull,' "
         JEGP, 65 (January 1966), 99-106.
2,728.   Riley, Thomas A. "Introduction," in his *ed.* of Th. M., *Der
         letzte Buddenbrook*, pp. v-[x] Boston: D. C. Heath [1965]
         Reviews: Brewster, item #456 — Weimar, item #3,436.
2,729.   Rilke, Rainer Maria. "Th. M's 'Buddenbrooks,' " in his
         Sämtliche Werke, Vol. 5, pp. 577-581. [Frankfurt a. M.]
         Insel, 1965. Previously published by Richard von Mises in his
         ed. of R. M. Rilke, *Bücher. Kunst. Theater*, pp. 14-18. [Wien,
         1934] Translated into English as "Th. M's 'Buddenbrooks' "
         by Henry C. Hatfield in item #1,229, pp. 7-9. [Cf. I, item
         #2,133]
2,730.   Rilla, Paul. "Vortrag Th. M's über 'Goethe und Tolstoi,' "
         Breslauer Neueste Nachrichten, Vol. 38, No. 13 (January 14,
         1925).
2,731.   ———. "Th. M's 'Tristan,' " in *Almanach des Deutschen
         P.E.N. Zentrums Ost und West; Deutsches Wort in dieser
         Zeit.* München: Das Schiff, 1954. Also in his *Essays*, pp. 266-
         283. Berlin: Henschel, 1955. [Cf. I, item #1,905]
2,732.   ———. "Notizen zu Th. M's 'Doktor Faustus,' " in his
         Essays, item #2,731, pp. 248-265. [Cf. I, item #2,819]
2,733.   ———. "Th. M. und sein Zeitalter," in his *Essays*, item #2,731,
         pp. 226-247. [Cf. I, item #332]
2,734.   Ringger, Kurt. "Ein Echo aus Th. M. in Giuseppe Tommasi di
         Lampedusas 'Gattopardo,' " *NZZ*, May 5, 1963. Expanded
         version in *GRM*, N. F., 13 (October 1963), 423-432.
2,735.   Rittenberg, Louis. "Th. M. Decries Hitlerism," *American-
         Hebrew Jewish Tribune*, September 17, 1934, pp. 289-312.

2,736. Rizzi, Silvio. "Archivierter Th. M.," *Du,* Vol. 20, No. 228
        (February 1960), pp. 54-57. [Th. M. Archive Zurich]

2,737. Rizzo, Franco. "L'Eletto di Th. M.," *Letterature Moderne,* 5
        (March-April, 1954), 223-228. [*Der Erwählte*]

2,738. ———. "Civiltà e poesia di Th. M.," in his *Nazionalismo e
        democrazia,* pp. [147]-150. Bari: L. Manduria, 1960.

2,739. ———. "Th. M. politico," in item #2,738, pp. [151]-160.

2,740. Robin, Pierre. Review of Th. M.-K. Kerényi, item #1,700c,
        Critique, 17 (1961), 216-225.

2,741. Robinson, Gladys Lloyd. "Th. M. in Hollywood," *Robert
        Wagner's Script,* Vol. 19, No. 457 (April 9, 1938), pp. 6-7,
        19. [Politics]

2,742. †Robinson, Walter Langridge. Name Characterization in the
        Works of Th. M. Ph. D. diss., University of Texas, 1959.

2,743. Rocca, Enrico. "Th. M. e il sud," *Il Mattino,* June 12, 1930.

2,744. Rodenburg, Carl. "Zum 250. Geburtstag Friedrichs des
        Grossen: Ein offener Brief," *Lübeckische Blätter,* Vol. 122,
        No. 8 (April 14, 1962), p. 106.

2,745. Roecker, Hans-Otto. "Th. M.: Doktor Faustus," *Weltstimmen,*
        Vol. 18, No. 6 (March 1949), pp. 1-10.

2,746. Roettger, Karl. "Ein Zeitdokument: Samuel zieht die Bilanz
        und Toni melkt die Kuh, oder zweier Könige Sturz . . . Mit
        einer 'Enderklärung' von Theodor Lessing über seinen Streit
        mit Th. M.," *Brücke,* 1 (1911/12), 150-157. [Cf. Th. Lessing,
        I, #657-658]

2,747. Rogalski, Aleksander. "Faust, Th. M. i Pawel Valéry," in his
        Literatura i Cywilizacja, pp. 26-32. Warsaw: Pax, 1956.
        [*Doktor Faustus* — Paul Valéry]

2,748. ———. "Opowiadanie Th. M. 'Die Betrogene,' " in item
        #2,747, pp. [163]-172.

2,749. ———. "Th. M. — pisarz i humanista," in item #2,747, pp.
        pp. [213]-230.

2,750. *———. *Most nad przepaścią o Tomaszu Mannie.* [Warsaw]
        Instytut Wydawniczy Pax, 1963. 418 pp.

2,751. Rohbra, Kurt Karl. "Die Buddenbrooks im Schabbelhaus," *Lübeckische Blätter,* Vol. 123, No. 3 (February 2, 1963), p. 34. [Collections]

2,752. Rohde, Peter P. "Th. M. og Nietzsche," in item #2,431, pp. 61-76.

2,753. Rolland, Jean. "Ce qui M. Th. M. est venu dire à Paris," *L'Eclair,* 13 (January 26, 1926), 1.

2,754. Rolland, Romain. "Th. M's 'Gedanken im Kriege,' " *Journal de Genève,* December 4, 1914. Abridged version in his *Au-dessus de la mêlée,* pp. 90-92. Paris: Olendorff, 1915. [Sharp attack upon Th. M's political attitude]

2,755. ———. "Th. M.," *Europe,* 31 (1953), 6-26. [Excerpt from his *Journal,* 1915]

2,756. Rollett, Edwin. "Alles Grosse steht als ein Trotzdem," *Neues Österreich,* June 5, 1955, pp. 9-10. [80th birthday]

2,757. Rolo, Charles J. "Of Love and Death," *Atlantic Monthly,* 194 (July 1954), 83. [*The Black Swan*]

2,758. Romains, Jules. "L'Allemagne peut le remercier," in item #1,493, p. 105. [80th birthday]

2,759. Rombach, Otto. "Th. M's 'Lotte in Weimar,' " *Standpunkt,* Vol. 1, No. 2 (1946), pp. 38-40.

2,760. Romberg, Bertil. "Th. M.: 'Doktor Faustus,' " in his *Studies in Narrative Technique of the First-Person Novel,* pp. 9-11 et al. Stockholm: Almqvist & Wiksell [1962]

2,761. Root, John G. "Stylistic Irony in Th. M.," *GR,* 35 (April 1960), 93-103.

2,762. Rose, Ernst. "Th. M.," in his *Faith from the Abyss: Hermann Hesse's Way from Romanticism to Modernity,* pp. 137-138 et al. [New York] New York University Press, 1965. [*Das Glasperlenspiel — Doktor Faustus*]

2,763. ———. Review of A. White, item #3,483, *GQ,* 38 (November 1965), 702-705.

2,764. Rose, William. Review of E. Heller, item #1,278, *Cambridge Journal,* January 24, 1959.

2,765. *Rosebrock, Theo. *Erläuterungen zu Th. M's 'Die Budden-brooks.'* Hollfeld: Bange [1960] 102 pp.

2,766. Rosenberg, Harold. "Myth and History," *Partisan Review,*
        Vol. 6, No. 2 (February 1939), pp. 19-39. [Politics —
        Mythology — *The Coming Victory of Democracy*]

2,767. ———. "The Comedy of the Divine," in his *The Tradition of
        the New,* pp. 126-132. New York: Horizon, 1959. [*Joseph
        and His Brothers*] [Cf. I, #2,539]

2,768. Rosenhaupt, Hans W. "Th. M's Interest in Translation,"
        History of Ideas Newsletter, 3 (July 1957), 60-63.

2,769. Rosenstein, Conrad N. "Th. M.," *Deutsche Rundschau,* 86
        (July 1960), 655-657. [Review of A. Hellersberg, item
        #1,285]

2,770. Rosiny, T. "Th. M. zwischen Geist und Leben," *Aachener
        Volkszeitung,* August 15, 1955. [Obit.]

2,771. Ross, Werner. "Landschaftsschilderung: Textanalyse als
        Hilfsmittel zur Aufsatzerziehung," *Deutschunterricht*
        (Stuttgart), 15 (December 1963), [90]-103. [On Th. M's
        Herr und Hund: pp. 98-102]

2,772. ———. "Briefschreiber Th. M.: Unvergessliche Stücke,"
        Rheinischer Merkur, Literaturblatt No. 31 (July 31, 1964),
        p. 15.

2,773. Rosteutscher, Joachim H. "Die Jünger des neuen Dionysos:
        Th. M.," in his *Die Wiederkunft des Dionysos; der
        naturmythische Irrationalismus in Deutschland,* pp. 254-257.
        Bern: Francke, 1947.

2,774. Rostosky, Fritz. "Mann: Mario und der Zauberer," *Die
        Schöne Literatur,* 31 (July 1930), 339-340.

2,775. Roth, F. E. "Goebbels antwortet Th. M.," *Sozialdemokrat,*
        May 23, 1937. [*Ein Briefwechsel. See also* item #74]

2,776. †Rothenfelder, Trudel. Th. M. als Erzähler in seinen frühen
        Novellen. Ph. D. diss., University of Mainz, 1953. 255 pp.

2,777. Rotsch, Lothar. Review of Admoni, item #8, *Germanistik,* 3
        (July 1962), 435-436.

2,778. Rouché, M. Review of J. Lesser, I, item #1,865, *Erasmus,* 9
        (1956), 88-90.

2,779. Rousseau, André. "Th. M. et son Faust," in his *Littérature du
        vingtième siècle,* pp. [124]-133. Paris: A. Michel [1953]

2,780. Roy, Michel. "Le Cas Th. M.," *Documents*, No. 7-8 (1949),
       pp. 695-702. [Concerns M's attitude toward Germany]
2,781. Deleted.

2,782. Rüdiger, Horst. "Th. M's 'Mario' als Melodrama," *Frankfurter
       Allgemeine Zeitung*, Vol. 8, No. 55 (March 5, 1956), p. 8.
       Also in *Welt*, March 8, 1956, *Stuttgarter Zeitung*, March 8,
       1956, *Standpunkt*, 10 (March 9, 1956), and *Universitas*, 11
       (May 1956), 553-554. [Concerns #3,362]
2,783. Rühle, Jürgen. "Die Republik der Unpolitischen: Zur 90.
       Wiederkehr des Geburtstages von Th. M.," *Forum*, 12 (June-
       July, 1965), 315-317; (August September, 1965) 380-383.
2,784. Rudolph, Johanna. "Die Forderung des Tages: Th. M. als
       Publizist," *Neue deutsche Presse*, Vol. 9, No. 10 (October
       1955), pp. 10-14. [Politics]
2,785. Ruhrberg, Karl. "Th. M. von Emil Barth angeregt: Ein
       Beispiel literarischer Entlehnung," *Düsseldorfer Nachrichten*,
       Vol. 82, No. 298 (December 23, 1961). [*Die Betrogene* and
       Emil Barth, *Der Wandelstern*]
2,786. Ruprecht, Erich. "Th. M.: Altes und Neues," *Erasmus*, 8
       (October 25, 1955), 606-608.
2,787. ———. "Doktor Faustus und die Krise des modernen Romans,"
       Die deutsche Literatur (Osaka, Japan), No. 9 (1963), pp. 1-
       28. [In German]
2,788. Rutra, Artur Ernst. "Th. M. über seine Reise nach Warschau,"
       Pologne Littéraire, Vol. 2, No. 7 (April 15, 1927).
2,789. Rychner, Max. "Briefwechsel Th. M.-Karl Kerényi," *Tat*,
       Vol. 10, No. 115 (April 28/29, 1945), p. 7. [Contains
       excerpts from #1,700 c]
2,790. ———. "Vom Umgang mit Göttern: Zu den Schriften von
       Karl Kerényi," *Tat*, Vol. 10, No. 163 (June 16/17, 1945),
       p. 5.
2,791. ———. "Th. M.: Essays," *Tat*, Vol. 11, No. 329 (November
       30, 1946), p. 13.
2,792. ———. "Th. M.: Doktor Faustus," *Tat*, Vol. 12, No. 286
       (October 18, 1947), pp. 1-2.

2,793.   ———. "Roman eines Romans: Th. M. *Die Entstehung des Doktor Faustus,*" *Tat,* Vol. 14, No. 332 (December 3, 1949), p. 15.

2,794.   ———. "Th. M.: Altes und Neues," *Tat,* Vol. 18, No. 98 (April 11, 1953), p. 11.

2,795.   ———. "Th. M.: Die Betrogene," *Tat,* Vol. 18, No. 352 (December 25, 1953), p. 11.

2,796.   ———. "Th. M.: Bekenntnisse des Hochstaplers Felix Krull," *Tat,* Vol. 19, No. 283 (October ᴵ6, 1954), p. 13.

2,797.   ———. "Th. M's neuer Roman: Bekenntnisse des Hochstaplers Felix Krull," *Universitas,* 9 (December 1954), 1271-1276.

2,798.   ———. "Th. M.: Zu seinem 80. Geburtstag," *Tat,* Vol. 20, No. 151 (June 4, 1955), p. 13.

2,799.   ———. "Th. M.: Rede zu seinem 80. Geburtstag," *Jahresring 55/56,* pp. 49-64. Stuttgart: DVA [1955]

2,800.   ———. "Gestalten und Beziehungen in den Romanen," *Neue Rundschau,* 66 (June 1955), 261-277.

2,801.   ———. "Der Kreis," *Aufbau* (New York), Vol. 21, No. 33 (August 19, 1955), p. 2. [Obit.]

2,802.   ———. "Th. M.," *Jezik,* 2 (1956), 49-64.

2,803.   ———. "Th. M's letztes Jahr. Ein Bericht von Erika Mann," *Tat,* Vol. 21, No. 142 (May 26, 1956), p. 13. [Review of item #2,059]

2,804.   ———. "Abschied von Th. M.," in Paul Schneider, *ed., Unsterblicher Geist. Deutsche Dichter im Andenken ihrer Freunde,* pp. 371-378. [Ebenhausen] Voss [1959]

2,805.   ———. "Th. M.-Karl Kerényi: Gespräch in Briefen," *Tat,* Vol. 25, No. 153 (June 4, 1960), p. 15. [Review of #1,700 c]

2,806.   ———. "Hinweise auf Bücher: Th. M. an Ernst Bertram," *Tat,* Vol. 25, No. 339 (December 10, 1960), p. 17. [Review of #1,575]

2,807.   ———. "Von der Politik der Unpolitischen: Die Briefe Th. M's an Paul Amann und Ernst Bertram," *Monat,* Vol. 13, No. 148 (January 1961), [45]-53. Also in his *Antworten: Aufsätze zur Literatur,* pp. 243-266. [Zurich] Manesse [1961] Review of item #1,575 and #3,426]

2,808. ———. "Th. M.: Briefe 1889-1936," *Tat*, Vol. 26, No. 350
(December 23, 1961), p. 17. [Review of *Briefe I*, #2,062]

2,809. ———. "Vorbemerkungen zum Briefwechsel Th. M.-Robert
Faesi," *Blätter der Th. M.-Gesellschaft Zürich*, No. 3 (1962),
pp. 3-4. [*See also* #833]

2,810. ———. "Th. M.: Briefe 1937-1947," *Tat*, Vol. 28, No. 354
(December 27, 1963), p. 17. [Review of *Briefe II*, #2,066]

2,811. S., H. D. "Neue Bücher," *Deutsche Arbeit*, 9 (1909/10),
264-267. [Concerns Th. M., *Königliche Hoheit*, and Heinrich
Mann, *Eine kleine Stadt*]

2,812. Saager, Adolf. "Ein tragisches Reiseerlebnis," *Landschäftler*,
Vol. 82, No. 189 (August 14, 1930). [*Mario und der
Zauberer*]

2,813. Sabais, Heinz-Winfried. "Th. M. zwischen Ost und West: Die
Hintergründe seiner Reise nach Weimar, 1949," *Heidelberger
Tageblatt*, February 11, 1953.

2,814. ———. "Don Quichote unseres Jahrhunderts," *Schwarzwälder
Bote*, December 25, 1954. [*Felix Krull*]

2,815. Sachs, Joseph. "Th. M. died recently in Switzerland: The
Hebraic Strain in Th. M,." *Jewish Affairs*, October 1955.
[Obit.]

2,816. Sador, H. B. "Al Doktor Faustus," *Molad*, Vol. 10, No. 59
(1953), p. 289.

2,817. Sadoveanu, Ion Marin. "Th. M.: 1875-1955," *Gazeta Literară*,
No. 34 (August 25, 1955), p. 6. [Obit.]

2,818. ———. "Destáinuiri scrittoricești sau Th. M. despre el însuși,"
Viața românească, No. 11 (November 1956), pp. 222-224.
["Schriftstellerische Selbstaussagen oder Th. M. über sich
selbst"]

2,819. ———. "Schitá de portret," *Secolul XX*, No. 6-7 (June-July,
1963), pp. 19-28.

2,820. Saenger, Samuel. "Betrachter oder Gestalter," *Neue Rundschau*,
44 (1933), 857-860. [*Leiden und Grösse Richard Wagners*]

2,821. Sagara, Kenichi. "Th. M's Novalis-Bild im Lichte seiner
Romantik-Kritik," *Doitsu Bungaku — Die deutsche Literatur*,

No. 27 (1961), pp. 92-100. [In German, with Japanese resumé]

2,822. †Sagave, Pierre-Paul. Un Problème littéraire redevenu actuel: Les discussions de Naphta et Settembrini dans la 'Montagne Magique" de Th. M. Mémoire, Diplome d'études supérieures, Université d' Aix-en-Provence, 1933. 80 pp.

2,823. ———. "L'Idée de l'Etat chez Th. M.," in item #1,493, pp. 123-130. Also in his *Recherches sur le roman social en Allemagne*, pp. 109-115. Aix-en-Provence: Ophrys [1960]

2,824. ———. "Th. M.: Huit lettres inédites à P.-P. Sagave," *Cahiers du Sud*, 43 (1956), [373]-386. Under the title "Quelques lettres de Th. M.," this French version was reprinted, together with Sagave's commentary, in his item #2,823, pp. [117]-127. [German original texts in Th. M., *Briefe I*, item #2,062, pp. 350-351 et al.]

2,825. ———. "Le Monde de la terreur chez Th. M.," *Les 4 Dauphins*, No. 1 (1956), pp. 47-56. [Reprint of I, item #1,367, pp. 67-71]

2,826. ———. "Th. M. et le monde latin," in *Mélange Etienne Gros*, pp. [261]-269. Aix-en-Provence, 1959.

2,827. ———. "Th. M.: Prix Nobel," in *Les Prix Nobel*, pp. 137-148. Monaco: Union européenne d'éditions, 1961.

2,828. ———. "Zum Bild des Luthertums in Th. M's 'Doktor Faustus,' " *Sinn und Form: Sonderheft Th. M.,* 1965, pp. 347-356.

2,829. Sakai, Shuji. "Georg Lukács' Haltung gegenüber Th. M.," *Doitsu Bungaku — Die deutsche Literatur,* No. 16 (1956), pp. 34-38. [In Japanese]

2,830. Salander, Martin [pseud.] "A propos," *National-Zeitung Basel,* December 15, 1936. [Concerns loss of Th. M's German citizenship]

2,831. Salis, Jean Rodolphe de. "Th. M. und die französische Literatur," *Basler Nachrichten,* Vol. 20, Sonntagsblatt No. 8 (February 21, 1926).

2,832. ———. "Th. M. zum 6. Juni 1950," in his *Im Laufe der Jahre,* pp. 302-308. Zürich: Orell Füssli [1962] [Cf. I, item #875 — 75th birthday]

2,833. *Saller, Karl, *ed. Th. M. zum 80. Geburtstag am 6. Juni 1955.* München: Deutscher Kulturring, 1955. 20 pp. [Contributions by H. Burgmüller, #518, Louis Fürnberg, #956, Stephan Hermlin, #1,341, Wolfgang Koeppen, #1,752, Hans Mayer, #2,173, Werner Warsinsky, #3,401 and Arnold Zweig, #3,613]

2,834. Samuel, Maurice. "The Brilliant Failure," in his *Certain People of the Book,* pp. 299-363. New York: Alfred A. Knopf, 1955. [*Joseph and IIis Brothers*] [Cf. I, #2,571]

2,835. *Sandberg, Hans-Joachim. *Th. M's Schiller-Studien: Eine quellenkritische Untersuchung.* [Oslo: Scandinavian University Books, 1965] 149 pp. [Ph. D. diss., University of Bergen]

2,836. Sands, Donald B. "The Light and Shadow of Th. M's 'Felix Krull,' " *Renascence,* 13 (1961), 119-124.

2,837. Sanesi, Roberto. "Omaggio a Tonio Kröger," *Aut aut,* No. 29 (September 1955), pp. 402-405.

2,838. Santarcangeli, Paolo. "Lettere di italiani," *Ponte,* 18 (November 1962), 1,531-1,534. [Review of L. Mazzucchetti, item #2,210]

2,839. Sapegno, Natalino. "Una ferma coscienza," *Il Contemporaneo,* Vol. 2, No. 23 (June 4, 1955), p. 5.

2,840. Sarnetzki, Detmar Heinrich. "Th. M.: Unordnung und frühes Leid," *Kölnische Zeitung,* November 9, 1926.

2,841. ———. "Th. M.: Zu seinem 80. Geburtstag am 6. Juni," *Kölnische Rundschau,* June 5, 1955, Feuilleton.

2,842. *Sato, Koichi. *Th. M.: Gesammelte Essays.* Tokyo: Taibuken, 1962. 286 pp. [In Japanese] Reviews: Aoki-Shigi, #126.

2,843. Saueressig, Heinz. "Die Welt des Doktor Faustus: Personen und Landschaften in Th. M's Roman," *Badische Bodensee-Zeitung,* September 15, 1962; *Schwäbische Zeitung,* No. 223 (September 26, 1962) ; and *Lesestunde,* Vol. 43, No. 1 (1966), pp. 72-75.

2,844. *————. *Die Entstehung des Romans 'Der Zauberberg': Zwei Essays und eine Dokumentation.* Biberach an der Riss: Wege und Gestalten [1965] 67 pp.
Contributors: E. R. Curtius, #615 — R. Kassner, #1,675 — M. Levy, #1,961 — N. J. Moschytz, #2,294 — A. Prüssian, #2,613 — H. Saueressig, #2,845-2,846.
Reviews: Anon., #99 — Anon., #122

2,845. ————. "Die Entstehung des Romans 'Der Zauberberg,' " in #2,844, pp. 7-24.

2,846. ————. "Die medizinische Region des 'Zauberberg,' " in #2,844, pp. 25-34. Also in *Münchener Medizinische Wochenschrift*, 107 (June 4, 1965), 1,169-1,173.

2,847. ————. "Eine Th. M.-Sammlung," *Börsenblatt für den Deutschen Buchhandel*, 21 (August 3, 1965), Aus dem Antiquariat, 1,525-1,531. [Collection of Hans-Otto Mayer]

2,848. ————. "Th. M. in seinen späten Briefen," *Schwäbische Zeitung*, No. 190 (August 19, 1965). [Review of *Briefe III*, #2,071]

2,849. ————. Review of Bürgin-Mayer, #504, *Bücherkommentare*, Vol. 17, No. 3 (September 15, 1965).

2,850. ————. "Die gegenseitigen Buchwidmungen von Heinrich und Th. M.," in G. Wenzel, item #3,472, pp. 483-490.

2,851. Saupe, Walther. "Drei Wege humanistischer Menschenbildung," in G. Wenzel, #3,453, pp. 129-133.

2,852. *Scarpa, Roque Esteban. *Th. M.: Una Personalidad y una Obra.* [Santiago de Chile] Editorial Universitaria, 1961. 452 pp.
Reviews: Dornheim, #708 — Subiotto, #3,201.

2,853. *Schaar, P. J. van der. *Dynamik der Pseudologie: Der pseudologische Betrüger versus den grossen Täuscher Th. M.* München: E. Rheinhardt, 1964. 100 pp. [*See* comments by E. E. Stein, #3,123, and W. Hellmann, #3,882]

2,854. Schab, Günter. "Roman eines Romans," *Rhein-Neckar-Zeitung*, April 29, 1949. [*Die Entstehung des Doktor Faustus*]

2,855. Schabbel, Otto. "Das Buddenbrook-Haus in Lübeck," *Hamburger Nachrichten*, Vol. 131, No. 110 (March 6, 1922).

2,856. Schaber, Will. "Das Ende des Bürgers: Zu Th. M's neuem
zeitkritischen Sammelband," *Das Freie Wort,* Vol. 2, No. 11
(March 16, 1930), pp. 27-30. [*Die Forderung des Tages*]

2,857. ———. "Brief an Th. M.," *Volksblatt,* Vol. 41, No. 251
(October 26, 1930). [Politics]

2,858. ———. "Zwischen den Jahrhunderten," *National-Zeitung*
Basel, Vol. 16, No. 248 (June 2, 1935), Sonntags-Beilage,
p. 2. [60th birthday — excerpt from I, item #785]

2,859. Schacht, Roland. "Lotte in Weimar," *Aufbau* (Berlin), 3
(1947), 369-370.

2,860. *Schädlich, Michael. *Th. M. und das christliche Denken: Eine*
Untersuchung über den Zusammenhang von Theologie und
Musik im 'Doktor Faustus.' [Berlin: A. Kietz, 1963] 23 pp.

2,861. Schaefer, K. "Zu Th. M's Anklagen gegen Lübeck," *Lübecker*
Nachrichten, Vol. 73, No. 91 (April 19, 1913). [Reply to
Th. M's letter, "Für Fritz Behn." Concerns Munich sculptor
and school-mate of Th. M. at the Katharineum in Lübeck]

2,862. Schaper, Eva. "Zwischen den Welten: Bemerkungen zu Th.
M's Ironie," in Hans-Joachim Schrimpf, *ed., Literatur und*
Gesellschaft vom 19. ins 20. Jahrhundert: Festgabe zum 60.
Geburtstag Benno von Wieses, pp. 330-364. Bonn: Bouvier,
1963.

2,863. Schauda, M. "Antwort an Th. M.," *Plan,* 1 (1945-46), 142-
144. [Politics — Th. M. as an emigré]

2,864. Schauer, Georg Kurt. "Das Äussere der Buddenbrooks," *S.*
Fischer Almanach: das 68. Jahr, pp. 92-[95] [Frankfurt a. M.]
1954.

2,865. †Schauer, Lucie. Untersuchungen zur Struktur der Novellen und
Romane Th. M's. Antithese und Synthese als Kategorien der
dichterischen Seinserfahrung. Ph. D. diss., Free University,
*Berlin, 1959. Also published as a monograph by Ernst Reuter-
Gesellschaft in Berlin-Dahlem, 1959, 203 pp.

2,866. Schaukal, Richard von. "Kritik: Vom Dichter," *Wiener*
Abendpost, Beilage No. 168 (July 25, 1903). [Tonio Kröger]

2,867. Schauwecker, Heinz. "Dann wird der Krieg nicht sein: Eine
Entgegnung an Th. M.," *Fränkischer Kurier,* No. 244

(Septmber 4, 1927). [Reply to Th. M's speech in the Warsaw
P.E.N. Club]

2,868. Scheffler, Herbert. "Zu Th. M's 2. Band der Joseph-Trilogie,"
Die liter. Welt, N. F., Vol. 10, No. 16 (1934), Beiblatt "Das
lebendige Buch," pp. 1-2.

2,869. †Scheidegger, Arnold. "Th. M.: Lotte in Weimar," in his
unpublished study Gestalten der deutschen Geistesgeschichte im
deutschen biographischen Roman des 20. Jahrhunderts, pp.
51-60. Ph. D. diss., University of Zurich, 1947.

2,870. †Scheiner, Peter Walter. "Th. M.," in his unpublished study
Oedipusstoff und Oedipusmotive in der deutschen Literatur,
pp. 309-317. Ph. D. diss., University of Vienna, 1964.

2,871. Scherrer, Paul. "Bruchstücke der Buddenbrooks-Urhandschrift
und Zeugnisse zu ihrer Entstehung, 1897-1901," *Neue
Rundschau*, 69 (August 1958), 258-291. Also special de luxe
ed. of twenty numbered copies, in slip-case, "Für Frau Katia
Mann zu ihrem 75. Geburtstag vom S. Fischer Verlag
überreicht."
Reviews: Siebenschein, #3,045.

2,872. ———. "Neues zur Entstehung der Buddenbrooks," *Zeit*,
No. 32 (August 8, 1958), p. 6. [Th. M's correspondence
with S. Fischer about the publication of his first novel,
excerpted from item #2,871]

2,873. ———. "Der Auktionsrummel um nachgelassene Hand-
schriften der Brüder Mann: Nachträgliche Richtigstellung von
Zürich aus," *Tages-Anzeiger*, December 20, 1958. [Comments
in item #231]

2,874. ———. "Vornehmheit, Illusion und Wirklichkeit," *Blätter
der Th. M.-Gesellschaft Zürich*, No. 1 (1958), 2-11. [*Felix
Krull*]

2,875. ———. "Zur Chronologie des Romans," *Librarium*, 2 (May
1959), 29-36. [*Buddenbrooks*]

2,876. ———. "Tony Buddenbrook: Die Hamburger Ehe," *Librarium*,
2 (August 1959), 123-136.

2,877. ———. "Aus Th. M's Vorarbeiten zu den Buddenbrooks,"
Blätter der Th. M.-Gesellschaft Zürich, No. 2 (1959). 32 pp.

Reprint of the two previous items.
Reviews: Hellmann, #1,291 — Leibrich, #1,898 — Matthias — #2,158

2,878. ———. "Th. M's Mutter liefert Rezepte für die Budden-brooks," in *Libris et Litteris: Festschrift für Hermann Tiemann*, pp. 325-337. Hamburg: Maximilians-Gesellschaft, 1959.

2,879. ———. "Th. M. in Zürich und Lübeck," *Lübeckische Blätter*, Vol. 119, No. 8 (April 24, 1959), pp. 81-83. [Concerns relations between Th. M. Archives in these two cities]

2,880. ———. "Th. M. und die Wirklichkeit," *Lübeckische Blätter*, Vol. 120, No. 7 (April 2, 1960), pp. 77-86.

2,881. ———. "Th. M.: 'Der Wille zum Glück,' " *Büchergilde*, No. 1 (1961), pp. 8-9.

2,882. ———. "Über den Sinn des Th. M.-Archivs," in item #2,644, pp. 10-16. Also in *Blätter der Th. M.-Gesellschaft Zürich*, No. 3 (1962), pp. 13-18.

2,883. Scheyer, Ernst. "Geistiges Leben in der Emigration," *Jahrbuch der Schlesischen Friedrich-Wilhelm-Universität zu Breslau*, 5 (1960), 271-295. [With Th. M's letter of April 13, 1948]

2,884. ———. "Über Th. M's Verhältnis zur Karikatur und bildenden Kunst," in G. Wenzel, item #3,472, pp. 143-168.

2,885. Schickele, René. "Berliner Abende: Des Ritters Ernst von Possart 'Andromache' bei Kroll. Th. M. als Gast des Vereins für Kunst," *Das Neue Magazin*, 73 (1904), 754-756.

2,886. ———. "Fünf Briefe an Th. M.," in H. Kesten, *ed.*, René Schickele, *Werke*, Vol. 3, pp. 1049-1050 et al. Köln: Kiepenheuer & Witsch, 1959.

2,887. Schiffer, Eva. "Manolescu's Memoirs: The Beginnings of Felix Krull," *Monatshefte*, 52 (November 1960), [283]-292.

2,888. †———. Parody in the Late Works of Th. M. — Ph. D. diss., Radcliffe College, Harvard University, 1962. [Cf. I, item #3,002]

2,889. ———. "Illusion und Wirklichkeit in Th. M's 'Felix Krull' und 'Joseph,' " *Monatshefte*, 55 (February 1963), [69]-81.

2,890. ———. Review of H. Koopmann, item #1,769, *Monatshefte*, 55 (February 1963), [83]-85.

2,891. ———. "Change in an Episode: A Note on 'Felix Krull,' "
MLQ, 24 (September 1963), 257-262.

2,892. ———. Review of G. Bergsten, #292, MLQ, 24 (December
1963), 415-418.

2,893. ———. Review of H. Hatfield, #1,229, Monatshefte, 57
(April-May, 1965), 208-210.

2,894. †Schikorra, Ursula. Die Gespräche in Th. M's 'Zauberberg.'
Ph. D. diss., University of Greifswald, 1958. 163 pp.

2,894a. Schileru, Eugen. "Prefața," in Th. M., Moartea la Veneția, pp.
iii-xxxviii. Bucharest: Colecția Biblioteca pentru toti, 1965.
[Death in Venice]

2,895. Schilling, Bernard N. "Tränen-Trieschke . . . Grünlich-
Permaneder," in his The Comic Spirit: Boccaccio to Th. M.,
pp. 194-216. Detroit: Wayne State University Press, 1965.
[Buddenbrooks]

2,896. ———. "Hanno, Kai and the 'Oil of Sorrow,' " in #2,895,
pp. 217-236. [Buddenbrooks]

2,897. †Schinkenberger, Ruth. Th. M's 'Joseph und seine Brüder.'
Eine morphologische Untersuchung. Ph. D. diss., University
of Bonn, 1956. 163 pp.

2,898. Schirmbeck, Heinrich. "Der amor fait eines grossen Spätlings,"
Neue lit. Welt, Vol. 4, No. 15 (August 10, 1953), p. 10.
[Altes und Neues]

2,899. Schirnding, Albert von. "Der Zauberer: Zu Th. M's Todestag,"
Nürnberger Nachrichten, August 10-11, 1957, p. 18. [poem]

2,900. Schirokauer, Arno. "Beiwerk: Zu Max Kapp: 'Th. M's
novellistische Kunst', Die lit. Welt, Vol. 5, No. 21 (1929),
p. 6. [Concerns I, item #1,877]

2,901. ———. "Bedeutungswandel des Romans," in his Gesammelte
Studien, pp. [149]-168. Hamburg: Hauswedell, 1957. [Cf.
I, item #2,619 — on Th. M's Lotte in Weimar: pp. 163-166]

2,902. Schlappner, Martin. "Du sense moraliste chez Th. M. et André
Gide," in item #1,493, pp. 131-148.

2,903. †Schleifenbaum, Waltraut. Th. M's 'Buddenbrooks.' Ein
Beitrag zur Gestaltanalyse von Dichtwerken. Ph. D. diss.,

University of Bonn, 1956. 213 pp.

2,904. Schlemmer, Hans. "Der Th. M.-Arbeitskreis," in G. Wenzel, item #3,453, pp. 166-168.

2,905. Schleswig-Holstein, Feodora von [pseud. Hugin]. "Unsere Fürsten und wir," *Kunstwart,* Vol. 23, No. 13 (April 1, 1910), pp. 1-3. [Cf. I, item #2,170 — *Königliche Hoheit. See also* Avenarius, item #151]

2,906. Schlocker, Georges. "Erneuerte Hochstapeleien und andere Wiederentdeckungen," *Schweizer Monatshefte,* 35 (July 1955), 251-253. [*Felix Krull*]

2,907. Schlüter, Wolfgang. "Einer ausserhalb des Elfenbeinturmes: Zum Gedenken an Th. M.," *Fränkische Tagespost,* August 7, 1965; also *Lübecker Morgen,* August 7/8, 1965. [10th anniversary of M's death]

2,908. Schlumberger, Jean. "Th. M.," *Figaro Littéraire,* Vol. 10, No. 487 (August 20, 1955), pp. 1, 7. [Obit.]

2,909. ———. "Gratitude personelle," in item #1,493, pp. 19-20.

2,910. Schmeisser, Marleen. "Friedrich der Grosse und die Brüder Mann," *NDH,* No. 90 (November-December, 1962), pp. 97-106. [Concerns Th. M's *Friedrich und die Grosse Koalition* and Heinrich Mann's *Der grosse König*]

2,911. Schmid, Karl. "Im Anfang war die Seele," *Domino,* No. 3 (March 1954), p. 5. [Review of Eichner, I, #159. *See also* #750]

2,912. ———. "Per Th. M.," *Svizzera Italiana,* Vol. 15, No. 112/113 (June-August, 1955), pp. 3-5. [Obit.]

2,913. ———. "Hesses 'Glasperlenspiel' und Th. M's 'Doktor Faustus,'" *Dichten und Trachten,* 9 (1957), 9-15.

2,914. Schmidt, Hannes. "Schrieb Th. M. vom Leben ab? Eine Bibliographie gibt Antwort," *Deutscher Forschungsdienst,* Vol. 5, No. 39 (1958), pp. 3-4. [Review of Bürgin, #502]

2,915. Schmidt, Rudolf. "Das Ringen um die Überwindung der Dekadenz in einigen Novellen von Th. M.," *Wissenschaftliche Zeitschrift der Universität Greifswald,* 11 (1962), [141]-153. [*Tristan — Der Tod in Venedig — Mario und der Zauberer*]

2,916. Schmitz, Oskar A. H. "Th. M.: 'Betrachtungen eines
        Unpolitischen,' " in his *Das rätselhafte Deutschland,* pp. 135-
        136. München: Müller, 1920.

2,917. Schmitz von Vorst, Josef. "Das 'Centro Th. M.': Über das
        Problem der deutschen Kulturarbeit in Italien," *Frankfurter
        Allgemeine Zeitung,* No. 132 (June 8, 1957).

2,918. ———. "Th. M., Papst und Teufel," *Frankfurter Allgemeine
        Zeitung,* No. 84 (April 9, 1963), p. 20.

2,919. Schnabel, Ernst. "Kein Abschied von Th. M.," *Welt,* July 17,
        1947. [Introduction to phonograph record of *Tonio Kröger*]

2,920. Schnack, Anton. "Der Redner Th. M.," *Berliner Tageblatt,*
        Vol. 59, No. 493 (October 18, 1930). [*Deutsche Ansprache*]

2,921. Schneditz, Wolfgang. "Th. M.," in his *Begegnungen mit
        Zeitgenossen,* pp. 20-25. München: Prestel [1959] [Cf. I,
        item #506]

2,922. Schneider, Karl-Ludwig. "Frommes Deutschtum: Th. M's
        Briefgespräche mit Ernst Bertram," *Zeit,* Vol. 15, No. 51
        (December 23, 1960), p. 13. [Review of item #1,575]

2,923. Schneider, Marcel. "Th. M. et Hermann Hesse," *La Table
        Ronde,* 50 (1950), pp. 139-144.

2,924. ———. "Th. M. et la musique," in item #1,493, pp. 111-114.

2,925. Schneider, Reinhold. "Th. M.: 'Doktor Faustus,' " *Freiburger
        Katholisches Kirchenblatt,* Zonenausgabe, April 11, 1948.
        Also in his *Begegnung und Bekenntnis,* pp. 112-116.
        Freiburg i. Br.: Herder [1963]

2,926. ———. "Th. M.: 'Nietzsches Philosophie,' " *Freiburger
        Katholisches Kirchenblatt,* Zonenausgabe, July 11, 1948. Also
        in his *Begegnung und Bekenntnis,* item #2,925, pp. 116-117.

2,927. ———. "Th. M.: 'Der Erwählte,' " in his *Begegnung und
        Bekenntnis,* item #2,925, pp. 118-120.

2,928. ———. "Kurzer Nachruf auf Th. M.," *Neue Rundschau,* 67
        (1956), 521-527. Also in his *Pfeiler im Strom,* pp. 327-335.
        [Wiesbaden] Insel [1958] Reprinted under the title
        "Gedenkworte für Th. M.," in Orden Pour le mérite für
        Wissenschaften und Künste, *Reden und Gedenkworte,* Vol.
        2, pp. 25-35. [Heidelberg: L. Schneider] 1958.

2,929. Schneider, Rolf. "Zu den beiden frühen Erzählungen Th. M's," *Aufbau* (Berlin), 11 (September 1955), 796-797. ["Der Wille zum Glück" — "Der Tod"]

2,930. ————. "Buddenbrooks," in his *Aus zweiter Hand: Literarische Parodien,* pp. [45-54] Berlin: Aufbau, 1958.

2,931. ————. "Th. M.: Aus 'Versuch über Knigge,' " in his *Aus zweiter Hand,* item #2,930, pp. 70-[74]

2,932. Schneider, Wilhelm. "Th. M.: Schriftstellersprache und Dichterwort," in his *Josef Ponten,* pp. 36-54. Stuttgart: DVA, 1924. [Cf. I, item #1,689]

2,933. Schneider, Wilhelm. "Th. M.," in his *Stilistische deutsche Grammatik,* pp. 22-23 et al. Basel: Herder [1959]

2,934. Schneller, Richard. "Th. M's 'Betrachtungen eines Unpolitischen,' " *Deutsche Rundschau,* 178 (1918), 274-282.

2,935. Schnitzler, Arthur. "Festgrüsse an Th. M.," *Neue Freie Presse,* No. 21, 814 (June 7, 1925), p. 29. [50th birthday]

2,936. Schöffler, Heinz. "Der Erde einen Menschensinn geben: Th. M. — Leben, Umwelt, Werk auf der Darmstädter Mathildenhöhe," *Deutsche Zeitung,* No. 74 (March 28, 1962), Feuilleton p. 12. [Exhibition]

2,937. ————. "Ein demokratisches Weltgewissen," *Tages-Anzeiger,* January 11, 1964. [Review of *Briefe II,* item #2,066]

2,938. Schömann, Milian. "Th. M. und die deutsche Sozialdemokratie," *Das Freie Wort,* Vol. 3, No. 27 (July 5, 1931), pp. 18-22.

2,939. Schoen, Ernst. "Einleitung," in Th. M., *Deutsche Hörer,* pp. 3-4. [London: Freier Deutscher Kulturbund in Grossbritannien, 1944]

2,940. ————. "Th. M. sprach in London," *Aufbau* (Berlin), 3 (November 1947), 355-356. ["Nietzsche im Lichte unserer Erfahrung"]

2,941. Schönberg, Arnold. "Further to the Schönberg-Mann Controversy," *Music Survey,* 2 (Autumn 1949), 77-80. [Cf. I, items #2,863-2,864]

2,942. ———. "Briefe an Th. M." [Nov. 1 and Nov. 8, 1930; Jan.
        2, 1950] in Erwin Stein, ed., Arnold Schönberg, Briefe,
        pp. 154-155 et al. Mainz: Schott [1958]
2,943. Schönherr, Hans. "Th. M.," in his Lübeck einst und jetzt,
        pp. 22-24. Lübeck: Verlag Lübecker Nachrichten [1959]
2,944. Schönwiese, Ernst. "Rahel spricht aus dem Grab zu Josef:
        Th. M. in Verehrung gewidmet," Österreichisches Tagebuch,
        Vol. 3, No. 11 (March 12, 1948), p. 17.
2,945. *Schörken, Rolf. Morphologie der Personen in Th. M's Roman
        'Joseph und seine Brüder.' Bonn: Rheinische Friedrich-
        Wilhelm-Universität, 1957. 234 pp. [Ph. D. diss., Bonn,
        1957]
2,946. Scholte, J. H. "Th. M.: Versuch über Schiller," Duitse Kroniek,
        No. 4 (November 1955), pp. 108-109.
2,947. Schoolfield, George C. "Th. M.," in his The Figure of the
        Musician in German Literature, pp. 171-190 et al. Chapel
        Hill: University of North Carolina Press, 1956.
2,948. ———. "Th. M. and the Honest Pagans," PQ, 36 (April
        1957), 280-285. [Concerns H. Weigand's study of Der
        Erwählte, I, item #2,933, and F. Gregorovius, Geschichte der
        Stadt Rom im Mittelalter]
2,949. ———. Review of Žmegač, item #3,600, JEGP, 61 (January
        1962), 136-138.
2,950. ———. "Th. M's 'Die Betrogene,' " GR, 38 (January 1963),
        [91]-120.
2,951. ———. Review of H. Levander, item #1,958, GQ, 38
        (November 1965), 698-702.
2,952. Schottlaender, Rudolf. "Der 'Antikomplex': Zu Th. M's 80.
        Geburtstag," Deutsche Universitätszeitung, Vol. 10, No. 11
        (June 8, 1955), pp. 5-6. [M's political attitude]
2,953. Schrem, Hans. "Mit Th. M. vor dem Buddenbrook-Haus,"
        Lübecker Nachrichten, Vol. 8, No. 133 (June 11, 1953), p. 9.
        [Biog.]
2,954. ———. " 'Wenn du meinst, Katja, natürlich . . .': Erinnerungen
        an Lübecks grössten Sohn in seiner Vaterstadt," Lübecker
        Nachrichten, August 14, 1955. [Biog.]

2,955. Schrenck-Notzing, Albert von. "Th. M.," in his *Die Phänomene des Mediums Rudi Schneider*, pp. 157-158. Berlin: De Gruyter, 1933.

2,956. Schroeder, Max. "Die Betrogene," *Aufbau* (Berlin), 10 (1954), 381-382. Also in his *Von Hier und Heute aus*, pp. 26-29. Berlin: Aufbau, 1957.

2,957. ———. " 'Leiden an Deutschland' und Erhebung: Zum Erscheinen der Gesammelten Werke von Th. M.," *NDL*, Vol. 3, No. 6 (June 1955), pp. 32-36. Also in his *Von Hier . . .,* #2,956, pp. 29-33.

2,958. ———. "In memoriam Th. M.: Die Kraft seines Werkes," *Sonntag*, No. 34 (August 21, 1955), p. 7. Also in his *Von Hier*, #2,956, pp. 37-38. [Obit.]

2,959. ———. "Th. M.: In Weimar (1949)," in his *Von Hier*, #2,956, pp. 22-23.

2,960. ———. "Der 75-Jährige,' in his *Von Hier*, #2,956, pp. 23-25.

2,961. ———. "Das Buddenbrookhaus," in his *Von Hier*, #2,956, pp. 33-37.

2,962. Schröder, Rudolf Alexander. "Th. M. zum 60. Geburtstag," in his *Gesammelte Werke*, Vol. 2, pp. 1000-1026. [Frankfurt a. M.] Suhrkamp, 1952. [Cf. I, item #786 — 60th birthday]

2,963. ———. "Th. M.: 'Leiden und Grösse der Meister,' " *Frankfurter Zeitung*, May 12, 1935. Also in item #2,962, pp. 1026-1036.

2,964. ———. "Verehrter, lieber Th. M.," *Der Bund; der kleine Bund*, Vol. 106, No. 254 (June 3, 1955), p. 6. [80th birthday]

2,965. Schröder, Wilhelm. "Th. M's 'Bekenntnisse des Hochstaplers Felix Krull,' " *Bücherei und Bildung*, Vol. 7, No. 11 (November 1955), pp. 724-725.

2,966. ———. Review of F. Lion, item #1,979, *Bücherei und Bildung*, Vol. 8, No. 7 (July 1956), 476.

2,967. ———. Review of R. Faesi, *Th. M.*, item #831, *Bücherei und Bildung*, Vol. 9, No. 7 (July 1957), p. 494.

2,968. ———. "Betrachtungen eines Unpolitischen," *Bücherei und Bildung*, Vol. 9, No. 7 (July 1957), p. 495. [Review of #2,058]

2,969.   Schroers, Paul. "Heinrich und Th. M. und ihre Verleger:
         Hinweis auf zwei Briefe und eine Briefsammlung," *Philobiblon*,
         2 (November 1958), 310-314.

2,970.   Schröter, Klaus. Literarische Einflüsse im Jugend- und
         Frühwerk von Heinrich Mann, 1892-1907: Ihre Bedeutung
         für sein Gesamtwerk. Ph. D. diss., University of Hamburg,
         1960. 234 pp. Published, in revised form, under the title
         *Anfänge Heinrich Manns: Zu den Grundlagen seines
         Gesamtwerks.* Stuttgart: J. B. Metzler, 1965. 198 pp.

2,971. *———. *Th. M. in Selbstzeugnissen und Bilddokumenten.*
         [Reinbeck] Rowohlt [1964] 173 pp. [Contains on p. 164
         important additions to Bürgin, #502]
         Excerpts:

   (a)   "Th. M. in Rom: Erste Begegnung 1896-1898," *Konkret,*
         No. 1 (January 1964), pp. 18, 20.

   (b)   "Th. M. und Paul Bourgets 'Dilettant,' " *Christ und Welt,*
         Vol. 17, No. 15 (April 10, 1964), p. 23.
         Reviews: Berendsohn, #279 — Haiduk, #1,152 — Heckmann,
         #1,246 — Hellmann, #1,308 — I. Jens, #1,578.

2,972.   ———. "Tempelwarte," *Welt der Literatur,* No. 14 (July 8,
         1965), p. 350. [Reply to Heckmann, #1,246]

2,973.   Schubert, Ludwig. "Goethe aus zweiter Hand," *Hamburger
         Akademische Rundschau,* 1 (1946), 251-253.

2,974. *Schütze, Sylvia. *Th. M. zum 80. Geburtstag.* Dortmund:
         Städtische Volksbüchereien, 1955. [7 pp. library catalogue]

2,975.   Schuh, Willy. "Th. M's letzte Prosa," *Allgemeine Zeitung
         für Württemberg,* November 17, 1956. [*Nachlese*]

2,976.   ———. "Zum Geleit," in Erika Mann, item #2,065, pp. 5-
         [10] [Richard Wagner]

2,977.   Schultes, Karl. "Bekenntnis zu Th. M.," *Vorwärts,* June 3,
         1955. [80th birthday]

2,978.   Schultz, H. Stefan. Review of H. Eichner, I, item #159,
         JEGP, 53 (July 1954), 494-497. [*See also* item #750]

2,979.   ———. Review of F. D. Hirschbach, item #1,429,
         Monatshefte, 48 (October 1956), 287.

2,980.   ————. Review of R. Hinton Thomas, item #3,273, *JEGP*, 56 (July 1957), 457-459.

2,981.   Schulz, Siegfried A. "Hindu Mythology in Th. M's Indian Legend," *CL*, 14 (1962), 129-142. [*Die Vertauschten Köpfe*]

2,982.   ————. " 'Die Vertauschten Köpfe': Th. M's indische Travestie," *Euphorion*, 57 (1963), [246]-271.

2,983.   ————. "Form and Style of Th. M's Indian Legend," in Alessandro S. Crisafulli, *ed.*, *Linguistic and Literary Studies in Honor of Helmut A. Hatzfeld*, pp. 365-373. Washington, D. C.: The Catholic University of America Press, 1964. [*Die Vertauschten Köpfe*]

2,984.   Schulze-Vellinghausen, Albert. "Stark aus Feinheit: Zum 80. Geburtstag Th. M's," *Frankfurter Allgemeine Zeitung*, Vol. 7, No. 128 (June 4, 1955). [80th birthday]

2,985.   Schumacher, Hans. "Zum 80. Geburtstag von Th. M.," *Basler Nachrichten*, Vol. 49, No. 22 (June 5, 1955), Sonntagsblatt. [80th birthday]

2,986.   Schuman, Robert. "Rencontre avec Th. M.," in item #1,493, p. 39.

2,987.   Schumann, Willy. "Theodor Storm und Th. M.: Gemeinsames und Unterschiedliches," *Monatshefte*, 55 (February 1963), [49]-68. Also in *Schriften der Theodor Storm-Gesellschaft*, No. 13 (1964), pp. 28-44.

2,988.   ————. Review of W. Hoffmeister, item #1,449, *GQ*, 38 (November 1965), 705-708.

2,989.   Schwabe, Walter. "Vorträge, Theater und Musik: 'Okkulte Erlebnisse,' " *Lübeckische Blätter*, Vol. 65, No. 51 (December 23, 1923), p. 599.

2,990.   Schwarz, Ruth. "Tony Buddenbrook — ein Frauenbildnis deutscher Spätbürgerlichkeit," *Spektrum*, 11 (1965), 205-209. [Elisabeth Mann — *Buddenbrooks*]

2,991.   Schweitzer, Albert. "Témoignage," in item #1,493, p. 37. [80th birthday]

2,992.   Schweizer, Hans. "Dostoievski et Nietzsche vus par Th. M.," *Journal de Genève*, No. 24 (January 29/30, 1955), p. 3.

2,993. Schweizer, Richard. "Heinrich Marti, ein Schweizer Vorfahre
        Th. M's," *Du,* Vol. 15, No. 6 (June 1955), pp. 49-51. [Biog.]
2,994. ———. "Trauerrede am Grabe Th. M's," in G. Wenzel,
        #3,453, pp. 91-92. Also in *Spektrum,* 11 (1965), 217-218.
2,995. ———. "Zürich als Stätte des Th. M.-Archivs," in item #2,644,
        pp. 17-23. Also in *Blätter der Th. M.-Gesellschaft Zürich,*
        No. 3 (1962), pp. 18-23.
2,996. Schwengeler, Arnold H. "Ein schweizerisches Geburtstags-
        geschenk: Zu Robert Faesis Buch über Th. M.," *Der Bund;*
        der kleine Bund, Vol. 106, No. 254 (June 3, 1955). [Review
        of #831]
2,997. ———. "Der Zauberer ist tot: Zum Hinschied Th. M's," *Der*
        Bund, Vol. 106, Morgenausgabe No. 377 (August 15, 1955),
        p. 1. [Obit.]
2,998. Schwerte, Hans. "Th. M's Schelmenroman: Zur Biographie des
        Felix Krull," *Erlanger Universität,* Vol. 8, No. 3 (May 11,
        1955), pp. 1-2.
2,999. ———. "Liebevolle Auflösung: Th. M's Hochstapler-
        Bekenntnisse. Zur 80. Wiederkehr seines Geburtstages,"
        Zeitwende; die neue Furche, 26 (June 1955), 399-405.
3,000. ———. "Dürers 'Ritter, Tod und Teufel,' eine ideologische
        Parallele zum Faustischen," in his *Faust und das Faustische;*
        ein Kapitel deutscher Ideologie, pp. 243-270. Stuttgart: E.
        Klett [1962]
3,001. Schyberg, Frederik. "Th. M. fylder 70," *Politiken,* June 6,
        1945, pp. 7-8. [70th birthday]
3,002. Scowcroft, Richard. "Th. M.: Felix Krull," *San Francisco*
        Chronicle, September 25, 1955, p. 16.
3,003. Seckelmann, Karlkuno L. "Ein deutscher Demokrat: Th. M.
        gestorben," *Saarbrücker Zeitung,* August 16, 1955. [Obit.]
3,004. Seeberger, Kurt. "Im Tonfall der Ironie," *Deutsche Zeitung,*
        November 20, 1955. [*Felix Krull*]
3,005. Seel, Otto. "Auseinandersetzung mit Th. M.," *Fränkischer*
        Kurier, No. 163 (June 14, 1931). [Politics]
3,006. Seelig, Carl. "Ein Frauenleben an der Seite von Th. M.: Zu

Katja Manns 75. Geburtstag," *Schweizer. Kaufmänn. Zentralblatt*, Vol. 62, No. 30/31 (July 25, 1958), pp. [447]-448.

3,007. ————. "Im Zauberbann von Th. M.: Eine Schatzkammer in der E. T. H.," *St. Galler Tagblatt*, Abendausgabe No. 124 (May 30, 1958). — "Im Geistesbanne Th. M's," *Tages-Anzeiger*, No. 185 (August 9, 1958), Bl. 10. — Rev. version, "Th. M.-Gedenkstätte in Zürich," *National-Zeitung Basel*, February 27, 1961.

Segebrecht, Wulf. *See* Lehnert, Herbert.

3,008. Seidenspinner, Clarence. "The Humanist in a World of Fury," *Northwestern University Alumni News*, Vol. 18, No. 4 (January 1939), pp. 22-25.

3,009. Seidler-von Hippel, Elisabeth. "Th. M.," in Paul Dormagen, *ed., Handbuch zur modernen Literatur in Deutschland*, pp. 59-74. Frankfurt a. M.: Hirschgraben, 1963. [Das Eisenbahnunglück — Buddenbrooks — Tonio Kröger — Tristan — Schwere Stunde — Königliche Hoheit — Der Tod in Venedig — Das Gesetz]

3,010. Seidlin, Oskar. "Stiluntersuchung an einem Th. M.-Satz," in his *Von Goethe zu Th. M.*, pp. 148-161. Göttingen: Vandenhoeck & Ruprecht [1963] [Cf. I, item #1,210]

3,011. ————. "Picaresque Elements in Th. M's Work," in his *Essays in German and Comparative Literature*, pp. [161]-181. Chapel Hill: University of North Carolina Press, 1961. German version, "Pikareske Elemente in Th. M's Werk," in item #3,010, pp. 162-184. [Cf. I, item #1,209]

3,012. ————. "Ironische Brüderschaft: Th. M's 'Joseph der Ernährer' und Laurence Sternes 'Tristram Shandy,' " *Orbis Litterarum*, 13 (1958), [44]-63. English version, "Laurence Sterne's 'Tristram Shandy' and Th. M's 'Joseph the Provider,' " in his *Essays*, #3,011, pp. [182]-202. Original German also in #3,010, pp. 185-207.

3,013. ————. Review of F. Kaufmann, item #1,683, *JEGP*, 58 (April 1959), 357-359.

3,014. ————. "The Shroud of Silence," in his *Essays*, item #3,011, pp. 228]-236. [Cf. I, item #1,044]

3,015. ————. "In the Beginning was . . . The Origin of Th. M's 'Joseph und seine Brüder,' " *MLN*, 77 (December 1962), 493-498.

3,016. Selander, Sten. "Inledning," in Th. M., *Tristan*, pp. 5-10. Stockholm: Ahlen, 1937.

3,017. Servicen, Louise. "Hommage de la traductrice," in item #1,493, p. 153.

3,018. Seuffert, Thea von. "Th. M.,' in her *Venedig im Erlebnis deutscher Dichter*, pp. 132-137. Köln: Petrarca-Haus; Stuttgart: DVA, 1937. [*Der Tod in Venedig*]

3,019. Seyppel, Joachim H. "Th. M. und die Barbarei: Eine kritische Betrachtung des 'Doktor Faustus,' " *Mittagsecho*, No. 60 (May 18, 1949).

3,020. ————. "Two Variations on a Theme: Dying in Venice. Th. M. and Ernest Hemingway," *Literature and Psychology*, Vol. 7, No. 1 (February 1957), pp. 8-12.

3,021. ————. "Adel des Geistes: Th. M. und August von Platen," *DVJS*, 33 (1959), 565-573.

3,022. Shabecoff, Philip. "1921 Mann letter denounced Nazis," *NYT*, January 16, 1966. [Concerns Th. M's letter about the Jewish question to the Munich paper *Der Neue Merkur*. See also Berendsohn, #284 — Hübinger, #1,510 — Stern, #3,139 — Tillmann, #3,282-3,282a.

Shigi, T. *See* Aoaki.

3,023. Shiroyama, Yoshihika. "Th. M. und Nietzsche," *Doitsu Bungaku — Die deutsche Literatur*, No. 8 (May 1952), pp. 50-53.

3,024. Shitahodo, Ibuki. "Das Leitmotiv in 'Tonio Kröger,' " *Osaka Furitsu-Daigaku-Kiyo*, 9 (1961), 87-108. [In Japanese]

3,025. ————. "Th. M. als Ironiker: Zum Problem des Künstlers," *Doitsu Bungaku — Die deutsche Literatur*, No. 27 (October 1961), pp. 70-78. [In Japanese, with German resumé]

3,026. Shuster, George N. "There is No Country," *Aufbau* (New York), Vol. 21, No. 33 (August 19, 1955), p. 1. [Obit.]

3,027. ————. "Art at War With the Good: Th. M's 'Death in Venice,' " in Robert M. MacIver, *ed., Great Moral Dilemmas in Literature, Past and Present,* pp. 25-36. New York: Harper, 1956.

3,028. ———. "Meaning of Mann," *America,* December 6, 1958. [Review of E. Heller, item #1,278]

3,029. ———. "Th. M's 'Last Essays,' " *America,* March 7, 1959.

3,030. ———. "Th. M.," in his *The Ground I Walked On,* pp. 144-146. New York: Farrar, Strauss, 1961. [Biog.]

3,031. Siebener, Karl. "Bekenntnis zu Th. M.," *Literarische Blätter,* No. 2 (June 25, 1946), pp. 1-3.

3,032. Siebenschein, Hugo, ed. *Th. M.: Tonio Kröger.* Prague: Staatliche Verlagsanstalt, 1932. 118 pp.

3,033. ———. "Biblická látka u Th. M.," *Radiojournal,* February 28, 1936. ["Der biblische Stoff bei Th. M."]

3,034. ———. "Mannův Kouzelný vrch," in Czech *ed.* of Th. M., *Der Zauberberg,* pp. 442-450. Prague, 1950.

3,035. ———. Review of V. Mann, I, #666, *Philologica,* 1 (1951), 13-14.

3,036. ———. "Th. M. zum 80. Geburtstag," *Sinn und Form,* 7 (1955), 358-368. [80th birthday]

3,037. ———. "Moje poslední setkání a Th. M.," *Světová literatura,* 2 (1955), 175-189. [About last meeting with Th. M. at Schiller Celebration in Weimar]

3,038. ———. "Th. M., demokrat a antifašista," *Tschechoslowakische Akademie der Wissenschaften,* December 5, 1955. [Politics]

3,039. ———. "Der Doppelbegriff Heinrich und Th. M.," *Philologica,* 4 (1957), 475-48.

3,040. ———. "Germanistické actuality," *Tschechoslowakische Akademie der Wissenschaften,* March 18, 1958. [Title in German: "Aktuelles in der Germanistik." Concerns Th. M. and Czechoslovakia]

3,041. ———. "Kouzelný vrch," *Časopis pro moderní filologii,* 3 (1958), 129-135. [Title in German: "Über Th. M's 'Zauberberg' "]

3,042. ———. "Humor bei Goethe und Th. M.," in *Filológiai Közlöny. Festschrift der Ungarischen Akademie der Wissen-*

schaften zu Ehren Professor Turóczi Trostlers, pp. 677-683.
Budapest, 1958.

3,043.   ———. Review of H. Bürgin, item #502, *Philologica,* 3
(1960), 243.

3,044.   ———. Review of I. Diersen, item #677, *DLZ,* 81 (1960),
1,009-1,012.

3,045.   ———. Review of P. Scherrer, item #2,877, *DLZ,* 82 (1961),
1,004-1,007.

3,046.   ———. "Über Th. M's Altershumor," in G. Wenzel, item
#3,461, pp. 196-203.

3,047.   ———. "Juvenilien," *Spektrum,* 11 (1965), 201-205.
["Gefallen" — *Der Kleine Herr Friedemann*]

3,048.   Sieburg, Friedrich. "Th. M's neuester Roman," *Welt,* March
15, 1951. [*Der Erwählte*]

3,049.   ———. "Auch ein Bildungsroman," *Gegenwart,* 9 (September
25, 1954), 622-623. Also in *Zeit,* Vol. 9, No. 40 (October 7,
1954), p. 6. Reprinted under the title "Kultur ist Parodie"
in his *Nur für Leser,* pp. 324-326. Stuttgart: DVA, 1955.
[*Felix Krull*]

3,050.   ———. "Im Zeichen der Vollendung," in his *Nur für Leser,*
#3,049, pp. 252-254. [Concerns *Altes und Neues.* — Cf. I,
#1,862]

3,051.   ———. "In der Sackgasse," in his *Nur für Leser,* item #3,049,
pp. 135-138. [Concerns *Der Erwählte.* Cf. I, #2,928]

3,052.   ———. "Höchster Anstandsunterricht," *Frankfurter
Allgemeine Zeitung,* January 28, 1961. [Review of Bertram,
#1,575]

3,053.   ———. "Ein Herr und Meister," *Frankfurter Allgemeine
Zeitung,* January 27, 1962. [*Briefe I,* #2,062]

3,054.   ———. "Der Geist der Erzählung," *Frankfurter Allgemeine
Zeitung,* May 4, 1963. [*Sämtliche Erzählungen*]

3,055.   ———. "Briefe an die Nacht," *Spiegel,* Vol. 18, No. 1-2
(January 8, 1964), pp. 66-67. [Review of *Briefe II,* item
#2,066]

3,056. Siedler, Wolf Jobst. "Über Käte Hamburgers *Th. M's Roman Joseph und seine Brüder,"* *Neue Zeitung,* July 5, 1950. [Review of I, item #2,450]

3,057. ———. "Spätlese im Verlagshaus Th. M's," *Tagesspiegel,* October 28, 1956. [*Nachlese*]

3,058. ———. "Buchsaison noch einmal im Schatten einer Th. M.-Novität," *Tagesspiegel,* December 10, 1961. [Review of *Briefe I,* item #2,062]

3,059. ———. Review of K. Sontheimer, item #3,097, *Bücherkommentare,* November 15, 1961.

3,060. ———. "Plädoyer für einen grossen Magen: Th. M. reist für Bonn durch die Welt," *Tagesspiegel,* May 17, 1962. [Th. M. Exhibit]

3,061. Siegmund, Georg. "Wie sich Davos geändert hat," *Rheinischer Merkur,* Vol. 19, No. 22 (May 26, 1964), p. 21. Also expanded version, "Davos — einst und jetzt: Der Zauberberg," *Erdkreis,* 14 (1964), 46-55.

3,062. Siemer, Heinrich. "Besuch bei Th. M.," *Lesestunde,* 7 (July 1, 1930), 226-228. [Biog.]

3,063. Siemsen, Anna. "Die Brüder Mann," in her *Literarische Streifzüge durch die Entwicklung der europäischen Gesellschaft,* pp. 178-183. Jena: Urania, 1925. [²1929, pp. 157-162] [Heinrich and Th. M.]

3,064. Sigoux, Gilbert. "Th. M. et le 'Docteur Faustus,' " *Preuves,* No. 133 (1962), pp. 86-90.

3,065. Silens, Peter. "Vom Geheimnis des Schöpferischen: Th. M. und 'Die Entstehung des Doktor Faustus,' " *Telegraf,* July 21, 1949.

3,066. ———. "Komödie der Sünde," *Telegraf,* March . . ., 1951. [*Der Erwählte*]

3,067. ———. "Letzte Prosa eines Grossen," *Telegraf,* November 18, 1956. [*Nachlese*]

3,068. ———. "Leiden an Deutschland von ehedem," *Telegraf,* August 26, 1962.

Silman, Tamara I., *see* items #8 and 9.

3,069. Silone, Ignazio. "Th. M. e il dovere civile," *Tempo Presente,* Vol. 3, No. 1 (January 1958), pp. [1]-5. Also in German,

"Die missverstandene Politik," *Forum,* 5 (June 1958),
219-222, and in French, "La pensée politique chez Th. M.,"
Preuves, No. 89 (July 1958), pp. 75-80. [*See also* reply by E.
M. Borgese, incorporated in item #3,070]

3,070. ———. "Rettifiche e conferme su Th. M.," *Tempo Presente,*
Vol. 3, No. 3 (March 1958), pp. [219]-225. [Cf. #406]

3,071. †Simon, John Donald. "Th. M. and the Franco-German
Reconciliation. M. A. thesis, University of Texas, 1961. [This
concerns the reaction of the French press to Th. M's visit to
Paris in February, 1926]

3,072. Simon, Ulrich. "The Theological Challenge of 'Doctor
Faustus,'" *Church Quarterly Review,* 159 (October-December,
1958), 547-553.

3,073. Sinclair, Upton. "Th. M.," in his *My Lifetime in Letters,* pp.
376-384. Columbia: University of Missouri Press [1960] [With
eight letters from Th. M. and one from Klaus M.]

3,074. Sinding-Larsen, Henning. "Th. M. arbetar på stort memoar-
verk," *Svenska Dagbladet,* August 4, 1953. [Interview]

3,075. Singer, Herbert. "Helena und der Senator: Versuch einer
mythologischen Deutung von Th. M's 'Buddenbrooks,'"
Stuttgarter Zeitung, No. 87 (April 13, 1963), Beilage 'Die
Brücke zur Welt.'

3,076. Single, Ernst. "Angst vor dem Gefühl: Das Beispiel von Th.
M's 'Doktor Faustus,'" *Stuttgarter Nachrichten,* Vol. 5, No. 9
(January 12, 1950), p. 9. [*Doktor Faustus.* Adds to I, item
#2,839]

3,077. Slochower, Harry. "Th. M.: 1875-1955," *Guide,* 2 (October
1955), pp. 12-14. [Obit.]

3,078. Smeed, J. W. "The Role of Professor Kuckuck in 'Felix Krull,'"
MLR, 59 (July 1964), 411-412.

3,079. †Smikalla, Karl. Die Stellung Th. Ms zur Romantik. Ph. D.
diss., University of Würzburg, 1953. 167 pp.

3,080. Sochaczewer, Hans. "Romane der Welt?" *Berliner Tageblatt,*
June 12, 1927, Beilage 'Literarische Rundschau.' [G. H.
Scheffauer and Th. M.]

3,081. Soenke, Jürgen. "Th. M.: Die Buddenbrooks," *Mindener Tageblatt*, Ausgabe B, Vol. 48, No. 116 (May 21, 1955).

3,082. *———. ed. *Wegweiser durch das Th. M.-Zimmer im Schabbelhaus der Kaufmannschaft zu Lübeck*. [Lübeck] 1962. 32 pp. illus.

3,083. Sørensen, Bengt Algot. "Th. M's 'Doktor Faustus,' Mythos und Lebensbeichte," *Orbis Litterarum*, 13 (1958), [81]-97.

3,084. ———. Review of Th. M.-K. Kerényi, item #1,700 c, *Orbis Litterarum*, 16 (1961), [122]-124.

3,085. ———. "Die symbolische Gestaltung in den Jugenderzählungen Th. M's," *Orbis Litterarum*, 20 (1965), [85]-97. [Tristan — Tonio Kröger   Der Tod in Venedig]

3,086. ———. Review of H. Weigand, item #3,432, *Orbis Litterarum*, 20 (1965), 159-160.

Soergel, Albert. *See* Hohoff, Curt.

3,087. Soeteman, Cornelis. "De Gregoriuslegende bij Hartmann von Aue en Th. M.," *Duitse Kroniek*, Vol. 4, No. 2 (June 1952), pp. 38-46. [*Der Erwählte*]

3,088. ———. "Driemaal Faust: zestiende eeuw — Goethe — Th. M.," *Duitse Kroniek*, Vol. 5, No. 1 (1953), pp. 8-17.

3,089. ———. "Th. M. tachtig jaar," *Duitse Kroniek*, Vol. 7, No. 2 (1955), pp. 50-51. [80th birthday]

3,090. ———. "Alter Wein in neuen Schläuchen: Über Stofferfindung und Stoffentlehnung in der deutschen Literatur," *Revue des Langues Vivantes — Levende Talen*, No. 205 (June 1960), pp. 360-371. [*See* esp. pp. 367-371 for a discussion of *Der Erwählte* and quotations from Th. M's letter to the author]

3,091. ———. "Th. M. en Duitsland," in his *Schrijver en Volk, zes lezingen*, pp. 109-127. Den Haag: Servire, 1963.

3,092. Sokel, Walter H. "Th. M.," in his *The Writer in Extremis*, pp. 78-82. Stanford: Stanford University Press, 1959. Also in German, "Th. M.: Doktor Faustus," in his *Der literarische Expressionismus*, pp. 102-107. München: A. Langen [1960]

3,093. Sommer, Elisabeth. "Th. M.," *Ansporn*, No. 18 (September 20, 1930), pp. 1121-1127. [Biog.]

3,094. Sommer, Heinz Erich. "Th. M. und Frankreich," *Frankfurter Neue Presse,* Vol. 17, No. 29 (February 3, 1962), Sonntagsbeilage.

3,095. Sommerhalder, Hugo. "Das Th. M.-Archiv der E. T. H. in Zürich," *Schweizer Monatshefte,* 40 (April 1960), 92-94. Also in Spanish, "El archivo de Th. M. en Zurich," *Humboldt,* Vol. 2, No. 6 (1961), pp. 74-75.

3,096. Sontheimer, Kurt. "Th. M. als politischer Schriftsteller," *Vierteljahrsschrift für Zeitgeschichte,* 6 (January 1958), [1]-44.

3,097. *————. *Th. M. und die Deutschen.* München: Nymphenburg [1961] 194 pp.
Excerpts:
(a) "Er sah, was not war: Th. M. als politischer Schriftsteller," *Kölner Stadtanzeiger,* No. 186 (August 12/13, 1961), Feuilleton.
(b) "Leiden an Deutschland," *Lübeckische Blätter,* Vol. 122, No. 10 (1962), pp. 131-134.
(c) "Th. M. als Politiker," *Welt und Wort,* 17 (1962), 74-76. Reviews: Becher, #208 — Faye, #839 — Hellmann, #1,300 — Henschel, #1,328 — Kantorowicz, #1,659 — Matter, #2,152 — Siedler, #3,059 — E. E. Stein, #3,122 — G. Stein, #3,126.

3,098. ————. "Heinrich und Th. M.," in Horst Lehner, *ed., Auf der Suche nach Frankreich,* pp. 141-158. [Herrenalb] H. Erdmann [1963]

3,099. Sorai, Yoshimi. "Über das Schicksal bei Th. M.," *Doitsu Bungaku — Die deutsche Literatur,* No. 24 (1960), pp. 42-47. [In Japanese, with German resumé]

3,100. Sorani, Aldo. "Colloquio con Th. M., il piú grande romanziero tedesco," *La Stampa,* March 8, 1925. [Interview-Biog.]

3,101. *Sós, Endre [and] Magda Vámos. *Th. és Heinrich Mann.* Budapest: Gondolat, 1960. 245 pp. Review: Zoltán, #3,606.

3,102. Spann, Meno. "Franz Kafka's Leopard," *GR,* 34 (April 1959), [85]-104. [Concerns Kafka's 'Ein Hungerkünstler' and Mann's 'Der Zauberberg'. *See* esp. pp. 103-104]

3,103. Specht, Richard. "Th. M's Essaywerk," *Neues Wiener Journal,* August 22, 1926. [*Bemühungen*]

3,104. ———. "Th. M's neue Novelle 'Mario und der Zauberer,' " *Neue Freie Presse,* May 12, 1930, Abendblatt.

3,105. ———. "Th. M. als französischer Autor," *Neue Freie Presse,* August 30, 1931. [Concerns *Sang réservé,* French translation of *Wälsungenblut*]

3,106. Speckner, Georg Joseph. "Th. M. — Tag für Tag," *Augsburger Allgemeine,* No. 281 (December 4, 1965), Literaturblatt, p. IV. [Review of Bürgin-Mayer, item #504]

3,107. Spender, Stephen. "Th. M's Irony," *Sunday Times,* October 12, 1958. [Review of E. Heller, item #1,278]

3,108. Spenlé, Jean Edouard. "Th. M. par M. Grützmacher dans les 'Preussische Jahrbücher,' " *Mercure de France,* 189 (July 1, 1926), 321-232. [Concerns I, item #1,621]

3,109. Spiel, Hilde. "Th. M's Briefwechsel," *Wort und Wahrheit,* 19 (1964), 646-648. [Review of *Briefe II,* item #2,066]

3,110. Sporn, Carl. "Nachwort," in Th. M., *Mario und der Zauberer,* pp. [63-64] Frankfurt a. M.: S. Fischer, 1953.

3,111. Stackmann, Karl. "Der Erwählte: Th. M's Mittelalter-Parodie," *Euphorion,* 53 (1959), [61]-74.

3,112. Stadelmeyer, Peter. "Degoutierliches aus bester Feder," *Frankfurter Hefte,* 8 (October 1953), 802-804. [*Die Betrogene*]

3,113. Stampfer, Friedrich. "Th. M's Vision: 'Vom künftigen Sieg der Demokratie,' " *Neue Volkszeitung,* September 24, 1938. [*The Coming Victory of Democracy*]

3,114. Stange, C. R. "Zum Tode von Th. M.," *Basler Nachrichten,* Beilage No. 343 (August 16, 1955). [Obit.]

3,114a. Starzycki, A. "Th. M's 'Doctor Faustus': A Contribution to the Studies of Musical Facts in Literature," *Zagadnienia rodzajów literackich,* 7 (1964), 27-41. [In Polish]

3,115. Stavenhagen, Lee. "The Name Tadzio in 'Der Tod in Venedig,' " *GQ,* 35 (January 1962), 20-23.

3,116. Stein, Ernst E. "Wir wollen Kafka nicht mit Mann verwechseln" [by Andreas Sattler, pseud.] *Zeit,* Vol. 13, No. 51 (December 19, 1958), p. 9. [Review of John [Hans] Kafka, *Welt und*

Kaffeehaus, which pretends to contain the original idea of
Felix Krull, and of H. P. Dorn, item #705, the "sequel" to
Felix Krull]

3,117.   ————. "Mann, Kafka und Thomas," *Zeit,* Vol. 14, No. 5
(January 30, (1959), p. 16. [Letter to the Editor by Andreas
Sattler, pseud., containing more information on the identity of
John Kafka and Hans Peter Dorn]

3,118.   ————. "Grosser Mann, was nun?" *Zeit,* Vol. 14, No. 52
(December 25, 1959), pp. 7-8. [Review of Amann, #3,426;
Bürgin, #502; Petriconi, item #2,522; E. Heller, #1,278; and
Erzählungen. See also Letters to the Editor by E. E. Stein,
#3,119, and K. Ziesel, #3,590]

3,119.   ————. "Brief an den Herausgeber," *Zeit,* Vol. 15, No. 5
(January 29, 1960), p. 20. [Refutation of K. Ziesel, #3,590]

3,120.   ————. "Das verdammte Entweder — Oder," *Zeit,* Vol. 15,
No. 23 (June 3, 1960), p. 11. [Review of A. Hellersberg, item
#1,285, and Th. M.-K. Kerényi, item #1,700 c]

3,121.   ————. "Zwölfmal Prestige," *Zeit,* Vol. 15, No. 52 (December
23, 1960), p. 8. [Review of 12-vol. *ed.* of Th. M's works by S.
Fischer, 1960]

3,122.   ————. "Politik — eine Kunstform: Th. M. und die
Deutschen," *Zeit,* Vol. 17, No. 38 (September 21, 1962), p. 24.
[Review of K. Sontheimer, item #3,097]

3,123.   ————. "Alles andere als krankhaft: Zur Berichtigung einiger
immer wiederkehrender Missverständnisse um Th. M.," *Zeit,*
Vol. 19, No. 52 (December 25, 1964). [Concerns
Joseph und seine Brüder and item #2,853]

3,124.   Stein, Gottfried. "Der Pädagoge Th. M.," *Pädagogisches Echo,*
Vol. 56, No. 7-8 (February 13, 20, 1926).

3,125.   ————. "Ich stelle mich der Freundschaft, dem Hass,"
Frankfurter Rundschau, Vol. 5, No. 176 (August 1, 1949),
p. 2. [Concerns Th. M's speech in Frankfurt's Paulskirche on
July 25, 1949. — Politics]

3,126.   ————. "Minutiöses Referat," *Frankfurter Hefte,* 20 (February
1965), 139-142. [Review of K. Sontheimer, item #3,097]

3,127. Stein, R. "Vom Geist der Medizin — und vom Geist der Literatur: Vier Jahrzehnte Zauberberg," *Zeitschrift für ärztliche Fortbildung,* Vol. 54, No. 1 (January 1965), pp. 82-87.

3,128. Steinbach, Ernst. "Gottes armer Mensch: Die religiöse Frage im dichterischen Werk von Th. M.," *Zeitschrift für Theologie und Kirche,* 50 (1953), 207-242.

Steinbömer, Gustav. *See* Hillard-Steinbömer.

3,129. Steiner, Gerhard. "Ein Wort zuvor," *Spektrum,* 11 (1965), 141-142. [90th birthday]

3,130. ———. 'Nachwort," in his *ed.* of Th. M., *Über deutsche Literatur: Ausgewählte Essays, Reden und Briefe,* pp. 355- [371] Leipzig: P. Reclam [1965]

3,131. Steiner, Jacob. "Weltbürgertum in der modernen deutschen Literatur," *Zürcher Student,* 29 (November 1951), 171-177.

3,132. ———. "Heinrich von Kleist und seine Erzählungen: Zu einem Vortrag Th. M's," *NZZ,* Vol. 175, No. 3058 (December 4, 1954).

3,133. ———. Review of G. Bergsten, item #292, *Samlaren,* 84 (1963), [292]-297.

3,134. Steinthal, Th. "Th. M. har faaet Nobelprisen," *Politiken,* November 13, 1929, p. 1. [Nobel Prize]

3,135. Stelzmann, Rainulf A. "Th. M's 'Death in Venice': Res et Imago," *Xavier University Studies,* 3 (1964), 160-167.

3,136. Stemmer, Konrad. "Themen und Variationen: Die neue Essaysammlung von Th. M.," *Neue Zeitung,* February 12, 1953. [*Altes und Neues*]

3,137. Stepanauskas, Leonas. "Kleine Perle in einem grossen Leben," *Wochenpost,* Vol. 12, No. 23 (June 5, 1965), p. 25. [Biog. — Nidden]. Enlarged version, entitled "Th. M. in Litauen," *Du,* Vol. 26, No. 299 (January 1966), pp. 61-62.

3,138. Stephan, Doris. "Th. M's 'Tod in Venedig' und Brochs 'Vergil,' " *Schweizer Monatshefte,* 40 (April 1960), 76-83.

3,139. Stern, Guy. "A Case for Oral Literary History: Conversations with or about Morgenstern, Lehmann, Reinacher and Th. M.," *GQ,* 37 (November 1964), 487-497. [*See* esp. pp. 490-492 on Th. M's "Gedanken über die Juden," announced as forth-

coming in the August 1921 issue of *Der Neue Merkur,* but
withdrawn before publication. — Cf. Berendsohn, #284 —
Hübinger, #1,510 — Tillmann, #3,282-3,282a]

3,140. Stern, J. Peter. "The Truthful Observer: Th. M's Appraisal of
Our Time," *Aspect,* No. 1 (February 1963), pp. 63-74.

3,141. Sternaux, Ludwig. "Th. M. und wir," *Berliner Lokalanzeiger,*
June 6, 1925. [50th birthday]

3,142. Sternberger, Dolf. "Die Liebe und das kalte Herz," *Gegenwart,*
10 (June 4, 1955), 378-379. [80th birthday]

3,143. Sternfeld, W. "Letzter Abschied: Zürich, 15. August 1955,"
AJR Information, Vol. 10 (September 1955) p. 4. [Obit.]

3,144. Stickelberger, Rudolf. "Th. M. gestorben," *Luzerner Neueste
Nachrichten,* Vol. 59, No. 187 (August 13, 1955), p. 1.
[Obit.]

3,145. Stieler, Hilde. "Erinnerung an Th. M. und seine Familie,"
Tat, Vol. 27, No. 4 (January 6, 1962), p. 17.

3,146. Stiemer, Felix. "Th. M.: Betrachtungen eines Unpolitischen,"
Menschen, Vol. 2, No. 2 (1919). [Poem]

3,147. Stillwell, Robert L. "Mann's Confessions of Felix Krull,"
Explicator, Vol. 20, No. 3 (1961).

3,148. Stock, E. M. "Th. M.: Leben und Wirken eines Dichters im
Exil," *Annabelle,* 5 (December 1942), 37-39, 104. [Biog.]

3,149. Stock, Irwin. "Mann's Christian Parable: A View of 'The
Holy Sinner,' " *Accent,* 14 (Winter 1954), 96-115. [*Der
Erwählte*]

3,150. Stockhammer, Morris. "Th. M's Job-Jacob," *Judaism,* 8 (1959),
242-246. [*Joseph and His Brothers*] Transl. from the German
by William Wolf.

3,151. ————. "Th. M. als Kantianer," in his *Kants Zurechnungsidee
und Freiheitsantinomie,* pp. 559-571. Köln: Kölner Univer-
sitätsverlag, 1961.

3,152. Stockum, Theodorus Cornelius van. Review of R. Hinton
Thomas, item #3,273, *Neophilologus,* 43 (April 1959), 171.

3,153. ————. "Der Künstler und das Leben," in his *Von Friedrich
Nicolai bis Th. M.,* pp. 301-319. Groningen: J. B. Wolters,
1962.

3,154. ———. "Savonarola, die historische Gestalt und ihre doppelte Spiegelung im Werke Th. M's," in item #3,153, pp. 320-333. ["Gladius Dei" — *Fiorenza*]

3,155. Stöcker, Jakob. "Th. M.: Der Wanderer zwischen den Welten," in his *Männer des deutschen Schicksals,* pp. 224-240. Berlin: Arnold, 1949.

3,156. Stöcklein, Paul. "Konträre Goethedeutungen," *Hochland,* 41 (August 1949), 587-593. ["Phantasie über Goethe"]

3,156a. ———. "In Bayern aufgewachsen: Ein Historiker unserer Tage," *Zwiebelfisch,* 18 (1963), 178-179. [Golo and Th. M.]

3,157. Störi, Fritz. "Ariels Echo," *Neue Schweizer Rundschau,* N. F., 16 (March 1949), 678-681. [*Doktor Faustus*]

3,158. ———. "Form als Ausdruck," *Basler Schulblatt,* 10 (September 9, 1949), 73-74. [*Doktor Faustus*]

3,159. Stössinger, Felix. "Zum 'Erwählten,' " *Neue Schweizer Rundschau,* N. F., 19 (1952), 461-462.

3,160. Stolpe, Sven. "De två fronterna," *BLM,* 8 (November 1939), 718-719. [*Das Problem der Freiheit — Frihetens problem*]

3,161. Stolte, Heinz. "In Eckermann-Haltung," *Neue lit. Welt,* No. 15 (August 10, 1953), [Review of J. Lesser, I, #1865]

3,162. Stommel, M. A. "Bürgerwelt im Schelmenlicht," *Rheinische Post,* No. 242 (October 16, 1954). [*Felix Krull*]

3,163. Storck, Joachim W. Review of P. Altenberg, #34, *Archiv,* 199 (1962), 190-191.

3,164. Storfer, A. J. "Th. M. und die Psychoanalyse," *Internationale Zeitschrift für Psychoanalyse,* 11 (1925), 247.

3,165. ———. "Th. M. entlarvt? — Und Sigmund Freud?," *Die psychoanalytische Bewegung,* 1 (July-August, 1929), 174-175. ["Die Stellung Freuds in der modernen Geistesgeschichte"]

3,166. Stout, Harry L. "Lessing's Riccaut and Th. M's Fitelberg," *GQ,* 36 (January 1963), 24-30. [Concerns Lessing's *Minna von Barnhelm* and Th. M's *Doctor Faustus*]

3,167. Strecker, Karl. "Th. M.: 'Betrachtungen eines Unpolitischen,' " *Velhagen und Klasings Monatshefte,* 33 (April 1919), [214]-216.

3,168. ———. "Der Zauberberg von Th. M.," *Weltstimmen*, 1
(April 1927), [2]-10. Also in *Velhagen und Klasings
Monatshefte*, 39 (March 1926), [109]-110.

3,169. Strenger, Hermann. "Dauernder Nachklang: Zu Th. M's
'Versuch über Schiller,' " *Stuttgarter Zeitung*, Vol. 11, No. 142
(June 25, 1955), p. 34.

3,170. Stresau, Hermann. "Th. M.: Weite und Grenzen seiner
geistigen Existenz," *Göttinger Universitäts-Zeitung*, August 15,
1947.

3,171. ———. "Kunst, Krankheit und Opfer," *Allgemeine Zeitung
Mainz*, No. 78 April 2-3, 1949, Literaturblatt. [*Doktor
Faustus*]

3,172. ———. "Biblisch und human," *Allgemeine Zeitung. Mainz*,
September 11, 1949. [*Joseph der Ernährer*]

3,173. ———. "Aus einem halben Jahrhundert," *Frankfurter
Allgemeine Zeitung*, Vol. 5, No. 170 (July 25, 1953).
[*Altes und Neues*]

3,174. ———. "Der Geist des Epischen," *S. Fischer Almanach: das
68. Jahr*, pp. 82-91. [Frankfurt a. M.] 1954. [80th birthday]
This has been incorporated in his monograph, item #3,181.

3,175. ———. "Die Buddenbrooks," *Neue Rundschau*, 66 (June
1955), 392-410.

3,176. ———. "Il motivo dell'irruzione nell'opera di Th. M.," *Il
Ponte*, 11 (June 1955), 888-894. [Transl. from the German by
Giovanni De Caria]

3,177. ———. "Th. M.," *Deutsche Universitäts-Zeitung*, Vol. 10,
No. 15/16 (August 29, 1955), pp. 3-4. [Obit.]

3,178. ———. "Sinn für Tatsächlichkeiten," *Frankfurter Allgemeine
Zeitung*, Vol. 8, No. 281 (December 1, 1956), p. 13.
[*Nachlese*]

3,179. ———. "Studie über frühe Novellen Th. M's," *Deutsche
Universitäts-Zeitung*, Vol. 12, No. 13/14 (1957), pp. 22-26.

3,180. ———. "Der Erwählte," *Deutsche Universitäts-Zeitung*, 14
(August 1959), 482-490. [*The Holy Sinner*]

3,181. *———. *Th. M. und sein Werk*. Frankfurt a. M.: S. Fischer,
1963. 284 Excerpt in item #3,174.

Reviews: Berendsohn, #276 — Hellmann, #1,307 — Pietsch, #2,553.

3,182. Strich, Christian, ed. *Der Autorabend: Dichteranekdoten von Rabelais bis Th. M.* Zurich: Diogenes, 1953.

3,183. *Strich, Fritz. *Th. M.* [Tokyo] Daigakusyrion [1931] 53 pp. [Text in German and in Japanese; translation by Toyotaro Seki]

3,184. ————. "Th. M. oder Der Dichter und die Gesellschaft," *Der Bund; der kleine Bund,* Vol. 106, No. 254 (June 3, 1955), pp. 5-7. Also in his *Kunst und Leben,* pp. [159]-168. Bern: Francke [1960] [80th birthday]

3,185. ————. "Tief ist der Brunnen der Vergangenheit," *NZZ,* Vol. 176, Sonntagsausgabe No. 1497 (28), June 5, 1955, p. 3. Also in his *Kunst und Leben,* item #3,184, pp. [152]-158.

3,186. ————. "Schiller und Th. M.," *Neue Rundschau,* 68 (May 1957), 60-83. Also in his *Kunst und Leben,* item #3,184, pp. [169]-190.

3,187. Stroh, Heinz. "Th. M's neue Novelle," *Berliner Börsenzeitung,* No. 140 (May 1930), pp. 7-8. [*Mario und der Zauberer*]

3,188. ————. "Th. M.: Sang réservé," *Berliner Börsenzeitung,* No. 192 (September 1931). [Concerns French edition of *Wälsungenblut*]

3,189. ————. "Th. M's jüdische Menschen," *Jüdische Revue,* 2 (March 1937), 172-175.

3,190. Stroman, Bernard J. H. "Materiaal voor en zelfportret van Th. M.," *Critisch Bulletin,* 22 (June 1955), 241-247.

3,191. Struc, Roman S. "The Threat of Chaos: Stifter's 'Bergkristall' and Th. M's 'Schnee,' " *MLQ,* 24 (December 1963), 323-332.

3,192. Strübel, Gustav. "Bekenntnisse des Hochstaplers Felix Krull," *Weltstimmen,* No. 1 (January 1955), pp. 2-6.

3,193. ————. "Der Dichter zwischen den Zeiten," *Deutsches Volksblatt,* June 4, 1955. [80th birthday]

3,194. Stuckenschmidt, Hans Heinz. "Schönbergs Versöhnung mit Th. M.," *Welt,* March 29, 1957. Also in his *Arnold Schönberg,* pp. 10-11. [Zurich] Atlantis [²1957] [With Th. M's letter of October 19, 1951, to Stuckenschmidt]

3,195.   ———. "Klaus Pringsheim zum 80. Geburtstag (24. Juli),"
          NZZ, Abendausgabe, Vol. 184, No. 2985 (July 23, 1963),
          pp. 1-2.

3,196.   ———. "Zwillinge achtzigjährig: Klaus Pringsheim und
          Katja Mann zum Geburtstag am 24. Juli," *Frankfurter
          Allgemeine Zeitung,* No. 168 (July 24, 1963), p. 20.

3,197.   Stucki, Clara. "Die Idee des Mythischen in Th. M's Joseph-
          roman," *Schule und Leben,* Vol. 47, No. 5 (1957), pp. 5-17.
          Also in *Jahresbericht der Töchterschule der Stadt Zürich,*
          Abt. I, 1956/57, pp. 23-37.

3,198.   Stuiveling, Garmt. "Th. M.," in his *Pantheon der Winnaars
          van de Nobelprijs voor Literatuur,* [26] pp. Hasselt: Heideland,
          1963.

3,199.   Sturm, Wilma. "Die Betrogene," *Schwäbische Landeszeitung,*
          October 24, 1953.

3,200.   Sturmann, Manfred. "Herr und Hund: Zu Th. M's 80.
          Geburtstag," *MB,* Vol. 23, No. 22 (June 3, 1955), p. 4.

3,201.   Subiotto, A. V. Review of Scarpa, item #2,852, *GLL,* N. S.,
          17 (October 1963), 170-172.

3,202.   Suchsland, Peter. "Künstlerproblematik und Realismus," *NDL,*
          8 (March (1960), 137-140. [Review of I. Diersen, item
          #677]

3,203.   Süskind, W. E. "Th. M.: Die neuen Kinder," *Uhu,* Vol. 2,
          No. 11 (August 1926), pp. 8-10. [Interview with Th. M.
          concerning Klaus Mann's article "Die neuen Eltern," in same
          issue of *Uhu,* pp. 4-8]

3,204.   ———. "Von Faust zu Faustus," *Weser-Kurier,* January 22,
          1949. [*Doktor Faustus*]

3,205.   ———. "Lotte in Weimar: Einige Bemerkungen zu Th. M's
          Roman," *Frankfurter Rundschau,* August 28, 1949, p. 4.

3,206.   ———. "Felix Krull lebt weiter," *Frankfurter Rundschau,*
          November 27, 1954. [Reprint of I, item #2,218]

3,207.   ———. "Th. M.: Der Tod und das Leben," *Süddeutsche
          Zeitung,* No. 131 (June 4-5, 1955). [80th birthday]

3,208.   ———. "Th. M.: Fürst und Zauberer. Versuch einer
         Würdigung zum 80. Geburtstag," *Main-Post,* Sonderbeilage
         Pfingsten 1955, p. 5. [80th birthday]
3,209.   ———. "Th. M.: Unser grösster Erzähler," *Deutsche Zeitung,*
         Vol. 10, No. 65 (1955), p. 14. [80th birthday]
3,210.   ———. "Th. M. gestorben," *Süddeutsche Zeitung,* No. 191/
         192 (August 13, 1955). [Obit.]
3,211.   ———. "Th. M. zum Abschied," *Süddeutsche Zeitung,* No.
         193 (August 16, 1955), p. 3. [Obit.]
3,212.   ———. "Abschied von Th. M.," *Welt und Wort,* 10
         (September 1955), 283-284. [Obit.]
3,213.   ———. "Abschied von Th. M.," *Süddeutsche Zeitung,* No. 300
         (December 15, 1956). [*Nachlese*]
3,214.   ———. "Th. M. als Briefschreiber," *Deutsche Zeitung,* No.
         155 (July 7/8, 1962), Lit. Rundschau. [*Briefe I,* #2,062]
3,215.   ———. "Die Zwillinge aus der Arcisstrasse," *Süddeutsche
         Zeitung,* No. 175 (July 23, 1963). [80th birthday of Katja
         Mann and Klaus Pringsheim]
3,216.   ———. "Die Zwillinge in der Arcisstrasse," *Süddeutsche
         Zeitung,* No. 190 (August 9, 1963). [Controversial discussion
         of #3,215 about 'Wälsungenblut.' *See also* K. Pringsheim,
         #2,608]
3,217.   ———. "Th. M. als Briefschreiber," *Süddeutsche Zeitung,*
         No. 290 (December 4, 1963). [*Briefe II,* #2,066]
3,218.   Suhrkamp, Peter. "Brief an Th. M. vom 29. Dezember 1947,"
         in Siegfried Unseld, *ed., Peter Suhrkamp: Briefe an die Autoren,*
         pp. 50-53. [Frankfurt a. M.: Suhrkamp, 1961] [²1963, pp.
         48-51]
3,219.   Sullivan, Daniel. "Two Humanisms," *Commonweal,* 29
         (December 30, 1938), 258-259.
3,220.   Sulzer, Elisabeth [i.e. Elisabeth Brock-Sulzer] "Pariser
         Rechenschaft," *Schweizer Monatshefte,* 6 (December 1926),
         [548]-553.
3,221.   Suter, Gody. "Der Repräsentant Th. M. und die Deutschen,"
         Weltwoche, Vol. 30, No. 1471 (January 19, 1962), p. 21.
         [Review of *Briefe I,* item #2,062]

3,222. Svanberg, Victor. "Th. M's ironi," *Tiden*, 21 (December 1929), 473-481.

3,223. ――――. "Tonio Kröger," *Stockholms-Tidningen*, August 30, 1953. Reprinted in his collection of essays, *Till nutidens liv*," pp. 228-231. Uppsala: Lindblad [1956]

3,224. ――――. "Roman om en roman," *Stockholms-Tidningen*, October 14, 1963, p. 7. [Review of G. Bergsten, item #292]

3,225. ――――. "Mann — Faust — Hitler," *Stockholms-Tidningen*, October 16, 1963. [*See also* John Landquist's reply, item #1,842, and Hans Levander, item #1,956]

3,226. ――――. "Dött och levande hos Th. M.," *Stockholms-Tidningen*, October 12, 1964. [Review of H. Levander, item #1,958]

3,227. Swales, M. W. Review of W. Hoffmeister, item #1,449, *MLR*, 61 (January 1966), 157-158.

3,228. Szabo, György. "Carte inedite di Th. M., Deszö Kosztolányi, Attila József," *L'Europa Letteraria*, Vol. 2, No. 7 (February 1961), pp. 8-14. [Includes first Italian publication of "Saluto a Th. M.," item #1,619]

3,229. Szentkuthy, Nikolaus. "Th. M's Joseph-Geschichten," *Sinn und Form: Sonderheft Th. M.*, 1965, pp. 205-217. Transl. from Hungarian by Pia Razgha.

3,230. *Szentmihályi, János [and] Jánosní Déri. *Th. M.-Bibliográfia*. Budapest, 1956. 32 pp.

3,231. Szigeti, Joseph. "The Phonograph in Th. M's 'The Magic Mountain,'" *American Music Lover*, Vol. 9, No. 2 (October 1942), pp. 27-29. Also in German in his *Zwischen den Saiten*, pp. 153-157. Zürich: Müller [1962] Transl. from English by Alexander J. Seiler and J. von Rezniceck.

3,232. Szondi, Peter. "Versuch über Th. M.," *Neue Rundschau*, 67 (1956), 557-563. [*Die Vertauschten Köpfe — Der Erwählte*]

3,233. ――――. "Th. M's Gnadenmär von Narziss," in his *Satz und Gegensatz: Sechs Essays*, pp. 71-78. Frankfurt a. M.: Insel, 1964. [*Der Erwählte*]

3,234. Tabarelli, Hans. "Th. M. über sich selbst; das Künstlertum des Bürgers," *Neues Wiener Journal*, October 30, 1926. [*Lübeck als geistige Lebensform*]

3,235. ———. "Th. M., der deutsche Patriot," *Neues Wiener Journal*, August 16, 1928, pp. 1-2.

3,236. Tachibana, Koichi. "Über den 'Tod in Venedig' von Th. M.," *University of Kanazawa Bulletin*, No. 3 (1955), pp. 74-89. [In Japanese]

3,237. Takahashi, Giko. "Th. M's Aufsätze über Sigmund Freud," *Studies in Literature*, No. 2 (1954), pp. 105-121. [Cf. I, item #1731]

3,238. Takahashi, Ryutaro, Hans Kroll, Koichi Sato, [and] Hans Erik Pringsheim. "Th. M.-Gedenkfeier," *Berichte der Japanisch-Deutschen Gesellschaft Tokio*, No. 23 (November 1955), pp. 1-20. [Obit.]

3,239. Takeda, Akira. " 'Doktor Faustus' von Th. M.," *Tōhoku Doitsu Bungaku Kenkyū*, No. 4 (1960), pp. 58-67; No. 5 (1961), pp. 50-71; No. 6 (1962), pp. 59-70.

3,240. Tamms, Werner. "Das Schicksalmotiv heisst Deutschland: Zu den Briefen 1889-1936," *Westdeutsche Allgemeine*, No. 203 (September 1, 1962).

3,241. Tanahashi, Kazuo. "Die Entstehung der Ironie — vor den 'Buddenbrooks,' " *Doitsu Bungaku — Die deutsche Literatur*, No. 16 (1956), pp. 39-44. [In Japanese]

3,242. Tansini, Giorgio. "Appunti su Th. M. interprete della Bibbia," *Humanitas*, 16 (December 1961), [993]-1019. [*Joseph and His Brothers*]

3,243. Tau, Max. "Til Th. M. på 80-årsdagen," in item #2,431, pp. vii-ix. [80th birthday]

3,244. ———. "Th. M.," in his *Das Land, das ich verlassen musste*, pp. 133-136 et al. [Hamburg] Hoffmann & Campe [1961]

3,245. Taubes, Jacob. "From Cult to Culture," *Partisan Review*, 21 (July 1954), [387]-400. [*Doktor Faustus* — Oskar Goldberg as model for "Dr. Chaim Breisacher"]
Taubner, A. *See* Holthusen, W.

3,246. Täufel, Richard. "Zu Th. M's Schillerbild," *Spektrum*, 11, (1965), 192-196. Enlarged version, entitled "Th. M's Verhältnis zu Schiller: Zur Thematik und zu den Quellen der Novelle 'Schwere Stunde,' " in G. Wenzel, item #3,472, pp.

207-233. [With facsim. of Th. M's letter to Editor of *Der Sonntag,* "Bericht über Entstehung der 'Schweren Stunde.' "]

3,247. Taucher, Franz. "Th. M. und die Humanität: Paraphrase zum *Zauberberg,"* in his *Die Wirklichen Freuden: Literarische Profile,* pp. 98-111. Wien: Forum [1958] [Cf. I, item #2367]

3,248. Tecchi, Bonaventura. "Th. M. e l'ultimo suo libro," *Gazzetta del Popolo,* July 3, 1930. Also in his *Scrittori tedeschi moderni,* pp. 53-57. Roma: Ed. di Storia e Letteratura, 1959. [Cf. I, item #2,060 — *Mario und der Zauberer*]

3,249. *———. *L'Arte di Th. M.* [Torino] Edizioni Radio Italiana, ³1961. 132 pp. [First published in 1956 — anthology of M's writings with Tecchi's introduction]

3,250. ———. "Th. M.," *Dizionario Letterario Bompiani degli Autori,* Vol. 2, pp. 615-621. Milano: Bompiani, 1957.

3,251. ———. "Th. M. narratore," in his *Scrittori tedeschi moderni,* item #3,248, pp. 47-52. [Cf. I, item #1888]

3,252. ———. "Come Th. M. ha visto Goethe," in item #3,248, pp. 59-62.

3,253. Teichmann, Alfred. "Th. M.," in his *Savonarola in der deutschen Dichtung,* pp. 89-90 et al. Berlin: De Gruyter, 1937. [*Fiorenza*]

3,254. Ter-Nedden, Eberhard. "Das schwere Glück des Humanismus," *Christ und Welt,* Vol. 14, No. 22 (June 2, 1961), p. 16. [Concerns Bertram, #1,575; Kerényi, #1,700 c]

3,255. ———. "Der gewissenhafte Korrespondent: Th. M.," *Christ und Welt,* Vol. 15, No. 15 (April 13, 1962), p. 25. [*Briefe I,* #2,062]

3,256. Térey, Edith. "Romain Rolland und Th. M.," *Pester Lloyd,* Morgenblatt, February 2, 1919, pp. 2-3.

3,257. ———. "Th. M's 'Rede und Antwort,' " *Pester Lloyd,* Morgenblatt, May 18, 1922, pp. 1-2.

3,258. ———. "Th. M.: Zu seinem 50. Geburtstag," *Pester Lloyd,* Morgenblatt, June 6, 1925, pp. 1-2.

3,259. ———. "Der neue Vater und das freie Kind," *Pester Lloyd,* Morgenblatt, November 22, 1926. [*Unordnung und frühes Leid*]

3,260. Tétaz, Numa F. "Une des consciences les plus hautes de notre temps: Th. M.," *Gazette Littéraire*, No. 196 (August 20/21, 1955), pp. 7, 10. [Obit.]

3,261. Thauer, Marianne. "Th. M.: Bekenntnisse des Hochstaplers Felix Krull," in Johannes Beer, *ed., Reclams Romanführer*, Vol. 1, pp. 578-579. Stuttgart: Reclam [1962]

3,262. Theile, Albert. "Die 'Deutschen Blätter,' " *Börsenblatt für den Deutschen Buchhandel*, Frankfurter Ausgabe, 14 (September 16, 1958), 1101-1106. [With discussion of Th. M s contributions to this German-language periodical in Chile]

3,263. Theunissen, Gert H. "Lotte in Weimar," *Sonntag*, Vol. 2, No. 8 (February 23, 1947), p. 7.

3,264. Thieberger, Richard. "Huldigung und Bekenntnis," *Stuttgarter Zeitung*, June 4, 1955, Sonntagsbeilage 'Die Brücke zur Welt.' [80th birthday]

3,265. ————. "Les derniers travaux sur Th. M.," *L'Allemagne d'Aujourdhui*, No. 4 (July-August, 1955), pp. [98]-105. [Survey of Th. M. studies]

3,266. ————. "Th. M. Studies," *L'Allemagne d'Aujourd'hui*, No. 5 (September-October, 1955), pp. 63-66. [Review of K. W. Jonas, item #1,605]

3,267. ————. "Französische Einstreuungen im Werk Th. M's," in *Deutschland-Frankreich: Ludwigsburger Beiträge zum Problem der deutsch-französischen Beziehungen*, Vol. 2, pp. [309]-318. Stuttgart: DVA, 1957.

3,268. Thiess, Frank. "Th. M's Lob der Bürgerlichkeit," in his *Erziehung zur Freiheit*, pp. 276-280. Stuttgart: Engelhorn, 1929.

3,269. ————. "Die Innere Emigration," *Münchner Zeitung*, August 18, 1945; *Neuer Hannoverscher Kurier*, September 14, 1945. Also in Grosser, item #1,090, pp. 22-[26] [Cf. I, item #1441]

3,270. ————. "Sehr geehrter Herr Johannes R. Becher!" [letter of March 20, 1946] in Grosser, item #1,090, pp. 102-108. [Concerns Th. M. as an emigré]

3,271. *Thirlwall, John C. *In Another Language: A Record of the Thirty-Year Relationship Between Th. M. and His English*

Translator, Helen Tracy Lowe-Porter. New York: Alfred A. Knopf, 1966. xx, 208, vii pp. *See* Hatfield, #3,874.

3,272. Thomas, R. Hinton. " 'Die Wahlverwandtschaften' and Mann's 'Der Tod in Venedig,' " *PEGS,* N. S., 24 (1955), 101-130.

3,273. *———. *Th. M.: The Mediation of Art.* Oxford: Clarendon Press, 1956. 188 pp. Reviews: Anon. #114 — Hatfield, #1,222 — Leibrich, #1,893 — Lohner, #1,999 — Lowry, #2,010 — Müller, #2,312 — Parry, #2,488 — Schultz, #2,980 — Stockum, #3,152 — Witte, #3,521.

3,274. Thomas, Walter. "Th. M.," in his *Richard Strauss und seine Zeitgenossen,* pp. 163-167, 276-[286] München: Langen [1964]

3,275. *The Thomas Mann Commemoration . . . Bryn Mawr, October 5, 1956.* Philadelphia: E. Stern, 1956. 46 pp. Contributions by Caroline Newton, items #2,402-2,403, and Mark Van Doren, item #3,345.

3,276. *The Th. M. Commemoration at Princeton University, October 24, 1964.* Princeton, N. J.: Princeton University Library, 1965. [37] pp. Contributions by Victor Lange, item #1,859, Caroline Newton, item #2,406, and Victor Zuckerkandl, item #3,609.

3,277. Thürer, Georg. "Th. M. und die Schweiz," *St. Galler Tagblatt,* Abendblatt No. 256 (June 4, 1955). [80th birthday]

3,278. Tillich, Paul. "Aus den Materialien zum 'Dr. Faustus': Paul Tillichs Brief an Th. M. 23. 5. 43," *Blätter der Th. M.- Gesellschaft Zürich,* No. 5 (1965), pp. 48-52.

3,279. Tilliette, Xavier. "Les confessions d'un grand écrivain: Th. M. et les Mémoires de Félix Krull," *Etudes,* 291 (October 1956), [88]-96.

3,280. ———. "Le grand écrivain Th. M.," in his *Existence et littérature,* pp. [47]-84. [Bruges] Desclée De Brouwer [1962]

3,281. ———. "Thomas l'Imposteur ou les aventures de Félix Krull," in #3,280, pp. [85]-101.

3,282. Tillmann, Curt. "Th. M.," in his *Sammlerglück mit Buchumschlägen,* p. 21. Mannheim: Privatdruck, 1951. [Concerns M's article "Über die Juden"]

3,282a. ———. "Zu leichtfertig? Wie Th. M. seinen Aufsatz 'Zur jüdischen Frage' zurückzog," *Frankfurter Allgemeine Zeitung,* Feuilleton No. 51 (March 9, 1966), p. 20.

3,283.   Tindall, William York. "Th. M.," in his *The Literary Symbol,* pp. 220-224. Bloomington: Indiana University Press [1955] [*Tonio Kröger — Death in Venice*]

3,284.   Tingsten, Herbert. "Th. M. som politiker," *Dagens Nyheter,* September 28, 1947.

3,285.   ———. "Th. M. som konservativ nationalist," *Dagens Nyheter,* September 30, 1947.

3,286.   ———. "Th. M. som radikal demokrat," *Dagens Nyheter,* October 4, 1947.

3,287.   ———. "Dam dör i Venedig," *Dagens Nyheter,* October 4, 1953. [*Die Betrogene*]

3,288.   ———. "Godhet och hjärtlöshet hos Th. M.," *Dagens Nyheter,* September 9, 1956. Also in his *På marknadstorget,* pp. 22-47. Stockholm: Wahlström & Widstrand, 1958.

3,289.   ———. "Kylan i Th. M's verk," *Dagens Nyheter,* September 17, 1956. Also in #3,288.

3,290.   ———. "Th. M's känslokyla i politiken," *Dagens Nyheter,* September 21, 1956. Also in #3,288.

3,291.   ———. "Th. M. inför nazism och kommunism," *Dagens Nyheter,* September 21, 1956. Also in #3,288.

3,292.   Törngren, Pehr Henrik. "En ledare," *Dagens Nyhter,* February 17, 1946. [Attack on Th. M. *See also* O. Holmberg's reply, #1,470]

3,293.   Tokuzawa, Yokuji. "Goethe und Th. M.: Zu Th. M's Essay über Goethes 'Faust,' " *Goethe-Jahrbuch,* 2 (1960), 36-50. [In Japanese]

3,294.   Toni, Gianantonio de. "Al lettore di 'Zauberberg,' " *Aut aut,* No. 29 (September 1955), 405-422.

3,295.   Torberg, Friedrich. "In Sachen Th. M.," in his *Pamphlete — Parodien,* pp. 70-83. München: Langen-Müller, 1964.

3,296.   ———. "Parodie Th. M.," in item #3,295, pp. 221-223.

3,297.   Torre, Guillermo de. "Th. M. y sus temas novelescos," *Insula,* Vol. 10, No. 118 (October 15, 1955), pp. 1, 5.

3,298.   Toynbee, Philip. "Th. M.," *Observer,* August 14, 1955. *Times,*
         August 15, 1955. Also in German, "Er sprach für seine Zeit,"
         Englische Rundschau No. 33 (1955), pp. 444-445. [Obit.]

3,299.   ———. "A German Galsworthy," *Encounter,* Vol. 5, No. 5
         (November 1955), pp. 71-74. [*Felix Krull* — *no* comparison
         with Galsworthy]

3,300.   ———. "Th. M's 'Joseph Novels,' " *Observer,* March 18,
         1956. Also in German, "Th. M's Meisterwerk," *Englische
         Rundschau,* No. 12 (1956), p. 150.

3,301.   ———. "A Response to Mann," *Observer,* September 28,
         1959. Also in German in *Englische Rundschau,* No. 22
         (1959) p. 344. [Review of E. Heller, #1,278]

3,302.   ———. "Marxist View of Mann: Essays on Th. M. by George
         Lukács," *Observer,* December 20, 1964. [Review of #2,035]

3,302a. Tracy, Gordon L. Review of Bergsten, #292, *Monatshefte,* 56
         (December 1964), 355-356.

3,303.   Tramer, Hans. "Felix Krull beginnt seine Weltbetörung,"
         MB, Vol. 23, No. 11 (March 1955), pp. 3-4.

3,304.   ———. "Geburtstagsgaben: Zu Veröffentlichungen von und
         über Th. M.," *MB,* Vol. 23, No. 31 (August 15, 1955) ;
         No. 33 (August 19, 1955) ; No. 34-35 (September 2, 1955).
         [80th birthday — Bibliographical survey of recent Th. M.
         literature]

3,305.   ———. "Ungekannte und Umgetaufte: Gustav Mahler und
         seine Zeit," *Bulletin . . . Leo Baeck Institute,* No. 10 (July
         1960), pp. 130-150. [*See* esp. pp. 132-133 on Th. M., Gustav
         Mahler and *Der Tod in Venedig*]

3,306.   ———. "Die mildere Zone Österreichs: Th. M. und Paul
         Amann" [by Zwi Altmann, pseud.] *Bulletin . . . Leo Baeck
         Institute,* No. 10 (July 1960), pp. 151-154. [Concerns Amann,
         #3,426]

3,307.   Traverso, Leone. "Intorno alla costruzione del 'Doktor
         Faustus,' " *Paragone,* Vol. 1, No. 4 (1950), pp. 17-22.

3,308.   ———. "In memoria di Th. M.," *Studi Urbinati di Storia,
         Filosofia e Letteratura,* 29 (1955), [139]-154.

3,309. Travi, Ernesto. "Nell'epistolario di Mann il nostro tempo è difficile," *L'Italia,* November 13, 1963, p. 3.

3,310. Trebitsch, Siegfried. "Freundschaft mit Th. M.," in his *Chronik eines Lebens,* pp. 262-265. Zurich: Artemis [1951]

3,311. ———. "Für Th. M. zum 80. Geburtstag," *Der Bund; der kleine Bund,* Vol. 106, No. 254 (June 3, 1955), p. 8. [80th birthday — facsim. of poem]

3,312. †Treffer, Günter. Studien zum Problem der Bildung in Th. M's Roman 'Der Zauberberg.' Ph. D. diss., University of Vienna, 1956.

3,313. Treich, Leon. "Un communiqué," *L'Eclair,* 13 (January 21, 1926), 2.

3,314. Trog, Hilda. "Das Th. M.-Archiv der Bibliothek der Eidgenössischen Technischen Hochschule in Zürich," *Domino,* No. 23 (October 1958), pp. 4-5.

3,315. †Trylich, Romana. The Reception of Th. M. in France, 1924-1930. M. A. thesis, University of Alberta, 1960. 89 pp.

3,316. Tschörtner, Heinz Dieter. "Gerhart Hauptmann und Th. M.," *Nation* (Berlin), 10 (1960), 715-728. Also in G. Wenzel, #3,461, pp. 87-105.

3,317. Tsuchiya, Akita. "Der dämmernde Schimmer der Erlösung in 'Doktor Faustus,' " *Doitsu Bungaku — Die deutsche Literatur,* No. 24 (1960), pp. 29-35. [In Japanese, with German resumé]

3,318. ———. "Literatur und Musik: Der Fall von Th. M.," *Doitsu Bungaku — Die deutsche Literatur,* No. 31 (1963), pp. 88-97.

3,319 *Turóczi-Trostler, József. *Th. M's Weg zum Mythos: Zum Joseph-Roman.* Budapest: G. Ranschburg, 1936. 14 pp. [Cf. I, #2569]

3,320. Tuska, Jon. "Th. M. and Nietzsche: A Study in Ideas," *GR,* 39 (November 1964), [281]-299.

3,320a. ———. "The Vision of Doktor Faustus," *GR,* 40 (November 1965), [277]-309.

3,321. Tutino, Saverio. "Begegnung mit Th. M. in Rom," *Tagebuch,* No. 11 (1953), pp. 1-2.

3,322. Uchigaki, Keiichi. "Th. M's Vorlesung 'Bekenntnisse des
        Hochstaplers Felix Krull,' " *Keisei*, No. 6 (1956), pp. 100-
        113. [In Japanese]

3,323. Ude, Karl. "Feindliche Brüder? Zu neu aufgefundenen Jugend-
        briefen Th. M's," *Welt und Wort*, 11 (July 1956), 211-212.
        [Heinrich and Th. M. — concerns letters now in the Heinrich
        Mann-Archive in the Deutsche Akademie der Künste in
        Berlin, edited by A. Kantorowicz, item #1,655]

3,324. Uhde-Bernays, Hermann. "Th. M.," in his *Im Lichte der
        Freiheit: Erinnerungen aus den Jahren 1880-1914*, pp. 264-
        265 et al. [München] Nymphenburg [²1963]

3,325. Uhse, Bodo. "Th. M. zum Gedenken," *Aufbau* (Berlin), 11
        (September 1955), 773-781. Also in his *Gestalten und
        Probleme*, pp. 149-[165] [Berlin: Verlag der Nation, 1959]
        [Obit.]

3,326. ————. "Ein Entsandter Deutschlands: Beim Besuch der Th.
        M.-Sammlung der Yale Universität, 1943," in item #3,325,
        pp. 31-34.

3,327. ————. "Vorwort," in Heinrich Mann, *Die traurige Geschichte
        von Friedrich dem Grossen*, pp. 5-15. Berlin: Aufbau, 1960.
        [Heinrich and Th. M.]

3,328. Uhse, M. "Th. M.: Tristan," *Leipziger Tageblatt*, No. 202
        (April 22, 1903).

3,329. Ullmann, Hermann. "Für das unliterarische Deutschland,"
        Deutsche Arbeit, 18 (1919), 310-313. [*Betrachtungen eines
        Unpolitischen*]

3,330. Ulrici, Helmuth. "Th. M's 'Zauberberg,' " *Klinische
        Wochenschrift*, Vol. 4, No. 32 (August 6, 1925), p. 1575.

3,331. Ulshöfer, Robert. "Die Wirklichkeitsauffassung in der
        modernen Prosadichtung: Dargestellt an Manns 'Tod in
        Venedig,' Kafkas 'Verwandlung' und Borcherts 'Kurz-
        geschichten,' verglichen mit Goethes 'Hermann und
        Dorothea,' " *Deutschunterricht* (Stuttgart), 7 (1955), [13]-
        40. [*See* esp. "Der Begriff der 'falschen Natur' in Th. M's
        'Tod in Venedig,' " pp. 19-27]

3,332. Unger, Hermann. "Ein zweiter Fall Nietzsche-Wagner: Aus einem Briefwechsel Mann-Pfitzner," *Hamburger Allgemeine,* November 30, 1949.

Unger, Wilhelm, in #2,501.

3,333. Ungermann, Peter. "Felix oder der letzte Europäer," *CIVIS,* Vol. 4, No. 30 (1957), pp. 47-48. [*Felix Krull*]

3,334. Unruh, Fritz von. "Ein letzter Gruss," *Aufbau* (New York), Vol. 21, No. 33 (August 19, 1955), p. 2. [Obit.]

3,335. Urdang, Constance. "Faust in Venice: The Artist and the Legend in 'Death in Venice,'" *Accent,* 15 (Autumn 1958), 253-267.

3,336. Uriarte, Fernando. "Th. M.: Aspectos de un modo de novelar," *Anales de la Universidad de Chile,* 117 (1959), 23-33.

3,337. Urzidil, Johannes. "Noch einmal: Th. M. über Adalbert Stifter," *Adalbert Stifter-Institut des Landes Oberösterreich,* Vol. 13, No. 1/2 (1964), p. 21.

3,338. Usui, Takejiro. "Über Th. M's Roman 'Doktor Faustus,'" *University of Kyoto Bulletin,* No. 1 (1952), pp. 26-46. [In Japanese]

3,339. Utsumi, Aki. "Homoerotik eines Künstlers," *Deutsche Sprache — Deutsche Literatur* (Tokyo), No. 2 (1959), pp. 18-24. [In Japanese]

3,340. Valangin, Aline. "Über Th. M's Roman 'Doktor Faustus,'" *Literarische Blätter,* Vol. 3, No. 17 (April 1948), pp. 3-7.

3,341. Valente, Vincenzo. "Th. M.: Una traversata con Don Chisciotte," *Ponte,* 16 (1960), 1004-1005. [*Meerfahrt mit Don Quichote*]

3,342. Vallentin, Antonina. "Propos d'un exilé: Th. M.," *Revue Hebdomadaire,* 44 (August 17, 1935), 338-346. [*Joseph und seine Brüder*]

3,343. ———. "Der Kobold des Hervorbringens," *Deutsche Zeitung,* Vol. 10, No. 44 (June 1955). Also in French, "Le Démon de la création," in item #1,493, pp. 67-74. [80th birthday]

3,344. Valmeroux, Jean-Martin. "En Lithuanie avec Th. M.," *Paris-Midi,* Vol. 23, No. 2474 (January 8, 1933), pp. 1, 3. [About Th. M. and Hans Reisiger in Nidden]

3,345. Van Doren, Mark. "Joseph and His Brothers: A Comedy in Four Parts," in item #3,275, pp. 14-46. Also in *American Scholar*, 26 (Summer 1957), 289-302. Reprinted in his *The Happy Critic*, pp. 71-87. New York: Hill & Wang [1961], and in Hatfield, #1,229, pp. 96-108.

3,346. Van Gelder, Robert. "Th. M. plaudert über sein jüngst fertiggestelltes Werk und seine nächsten Pläne," in his *Prominente plaudern*, pp. 54-56. Wien: Humboldt [1948] [Cf. I, item #711, transl. into German by Gottfried von Ippisch]

3,347. Vecchiato, Giorgio. "Th. M. è morto nel pieno della sua grandezza," *Il Popolo*, Vol. 12, No. 224 (August 13, 1955), p. 3. [Obit.]

3,348. Vegesack, S. von. "Th. M.: 'Tankar i kriget,' " *Nya Dagligt Allehanda*, August 30, 1915. ["Gedanken zum Kriege" — *Friedrich und die Grosse Koalition*]

3,349. Vené, Gian Franco. "Osservazioni sul concetto di libertà nel realismo di Th. M.," *Nuova Corrente*, No. 9-10 (April 1958), pp. 85-96.

3,350. *Venohr, Lilli. *Th. M's Verhältnis zur russischen Literatur*. Meisenheim: Hain, 1959. 95 pp. [Ph. D. diss., University of Marburg, 1957] Reviews: Gronicka, #1,087 — Hellmann, #1,289

3,351. ———. Review of A. Hofman, item #1,450, *Zeitschrift für Slawistik*, 7 (1962), 415-421.

3,352. Ventzki, Rudolf. "Für und wider Th. M.: Eine Entgegnung," *Stuttgarter Zeitung*, Vol. 14, No. 119 (May 27, 1958), p. 15. [Reply to article "Manfred Hausmanns Austritt aus der Akademie," *Stuttgarter Zeitung*, April 30, 1958]

3,353. Vermeil, Edmond. "Civilisation et germanisme; réponse à M. Ernst Robert Curtius," *Revue de Genève*, February 1927, pp. 164-175. [*Betrachtungen eines Unpolitischen*]

3,354. ———. "Th. M.," *Allemagne*, Vol. 7, No. 37 (June-July), 1955), p. 1. [80th birthday]

3,355. ———. "Le Domaine du diable," in item #1,493, pp. 75-82.

3,356. ———. "Th. M.," in L. J. Ludovici, ed., Nobel Prize Winners, pp. 116-127. London: Arco; Westport, Conn.: Associated Bookseller [1957] [Transl. from the French by L. J. Ludovici]

3,357. Vetrano, Giuseppe. "La Dinastia borghese dei Mann," Comunità, Vol. 15, No. 91 (July 1961), pp. 78-88.

3,358. Victor, Walther. "Ein literarischer Aktivist: Wall Schaber," Das Wort, Vol. 2, No. 2 (1937), pp. 91-92.

3,359. ———. "Th. M.: Lotte in Weimar," Das Buch, No. 8 (March 1940), pp. 11-12.

3,360. Viereck, George Sylvester. "The New Paganism," New York American, December 8, 1929. [Interview — Politics]

3,361. Vil'mont, Nikolaj Nikolaevič. "Th. M.," Inostrannaja Literatura, 4 (1957). Condensed German version, translated by Eva-Maria Pietsch, "Die Tragödie des Komponisten Adrian Leverkühn," Geist und Zeit, No. 4 (1960), pp. 106-126. [Music — Doctor Faustus]

3,362. *Visconti, Luchino. Mario e il Mago. Milano: Edizioni Suvini Zerboni [1954] 19 pp. [Subtitle: "Azione correografica in due atti; musica di Franco Mannino"] See comments by H. Rüdiger, #2,782.

3,362a. Vitner, Ion. "Mitul faustic," in his Meridiane literare, pp. 248-253. Bucharest: Espla, 1960. [In Rumanian]

3,362b. ———. "Destinul lui Adrian Leverkühn," in #3,362 a, pp. 254-260.

3,363. ———. "Arta și umanul," in #3,362 a, pp. 261-269.

3,364. Vogler, Lewis. "Th. M. Offers a New Novel About an Aging Woman," San Francisco Chronicle, June 27, 1954, p. 17. [The Black Swan]

3,365. Vordtriede, Werner. "A Case of Transposed Heads in Th. M's 'Königliche Hoheit,'" MLN, 74 (January 1959), 49-51.

3,366. ———. "Richard Wagners 'Tod in Venedig,'" Euphorion, 52 (1959), 378-396. [See esp. pp. 383-396 on Th. M.]

3,367. Vossen, Peter. "Die 'indirekte Rede bei Th. M.," *Neue Stenographische Praxis,* 1 (1953), 6-10.

3,368. Waddell, Joan. "Two Illustrations for 'Death in Venice,' " *Trend,* Vol. 1, No. 2 (February 1942), pp. 15-17. [With excerpt from Th. M's letter to the artist's teacher, Wolfgang Born]

3,369. Wägner, Harald. "Inledning," in Th. M., *Tristan,* pp. iii-xi. Stockholm: Ahlen & Akerlund, 1921.

3,370. Wälder, Robert. "Die Psychoanalyse im Lebensgefühl des modernen Menschen," in A. J. Storfer, *ed., Almanach für das Jahr 1929,* pp. 47-62. Wien: Psychoanalytischer Verlag, 1929. [For a discussion of *Der Zauberberg see* pp. 52-53]

3,371. Wagner, Friedrich A. " 'Diese vom Genie geadelte Stadt': Die Feierlichkeiten des Deutschen Schiller-Komitees in Weimar mit Th. M.," *Frankfurter Allgemeine Zeitung,* Vol. 7, No. 115 (May 18, 1955), p. 9. [Th. M. in Weimar]

3,372. Wagner, Klaus. "Th. M. auf der Tanzbühne," *Musica,* 11 (July-August, 1957), 441. [Concerns ballet 'Mario und der Zauberer']

3,373. Wahnes, Günther. "Th. M.-Gymnasium," in Paul Brockhaus, *ed., Der Wagen,* pp. 140-142. Lübeck: Schmidt-Römhild, 1960.

3,374. Waidson, Herbert Morgan. "The Recent German Novel: Some Themes and Directions," in John Wain, *ed., International Literary Annual,* 1 (1958), 29-46. [*See* pp. 31-33 on Th. M.]

3,375. ————. "Irony and Conviction," in his *The Modern German Novel,* pp. 51-61. London: Oxford University Press, 1959.

3,376. ————. "Th. M.," in his *German Short Stories 1900-1945,* pp. viii-xi, 1-2. Cambridge: University Press, 1959.

3,377. ————. "Th. M.," in his rev. *ed* of E. K. Bennett's *A History of the German Novelle,* pp. 252-259. Cambridge: University Press, 1961. [Cf. I, item #1870]

3,378. ————. "Th. M.," in his *The Changing Pattern of the German Novel,* pp. 15-17. [Swansea] University College of Swansea, 1961.

3,379. Wain, John. "The Mind of *Autolycus,*" *Spectator,* 195 (November 11, 1955), 624-625. [*Felix Krull*]

3,380. Wais, Kurt. "Zur Auswirkung des französischen naturalistischen Romans auf Deutschland," in *Deutschland-Frankreich: Ludwigsburger Beiträge zum Problem der deutsch-französischen Beziehungen,* pp. 149-168. Stuttgart: DVA, 1954. [*Tonio Kröger*]

3,381. Waldemar, Charles. "Letzte Unterredung mit Th. M.," *Frankfurter Allgemeine Zeitung,* No. 204 (September 3, 1955).

3,382. Walden, Herwarth. "Deutsche Meisterehrung: Polemik gegen einen Bericht des Feuilletonisten Zarek über einen geselligen Abend bei Th. M.," *Sturm,* 15 (1924), 117-121.

3,383. Waldinger, Ernst. "Th. M. im Exil," *Austro-American Tribune,* Vol. 4, No. 2 (September 1945), p. 10. [Cf. I, item #680 — Review of W. Perl]

3,384. †Waldner, Gerhard. Der Erwählte von Th. M., die Quellen des Romans und seine Beziehungen zum Gesamtwerk des Dichters. Ph. D. diss., University of Innsbruck, 1954. 107 pp.

3,385. Waldstein, Wilhelm. "Th. M. als Erzähler," in his *Kunst und Ethos: Deutungen und Zeitkritik,* pp. 194-209. Salzburg: O. Müller [1954]

3,386. Wallmann, Jürgen P. "Eine retouchierte Autobiographie," *Tat,* Vol. 31, No. 6 (January 7, 1966), p. 30. [Review of Bürgin-Mayer, item #504]

3,387. Walter, Bruno. "Glückwunsch für Th. M.," *Neue Volkszeitung,* June 6, 1940, p. 4. [65th birthday]

3,388. ———. "Für Katja Mann," *NZZ,* Vol. 174, No. 1709 (June 24, 1953). [Written for her 70th birthday]

3,389. ———. "An Th. M.," *Neue Rundschau,* 66 (June 1955), 258-260. [80th birthday]

3,390. ———. "Th. M.," in his *Thema und Variationen: Erinnerungen und Gedanken,* pp. 272-277 et al. [Frankfurt a. M.] S. Fischer, 1960. [First published in English, I, item #715. — Biog.]

3,391. Walter, Friedrich. "Huldigung," *Ruf,* No. 14 (October 1, 1945), p. 4. [70th birthday. — Cf. I, item #848]

3,392. Walter, Hans-Albert. "Die Helfer im Hintergrund: Zur
        Situation der deutschen Exilverlage 1933-1945," *Frankfurter
        Hefte,* 20 (February 1965), 121-132.

3,393. Walter, Hilde. "Th. M's neueste Erklärungen," *Staats-Zeitung
        und Herold,* May 13, 1951, p. A 7. [Controversy with E.
        Tillinger — charge of Communism]

3,394. Walter, Marie. "Concerning the Affair Wälsungenblut," *Book
        Collector,* 13 (Winter 1964), 463-472.

3,395. Walter, Wolfgang. "Die Th. M.-Ausgabe des Aufbau-
        Verlages," *Börsenblatt für den Deutschen Buchhandel*
        (Leipzig), 132 (May 28, 1955), 392-393.

3,396. Walzel, Oskar. "Th. M.," in Wilhelm Scherer [and] Oskar
        Walzel, eds., *Geschichte der deutschen Literatur,* pp. 673-676
        et al. Berlin: Askanischer Verlag, ³1921.

3,397. ———. "Die Brüder Mann," in his *Die deutsche Literatur von
        Gottsched bis zur Gegenwart,* Vol. 2, pp. 342-343. Potsdam:
        Athenaion [1930]

3,398. Warburg, Frederick C. "Banned by the Censor," *TLS,* March
        23, 1956, p. 181. [Letter to the Editor concerning *Felix Krull*
        which has been banned in Ireland]

3,399. ———. "Th. M.," in his *An Occupation for Gentlemen,* pp.
        187-189 et al. London: Hutchinson [1959]

3,400. Warnecke, Robert. "Th. M. zum Gruss!" in *Th. M.: Zur
        Erinnerung an seinen Vortragsabend am 8. Juni 1926,* pp. 4-5.
        Altona: [Lübkert] 1926. [Cf. #495]

3,401. Warsinsky, Werner. "Vom Berge Nebo — das weite Land:
        Dem 80-jährigen Th. M.," in #2,833, pp. 6-7.

3,402. Wassermann, F. M. Review of *Briefe II,* item #2,066, *Books
        Abroad,* 38 (Autumn 1964), 408.

3,403. Wasserstrom, William. "In Gertrude's Closet," *Yale Review,*
        48 (December 1958), [245]-265. [Concerns Oedipal patterns
        in the works of Gide, Th. M., Joyce, Kafka, Camus and others;
        see esp. pp. 250-253 for discussion of *Doktor Faustus*]

3,404. Watts, Harold H. "Th. M. and the Earthly Crew," in his
        Hound and Quarry, pp. 129-146. [London] Routledge, Kegan
        Paul [1953] [Cf. I, item #1641]

3,405. ———. "The Thrice-Told Tale: M's Myth for his Time," in item #3,404, pp. 147-157. [Cf. I, item #2572]

3,406. ———. "Th. M. and the Opposites," in item #3,404, pp. 158-173. [Cf. I, item #389]

3,407. Weaver, John D. "Artist in Exile: Th. M.," *University Review* (Kansas City, Mo.), 5 (Spring 1939), [208]-213.

3,408. Weber, Hans von. "Th. M.: Betrachtungen eines Unpolitischen," *Zwiebelfisch,* Vol. 9, No. 6 (November 1918).

3,409. Weber, Werner. "Th. M. vor den Zürcher Studenten," *NZZ,* Vol. 170, Morgenausgabe No. 1288 (June 23, 1949), Bl. 2. [*Der Erwählte*]

3,410. ———. "Neues von Felix Krull," *NZZ,* Vol. 173, No. 2036 (September 20, 1952), Bl. 1, pp. 1-2.

3,411. ———. "Auf den Spuren Felix Krulls," *NZZ,* Vol. 174, No. 950 (April 25, 1953), Bl. 1.

3,412. ———. "No Stage Fright Today: Zu Th. M's 80. Geburtstag," *NZZ,* Vol. 176, Morgenausgabe No. 1487 (June 4, 1955), Bl. 1. [80th birthday]

3,413. ———. "Th. M. gestorben," *NZZ,* Vol. 176, Sonntagsausgabe No. 2124 (August 14, 1955), Bl. 2. [Obit.]

3,414. ———. "Die Begräbnisfeier für Th. M.," *NZZ,* Vol. 176, Morgenausgabe No. 2147 (August 17, 1955), Bl. 1. Also Fernausgabe No. 266 (August 18, 1955), Bl. 2. [Obit.]

3,415. ———. "Zum Gedenken an Th. M.," *NZZ,* Vol. 177, Morgenausgabe No. 1584 (June 2, 1956), Bl. 1. [Review of Erika Mann, item #2,059, and Monika Mann, item #2,100]

3,416. ———. "Wieder zu haben: 'Gesang vom Kindchen.' Zu einer Neuausgabe von Th. M's Vers-Idylle," *NZZ,* Vol. 180, Morgenausgabe No. 3303 (October 31, 1959), Bl. 1.

3,417. ———. "70 Jahre 'Die Neue Rundschau,' " *S. Fischer Almanach: Das 73. Jahr,* pp. 21-30. Frankfurt a. M., 1959.

3,418. ———. "Der Briefwechsel Th. M.-K. Kerényi," *NZZ,* Vol. 181, Morgenausgabe No. 2003 (June 11, 1960), Bl. 1. [Review of item #1,700 c]

3,419. ———. "Th. M. an Ernst Bertram," *NZZ,* Vol. 181, No. 3626 (October 22, 1960), Bl. 1. [Review of item #1,575]

3,420. ———. "Gruss an Katja Mann," *NZZ*, Vol. 184, Morgenausgabe No. 2992 (July 24, 1963), Bl. 4.

3,421. ———. "Th. M. und Emil Preetorius," *NZZ*, Vol. 185,
Abendausgabe No. 1342 (March 31, 1964). [About H.
Wysling's *ed.* of their correspondence, item #3,548]
———. *See also* #937.

3,422. Wedderkop, H. von. "Th. M's Zauberberg," *Querschnitt*, 5
(December 925), 1078-1079.

3,423. ———. "Der Alte aus Lübeck," *Querschnitt*, 6 (July 1926),
559-560. [*Lübeck als geistige Lebensform*]

3,424. Wedekind, Frank. "Fiorenza," *Sturm*, 1 (1910/11), 149.

3,425. Wedesweiler, Otto. "Th. M.," *Lions*, No. 5 (1957),
pp. 16-166.

3,426. *Wegener, Herbert. "Einleitung," in his *ed.* of Th. M., *Briefe an
Paul Amann, 1915-1952*, pp. 7-21. Lübeck: M. Schmidt-
Römhild 1959] Also in English, transl. by Richard and Clara
Winston, pp. 3-30. Middletown: Wesleyan University Press
[1960]
Reviews: Anon., #103 — M. Bloch, #355 — Blöcker, #363
— Böhmer, #389 — Dach, #623 — Grimm, #1,081 —
Gronicka, #1,087 — Hamburger, #1,178 — Johann, #1,594
— Klessmann, #1,733 — Morton, #2,291 — Paoli, #2,483 —
Redman, #2,647 — Reuter, #2,689 — Rychner, #2,807 —
E. E. Stein, #3,118 — Tramer, #3,306.

3,427. Wegner, Michael. "Th. M. und die klassische russische
Literatur," *Urania*, 23 (April 1960), 121-124.

3,428. Weigand, Hermann J. "Thoughts on the Passing of Th. M.,"
GR, 31 (October 1956), 163-175. [*See also* supplement,
#3,429] Expanded German version, "Th. M. zum Gedächtnis,"
Neophilologus, 40 (July 1, 1956), [162]-179.

3,429. ———. "Th. M. and Goethe: A Supplement and a Correction,"
GR, 32 (February 1957), 75-76. [Letter to the Editor about a
misstatement in his article, #3,428]

3,430. ———. Review of F. Kaufmann, #1,683, *GR*, 33 (October
1958), 236-237.

3,431. ———. "Th. M's 'Royal Highness' as Symbolic Auto-
biography," in Hatfield, #1,229, pp. 35-45. Transl. from the
German by H. Hatfield. [Cf. I, #2,189]

3,432. *———. *The Magic Mountain: A Study of Th. M's Novel
'Der Zauberberg.'* Chapel Hill: University of North Carolina
Press, 1964. xi, 183 pp. [Reprint of I, #2,378, except for
corrections of a few misprints]
Reviews: Sørensen, #3,086.

3,433. Weigand, Paul: "Th. M's 'Tonio Kröger' and Kleist's 'Über
das Marionettentheater,' " *Symposium,* 12 (Spring-Fall, 1958),
133-138.

3,434. Weigand, Wilhelm. "Th. M's 'Walsungenblut,' " in his *Welt
und Weg: Aus meinem Leben,* pp. 255-257. Bonn: Röhrscheid
[1940]

3,435. Weimar, Karl S. "Introduction," in Th. M., *Tristan,* pp. vii-xv.
[Boston] Ginn [1960] Reviews: F. Braun, #438 —
Kirchberger, #1,720.

3,436. ———. Review of Thomas A. Riley, item #2,728, *GQ,* 38
(November 1965), 709-710.

3,437. Weinreich, Marcel. "La Cultura europea en la obra de Th. M.,"
Isla, Vol. 2, No. 4 (April 1940), pp. 8-9, 16. [Part I]

3,438. ———. "Th. M. y el pensamiento occidental," *Luminar,* 5
(November 4, 1941), 384-407.

3,439. Weintraub, Stanley. " 'Castle Corner': Joyce Carey's 'Buddenbrooks,' " *Wisconsin Studies in Contemporary Literature,* Vol.
5, No. 1 (Winter-Spring, 1964), pp. 54-63.

3,440. Weiskopf, Franz Carl. "Unsere Meinung: Zum Austritt Hans
Grimms aus der Schiller-Gesellschaft wegen Th. M's Rede zur
Schillerfeier," *NDL,* Vol. 3, No. 6 (June 1955), pp. 3-4.

3,441. Weiss, Julian. "Th. M. in Budapest: Vorwort zu seiner
Vorlesung," *Pester Lloyd,* Morgenblatt, January 11, 1922,
pp. 1-2.

3,442. *Weiss, Walter. *Th. M's Kunst der sprachlichen und
thematischen Integration.* Düsseldorf: Pädagogischer Verlag
Schwann [1964] 100 pp.

3,443. Weisstein, Ulrich. "Th. M.," in his *Heinrich Mann*, pp. 4-16
        et al. Tübingen: H. Niemeyer, 1962.

3,444. Welter, Marianne. "Späte Liebe," *Spektrum*, 11, (1965), 210-
        215. [*Der Tod in Venedig — Die Betrogene*]

3,445. Welti, Jakob Rudolf. "Das Th. M.-Archiv der E.T.H.," *Basler
        Nachrichten*, Vol. 115, No. 57 (February 7-8, 1959), Beilage
        'Maske und Muse,' No. 3.

3,446. Weltmann, Lutz. "Th. M's 'Doktor Faustus,' " *AJR Informa-
        tion*, July 1949, p. 4.

3,447. ————. "Tiefgründig-Deutsches — europäisch artikuliert,"
        Neue Zeitung, November 8-9, 1952. [Review of J. Lesser, I,
        item #1865]

3,448. Wenclowa, Antanas. "Gruss an Th. M.," *Sinn und Form*,
        7 (July 1955), 348-350. [80th birthday]

3,449. Wenger, Paul Wilhelm. "Th. M's Faustroman," *Das Goldene
        Tor*, 3 (1948), 635-643. [*Doktor Faustus*]

3,450. Wentinck, Ch. "Nieuwe misdrijven van Felix Krull," *Nieuwe
        Rotterdamsche Courant*, Vol. 111, No. 267 (November 13,
        1954), p. 2.

3,451. Wenzel, Georg. "Gedenkwort zum Ableben Th. M's,"
        Potsdamer Tagespresse, August 19, 1955. Also in #3,453,
        p. 165. [Obit.]

3,452. ————. "Bemerkungen zur Th. M.-Ehrung," *Aussprache*, Vol.
        10, No. 4 (April 1955), pp. 59-60.

3,453. *————. *ed., Th. M. zum Gedenken*. Potsdam: Th. M.-
        Arbeitskreis, 1956. 171 pp.
        Contributors: Basler, #192 — J. R. Becher, #213 — Fedin,
        #843 — Goes, #1,032 — Hecht, #1,245 — E. Heller, #1,276
        — Hesse, #1,360 — G. Hoffmann, #1,447 — A. Kaufmann,
        #1,678 — Martini, #2,130 — Mercanton, #2,234 — Saupe,
        #2,851 — Schlemmer, #2,904 — Schweizer, #2,994 —
        Wenzel, #3,454, 3,456-3,457 — A. Zweig, #3,616.

3,454. ————. "Vorwort," in #3,453, pp. 5-6.

3,455. ————. "Wir ehrten Th. M.," *Aussprache*, Vol. 11, No. 6
        (June 1956), pp. 88-90.

3,456. ———. "Brief an Th. M., 22. Februar 1955," in #3,453, pp. 40-43. [Concerns "Th. M.-Arbeitskreis" in Potsdam]

3,457. ———. "Th. M. — Adel des Geistes," in #3,453, pp. 103-128.

3,458. ———. "Begegnungen mit der Th. M.-Brigade der Berliner Druckerei," *Spektrum* 7 (1961), 270-271.

3,459. ———. "Das Th. M.-Archiv der Deutschen Akademie der Wissenschaften zu Berlin," *Marginalien,* No. 11 (1961), pp. 54-56.

3,460. ———. Review of P. Altenberg, #34, *DLZ,* 83 (May 1962), 407-410.

3,461. *———. ed., *Vollendung und Grösse Th. M's: Beiträge zu Werk und Persönlichkeit des Dichters.* Halle/Saale: Sprache und Dichtung, 1962. 340 pp.
Contributors: Albrecht, #25 — Braemer, #423 — Dobbek, #695 — Esche, #805 — Haiduk, #1,148-1,149 — E. Heller, #1,276 — Hilscher, #1,414 — Kirsch, #1,723 — Mater, #2,140 — Matlochóva, #2,145 — Matter, #2,151 — Mercanton, #2,234 — J. Müller, #2,314 — Pietsch, #2,551 — B. Richter, #2,711 — Siebenschein, #3,046 — Tschörtner, #3,316 — Wenzel, #3,462-3,464 — A. Zweig, #3,617.
Reviews: Hellmann, #1,303 — Hilscher, #1,416.

3,462. ———. "Vorwort," in #3,461, pp. [9-10]

3,463. ———. "Bemerkungen zu Th. M's Erzählung 'Die Betrogene,' " in #3,461, pp. 275-279.

3,464. ———. "Im Dienste Th. M's," in #3,461, pp. 312-313. [Concerns "Th. M.-Kreis Potsdam"]

3,465. ———. "Th. M's Bedeutung," *Spektrum,* 11 (1965), 144-156. Enlarged, rev. version in *Th. M.: Werk und Bedeutung.* Berlin: Deutscher Kulturbund, 1965. 43 pp.

3,466. ———. "Th. M. an Arthur Baumgarten," *Spektrum,* 11 (1965), [175] [With facsim. of Th. M's letter of May 30, 1939]

3,467. ———. "Nachbericht," *Spektrum,* 11 (1965), 219-220. [Bibliogr.]

3,468.   ———. "Im Dienste des Werkes Th. M's: Das Th. M.-Archiv
         der Deutschen Akademie der Wissenschaften zu Berlin,"
         Börsenblatt für den Deutschen Buchhandel, (Leipzig), No. 21
         (May 1965), pp. 433-435.

3,469.   ———. "Mit dem Willen zu rettender Ehrfurcht: Werk und
         Vermächtnis Th. M's," *Neue Zeit,* Vol. 21, No. 130 (June 5,
         1965), p. 3, Berliner Ausgabe. [90th birthday]

3,470.   ———. "Th. M.: Ausstellung aus Anlass seines 90. Geburts-
         tags," Berlin: Deutsche Staatsbibliothek, 1965. [6 pp. —
         Exhibit]

3,471.   ———. "Nachlese zur Th. M.-Ausstellung in Berlin,"
         Spektrum, 11 (1965), 393-398. [Exhibit]

3,472. *———. ed. *Betrachtungen und Überblicke zum Werk Th. M's:
         Aufsätze. Texte. Rezensionen. Bibliographien.* Berlin: Aufbau,
         1965. 678 pp.
         Contributors: Admoni, #9 — Beck, #223 — Bürgin, #2,389
         — Fourrier, #906 — Geerdts, #978 — Haiduk, #1,151-1,152
         Hamburger, #1,184 — Hofman, #1,456 — I. Jens, #1,577 —
         W. Jens, #1,585 — Jonas, #1,616 — Lehnert, #1,883 —
         Lesser, #1,941 — Mater, #2,141-2,142 — Matter, #2,153 —
         Neumann, #2,389 — Pietsch, #2,553 — K. Pringsheim,
         #2,607 — Reichart, #2,389 — Richter, #2,712 — Saueressig,
         #2,850 — Scheyer, #2,884 — Silman, #9 — Täufel, #3,246
         — Wenzel #3,473-3,475 — Žmegač, #3,603. (*See* #3,900.)

3,473.   ———. "Vorwort," in item #3,472, pp. 5-7.

3,474.   ———. "Th. M's Beiträge aus dem *Frühlingssturm* und
         Gedichte," in item #3,472, pp. 421-423.

3,475.   ———. "Th. M.-Heinrich Mann: Briefe an den Bruder,
         1900-1949," in item #3,472, pp. 473-479.

3,476.   Werner, Alfred. "Th. M.: Priest of Culture," *Chicago Jewish
         Forum,* 14 (Summer 1956), 214-220. [Review of K. W. Jonas,
         item #1,605]

3,477.   Werner, Bruno E. "Th. M's neuer Roman 'Dr. Faustus,'"
         Rhein-Pfälzische Rundschau, February 19, 1948.

3,478. Werner, Otto. "Mann über Bord," *Gewissen,* 4 (October 23, 1922). [Sharp attack upon Th. M. because of his address *Von Deutscher Republik*]

3,479. Wertheimer, Julius. "Fiorenza," *Schaubühne,* 3 (1907), 558-559.

3,480. Wescott, Glenway. "Th. M.: Will Power and Fiction," in his *Images of Truth: Remembrances and Criticism,* pp. 164-241. New York: Harper [1962] [*The Magic Mountain — Doctor Faustus*]

3,481. West, Paul. "Th. M's Verlegenheit," *Sinn und Form: Sonderheft Th. M.,* 1965, pp. 224-237. [Transl. from English by Elga Abramowitz]

3,482. *White, Andrew. *Die Verfluchten und Gesegneten: Eine Studie über die Helden Th. M's als Betreter des Verbotenen und Vertreter des Bösen.* Köln: Riehl, 1960. [Ph. D. diss., University of Munich, 1960. 169 pp.]

3,483. *————. *Th. M.* Edinburgh: Oliver & Boyd; New York: Grove Press [1965] 122 pp.
Reviews: E. Rose, #2,763.

3,484. Widmer, Johannès. "Th. M.: Pariser Rechenschaft," *Bibliothèque Universelle et Revue de Genève,* 2 (December 1926), [813]-814.

3,485. Wiemann, H. "Th. M. and 'Doctor Faustus,' " *AUMLA,* No. 4 (1956), pp. 39-45.

3,486. Wien, Wilhelm. "Th. M.: 80 Jahre Zeitgenosse," *Bremer Nachrichten,* No. 127 (June 4, 1955), p. 13. [80th birthday]

3,487. ————. "Von der Durststrecke eines versprengten Lebens," *Westdeutsche Zeitung,* January 25, 1964. Under the title "Vom Leiden an Deutschland" also in *Bremer Nachrichten,* January 25, 1964. [*Briefe II,* #2,066]

3,488. Wiese, Benno von. "Bild-Symbole in der deutschen Novelle," *PEGS,* N. S., 24 (1955), 131-158. [*See* esp. pp. 151-158 on *Der Tod in Venedig*]

3,489. ————. "Th. M.: 'Der Tod in Venedig,' " in his *Die deutsche Novelle von Goethe bis Kafka,* pp. 304-324. Düsseldorf: Bagel [1956]

Wiesengrund-Adorno, Theodor. *See* Adorno.

3,490. Wildbolz, Rudolf. "Th. M. als Romancier," *Der Bund; der kleine Bund,* Vol. 106, No. 254 (June 3, 1955), pp. 7-8. [80th birthday]

3,491. Wilder, Thornton. "Th. M.: 1875-1955," *Proceedings of the American Academy of Arts and Letters,* 2nd Series, No. 7 (1957), pp. 123-128. [Obit.]

3,492. †Wilhelm-Billig, Gertraude. Sprachimitation in Th. M's Roman 'Der Erwählte.' Ph. D. diss., University of Munich, 1961. 141 pp.

3,493. Wilkinson, Elizabeth M. "Aesthetic Excursus on Th. M's *Akribie,*" *GR,* 31 (October 1956), 225-235.

3,494. ———., Hans Flesch [and] Michael Hamburger. "Addresses at the Memorial Meeting for Th. M., October 5, 1955," *P.E.N. News,* No. 192 (April 1956), pp. 25-33. [Obit.]

3,495. ———. "Tonio Kröger: An Interpretation," in Hatfield, item #1,229, pp. 22-34. [Reprint of I, item #1,927]

3,496. Willecke, Frederick W. "Th. M. und Luther," *KFLQ,* 5 (1958), [154]-162.

3,497. Williams, W. D. "Th. M's 'Dr. Faustus,' " *GLL,* N. S., 12 (July 1959), 273-281.

3,498. ———. Review of E. Heller, item #1,278, *MLR,* 55 (1960), 132-134.

3,499. Willnauer, Franz. "Der Zeitgenosse Adrian Leverkühn: Fiktion und Faktizität im Musiker-Roman," *Deutsche Rundschau,* 89 (1963), 56-64. [*Doktor Faustus*]

3,500. Willoughby, Leonard Ashley. Review of Th. M., 'Mass und Wert,' " *GLL,* 2 (July 1938), 310-311.

3,501. ———. Review of K. W. Jonas, item #1,605, *GLL,* N. S., 9 (April 1956), 228-229.

3,502. Willson, A. Leslie. "Th. M's 'Die Vertauschten Köpfe;' The Catalyst of Creation," *Monatshefte,* 49 (November 1957), [313]-321. [*The Transposed Heads*]

3,503. Winkler, Rudolf. "Nachwort," in Th. M., *Tonio Kröger,* pp. 85-95. Leipzig: Reclam, 1963.

3,504. Winn, Joseph A., [and] Th. M. "Th. M. und die
Tschechoslowakei: Ein Briefwechsel," *Aufbau* (New York),
Vol. 11, No. 46 (November 16, 1945), p. 4. [Concerns Th. M.
as an emigré]

3,505. Winston, Richard. "Th. M's Latest Novel Reveals Him as a
Great Humorous Writer," *NYHT Books,* September 18, 1955,
pp. 1, 11. [*Felix Krull*]

3,506. Winter, Cecil. "Letter to the Editor," *New Statesman and
Nation,* N. S., 6 (1933), 383. [Reply to I, item #1,771, W.
J. Turner, "Th. M. and Wagner."] *See also* item #88.

3,507. Wintzen, René. "Pour le quatre-vingtième anniversaire de
Th M.," *Documents,* 10 (June-July 1955), 769-774. [80th
birthday]

3,508. ————. "Hommage de la France à Th. M.," *Documents,* 10
(September 1955), 1198. [Review of item #1,493]

3,509. Wirpsza, Witold. "Arbetet med den store ironikern,"
Tidskriften Polen, No. 3 (1964), pp. 16-17. [About translations of *Doktor Faustus* into Polish. This article was also
published in English, French, German, Polish, and Spanish]

3,510. †Wirtz, Erika A. Der sprachliche Ausdruck der Ironie in Th.
M's 'Zauberberg' und ihre geistigen Grundlagen. M. A.
thesis, University of Liverpool, 1954. 252 pp.

3,511. ————. "Stilprobleme bei Th. M.," in Paul Böckmann, *ed.,*
Stil- und Formprobleme in der Literatur, pp. [430]-435.
Heidelberg: C. Winter, 1959.

3,512. ————. "Die Bedeutung des Sprachstils für den Sinnzusam-
menhang in Th. M's 'Zauberberg,' " *Wirkendes Wort,* 12
(1962), 161-167.

3,513. ————. Review of V. Žmegač, item #3,600, *GLL,* N. S., 16
(January 1963), 153-157.

3,514. †Wiseman, Richard W. Music and the Problem of Evil: Music
as a Means to New Vision in the Work of Th. M. and Hermann
Hesse. Ph. D. diss., University of California, Berkeley, 1960.

3,515. Wistinghausen, Curt von. "St. Gregorius auf dem Stein,"
Christengemeinschaft, 24 (February 1952), 63-64. [*Der
Erwählte*]

3,516. Witkop, Philipp. "Th. M.: Zu seinem 50. Geburtstag," *West-deutsche Illustrierte*, June 1925.

3,517. Witsen Elias, Jan W. J. "Th. M., de boarger en de kunstner," *De Tsjerne*, 10 (October 1955), 329-333.

3,518. Witte, William. "Faust and Doctor Faustus," *Aberdeen University Review*, 33 (Autumn 1949), 113-117.

3,519. ———. "Introduction," in his *ed*. of Th. M., *Two Stories*, pp. xi-xxiv. London: T. Nelson [1957] New York: Rinehart [1959] [*Unordnung und frühes Leid — Mario und der Zauberer*]

3,520. ———. "Th. M. and Schiller," *GLL*, N. S., 10 (July 1957), 289-297. Reprinted in his *Schiller and Burns, and Other Essays*, pp. 57-66. Oxford: Blackwell, 1959.

3,521. ———. Review of R. Hinton Thomas, #3,273, *GLL*, N. S., 11 (January 1958), 153-154.

3,522. Wittek, Bernhard. "Th. M.: Deutsche Hörer," in his *Der britische Aetherkrieg gegen das Dritte Reich: Die deutsch-sprachigen Kriegssendungen der British Broadcasting Corporation*, pp. 59, 95 et al. München: Fahle, 1962. [Ph. D. diss., Munich]

3,523. Wittkowski, Victor. "Encantro con Th. M.," *Sintese*, Vol. 8, No. 22 (October 1943). [Biog.]

3,524. ———. "Soggiorni romani di Th. M.: Un borghese e la classicità," *Fiera Letteraria*, Vol. 8, No. 43 (October 25, 1953), pp. 1, 6. [Biog.]

3,525. Wizelius, Ingemar. "En okänd Mann," *Dagens Nyheter*, July 18, 1956. [*Leiden an Deutschland*]

3,526. Woehe, Kurt. "Der pädagogische Gedankengehalt in Th. M's 'Zauberberg,'" *Vierteljahrsschrift für Philosophische Pädagogik*, 7 (May 1927), [156]-161.

3,527. Wörme, Friedrich. "Das Menschenbild der zeitgenössischen Dichtung: Dargestellt an Th. M., Ernst Wiechert, Werner Bergengruen," *Die ärztliche Praxis*, 93 (1953), 259-273.

3,528. Wörner, Karl H. "Ein Dichter über Musik: Th. M. in seinem Roman 'Doktor Faustus,'" *Musica*, 2 (September-October, 1948), 229-237. [Followed by an excerpt from *Doctor Faustus*, entitled "Beethoven und die Fuge," on pp. 237-242]

3,529. Wohlfarth, Paul. "Stil und Sprache in Th. M's Hochstapler-novelle," *Muttersprache*, No. 6 (1955), pp. 202-207. [*Felix Krull*]

3,530. Wolf, Alois. "Gnade und Mythos: Zur Gregoriuslegende bei Hartmann von Aue und Th. M.," *Wirkendes Wort*, 12 (July 1962), 193-209. [*Der Erwählte*]

3,531. *————. *'Gregorius' bei Hartmann von Aue und Th. M.: Interpretationen.* München: Oldenbourg, 1964. 96 pp. Reviews: Brandstetter, #430 — Brandt, #432.

3,532. *Wolff, Hans M. *Th. M.: Werk und Bekenntnis.* Bern: Francke [1957] 143 pp. Reviews: Altenberg, #32 — Hirschbach, #1,430 — Landsträsser, #1,844 — Loose, #2,002 — Remak, #2,683.

3,533. Wolffheim, Hans. "Das 'Interesse' als Geist der Erzählung: Ein Beitrag zur Stilphysiologie Th. M's," *Euphorion*, 47 (1953), [351]-389.

3,534. ————. "Seltener Glücksfall und Wohltat des Geistes: Der Briefwechsel Th. M. — K. Kerényi," *Hamburger Echo*, December 17, 1960. [Review of Kerényi, #1,700 c]

3,535. ————. "Von der Gefährlichkeit des Idealisten: Über Briefe Th. M's an Ernst Bertram," *Hamburger Echo*, July 8, 1961. [Review of Bertram, #1,575]

3,536. Wolfradt, Willi. "Th. M's Bekenntnis," *Der Neue Merkur*, 3 (April 1919), [69]-70. [Cf. I, #1,546 — *Betrachtungen eines Unpolitischen*]

3,537. Wolfskehl, Karl. "Brief an Th. M. vom 12. Juni 1946," in Margot Ruben, *ed., Zehn Jahre Exil: Briefe aus Neuseeland 1938-1948*, pp. 266-267. Heidelberg: L. Schneider, 1959.

3,538. Wooley, E. O. "Four Letters from Th. M. to E. O. Wooley," *Monatshefte*, 56 (January 1964), [15]-17. German original text also in *Schriften der Theodor Storm-Gesellschaft*, No. 13 (1964), pp. 45-46. [Theodor Storm and Th. M.]

3,539. Worm, Walter. "Leisewitzens Zahnschmerzen," *Zahnärztliche Rundschau*, Nos. 44-46 (November 9, 16, 23, 1922), pp. 668-669, 683-684, 701-702. [*Buddenbrooks*]

3,540. Wunderlich, Eva C. "Zweimal Gregorius: Th. M. und Hanna
        Stephan," *GQ*, 38 (November 1965), 640-651.

3,541. Wuthenow, Rainer. "Ein Nachruf für Th. M.," *Hersfelder
        Volkszeitung*, August 17, 1955. [Obit.]

3,542. ————. "Der Fall Ernst Bertram: Philologie und Vorurteil,"
        NDH, No. 86 (March-April 1962), pp. 89-96. [Review of
        item #1,575]

3,543. Wymetal, Wilhelm von. "Th. M.: Tristan," *Tagesbote für
        Mähren und Schlesien*, June 20, 1903.

3,544. ————. "Th. M's Buddenbrooks," *Die Woche: Wiener
        Montags-Zeitung*, No. 37 (August 24, 1903).

3,545. Wyrsch, Jakob. "Sigmund Freud und Th. M.," *NZZ*, Vol. 157,
        No. 1785 (October 17, 1936), Bl. 3. [Freud und die Zukunft]

3,546. Wysling, Hans. "Th. M's Technik der Montage," *NZZ*, Vol.
        184, Fernausgabe No. 155 (June 8, 1963), Bl. 19. [Concerns
        G. Bergsten, item #292]

3,547. ————. "Die Technik der Montage: Zu Th. M's 'Erwähltem,' "
        Euphorion, 57 (1963), [156]-199.

3,548. ————. ed. "Aus dem Briefwechsel Th. M. — Emil
        Preetorius," *Blätter der Th. M.-Gesellschaft Zürich*, No. 4
        (December 1963). [With his commentary on pp. 3-8.
        Discussed in W. Weber, item #3,421] *See also* #2,599.

3,549. ————. "Heiteres Nachspiel zum Briefwechsel Th. M. — Emil
        Preetorius," *Blätter der Th. M.-Gesellschaft Zürich*, No. 5
        (1965), pp. 16-21. [With the text of Th. M's review of
        Chamisso's *Peter Schlemihl* as published in *Berliner Tageblatt*,
        December 25, 1910]

3,550. ————. "Archivalisches Gewühle: Zur Entstehungsgeschichte
        des Hochstapler-Romans," *Blätter der Th. M.-Gesellschaft
        Zürich*, No. 5 (1965), pp. 24-44. [With the text of Th. M's
        introduction to *Felix Krull* as read in the Schauspielhaus Zurich
        on September 24, 1951]

3,551. ————. "Th. M's Tagebücher: Aus den Notizen zur
        'Entstehung des Faustus,' " *Blätter der Th. M.-Gesellschaft
        Zürich*, No. 5 (1965), pp. 44-47.

3,552. ————. "Th. M.: Geist und Kunst. Aus Notizen zu einer 'Abhandlung über das Literarische,' " *S. Fischer Almanach: das 79. Jahr,* pp. 15-[34] [Frankfurt a. M.] 1965.

3,553. Wyss, Heinz. Review of H. Eichner, #750, *L'Ecole Bernoise,* No. 43-44 (February 10, 1962), p. 813.

3,554. Yamamoto, Atsushi. "Über das mythische Element in 'Der Tod in Venedig,' " *Doitsu Bungaku — Die deutsche Literatur,* No. 24 (1960), pp. 21-28. [In Japanese, with German resumé]

3,554a. ————. "Versuch über den Roman 'Dr. Faustus' von Th. M.," *Doitsu Bungaku — Die deutsche Literatur,* No. 33 (1964), pp. 60-80. [In Japanese]

3,555. Yamanaka, Hiroshi. "Über Mythus und den Typus in 'Joseph und seine Brüder,' " *Doitsu Bungaku — Die deutsche Literatur,* No. 24 (1960), pp. 21-28. [In Japanese]

3,556. Yamato, Teruyasu. "Der neue Humanismus Th. M's und die russische Literatur," *Osaka-Kobe,* 4 (1962), 30-43. [In Japanese, with German resumé]

3,557. Yanagawa, Shigeo. "Der moderne deutsche Roman — im Falle Th. M's," *Bulletin, University of Tokyo-Toritsu,* No. 5 (1951), pp. 48-54. [In Japanese]

3,558. ————. "Th. M's Nietzsche-Erlebnis," *Bulletin, University of Tokyo-Toritsu,* No. 13 (1956), pp. 115-135. [In Japanese]

3,559. Yao-Mien, Huang. "Gruss an Th. M.," *Sinn und Form,* 7 (July 1955), 350. [80th birthday]

3,560. Yates, Peter. "Leverkühn and the Magician," *Saturday Review,* Vol. 32, No. 9 (February 26, 1949), pp. 47-48. [*Doktor Faustus* — Schönberg Controversy]

3,561. Yoshida, Jiro. "Kunst und Künstlerproblem in Th. M's Werk," *Doitsu Bungaku Kyoto,* No. 4 (1955), pp. 1-16. [In Japanese]

3,562. ————. "Der moderne Faust: Th. M's 'Doktor Faustus,' " *Shiso,* No. 382 (April 1956), pp. 79-89. [In Japanese]

3,563. ————. "Aus der neuesten Th. M.-Forschung," *Doitsu Bungaku Kyoto,* No. 10 (1961), pp. 60-76. [In Japanese]

3,564. Yoshida, Sentaro. "Politik und Ironie im Falle Th. M's," *Bulletin, University of Okayama,* No. 2 (1953), pp. 47-59. [In Japanese]

3,565. Yoshinori, Takao. "Der moderne Faust und die Theodizee,"
        Doitsu Bungaku — Die deutsche Literatur, No. 12 (1954),
        pp. 56-59. [In Japanese]
3,566. Yourcenar, Marguerite. "Humanisme de Th. M.," in item
        #1,493, pp. 23-33. Expanded English version by Grace Frick,
        "Humanism in Th. M.," *Partisan Review,* 23 (Spring 1956),
        [153]-170. Again expanded, under the title "Humanisme et
        hermétisme chez Th. M.," in her book *Sous bénéfice
        d'inventaire,* pp. 224-271. [Paris] Gallimard [1962]
3,567. Yur'eva, L. M. "Th. M. and Gorkij," in his *M. Gorkij and the
        Progressive German Writers of the Twentieth Century,* pp. 43-
        67. Moscow: Academy of Sciences of the U.S.S.R., 1961.
        [In Russian]
3,568. Zachäus, Herbert. "Mann gegen Mann," in Grosser, item
        #1,090, pp. 121-[132]
3,569. Zaloscer, Hilde. "De la composition musicale dans les oeuvres
        littéraires," *Rhythme,* 2 (October 1953), [15]-22. [*See* esp.
        pp. 18-22 for a discussion of *Buddenbrooks* and *Doctor
        Faustus*]
3,570. ———. "Die Antithetik im Werke Th. M's," *Bulletin de la
        Faculté des Lettres,* 8 (1959), 47-96.
3,571. ———. "Les hypostases du temps dans l'oeuvre de Th. M.,"
        Revue du Caire, Vol. 43, No. 227-228 (July-August, 1959),
        pp. [1]-20.
3,572. Zampa, Giorgio. "Th. M. e i critici," *Il Mondo,* Vol. 6,
        (May 2, 1954).
3,573. ———. "Parodia e verità," *Il Mondo,* Vol. 7, No. 34 (August
        23, 1955), p. 3.
3,574. Zanders, Janis. "Jazeps-trimdinieks," *Cela zimes,* No. 21
        (September 1954), pp. 347-353.
3,575. Zanker, Arthur. "An Th. M.: Zum 50. Geburtstag," in his
        Die Ernte mit den vier Geräten, p. 117. Wien: Saturn, 1935.
        [50th birthday]
3,576. Zarek, Otto. "Th. M. und die Ärzte," *Tagebuch,* 6 (June 6,
        1925), 845-847. [Attack upon article by Dr. Schelenz on
        Der Zauberberg, cf. I, item #2,344]

3,577. ———. "Biblische Stoffe in der neuen deutschen Dichtung," *Pester Lloyd*, Morgenblatt, (March 24, 1934), pp. 1-3. [*Die Geschichten Jaakobs — Der Junge Joseph*]

3,578. ———. "Begegnung in Berlin: Frau Katia Mann," *Allgemeine Wochenzeitung der Juden in Deutschland*, Vol. 12, No. 6 (May 10, 1957), Feuilleton.

3,579. Zarins, Guntis. "Einige europäische Kulturprobleme in den Werken Th. M's," *Cela zimes*, No. 27 (September 1955), pp. 358-364.

3,580. Zeller, Bernhard. "Erläuterungen," in Gunter Böhmer, item #388 [2 pp.]

3,581. Zeller, Reimar. "Mythos und Modernität: Zu Th. M's Roman 'Joseph und seine Brüder,' " *Kirche in der Welt*, Vol. 20, No. 5 (May 1965), pp. 213-217.

3,582. Zendelwald. "Zwei Brüder," *Eiserne Blätter*, 1 (December 7, 1919), 422-424. [Heinrich and Th. M.]

3,584. Zerner, Marianne. "Th. M's 'Der Bajazzo': A Parody of Dostoevski's 'Notes from the Underground,' " *Monatshefte*, 56 (November 1964), [286]-290.

3,585. Zeydel, Edwin H. Review of J. G. Brennan, I, item #140, *MLJ*, 27 (1943), 224. [Cf. #450]

3,586. ———. "Th. M. and Gregorius," in his *Hartmann von Aue: Gregorius*, pp. 6-8. Chapel Hill: University of North Carolina Press, 1955. [*Der Erwählte*]

3,587. Ziegler, K. "Th. M.: Versuch über Schiller," *Wirkendes Wort*, 6 (1955/56), 58.

3,588. Ziegler, Leopold. "Th. M. in Briefen Leopold Zieglers an die Bayerische Akademie der Schönen Künste, 1949," in his *Briefe 1901-1958*, pp. 123-129. München: Kösel [1963]

3,589. Ziesel, Kurt. "Th. M.," in his *Das verlorene Gewissen*, pp. 125-127. München: J. F. Lehmann [1958] [*See* esp. 8th ed., 1962] Also in his *Der rote Rufmord: Eine Dokumentation zum kalten Krieg*. Tübingen: F. Schlichtenmayer, ³1961. [Concerns controversy Th. M. — Manfred Hausmann]

3,590.   ———. "Th. M. und Hausmann," *Zeit*, Vol. 15, No. 2
         (January 8, 1960), p. 16. [*See also* E. E. Stein, #3,119]

3,591.   Ziessler, Albrecht. "Th. M.: Zu seinem 75. Geburtstag,"
         Lübecker Freie Presse, June 6, 1950.

3,592.   ———. "Th. M. besucht Lübeck: Eine Versöhnung nach 50
         Jahren," *Welt*, March 12, 1955.

3,593.   ———. "Th. M. zu seinem 80. Geburtstag," *LFP am
         Wochenende*, No. 128 (June 4, 1955).

3,594.   ———. "Ich gestehe, ich bin recht ergriffen . . . Notizen zu
         einem Besuch Th. M's in Travemünde," in *Hansestadt Lübeck:
         Der Lebens-und Daseinskampf einer Stadt*, pp. 72-75. [Lübeck,
         1955]

3,595.   Zimmermann, R. Chr. "Wenn Wissenschaft von Stil
         überspielt wird," *Die Welt der Literatur*, No. 12 (June 10,
         1965), p. 288. [Review of Baumgart, item #204]

3,596.   Zimmermann, Werner. "Th. M.: Tonio Kröger," in his
         Deutsche Prosadichtungen der Gegenwart, Vol. 1, pp. 157-185.
         Düsseldorf: Schwann [⁴1962]

3,597.   ———. "Th. M.: Königliche Hoheit," in item #3,596,
         pp. 186-228.

3,598.   Zinberg, Dorothy S., [and] Norman E. Zinberg. "Hans
         Castorp: Identity Crisis Without Resolution," *American Imago*,
         20 (1963), 393-402.

3,599.   Ziolkowski, Theodore. "Th. M.," in his *The Novels of
         Hermann Hesse*, pp. 283-284 et al. Princeton University Press,
         1965.

3,600.   *Žmegač, Viktor. *Die Musik im Schaffen Th. M's*. Zagreb:
         Philosophische Fakultät der Universität, 1959. 109 pp.
         [Transl. from Serbo-Croatian. Originally written as a Ph. D.
         diss., University of Zagreb]
         Reviews: Grandi, #1,058 — Hellmann, #1,287 — Leibrich,
         #1,900 — Schoolfield, #2,949 — Wirtz, #3,513

3,601.   ———. "Zum Problem des Erzähleinsatzes bei Th. M.,"
         Filologija, 4 1963), 205-220. [In German, with resumé in
         Serbo-Croatian]

3,602. ⸻. "Zur Form und Funktion des Erzähleinsatzes bei Th. M.," *Sinn und Form: Sonderheft Th. M.,* 1965, pp. 255-267.

3,603. ⸻. "Konvention — Modernismus — Parodie: Bemerkungen zum Erzählstil Th. M's," in G. Wenzel, item #3,472, pp. 107-119.

3,604. Zöller, Josef Othmar. "Der Schwanengesang eines Hedonisten," *Deutsche Tagespost,* Vol. 6, No. 114 (September 26/27, 1953), p. 7. [*Die Betrogene*]

3,605. Zolla, Elémire. "Th. M.: Disegno della personalità. Il Dottor Faustus," *Letterature Moderne,* 4 (March-April, 1953), 146-153.

3,606. Zoltán, Paulinyi. Review of Sós-Vámos, item #3,101, *Germanistik,* 2 (1961), 619-620.

3,607. Zuchardt, Karl. "Künstler und Mensch: Zur Vortragsreise Th. M's," *Deutsche Warte — Atalaya Alemaña,* Vol. 8, No. 13 (March 31, 1923), pp. 5-6.

3,608. ⸻. "Un novelista notable," *La Vanguardia,* May 3, 1923, p. 5.

3,609. Zuckerkandl, Victor. "Th. M. the Musician," in item #3,276, pp. 13-[33] Also in German, "Th. M., der Musiker," *NZZ,* Vol. 186, No. 277 (October 9, 1965), p. 20.

3,610. Zuckerman, Elliott. "Th. M.," in his *The First Hundred Years of Wagner's 'Tristan,'* pp. 136-148 et al. New York: Columbia University Press, 1964.

3,611. Zuckmayer, Carl. "Worte des Abschieds," *Welt,* August 15, 1955. [Obit.]

3,612. Zurkuhlen, H. "Das Th. M.-Archiv," *Sonntag,* July 17, 1955. [Berlin Archive]

3,613. Zweig, Arnold. "Brief an Th. M.," *NDL,* Vol. 3, No. 6 (June 1955), pp. 13-14 [facs.] Under the title "Glückwunsch an Th. M." in his *Früchtekorb,* pp. 87-88. Rudolstadt: Greifenverlag, 1957. [80th birthday] Also in item #2,833.

3,614. ⸻. "Über den 80-jährigen Th. M. werden jetzt überall Aufsätze erscheinen," in *Th. M.: Leben und Werk,* 297, pp. 8-9. [Halle: Freiheit-Verlag, 1955]

3,615. ———. "Passione armata," *Il Contemporaneo*, Vol. 2, No. 23
(June 4, 1955), p. 5. [80th birthday]

3,616. ———. "Abschied von Th. M.," *Neues Deutschland*, Vol. 10,
No. 189 (August 14, 1955), p. 4. Reprinted in G. Wenzel,
item #3,453, pp. 61-63. Also in Arnold Zweig's *Früchtekorb*,
item #3,613, pp. 91-94, and in *Th. M.: Leben und Werk*,
item #297, pp. 5-6. [Obit.]

3,617. ———. "Th. M's Bedeutung," in his *Früchtekorb*, item
#3,613, pp. 88-91. Also in his *Essays*, Vol. 1, pp. 305-[308]
Berlin: Aufbau, 1959. Reprinted in G. Wenzel, item #3,461,
pp. 13-15.

3,618. ———. "Th. M.: Zum 40. Geburtstag," in his *Essays*, Vol. 1,
pp. 279-304 [item #3,617] Cf. first publication, I, item
#2,150.

3,619. ———. "Lebensweg mit Th. M. — Th. M. starb am 12. 8.
1955," *NDL*, 13 (August 1965), 167-179.

3,620. Zweig, Stefanie. "Von der Unendlichkeit des Grossen,"
Allgemeine Wochenzeitung der Juden in Deutschland, Vol. 10,
No. 9 (June 3, 1955), Feuilleton. [80th birthday]

3,621. Zygulski, Zdzislaw. "Th. M. (1875-1955)," *Kwartalnik
Neofilologiczny*, No. 2 (1957), pp. 121-138.

RESEARCH IN PROGRESS

3,622. Anderson, Birgit (Marburg a.d.L.). Die Bedeutung des
Demetermythos für das Alterswerk Th. M's.

3,623. Bartholomeczik (Mainz). Das Selbstverständnis des Deutschen
bei George, Ernst Bertram und Th. M.

3,624. Beal, M. (London). Irony and Humor in Th. M's Novels and
Novellen. An Investigation of their Relevance to his Style,
Artistic Methods and Ideas. [Completed]

3,625. Becker, Hans-Jürgen (Frankfurt a. M.). Der *Felix Krull* von
Th. M. und seine Roman-Vorbilder.

3,626. Berger, Willy (Bonn). Der Mythos und seine Motive in Th.
M's Roman *Joseph und seine Brüder*.

3,627. Berthel, Werner (Marburg a.d.L.). Die Entwicklung der Form
der Ironie im Werke Thomas Manns, aufgezeigt an den
Romanen *Buddenbrooks, Der Zauberberg* und *Der Erwählte*.

3,628. Deleted.

3,629. Bulhof, Francis (University of Texas). A Word Index to
        Th. M's Novel *Der Zauberberg.* [Supplement to #509]

3,630. Dierks, Manfred (Freiburg i. Br.). Mythos und Psychologie
        in Th. M's Joseph-Roman.

3,631. Dittmann, Ulrich (München). Sprachbewusstsein und Rede-
        formen im Werk Th. M's.

3,632. Eilers, Egon (Marburg a.d. L.). Th. M's *Fiorenza.*

3,633. Franses, Alison M. (Hull). Th. M's *Betrachtungen eines
        Unpolitischen* und Stefan Zweigs *Die Welt von Gestern.*

3,634. Gaier, Konrad (Freiburg i. Br.). Figur und Rolle des Erzählers
        im Spätwerk Th. M's.

3,635. Gaudigs, Joachim (Hamburg). Das Sprachproblem bei Th. M.

3,636. Geibel, Erika (Marburg a.d.L.). Th. M's *Doktor Faustus* und
        das Volksbuch.

3,637. Geiser, Christoph (Basel). Studien zum Problem des
        Symbolismus bei Th. M.

3,638. Gübel, Hans-Dieter (Marburg a.d.L.). Die Bedeutung Ägyptens
        für die Interpretation von Th. M's Romanzyklus *Joseph und
        seine Brüder.*

3,639. Haug, Hellmut (Tübingen). Die Zeitstruktur des Erzählens
        im Werk Th. M'.

3,640. Honsza, Norbert (Wroclaw). Die Entwicklung der politischen
        und gesellschaftlichen Ideen im Gesamtwerk von Th. M.
        [Habil.-Schr.]

3,641. Jonas, Ilsedore B. (Pittsburgh). Th. M. und Italien.

3,642. Juill, J. M. (Cambridge). Th. M. and the Russian Writers.

3,643. Kaminski, Manfred (Würzburg). Th. M's Gestaltung
        religiös-christlicher Thematik im *Doktor Faustus* und im
        Erwählten.

3,644. Keller, Erkme (Marburg a.d. L.). Die Kritik der Werte in
        Th. M's *Zauberberg.*

3,645. Kiefer, Margrit (Marburg a.d. L.). Groteske Formelemente
        im Werke Th. M's.

3,646. Kirkwood, Henry (Edinburgh). Th. M's Relationship to the
        English Language and to Anglo-Saxon Culture.

3,647. Kleinberg, Helmut (Göttingen). Das Dämonische bei Th. M.

3,648. Klynne, Hilding (Stockholm). Übersetzungstechnische Probleme an Hand der schwedischen Übersetzungen der Werke von Th. M.

3,649. Kokemüller, Klaus (Freiburg i. Br.). Die Raumstruktur im Werke Th. M's.

3,650. Kücking, Marlies (Köln). Das Motiv der Krankheit und die Frage nach dem Sinn des Menschen im Werke Th. M's.

3,651. Lindemann, Karin (Erlangen). Das Problem des Verhältnisses von Ich und Wirklichkeit bei spätromantischen Künstlerfiguren von E. T. A. Hoffmann, Kierkegaard, und Th. M. [Completed]

3,652. Losch, Yvonne (Harvard). Kälte als Thema und Motiv bei Th. M.

3,653. Petersen, Jürgen (Köln). Das Verhältnis von Bewusstsein und Leben in der Erzählhaltung des frühen Th. M.

3,654. Philipson, Wendy (London). The Problem of Good and Evil in Th. M.

3,655. Raffenberg, Manfred (Münster i. W.). Die Fiktion des Erzählers als ästhetisches Problem bei Th. M.

3,656. Randlesome, C. (Nottingham). Th. M's Use of 'Leitmotiv' in Der Zauberberg.

3,657. Reiss, Gunter (München). Formprobleme der Allegorisierung im Werk Th. M's.

3,658. Rümpele, Doris (Freiburg i. Br.). Die Namensgebung im Werk Th. M's.

3,659. Scharfschwerdt, Jürgen (München). Th. M's Zauberberg und der deutsche Bildungsroman.

3,660. Scheltinga Koopman, E. Th. (Amsterdam). Die Musik in Th. M's Erzählkunst und in der Erzählkunst der Romantik.

3,661. Scherrer, Anton (Fribourg). Novellistik in der Nachfolge Th. M's.

3,662. Schmidt, Renate (Frankfurt a. M.). Die Gegenposition zur Dekadenz in der mittleren Schaffensperiode Th. M's.

3,663. Schmitt, Gerhard (Bonn). Der Anteil Schopenhauers und Nietzsches am Weltbild Th. M's.

3,664. Schönebeck, Uwe (Göttingen). Die Erzählfunktion des Mythos bei Th. M. [Completed]
3,665. Stapanauskas, Leonas (Humboldt University, Berlin). Th. M. und Litauen.
3,666. Vaupel, Kurt (Hamburg). Elemente der Schopenhauerschen Philosophie im Werke Th. M's.
3,667. Voss, Lieselotte (Tübingen). Studien zu Th. M's *Doktor Faustus.*
3,668. Vulpius, Klaus-Peter (Tübingen). Jugendstil in der deutschen Dichtung. Versuch einer Stilanalyse unter besonderer Berücksichtigung der Frühschriften Th. M's.
3,669. Wegner, Klaus-Jürgen (Free University of Berlin). Th. M's Stellung zur Literatur.
3,670. Wilhelmi, Carl-Michael (Frankfurt a. M.). Der Aspekt des Bösen im *Doktor Faustus* von Th. M.
3,671. Williams, A. (Keele). Th. M. and 'Deutschtum.'
3,672. Wilson, Eric (Stanford University). A New Look at Th. M's *Felix Krull.*

Appendix

In May, 1966, copy for the final manuscript of *Thomas Mann Studies* Volume II was sent to the printer for typesetting. This consisted of the Preface, the note on Thomas Mann Collections, and the main part—the bibliography of 3,672 items, including research in progress.

In the following months, the authors were privileged to spend some time in the Thomas Mann Archives in Zurich as well as in other European libraries. Between May and September, 1966, a considerable amount of material was discovered by them which, it was felt, should by all means be included. These items fall into three categories and are arranged accordingly:

Part A contains those studies which were completed before 1955 and should, ideally, have been included in Vol. I, *Fifty Years of Thomas Mann Studies.*

Part B lists more recent materials completed between 1955 and 1966.

Part C, based on Peter Mollenhauer's excellent survey [*Monatshefte*, 58 (Fall 1966), 258-267], deals with additional dissertations currently in progress.

During the year 1966, requests have come to us from all parts of the world, urging us to bring this bibliographical record as much up to date as possible. We are therefore especially grateful to Mr. Gordon Hubel, Director, University of Pennsylvania Press, for his permission to record our most recent findings in the following Appendix.

My personal thanks go to Dr. Frank W. Wadsworth, Dean, Division of Humanities, University of Pittsburgh, for his many kindnesses and his unfailing support of my research efforts. I also wish to acknowledge the generous assistance of the Ford Foundation's International Dimension Program which, through the award of a research grant, enabled me to work in European libraries in the summer of 1966.

K. W. J.

Pittsburgh, Pa., January 1967.

PART A

ADDENDA 1901-1954

3,673. Aders, Egon F. M. "Brief an Th. M.," *Berliner Lokal-Anzeiger*, No. 167 (April 8, 1927).

3,674. Andersch, Alfred. "Einleitung," in Th. M., *Politische Dokumente 1930-1950*, pp. 7-34. [Frankfurt a. M.] S. Fischer, 1950. [Identical with item #46. Withdrawn before publication, only one copy of this book known to be extant]

3,675. Angelloz, J. F. "Die Betrogene," *Mercure de France*, May 1, 1954.

3,676. Anon. "Th. M's 'Buddenbrook' Saga in Translation," *NYT Book Review*, February 17, 1924, p. 6.

3,677. Anon. "Ohne Th. M.?" *Der Ruf*, Vol. 2, No. 11 (1947), pp. 1-2.

3,678. Bab, Julius. "Der italienische Zauber," *Berliner Volkszeitung*, Vol. 78, No. 214 (May 8, 1930). [*Mario und der Zauberer*]

3,679. Bahr, Hermann. "Th. M.: Zum 50. Geburtstag," *Neue Freie Presse*, June 7, 1925. [Cf. #168]

3,680. Baldus, Alexander. "Th. M.: Kritik und Bekenntnis," *Allgemeine Rundschau*, No. 23 (June 9, 1928). [Cf. I, item #111]

3,681. Ballin, Fritz. "Th. M. und die Freimaurerei," *Eklektisches Bundesblatt*, 6 (July-August 1930), 238-242. [Concerns *Der Zauberberg*. With a letter from Th. M., May 15, 1930]

3,682. Basler, Otto. "Th. M. und Goethe," *National-Zeitung. Basel*, No. 527 (November 13, 1949). [Review of B. Blume, I, item #1700]

3,683. Bergmann, Gertrud. "Th. M. bei den Juden," *Der Angriff*, No. 85 (October 23, 1930). [*Deutsche Ansprache*]

3,684. Bessell, Georg. "Nietzsche, Spengler, Th. M.," *Weser-Zeitung*, October 25, 1922.

3,685. Billo, A. F. "Th. M. und sein Interview," *Schweizer Freie Presse,* No. 238 (October 13, 1926). [With a letter from Th. M.]

3,686. Björkman, Carl. "Th. M.," *Nya Dagligt Allehanda,* November 13, 1929. [Nobel Prize]

3,687. Blumenthal, W. "Th. M.-Biographie," *Berliner Tageblatt,* July 12, 1925. [Review of A. Eloesser, I, item #619]

3,688. Bondy, François. "Weimar bei Hollywood," *Weltwoche,* Vol. 17, No. 798 (February 25, 1949), p. 15.

3,689. ———. "Th. M. in Weimar," *Weltwoche,* Vol. 17, No. 821 (August 5, 1949), p. 5.

3,689a. Boyd, Ernest. "A Great German Novelist," *New York World,* February 8, 1925. [*Death in Venice*]

3,690. Brentano, Bernard von. "Th. M.," in his *Das Land der Liebe,* pp. 21-44. Tübingen: R. Wunderlich [1952]

3,691. Brion, Marcel. "Souffrances et grandeur des maîtres," *Nouvelles Littéraires,* August 24, 1935. [*Leiden und Grösse der Meister*]

3,692. Brod, Max. "Ein Buch, zu dem man zurückkehrt," *Prager Tagblatt,* August 24, 1930. [*Der Zauberberg*]

3,693. Bruno, Francesco. "Pregiudizi di Tommaso Mann," *Augustea,* Vol. 6, No. 13 (July 15, 1930), p. 414. [*Mario und der Zauberer*]

3,694. Burgmüller, Herbert. "Die Krise der bürgerlichen Kultur," *Fähre,* 2 (1947), 509. [Review of A. Bauer, I, item #113]

3,695. Caroli, Annelise. "Süsser Schlaf," *Vossische Zeitung,* December 14, 1930.

3,696. Czachowski, Kazimierz. "Autoportret Tomasza Manna," *Wiadomósci literackie,* No. 48 (November 28, 1926).

3,697. Deubel, Werner. "Th. M.: Der Zauberberg," *Frankfurter Nachrichten,* December 23, 1924, 2. Beiblatt.

3,698. Diebold, Bernhard. "Senior und Junior: Ein ganz unliterarisches Kapitel," *Frankfurter Zeitung,* No. 902 (December 4, 1926). [*Unordnung und frühes Leid*]

3,698a. Dollinger, Hermann. "Th. M.: Zu des Dichters 50. Geburtstag," *Nürnberg-Fürther Morgenpresse,* June 6, 1925.

3,699. Durieux, Louis. "Un entretien avec Th. M.," *Comedia,* Vol. 22, No. 5503 (January 31, 1928).

3,700. Ebermayer, Erich. "Hochstapler Krull: Zu Th. M's Geburtstag am 6. Juni," *Leipziger Tageblatt,* June 6, 1925.

3,701. Eisner, Pavel. "Th. M.," *Literární rozhledy,* Vol. 14, No. 3 (December 1929), pp. 76-77. [Nobel Prize]

3,702. Emrich, Wilhelm. "Th. M.: Lebensabriss," *Buch- und Kunstrevue,* Beilage zur *Wirtschaftskorrespondenz für Polen,* July 5, 1930.

3,703. ————. "Th. M. spricht," *Buch- und Kunstrevue,* Beilage zur *Wirtschaftskorrespondenz für Polen,* January 10, 1931. [*Deutsche Ansprache*]

3,704. ————. "Vom Beruf des Schriftstellers in unserer Zeit," *Buch- und Kunstrevue.* Beilage zur *Wirtschaftskorrespondenz für Polen,* May 23, 1931. [Th. and Heinrich Mann]

3,705. Eulenberg, Herbert. "Th. M.: Zu seinem 50. Geburtstag," *Hamburger Anzeiger,* June 6, 1925. [Cf. I, item #739]

3,706. Fangen, Ronald. "Th. M.," *Tidens Tegn,* No. 10 (March 12, 1926). [*Der Zauberberg*]

3,707. Fiedler, Kuno. "Eine Einladung mit Hintergründen: Offener Brief an Th. M.," *Volksstimme,* Vol. 42, No. 117 (May 21, 1946), pp. 1-2.

3,708. Fischer, Hanns. "Th. M's künstlerische Sendung," *Rundschau,* Vol. 6, No. 291 (June 4, 1945), p. 1. [70th birthday]

3,709. Flach, Józef. "Th. M.," *Gazeta lwowska — Lemberger Zeitung,* No. 110 (May 14, 1903).

3,710. Fratzscher, A. Review of G. Jacob, I, item #517, *Bücherwurm,* Vol. 12, No. 6 (June 1926). [Bibl.]

3,711. Frey, Alexander M. "Begegnungen: Th. M. 1952," *St. Galler Tagblatt,* August 20, 1952.

3,712. ————. "Th. M. in Zürich," *National-Zeitung Basel,* March 17, 1953. [*Die Betrogene*]

3,713. Geck, Rudolf. "Blau oder braun? Ein Brief von Th. M.," *Frankfurter Zeitung,* June 24, 1925. [Concerns *Unordnung und frühes Leid. See also* E. Korrodi, item #1,774]

3,714. George, Manfred. "Th. M.: Unordnung und frühes Leid," *8-Uhr-Abendblatt,* November 3, 1926.

3,715. ———. "Unfruchtbarkeit des Radikalismus: Th. M. gegen politisches und kulturelles Obskurantentum," *Neue Leipziger Zeitung,* June 13, 1930.

3,716. ———. "Vernunft und Moral erobern den Frieden," *Aufbau* (New York), May 5, 1950, p. 5. [*Meine Zeit*]

3,717. Goldstein, Ludwig. "Th. M. im Pen-Club," *Königsberger Hartungsche Zeitung,* No. 596 (December 20, 1929).

3,718. Greeven, Erich August. "Th. M's 'Zauberberg,' " *DAZ,* January 4, 1923.

3,719. Grossmann, Rudolf. "Die Romanzwillinge: Th. und Heinrich Mann," *Berliner Tageblatt,* No. 66 (February 9, 1926).

3,720. Groth, W. "Nobelpreisträger Th. M.: Unterredung mit dem Dichter," *Hannoverscher Kurier,* Beilage No. 534 (November 13, 1929). [Interview — *Joseph und seine Brüder*]

3,721. Gumppenberg, Hanns von. "Im Akademisch-dramatischen Verein las am Montag Th. M.," *Münchner Neueste Nachrichten,* Vol. 54, No. 539 (November 20, 1901), p. 4. [*Buddenbrooks* —Gladius Dei]

3,722. Harbeck, Hans. "Der gläubige Thomas," *Nürnberger Zeitung,* February 6, 1931. [Poem]

3,723. Hausegger, Siegmund von. "Offener Brief an 'Die Neue Rundschau,' " *Münchner Neueste Nachrichten,* Vol. 86, No. 124 (May 6, 1933). [Concerns 'Leiden und Grösse Richard Wagners']

3,724. ———. "Um Th. M's Wagner-Rede," *Münchner Neueste Nachrichten,* June 1, 1933. [Letter to Peter Suhrkamp]

3,725. Hausmann, Manfred. "Manfred Hausmanns Antwort," *Neue Zeitung,* July 11, 1947. [Cf. I, item #1,237]

3,726. Heilborn, Ernst. "Herr und Hund. — Gesang vom Kindchen," *Das lit. Echo,* 22 (1919/20), 753.

3,726a. Hellwig, Albert. "Dichter und Hochstapler," *Reclams Universum,* 40 (April 1924), [2 pp.] [*Felix Krull*]

3,727. Hengstenberg, Ernst. "Th. M. in Paris," *Rheinischer Beobachter,* Vol. 5, No. 13 (July 1, 1926).

3,728.   Herzfeld, Günther. "Sanatoriums-Romane," *Bund,* November 26, 1924. [*Der Zauberberg*]

3,729.   Hoffa, Lizzie. "Der Zauberberg von Th. M.," *Nordbayrische Zeitung,* August 24, 1925. [Also in *Frankfurter Zeitung,* August 24, 1925]

3,730.   Holländer, Friedrich. "Blick in den Zauberberg," *Stachelschwein,* No. 4 (February 1925), pp. 19-21.

3,731.   Holmberg, Olle. "Människans värdighet," *Dagens Nyheter,* May 19, 1930. [*Mario und der Zauberer*]

3,732.   Hotzel, Curt. "Der Fall Th. M.," *Standarte,* 3 (March 11, 1928), 112-113. [Typical Nazi attitude]

3,733.   ———. "Th. M. 'politisch,' " *Deutsche Tageszeitung,* October 18, 1930. [*Deutsche Ansprache*]

3,734.   Hübscher, Arthur. "Offener Brief an Th. M.," *Deutsche Presse,* Vol. 2, No. 93 (May 23, 1924).

3,735.   Hussong, Friedrich. "Eine Viertelstunde zu spät," *Berliner Lokal-Anzeiger,* No. 506 (October 26, 1930). [Concerns M's political writings]

3,735a. Hyman, Stanley Edgar. Review of C. Neider, I, #297, *Hudson Review,* 2 (Spring 1949), 141-143.

3,736.   Ignotus, Hugo. "Die Hochstaplernovelle Th. M's," *Bühne,* Vol. 2, No. 42 (August 27, 1925).

3,737.   Isolani, Gertrud. "Besuch bei Th. M. in Erlenbach," *National-Zeitung Basel,* July 16, 1953.

3,738.   Jancke, Oskar. "Bekenntnisse des Hochstaplers Felix Krull," *Aachener Post,* January 28, 1924.

3,739.   Jundt, Karl. "Gespräch mit dem Dichter," *Vossische Zeitung,* No. 271 (November 13, 1929). Also in *Tempo* (Berlin), Vol. 2, No. 265 (November 13, 1929). [Nobel Prize]

3,740.   Kahn, Máximo José. "Th. M.: Pariser Rechenschaft," *Gaceta literaria,* November 15, 1927.

3,741.   Kiaulehn, Walther. "Stürmischer Jubel um Th. M.," *Münchner Merkur,* No. 252 (October 20, 1952). [*Felix Krull*]

3,742.   Klugkist, Kurt. "Lübeck als geistige Lebensform," *Lübecker Nachrichten,* April 5, 1953. [*Altes und Neues*]

3,743. Knittel, Jean. "Th. M.: Ein deutscher Patriot," *Neueste Nachrichten* (Strassburg), January 20, 1937. [*Ein Briefwechsel*]

3,744. König, Otto. "Wien und seine Dichter: Ein Gespräch mit Th. M.," *Neues Wiener Journal*, November 1, 1923.

3,745. ———. "Th. M's Wiener Eindrücke: Abschiedsbesuch bei dem Dichter," *Neues Wiener Journal*, November 6, 1928.

3,746. Leuteritz, Gustav. "Th. M. und die deutsche Musik," *Hamburger Anzeiger*, June 6, 1925. [Cf. I, item #1154]

3,747. Lissauer, Ernst. "Zum Bilde Th. M's: Anlässlich seines Hochstapler-Romans," *Neues Wiener Tagblatt*, March 27-29, 1923. [*Felix Krull.* — Cf. I, #2,206]

3,748. Litzmann, Berthold. "Th. M's neuer Roman," *Hannoverscher Kurier*, Unterhaltg. — Beilage No. 508/509 (December 4, 1924). [*Der Zauberberg*]

3,749. Lüth, Ernst. "Der Zauberberg: Der neue grosse Roman von Th. M.," *Hamburger Anzeiger*, February 9, 1925.

3,750. Luft, Friedrich. "Th. M.: Lotte in Weimar," *Athena*, Vol. 1, No. 4 (1946/47), pp. 87-88.

3,751. Mann, Heinrich. "Mein Bruder Th. M. und ich," *Neue Freie Presse*, October 29, 1926.

3,752. Marcus, Carl David. "Th. M's nya roman 'Der Zauberberg,' " *Nya Dagligt Allehanda*, December 9, 1924.

3,753. Marcuse, Ludwig. "Th. M's 'Okkulte Erlebnisse,' " *Berliner Börsen-Courier*, Abend-Ausgabe, December 14, 1923.

3,754. Martens, Kurt. "Die Brüder: Ein Nachwort zur Th. M.-Feier," *Neue Badische Landeszeitung*, June 15, 1925. [50th birthday]

3,755. Maync, Harry. "Th. M.," *Bund*, January 20, 1921.

3,756. Miethe, Käthe. "Goethe und Tolstoi: Ein Vortrag von Th. M.," *DAZ*, September 9, 1921.

3,757. ———. "Die Entstehung der Buddenbrooks," *DAZ*, September 9, 1926. [*Lübeck als geistige Lebensform*]

3,758. Morandotti, A. "Fiorenza," *Corriere della Sera*, January 23, 1913.

3,759. Mühlberger, Josef. "Der Salto mortale ins Nichts," *Esslinger Zeitung*, December 3, 1954. [*Felix Krull*]

3,760. Mühsam, Heinrich. "Disputatio spiritualis: Naptha kontra Settembrini," *Vossische Zeitung*, Unterhaltungsblatt No. 188 (April 22, 1925). [*Der Zauberberg*]

3,761. Natonek, Hans. "Gespräch mit einem berühmten Mann," *Berliner Tageblatt*, February 5, 1925.

3,762. Neumann, Alfred. "Gespräch mit Th. M.," *Münchner Sonntagszeitung*, Vol. 1, No. 14 (July 4, 1920).

3,763. Nobel, Alphons. "Der Zauberberg," *Der Deutsche*, February 20, 1925.

3,764. Noël, Maurice. "Th. M. remercie les nazis," *Le Figaro*, January 25, 1937. [*Ein Briefwechsel*]

3,765. Osborn, Max. "Die 'gutmütige' Republik," *Vossische Zeitung*, February 21, 1933. [Concerns "Bekenntnis zum Sozialismus"]

3,766. Pfeiffer-Belli, Erich. "Lotte in Weimar," *Der Ruf*, Vol. 1, No. 6 (1946/47), pp. 87-88.

3,767. Pinthus, Kurt. "Th. M.: Das Wunderkind. Novellen," *Zeitschrift für Bücherfreunde*, N. F., 6 (1915), Beiblatt, p. 409.

3,768. Platzer, Martin. "Der Zauberberg," *National-Zeitung Basel*, Vol. 6, No. 47 (November 22, 1925), Sonntags-Beilage "Der Basilisk," pp. 1-2.

3,769. Poeschel, Erwin. "Echo vom Zauberberg," *Stachelschwein*, No. 4 (February 1925), pp. 15-19. [Adds to I, item #2,327]

3,770. Pollatschek, Walther. "Th. M's 'Neue Studien,'" *Ost und West*, No. 9 (1948), pp. 88-89.

3,771. Ponten, Josef. "Die Frau des Dichters," *Münchner Neueste Nachrichten*, June 13, 1925. [Th. and Katja Mann]

3,772. Puccini, Mario. "Ritratto di Tonio Kröger," *Il Secolo*, June 11, 1924. [Cf. #2,616]

3,773. ———. "Tommaso Mann," *Il Resto del Carlino*, November 20, 1926.

3,774. Raphael, Gaston. "Un roman de Th. M.," *L'Europe Nouvelle*, No. 388 (June 20, 1925). [*Der Zauberberg*]

3,775. Rency, Georges. "Tristan par Th. M.," *L'Indépendance belge*, March 28, 1926.

3,776. Richter, Georg Martin. "Königliche Hoheit," *Münchner Neueste Nachrichten,* Vol. 62, No. 504 (October 28, 1909).

3,777. Rossen, Evelyn. "Gespräch mit Th. M.," *Neues Wiener Journal,* No. 12244 (December 25, 1927).

3,778. Salingré, Ulrich. "Th. M. und die Nationalsozialisten," *Berliner Montagspost,* No. 40 (October 20, 1930). [*Deutsche Ansprache*]

3,779. Sander, Ernst. "Der Zauberberg," *Reclams Universum,* 40 (December 1924), [321]-322.

3,780. Schaber, Will. "Th. M. über Bürgertum und Sozialismus," *Neckar-Echo,* Vol. 21 (December 12, 1928).

3,781. Schacht, Dr. "Th. M's 'Zauberberg,' " *Freie Deutsche Bühne,* 6 (1924), 297-302. [*Der Zauberberg*]

3,781a. Schneider, Franz. "Quarterly German Book-Letter," *Modern Language Bulletin,* Vol. 10, No. 3-4 (June-October 1925), [2 pp.] [*The Magic Mountain*]

3,782. Schnitzler, Arthur. "Herrn Th. M.," *Münchner Zeitung,* October 16, 1922. [*Von Deutscher Republik*]

3,783. Schwedhelm, Karl. "Mit und ohne Politik," *Rheinische Post,* April 11, 1953. [*Altes und Neus*]

3,784. Seckel, Helmut. "Der Roman des Mediziners," *Vossische Zeitung,* July 5, 1925. [*Der Zauberberg*]

3,785. Specht, Richard. "Th. M. als französischer Autor," *Neue Freie Presse,* August 30, 1931. [*Wälsungenblut — Sang réservé*]

3,786. Spiero, Heinrich. "Th. M.," in his *Deutsche Köpfe,* pp. 138-140. Darmstadt: E. Hofmann, 1927.

3,787. Steiger, Edgar. "Th. M.: Fiorenza," *Tag,* December 20, 1907.

3,788. Stroh, Heinz. "Th. M's Rechenschaft," *Berliner Börsen-Zeitung,* October 16, 1926. [*Lübeck als geistige Lebensform — Pariser Rechenschaft*]

3,789. ————. "Th. M. liest," *Berliner Börsen-Zeitung,* No. 574 (December 9, 1929). [*Mario und der Zauberer*]

3,790. Sturm, Vilma. "Die Bekenntnisse des Hochstaplers Felix Krull," *Schwäbische Landeszeitung,* November 20, 1954.

3,791. Tilgher, Adriano. "L'estetica di Th. M.," *Il Mattino,* November 27, 1929.

3,792. Tucholsky, Kurt. "Europäische Kinderstube" [by Peter Panter, pseud.] *Weltbühne,* Vol. 27, No. 33 (August 18, 1931).

3,793. Van Gils, J. B. F. "Th. M.: Der Zauberberg," *Nederlands Tijdschrift voor Geneeskunde,* November 29, 1925, pp. [2430]-2433.

3,794. Wälder, Robert. "Der 'Zauberberg' im Freudschen Licht," *Vossische Zeitung,* No. 250 (October 19, 1928).

3,795. Walzel, Oskar. "Th. M.: Zum 50. Geburtstag des Dichters," *Nürnberger Zeitung,* June 6, 1925. [Cf. I, item #761]

3,796. Wegwitz, Paul. "Menschlichkeit — Humanität: Zu Th. M's gesammelten Abhandlungen und kleinen Aufsätzen," *Tat,* 18 (1927), 964-966. [*Rede und Antwort — Bemühungen*]

3,797. Weiss, Ernst. "Th. M's 'Zauberberg,' " *Berliner Börsen-Courier,* November 27, 1924.

3,798. Werner, Bruno E. "Ein europäischer Roman," *Neue Zeitung,* December 29, 1947, p. 3. [*Doktor Faustus*]

3,799. Wien, Werner. "Ironie als Lebenshaltung," *Bremer Nachrichten,* November 2, 1954. [*Felix Krull*]

3,800. Winterfeld, Achim von. "Th. M.: Zu seinem 50. Geburtstag," *Neue Preuss. Kreuz-Zeitung,* June 6, 1925. [Cf. I, item #762]

3,800a. Wittmer, Victor. "Gespräch mit Th. M.," *Neues 8-Uhr-Blatt,* January 10, 1922. [Interview in Vienna]

3,801. Wolf, Herman. "Het nieuwe boek van Th. M.," *Nieuwe Rotterdamsche Courant,* No. 160 (January 17, 1925). [*Der Zauberberg*]

3,802. Wust, Peter. "Th. M. in seiner Gesamterscheinung," *Eichendorff-Blätter,* Monatsbeilage der *Neisser Zeitung,* Vol. 1, No. 6 (June 1925). [50th birthday]

3,803. Zerkaulen, Heinrich. "Th. M. im Essener Kunstverein," *Essener Volkszeitung,* January 9, 1918.

3,804. Zweig, Arnold. "Glückwunsch an Th. M.," *Schriftsteller,* Vol. 17, No. 10 (December 1929). [Nobel Prize]

PART B

ADDENDA 1955-1966

3,805. Amoroso, Ferruccio. "Mann e Neumahn," *Il Mondo*, October 31, 1961. [Concerns *Felix Krull* and Robert Neumann's *Olympia*]

3,806. Anon. "Das Th. M.-Archiv in Zürich: Die Eröffnungsfeier," *NZZ*, Vol. 182, Morgenausgabe No. 707 (February 27, 1961), Bl. 1.

3,807. Anon. "Alleged Plagiarism by Th. M.," *Times*, May 19, 1957. [*Felix Krull*]

3,808. Anon. "Myth and Fiction," *TLS*, January 27, 1961, p. 56. [Concerns P. Amann, #3,426, and K. Kerényi, #1,700c]

3,809. Anon. "Th. M. in Übersetzungen: Bibliographie," in #3,933, pp. 25-61.

3,809a. †Artes, Irene Isabel. "Th. M.," in her unpublished study *The Essay as an Art Form: A Study of Selected German Essays.* Ph. D. diss., University of Manitoba, 1965.

3,810. Bachler, Karl. "Th. M's kritische Ironie," *Badische Neueste Nachrichten*, Vol. 18, No. 28 (February 2, 1963), p. 3.

3,810a. Baden, Hans Jürgen. "Die Mythologie Th. M's," *Rheinische Post*, November 28, 1964. [*Joseph und seine Brüder*]

3,811. Basler, Otto. "Rund um Th. M.," *NZZ*, Vol. 186, Morgenausgabe No. 5165 (December 2, 1965), Bl. 8. [Review of Bürgin-Mayer, #504; Berendsohn, #283; and Lindtke, #1,975]

3,812. Bauer-Heyd, Walter. "Th. M. und der Nobelpreis," *Tages-Anzeiger*, No. 56 (March 7, 1962), Bl. 7.

3,813. Baum, Georgina. "Ironie und Th. M's Erzählung 'Die Vertauschten Köpfe,' " *Weimarer Beiträge*, No. 3 (1966), pp. [446]-459.

3,814. Baumgart, Reinhard. "Th. M. wiedergelesen," *Sprache im Technischen Zeitalter,* No. 17-18 (January-June 1966), pp. 56-64.

3,815. ———. "Th. M. von weitem," in his *Literatur für Zeitgenossen: Essays,* pp. 151-162. Frankfurt a. M.: Suhrkamp [1966] [First published in *Sinn und Form.* Cf. #206]

3,816. Becher, Johannes R. "Hochverehrter Th. M.!" [item #217 also in #660, pp. 5-6]

3,816a. Bercovitch, Sacvan. "Th. M's 'Heavenly Alchemy': The Politics of *The Holy Sinner,*" *Symposium,* 20 (Winter 1966), 293-305.

3,817. Berczik, Arpád. "Unveröffentlichter Brief Th. M's," *Weimarer Beiträge,* No. 3 (1966), pp. 459-460. [With Th. M's letter of January 14, 1950, to Dr. Edith Apáthy, née Görgényi]

3,818. Berthold, Werner. "Th. M.," in his *Exil-Literatur 1933-1945,* pp. 254-256 et al. Frankfurt a. M.: Buchhändler-Vereinigung, 1965.

3,819. Bihalji-Merin, Otto. "Th. M.," in his *Die Architekten des modernen Denkens in der Literatur und Kunst,* pp. 115-144. Beograd: Prosveta, 1965. [In Serbo-Croatian]

3,820. Deleted

3,821. *Bisdorff, Ernest. *Th. M. und die Politik.* Luxembourg: Editions du Centre, 1966. 71 pp. [Second, enl. edition. First published by "Section des Arts et des Lettres de l'Institut Grand-Ducal"]

3,822. Blöcker, Günter. "Th. M's letzte Briefe (1948-1955)," *Welt und Wort,* 21 (June 1966), 191-192. [Review of *Briefe III.* First published in #361]

3,823. Blume, Bernhard. "Th. M's Altersbriefe," *Stuttgarter Zeitung,* March 5, 1966. [*Briefe III,* item #2,071]

3,824. Bo, Carlo. "Salderemo nel '75 il vecchio debito con Mann," *L'Europeo,* July 11, 1965.

3,824a. Böök, Frederik. "Discours de réception . . . lors de la remise du Prix Nobel de Littérature à Th. M., le 10 décembre 1929," in K. Strömberg, item #3,983 c, pp. 21-[24]

3,825. Braun, Frank X. "A Lesson in Articulation in Th. M's 'Zauberberg,'" *Monatshefte,* 58 (Summer 1966), [124]-130.

3,825a. ———. Review of Ernst Keller, item #1,696, *Monatshefte*, 59 (Spring 1967), 79-80.

3,826. Breitenstein, Jørgen. "Forord," in Th. M., *Lübeck som aandelig livsform*, pp. 7-[20] Copenhagen: Hasselbach, 1964.

3,827. Brion, Marcel. "Les idées politiques de Th. M.," *Le Monde*, February 10, 1960, p. 8.

3,827a. ———. "La correspondance de Th. M.: Une clé pour son oeuvre," *Le Monde*, March 19, 1966.

3,828. Brües, Otto. "Th. M's 'Seemannsgarn,' " *Lübecker Nachrichten*, No. 130 (June 4, 1960), p. 9. [85th birthday. Cf. #492]

3,829. Carlsson, Anni. "Der Roman als Anschauungsform der Epoche: Bemerkungen zu Th. M. und Günter Grass," *NZZ*, Vol. 185, Sonntagsausgabe No. 5007 (129), November 22, 1964, Bl. 5. [Cf. #542] [Concerns *Doktor Faustus* and *Hundejahre*.]

3,830. Carstensen, Jens. "Einflüsse auf Th. M's Schaffen; Dokumentarisches und Archivalisches," *Lübeckische Blätter*, 126 (September 3, 1966), 218-220.

3,831. *Cases, Cesare. *Th. M.* Milano: C. E. I. [1965] (I Protagonisti della Storia Universale, No. 49, pp. 281-308).

3,831a. Conley, John. "Th. M. on the Sources of Two Passages in *Death in Venice*," *GQ*, 40 (January 1967), 153-155. [Cf. Th. M's letter of Nov. 20, 1946, to John Conley, *English Notes*, Vol. 4, No. 13 (February 20, 1956), p. 1]

3,832. Connolly, Cyril. "Mann — the German Galsworthy," *Sunday Times*, May 7, 1961. [*Stories of a Lifetime*]

3,833. Dach, Charlotte von. "Briefe von Th. M.," *Bund*, No. 348 (August 13/14, 1965), pp. 7-8. [*Briefe II*, item #2,066]

3,834. ———. "Werkstattzeugnisse: Neues aus den 'Blättern der Th. M.-Gesellschaft,' " *Bund*, No. 463 (October 29-30, 1965). [Concerns O. Basler, item #197, and H. Wysling, item #3,550]

3,835. ———. "Th. M's letzte Jahre," *Bund*, No. 185 (May 12, 1966). [*Briefe III*, item #2,071]

3,836. Daemmrich, Horst S. "Th. M's *Schwere Stunde* Reconsidered," *Papers on Language and Literature*, 3 (Winter 1966-1967), [34]-41.

3,836a. ————. "Mann's Portrait of the Artist: Archetypal Patterns," *Bucknell Review,* 14 (December 1966), 27-43.

3,837. David, Claude. "Th. M.," in his *Histoire de la littérature allemande sous la direction de Fernand Mossé,* Vol. 5, pp. 833-841. Paris: Aubier, 1959. [Cf. German transl. by Hermann Stiehl, #641]

3,837a. Davydov, J. "Der Teufel des Adrian Leverkühn: Die Entfremdung der Kunst im Spiegel der bürgerlichen Kultursoziologie und Philosophie," *Weimarer Beiträge,* 12 (1966), 210-236.

3,838. Dettmering, Peter. "Die Problematik der Suizide im Werke Th. M's," *Psyche,* 19 (December 1965), 547-569.

3,839. ————. "Die Inzestproblematik im späteren Werk Th. M's," *Psyche,* 20 (June 1966), 440-465.

3,840. *Deutsche Akademie der Künste, Berlin, ed. *Th. M.-Heinrich Mann.* Berlin: Aufbau, 1965. [Correspondence between H. and Th. M., with postscript by Ulrich Dietzel]. [*See* comments by W. Schütte, #3,973]

3,841. Donker, Anthonie. "Na tien jaren," *Critisch Bulletin,* 22 (October 1955), 456-458.

3,842. Duwe, Wilhelm. "Th. M.," in his *Ausdrucksformen deutscher Dichtung,* pp. 62-64 et al. [Berlin] E. Schmidt [1965]

3,843. Ebermayer, Erich. "Th. M.," in his ". . . und morgen die ganze Welt," pp. 24-27 et al. [Bayreuth] Hestia [1966] [Biog.]

3,844. Egri, Péter. "A Survey of Criticism on the Relation of James Joyce and Th. M.," *Angol Filológiai Tanulmányok — Hungarian Studies in English,* 2 (1965), 105-120.

3,845. ————. "James Joyce and Adrian Leverkühn: Decadence and Modernity in the Joycean Parallels of Th. M's Doktor Faustus," *Acta Litteraria Academiae Scientiarum Hungaricae,* 8 (1966), 195-238; 421-444.

3,846. Eiberling, Curt. "Goethe och Tolstoj," *Samtid och Framtid,* 21 (1964), 212-215. [Concerns Th. M's essay]

3,847. Emrich, Wilhelm. "Das Bild Italiens in der deutschen Dichtung," in his *Geist und Widergeist,* pp. 258-[286] Frankfurt a. M.: Athenäum, 1965. [Cf. #771a]

3,848. Enders, Horst. "Der doppelte Beginn mit Hans Castorp: Zu
        Th. M's 'Der Zauberberg,' " *Sprache im Technischen
        Zeitalter*, No. 17-18 (January-June 1966), pp. 81-109.
        [Cf. #776]

3,849. Eschenburg, Theodor. "Nachlese zu den Buddenbrooks,"
        Lübeckische Blätter, 124 (August 15, 1964), 210-214.
        Reprinted in *Universitas*, 21 (March 1966), 273-282. Also
        published as a pamphlet, Tübingen, 1964. [Cf. #806]

3,850. Fabian, Walter. "Die Briefe Th. M's an Ernst Bertram," *Tages-
        Anzeiger*, No. 284 (December 2, 1960), Bl. 7. [Review of
        #1.575. Cf. #827]

3,851. Fernau, Rudolf. "Ein Schauspieler hört Th. M.," *S. Fischer
        Almanach: Das 80. Jahr*, pp. 38-[39] [Frankfurt a. M.] 1966.

3,852. *Feuerlicht, Ignace. *Th. M. und die Grenzen des Ich*. Heidelberg:
        C. Winter, 1966. 222 pp. [Includes items #860-861]

3,853. Fiedler, Kuno. "Zum 6. Juni 1955: Der achtzigjährige Th. M.,"
        Volksstimme, Vol. 51, No. 128 (June 4, 1955).

3,854. ————. "Th. M. und Graubünden," *Bündner Jahrbuch 1966*,
        pp. 142-144. Chur: Bischofberger, 1966.

3,855. Fietz, Lothar. "Strukturmerkmale der hermetischen Romane
        Th. M's, H. Hesses, H. Brochs und H. Kasacks," *DVJS*, 40
        (June 1966), [161]-183.

3,856. Fröberg, Paul. "Th. M's *Doktor Faustus* i ny belysning,"
        Samtid och Framtid, 19 (1963), 220-223. [Review of G.
        Bergsten, #292]

3,857. Fussenegger, Gertrud. "Josephslegende," *Zeitwende*,
        (December 1965), pp. [843]-844.

3,858. Geerdts, Hans Jürgen. "Der Künstler und die Gesellschaft,"
        NDL, (March 1966), pp. 143-145. [Review of E. Hilscher,
        #1,420]

3,859. Goff, Penrith. Review of G. Bergsten, #292, *Modern
        Philology*, 64 (November 1966), 177-179.

3,859a. Golik, I. E. "Th. M. — ein kämpferischer Humanist," in
        Probleme des sozialistischen Realismus, pp. 462-509. Moscow,
        1959. [In Russian]

3,859b. †————. Th. M. und sein 'Doktor Faustus.' Ph. D. diss.,
Moscow, 1965. 259 pp. [In Russian] [Cf. review by R. Schröder,
#3,972]

3,860. Grandi, Hans. "Musikhinweise," in item #660, pp. 108-113.

3,860a. Grimm, Reinhold. "Dicht am Wort: Eine Studie über Th.
M's Sprache," *Frankfurter Allgemeine Zeitung,* January 30, 1967.
[Review of W. Weiss, #3,442]

3,861. Günther, Joachim. Review of Th. M., *Reden und Aufsätze,*
I-II, *NDH,* Vol. 13, No. 1 (109), 1966, pp. 163-167.

3,862. ————. Review of Th. M., *Briefe III, NDH,* Vol. 13, No. 2
(110), 1966, pp. 180-187.

3,863. ————. "Liebe zu Th. M. auf seltsamen Wegen: Anmerkungen
zu einem Aufsatz von Sebastian Haffner," *Tagesspiegel,*
No. 6231 (March 10, 1966), p. 4. [Reply to item #3,866,
concerning *Briefe III*]

3,864. Haas, Willy. "Th. M. als Briefschreiber," *Welt,* March 31,
1966. [*Briefe III,* item #2,071]

3,865. Habe, Hans. "Th. M.," in his *Im Jahre Null,* pp. 79-80,
92-93 et al. München: Desch, 1966.

3,866. Haffner, Sebastian. "Th. M's Briefe," *Konkret,* No. 2
(February 1966), pp. 42-43. [*See* J. Günther, #3,863]

3,867. Hamberg, Lars. "Th. M.," *Horisonts småskrift,* No. 7 (1966),
pp. 33-34.

3,868. Hamburger, Käte. "Th. M's Humor," *Sprache im Technischen
Zeitalter,* No. 17-18 (January-June 1966), pp. 50-56. [Excerpt
from #1,186]

3,869. Hamburger, Michael. "The Conscience of a Bourgeois,"
Spectator, No. 7124 (January 8, 1965), pp. 45-46. [Review of
G. Lukács, #2,035]

3,870. Hartung, Günter. "Bertolt Brecht und Th. M.: Über
Alternativen in Kunst und Politik," *Weimarer Beiträge,* No. 3
(1966), pp. [407]-435.

3,871. Hartung, Rudolf. "Tagebuch-Notizen" (III), *Neue Rundschau,*
77 (1966), 272-[281] [*See* esp. pp. 275-276 for negative
criticism by Holthusen, I, #2,746, Muschg, #2,349, and
Sieburg, #3,049-3,051]

3,872. Hatfield, Henry. Review of G. Bergsten, #292, *Zeitschrift für deutsches Altertum und deutsche Literatur,* 93 (1963), 141-143.

3,873. ———. Review of R. Gray, #1,059, *GR,* 41 (November 1966), 311-315.

3,874. ———. Review of J. C. Thirlwall, #3,271, *GR,* 41 (November 1966), 315-316.

3,874a. ———. Review of K. Hamburger, #1,186, *GQ,* 40 (March 1967), 274-276.

3,875. Haug, Hellmut. "Noch immer kein Schlusswort zu Th. M.," *Stuttgarter Zeitung,* No. 11 (January 15, 1966), p. 86.

3,876. Haussherr, Reiner. "Texte über die Pietà Röttgen," *Bonner Jahrbücher,* 165 (1965), 145-155. [*Der Zauberberg*]

3,877. Heimann, Heidi. Review of R. D. Miller, #2,260, *GLL,* N. S., 19 (April 1966), 225-226.

3,878. Helbling, Carl. "Briefe Th. M's," *NZZ,* Vol. 187, Morgenausgabe No. 2655 (June 16, 1966), Bl. 6. [*Briefe III,* item #2,071]

3,879. Heller, Erich. "Fausts Verdammnis," in his *Die Reise der Kunst ins Innere und andere Essays,* pp. [15]-54. Frankfurt a. M.: Suhrkamp, 1966. [*See* esp. pp. 49-52]

3,880. ———. "Th. M.: Buddenbrooks," in Jost Schillemeit, *ed., Deutsche Romane von Grimmelshausen bis Musil, pp.* 230-268. [Frankfurt a. M.] Fischer Bücherei [1966] (Interpretationen, #3). [Excerpt from #1,278, German *ed.,* pp. 9-60]

3,880a. Heller, Peter. "Mann: Sphere of Ambiguity," in his *Dialectics and Nihilism: Essays on Lessing, Nietzsche, Mann, and Kafka,* pp. 151-226. Amherst: University of Massachusetts Press, 1966.

3,881. Hellmann, Winfried. Review of V. Mann [2nd ed.], item #2,106, *Germanistik,* 7 (April 1966), 320.

3,882. ———. Review of P. J. van der Schaar, item #2,853, *Germanistik,* 7 (April 1966), 320-321.

3,883. *Henning, Margrit. *Die Ich-Form und ihre Funktion in Th. M's 'Doktor Faustus.'* Tübingen: M. Niemeyer, 1966. vi, 242 pp.

3,884.   Hermsdorf, Klaus. "Th. M.," in #660, pp. 11-24.

3,885.   ―――. Review of H. Koopmann, #1,769, *DLZ*, 85 (1963), 1006-1009.

3,886.   ―――. "Die Geburt eines Schelmen: Zu Th. M's *Krull*-Fragment von 1911," *Weimarer Beiträge*, No. 1 (1965), pp. 102-117.

3,887.   ―――. Review of K. Hamburger's *ed.* of Th. M., *Das Gesetz*, #1,183, *Weimarer Beiträge*, No. 1 (1966), pp. 160-161.

3,888.   Hertling, Gunter H. "Selbstbetrug und Lebenskunst: Gerhart Hauptmanns Lorentz Lubota und Th. M's Felix Krull," *Orbis Litterarum*, 20 (1965), [205]-216. [Concerns Hauptmann's *Phantom* and Th. M.]

3,888a.   Heuschele, Otto. "Th. M's Werk: Neue Beiträge zu seiner Deutung," *NZZ*, December 16, 1966. [Review of H. Lehnert, #1,882; K. Hamburger, #1,186; E. Keller, #1,696]

3,889.   Hildenbrandt, Fred. "Begegnung mit Th. M.," in his *Ich soll dich grüssen von Berlin: Berliner Erinnerungen*, pp. 187-189. München: Ehrenwirth [1966] [Biog.]

3,890.   Hillard-Steinbömer, Gustav. "Parodistische Legende," in his *Recht auf Vergangenheit*, pp. 156-160. Hamburg: Hoffmann & Campe, 1966. [Cf. #1,388]

3,891.   ―――. "Th. M. zum zehnjährigen Todestag," in item #3,890, pp. 161-163. [Cf. #1,395]

3,892.   ―――. "Die Zürcher Gedenkstätten für Th. M.," in item #3,890, pp. 164-167. [Cf. #1,394]

3,892a.   *Hilscher, Eberhard. *Th. M. Élete és müve*. [Budapest] Kossuth Könyvkiadó, 1966. 343 pp. [Hungarian transl. of #1,420 by Béla Székely]

3,893.   Höllerer, Walter. "In Sachen Th. M. ― Aussicht," *Sprache im Technischen Zeitalter*, No. 17-18 (January-June 1966), pp. 110-113.

3,893a.   *Hofman, Alois. *Th. M. und die Welt der russischen Literatur*. Berlin: Akademie-Verlag, 1967. 428 pp. [Tolstoy ― Dostoevski ― Turgenev ― Gontscharow ― Chekhov]

3,894. Hofmiller, Josef. "Th. M's 'Tod in Venedig,' " in Jost Schillemeit, ed., *Deutsche Erzählungen von Wieland bis Kafka*, pp. 303-318. [Frankfurt a. M.] Fischer Bücherei [1966] (Interpretationen, #4). [Cf. #1,457]

3,895. Honsza, Norbert. "Die Gestalt Goethes im biographischen Roman Th. M's," *Acta Universitatis Wratislaviensis — Germanica Wratislaviensia*, Vol. 10, No. 45 (1966), pp. 163-187. [In Polish, with German resumé]

3,895a. Ianosi, Ion. "Prefata," in Th. M., *Doctor Faustus*, pp. 5-[32] Bucharest: Editura Pentru, 1966. [Rumanian transl. by Eugen Barbu and Andrei Ion Deleanu]

3,896. Isolani, Gertrud. "Meine Begegnungen mit Th. M.," *Allgemeine Wochenzeitung der Juden in Deutschland*, Vol. 20, No. 26 (September 24, 1965), pp. 35, 37, 39. [Biog.]

3,897. *Itoh, Tsutomu. *Goethe und Th. M.* Gifu-City (Japan), 1962. 36 pp. [In Japanese. Cf. #1,547a]

3,898. Jørgensen, Aage. "Th. M's Doktor Faustus," *Orbis Litterarum*, 20 (1965), [165]-175. [Concerns G. Bergsten, #292]

3,899. Johann, Ernst. "Die Erstausgaben Th. M's," *Frankfurter Allgemeine Zeitung*, June 24, 1955.

3,900. ————. "Th. M. - Ost," *Frankfurter Allgemeine Zeitung*, No. 247 October 24, 1966), p. 23. [Review of G. Wenzel, item #3,472]

3,901. Jonas, Klaus W. Review of Bürgin-Mayer, #504, *Monatshefte*, 59 (Spring 1967), [54]-56.

3,902. Kakabadse, Nodar. "Paul Thomas macht Verse oder Kommentare zur Lyrik des jungen Th. M.," *Wissenschaftliche Zeitschrift der Tbilisser Universität*, No. 115 (1965), pp. [311]-323. [In Russian] Also in German, *Weimarer Beiträge*, No. 3 (1966), pp. 461-470.

3,903. Kesten, Hermann. "Th. M., die Juden und die Deutschen," *Aufbau* (New York), Vol. 32, No. 26 (July 1, 1966), p. 28. [Review of W. A. Berendsohn, #284]

3,904. Kirchberger, Lida. " 'Death in Venice' and the Eighteenth Century," *Monatshefte*, 58 (December 1966), 321-334.

3,905.   ———. Review of H. Lehnert, item #1,882, *Monatshefte*, 58
          (December 1966), 355-357.

3,906.   Köttelwesch, Clemens. "Th. M.," in H. W. Eppelsheimer and
          his *Bibliographie der deutschen Literaturwissenschaft*, Vol. 6,
          1963-1964, pp. 265-272. Frankfurt a. M.: Klostermann [1965]

3,907.   Koppen, Erwin. " 'Quest' idioma celeste . . .' Th. M's Rezeption
          der italienischen Sprache," *Arcadia*, 1 (1966), [192]-209.

3,908.   Korlén, Gustav. "Vom Elend und Glanz der schwedischen
          Übersetzungen moderner deutscher Literatur," *Nerthus:
          Nordisch-deutsche Beiträge*, 1 (1964), pp. 195-201. [Th. M.:
          Der Erwählte. — H. Hesse: *Das Glasperlenspiel* — G. Grass:
          Die Blechtrommel]

3,908a.   ———. "Konstruktive Übersetzungskritik als Aufgabe der
          schwedischen Universitätsgermanistik," *Babel*, 12 (1966),
          26-31.

3,909.   Lask, Thomas. "The Story of a Novel," *NYT*, August 30, 1961.
          [*Die Entstehung des Doktor Faustus*]

3,910.   Lehnert, Herbert. "Zur Theologie in Th. M's 'Doktor Faustus':
          Zwei gestrichene Stellen aus der Handschrift," *DVJS*, 40
          (June 1966), [248]-256.

3,911.   ———. "Th. M.-Forschung: Ein Bericht" [I. Teil], *DVJS*, 40
          (June 1966), [257]-297.

3,911a.   ———. "Th. M's Josephstudien 1927-1939," *Jahrbuch der
          Deutschen Schiller-Gesellschaft*, 10 (1966), [378]-406.

3,912.   Leibrich, Louis. "Th. M. 1965," *EG*, 21 (April-June 1966),
          254-261. [Bibliogr. survey of recent criticism]

3,913.   Leonhardt, Rudolf Walter. "Mann Yesterday and Today,"
          NYT Book Review, July 10, 1966, pp. 1, 52. [Review of
          J. C. Thirlwall, item #3,271]

3,914.   Levin, Bernard. "The Wandering Gentile," *Truth*, August 19,
          1955, pp. 1049-1050. [Obit.]

3,914a.   Lindemann, Reinhold. "Vernunft gegen Schwarmgeisterei,"
          Rheinische Post, November 22, 1966. [*Reden und Aufsätze
          I-II*]

3,915.   Lodemann, Jürgen. "Th. M. und seine Namen," *Welt*,
          No. 185 (August 12, 1965), p. 5.

3,916. Lowe-Porter, Helen T. "On Translating Th. M.," in J. C. Thirlwall, item #3,271, pp. 178-[209] [Complete text. See also shorter version, item #2,008]

3,917. ————. "Doctor Faustus" (1948), in J. C. Thirlwall, item #3, 271, pp. 151-177.

3,917a. Lukács, György. "Th. M. im heutigen öffentlichen Leben," in Th. M., Novellák, Vol. 1, pp. 7-[15] Budapest: Európa Könyvkiadó, 1957. [In Hungarian. Cf. German version, item #2,027]

3,918. Maatje, Frank C. "Die Duplikation der Zeit in Th. M's 'Doktor Faustus,' " in his Der Doppelroman: Eine literatursystematische Studie über duplikative Erzählstrukturen, pp. 66-77. Groningen: J. B. Wolters, 1964.

3,919. ————. "Fiktionalität und Funktionalität des Ich-Erzählers im Doppelroman," in item #3,918, pp. 81-91. [See esp. pp. 84-88 on Der Erwählte and Doktor Faustus]

3,919a. Mampell, Klaus. "Th. M. und die 47 er," Zeit, No. 28 (July 8, 1966). [Concerns "Gruppe 47"]

3,920. Mann, Erika. "Das Rätsel um Rudi," Spiegel, Vol. 19, No. 50 (December 8, 1965), pp. 148-151. [Briefe III, item #2,071]

3,921. ————. "Wer läutet?," in S. Fischer Almanach: Das 80. Jahr, pp. 48-[55] [Frankfurt a. M.] 1966. [Der Erwählte]

3,922. Mann, Heinrich. "Mein Bruder," in item #660, pp. 6-7. [Cf. #2,081]

3,922a. Mann, Katja. "Bilder aus Lübeck: Letter to the Editor," Stern, No. 4 (January 22, 1967), p. 7. [Concerns K. G. Simon, #3,979a]

3,923. Markwardt, Bruno. "Die grossen Einzelgänger," in his Geschichte der deutschen Poetik, Vol. 5, pp. 498 ff. Berlin: De Gruyter, 1966. [Concerns F. Wedekind, G. Hauptmann, Th. and Heinrich Mann, Hesse]

3,924. Maurina, Zenta. "Th. M. und Agnes Meyer," in her Verfremdung und Freundschaft: Essays, pp. 100-113. Memmingen: M. Dietrich, 1966.

3,925.   Mauz, Gerhard. "Einst überlas man das Ende," *Merian: Lübeck,*
         Vol. 17, No. 6 (June 1964), pp. 49-53. [*Buddenbrooks*]
3,926.   Mayer, Hans. "La vie et l'oeuvre de Th. M.," in Kjell
         Strömberg, *ed.,* in item #3,983, pp. 27-44. [French transl. by
         Pierre Barkan]
3,927.   ————. "Anmerkungen zum 'Doktor Faustus' von Th. M.,"
         Sprache im Technischen Zeitalter, No. 17-18 (January-June
         1966), pp. 64-69.
3,927a. ————. "Rückblicke auf Th. M.," in his *Zur deutschen
         Literatur der Zeit: Zusammenhänge, Schriftsteller, Bücher,* pp.
         54-74. Reinbeck: Rowohlt, 1967.
3,927b. ————. "Th. M. oder der Wendepunkt," in item #3,927a,
         pp. 261-269.
3,928.   Mazzucchetti, Lavinia Jollos. "Th. M. l'Europeo," in Luigi
         Rognoni's *ed.* of her *Cronache e Saggi,* pp. 321-463. [Milano]
         Il Saggiatore [1966] [Contains her collected articles on Th.
         M., 1924-1964]
3,929.   Meyer, Heinrich. "Mann und Rilke und der Eugen-Diederichs-
         Komplex," in his *Was bleibt: Bemerkungen über Literatur und
         Leben,* pp. 44-47 et al. Stuttgart: H. E. Günther [1966]
3,930.   *Middell, Eike. *Th. M.: Versuch einer Einführung in Leben und
         Werk.* Leipzig: P. Reclam [1966] 291 pp.
3,931.   †Mietusch, Harry. Der kritische Empfang Th. M's in
         Ostdeutschland. Ph. D. diss., Cornell University, 1966.
3,932.   Moeller, Hans-Bernhard. "Th. M's venezianische Götterkunde,
         Plastik und Zeitlosigkeit," *DVJS,* 40 (June 1966), [184]-205.
3,933.   *Mönnig, Richard, *ed. Th. M.* Bonn: Inter Nationes, 1965. 61
         pp. [Contents: Anon., item #3,809, and G. Mann, item
         #2,074]
3,933a. Mohrt, Michael. "Confessions d'un chevalier de la littérature,"
         Figaro Littéraire, February 16, 1967, p. 6. [*Lebensabriss*]
3,934.   Mutini, Claudio. "In margine di una dimenticata recensione di
         Th. M.: Le ultime *Rime* di Michelangelo," *Filologia e
         Letteratura,* 11 (1965), 84-112.
3,935.   †Nelson, Donald F. Stylistic Unity and Change in Th. M's *Felix
         Krull.* Ph. D. diss., University of Minnesota, 1966.

3,936. Neveux, Jean B. Review of A. Rogalski, item #2,750, *EG*, 19 (July-September 1964), 324-325.

3,937. Nielsen, Birger Hassing. "Th. M's Vorarbeiten zu einem Drama über Luthers Hochzeit (1955)," *Orbis Litterarum*, 20 (1965), [98]-127.

3,938. Nielsen, Birgit S. "Adrian Leverkühns Leben als bewusste mythische imitatio des Dr. Faustus," *Orbis Litterarum*, 20 (1965), [128]-158.

3,939. Olsen, Henry. "Der Patient Spinell," *Orbis Litterarum*, 20 (1965), 217-221.

3,940. Oplatka, Andreas. "Th. M. und Richard Wagner," *Schweizer Monatshefte*, 45 (October 1965), 672-679.

3,941. ———. "Chronik eines Lebens," *Weltwoche*, Vol. 34, No. 1,684 (February 18, 1966), p. 26. [Review of *Briefe III*, item #2,071, and Bürgin-Mayer, #504]

3,942. Orlowski, Hubert. "Zur Problematik der 'Betrachtungen eines Unpolitischen' von Th. M.," *Filologia* (Poznan), No. 6 (1964), pp. 223-244.

3,943. Paci, Enzo. "Musica, Mito e Psicologia in Th. M.," in his *Relazioni e Significati*, Vol. II: *Kierkegaard e Th. M.*, pp. [242]-261. Milano: Lampugnani Nigri, 1965. [Cf. #2,471]

3,944. ———. "Mann e la filosofia," in item #3,943, pp. [262]-284. [Cf. #2,470]

3,945. ———. "Due momenti fondamentali nell'opera di Mann," in item #3,943, pp. [285]-306. [Cf. #2,475]

3,946. ———. "L'ironia di Mann," in item #3,943, pp. [307]-319. [Cf. #2,474]

3,947. ———. "Su Altezza Reale," in item #3,943, pp. [320]-326. [First published in *Aut aut*, 1956]

3,948. ———. "Ricordo e Presenza dei Buddenbrook," in item #3,943, pp. [327]-341. [Cf. #2,478]

3,949. Peacock, Ronald. "Much is Comic in Th. M.," *Euphorion*, 59 (1965), [345]-360. [Rev. version of #2,495]

3,950. Perez, Hertha. "Traditii democratice ale clasicismui German in interpretarea lui Th. M.," *Orizont*, Vol. 17 (148), No. 8 (August 1966), pp. 53-59.

3,951. ———. "Th. M. despre munca de creatie artistica," *Iasul Literar*, No. 10 (October 1966), pp. 67-70.

3,952. Pietsch, Eva-Maria. Review of Bürgin-Mayer, #504, *Universitas*, 21 (May 1966), 539-540.

3,953. Pongs, Hermann. "Th. M.: 'Doktor Faustus,' " in his *Dichtung im gespaltenen Deutschland*, pp. 166-183. Stuttgart: Union Verlag [1966]

3,954. Pringsheim, Klaus H. "Th. M. in Amerika," *NDH*, Vol. 13, No. 1 (109), 1966, pp. 20-46. [German version of #2,609]

3,955. Deleted.

3,956. Rattner, Josef. "Psychologische Notiz zu Th. M's Hochstaplerroman 'Felix Krull,' " *Psychologische Menschenkenntnis*, 2 (March 1966), 281-288.

3,957. Rauter, Herbert. "Th. M. in Frankreich," *Rotarier*, 16 (November 1966), 657-661.

3,958. Reich-Renicki, Marcel, et al. "Diskussion zu 'In Sachen Th. M.,' " *Sprache im Technischen Zeitalter*, No. 17-18 (January-June 1966), pp. 70-79. [Other participants: Walter Jens, Ivan Nagel, Erich Fried, Werner Kraft, Hans Mayer, and Reinhard Baumgart]

3,959. Reichart, Walter A. "Th. M.," *PMLA*, 81 (May 1966), 320-322. [Bibliog.]

3,960. Requadt, Paul. "Jugendstil im Frühwerk Th. M's," *DVJS*, 40 (June 1966), [184]-205.

3,961. Reuter, Ernst. "Briefe an Th. M.," in Hans E. Hirschfeld [and] Hans J. Reichardt, *eds., Ernst Reuter: Aus Reden und Schriften*, pp. 64-74. Berlin: Colloquium [1963] [Cf. item #2,687]

3,962. Reutimann, Hans. "In Kummer geborene Heiterkeit," *Tages-Anzeiger*, January 19, 1966, p. 19. Also *Zürichsee-Zeitung*, January 21, 1966. [*Briefe III*, item #2,071]

3,963. Roth, Maria. "Mynheer Peeperkorn in the Light of Schopenhauer's Philosophy," *Monatshefte*, 58 (December 1966), 335-344.

3,964. Royer, Jean. "Lübecker Gotik und Lübecker Strassenbild als Leitmotiv in den 'Buddenbrooks,' " *Nordelbingen: Beiträge zur Kunst — und Kulturgeschichte,* 33 (1964), 136-150.

3,965. Rump, Torben. Review of M. Flinker, item #887, *Orbis Litterarum,* 20 (1965), 228-231.

3,966. Sander, Rolf. "Feierstunde im Th. M.-Gymnasium," *Lübeckische Blätter,* 126 (October 1, 1966), 246-249.

3,967. Schaper, Eva. "A Modern Faust: The Novel in the Ironic Key," *Orbis Litterarum,* 20 (1965), [176]-204.

3,968. Scheltinga Koopman, E. Th. "Die Funktion der Musik in Th. M's 'Tristan' und 'Zauberberg,' " *Duitse Kroniek,* Vol. 17, No. 3 (1965), pp. 82-100; No. 4 (1965), pp. 130-142.

3,969. Schiffer, Eva. Review of A. Wolf, item #3,531, *Monatshefte,* 58 (June 1966), 169-170.

3,969a. ————. Review of H. J. Sandberg, item #2,835, *Monatshefte,* 59 (Spring 1967), 74-76.

3,970. Schirmbeck, Heinrich. "Mythos und Demokratie," in his *Die Formel und die Sinnlichkeit,* pp. 272-282. München: List [1964] [Th. and Klaus M.]

3,971. Schreiber, William I. Review of E. Hilscher, item #1,420, *MLJ,* 50 (October 1966), 436-438.

3,972. Schröder, Ralf. Review of I. Golik. "Th. M. und sein Doktor Faustus," *Weimarer Beiträge,* No. 1 (1966), pp. 161-163. [Review of #3,859b]

3,973. Schütte, Wolfram. "Der Briefwechsel zwischen Th. M. und Heinrich Mann," *NZZ,* Vol. 187, Morgenausgabe No. 3387 (August 11, 1966), Bl. 3. [Review of U. Dietzel, #3,840]

3,974. Schumann, Willy. "Wiederkehr der Schelme," *PMLA,* 81 (December 1966), 467-474. [*Felix Krull*]

3,975. Seelig, Carl. "Neue Gedenkstätte für einen grossen Dichter," *Tages-Anzeiger,* No. 43 (February 20, 1961), Bl. 6. [Thomas Mann Archive Zurich. Cf. #3,007]

3,976. ————. "Eröffnungsfeier des Th. M.-Archivs," *Tages-Anzeiger,* February 27, 1961.

3,977.   ———. "Die 'tschechische Episode' in Th. M's Leben," *Tages-
          Anzeiger*, No. 54 (March 4, 1961), Bl. 20. [Concerns Th. M.
          and Rudolf Fleischmann]

3,978.   Shitahodo, Ibuki. "Das Problem des Künstlers bei Th. M.,"
          Wissenschaftliche Berichte der Präfektur-Universität Osaka,
          Vol. 8 (1960), pp. 25-40. [In Japanese]

3,979.   Sieburg, Friedrich. "Ein Herr und Meister," in his *Verloren ist
          kein Wort*, pp. 334-346. Stuttgart: DVA [1966] [Contains
          items #3,052-3,055]

3,980.   Simon, Karl Günter. "Marzipan und Th. M.: 'Das
          Weihnachtsfest war entzückend,' " *Stern*, No. 52 (December 25,
          1966), pp. 26-38. [*See* comments by Katja Mann, item
          #3,922a]

3,981.   Sora, Mariana. "Th. M.," in Th. M., *Casa Buddenbrook*, Vol. 1,
          pp. v-lx. Bucharest: Editura Pentru Literatura, 1966.

3,982.   Stähle, Peter. "Nur ein Satyrspiel? Th. M. und die Universität
          Bonn," *Zeit*, No. 51 (December 17, 1965), p. 31.

3,983.   Stamm, Edith Perry. "Mann's 'Gladius Dei,' " *Explicator*, 23
          (1965), 60.

3,983a.   Stein, Ernst. "Niemals Aussenseiter seiner Zeit: Zu neuer
          Th. M.-Literatur," *Zeit*, January 27, 1967, pp. 22-23. [Review
          of Berendsohn, #284; Bürgin-Mayer, #504; Hohmeyer,
          #1,459; Keller, #1,696; Lehnert, #1,882; Michael Mann,
          #2,094; Saueressig, #2,844]

3,983b.   Stenzel, Jürgen. "Th. M's 'Tristan,' " in his *Zeichensetzung:
          Stiluntersuchungen an deutscher Prosadichtung*. Göttingen:
          Vandenhoeck & Ruprecht, 1966. [Style]

3,983c.   Strömberg, Kjell. "Th. M.," in his *ed.* of La '*petite histoire' de
          l'attribution du Prix Nobel à Th. M.*, pp. 9-[17] Bruge: Impr.
          Ste. Catherine, 1962.

3,984.   Strothmann, Dietrich. "Th. M.," in his *Nationalsozialistische
          Literaturpolitik*, pp. 310-313 et al. Bonn: Bouvier, ²1963.

3,985.   Stuckenschmidt, Dierk. " 'Schlüsselbilder' in Th. M's
          'Zauberberg,' " *Monatshefte*, 58 (December 1966), 310-320.

3,985a.   Suchkov, B. "Th. M.," in Th. M., *Buddenbrooks*, pp. 5-[62]
          Moscow, 1959. [In Russian. Vol. 1 of M's collected works]

3,986. Süskind, W. E. "Hermes kommt zu Apoll: Zum Briefwechsel
Th. M.-Karl Kerényi," *Süddeutsche Zeitung,* June 7, 1960.
[Concerns #1,700c]

3,987. ———. "Viermal: Das Th. M.-Buch," *Süddeutsche Zeitung,*
No. 85/86 (April 9-11, 1966). [Review of Michael Mann,
item #2,094; Bürgin-Mayer, item #504; *Briefe III,* item
#2,071, and Th. M., *Reden und Aufsätze*]

3,988. ———. "Das Haus Th. M.," in Hermann Proebst und Karl
Ude, *eds., Denk ich an München,* pp. 135-142. München:
Gräfe & Unzer [1966] [Biog.]

3,989. *Szemere, Samuel. *Kunst und Humanität: Eine Studie über Th.
M's ästhetische Ansichten.* Berlin: Akademie-Verlag; Budapest:
Akademiai Kiadó, 1966. 171 pp.

3,990. Szenessy, Mario. "Über Th. M's 'Die Betrogene,' " *DVJS,* 40
(June 1966), [206]-216.

3,991. Theodor, Erwin. "Th. M.," in his *Temas alemaes.* Sao Paolo:
Consuelho Estadual de Cultura [1965]

3,992. Thomas, R. Hinton. Review of G. Bergsten, item #292, *GLL,*
N. S. 19 (April 1966), 222-223.

3,993. Toynbee, Philip. "The Wound and the Bow," *Observer,* April
26, 1959. [*Last Essays*]

3,994. ———. "The Patriotic Mann," *Observer,* January 22, 1961,
p. 29. [*A Sketch of My Life.* — *Letters to P. Amann,* #3,426]

3,995. Traschen, Isadore. "The Uses of Myth in *Death in Venice,*"
MFS, 11 (1965), 165-179.

3,996. †Tribus, Helmut M. Sprache und Stil in Th. M's 'Buddenbrooks.'
Ph. D. diss., Ohio State University, 1966.

3,996a. Verdaguer, Mario. "Palabras Preliminares del Traductor," in his
transl. of La Montaña Magica, pp. [5]-6. Barcelona: Plaza &
Janés [1962]

3,996b. Virchow, Christian. "Geschichten um den 'Zauberberg,' "
Deutsches Ärzteblatt, No. 5 (1967), pp. 263-265; No. 6
(1967), pp. 316-319.

3,997. Walter, Bruno. "An Th. und Katja Mann," *S. Fischer
Almanach: Das 80. Jahr,* pp. 56-58. [Frankfurt a. M.] 1966.
[Letter of December 12, 1946]

3,998. Walter, Hans-Albert. "Der engagierte Asthet: Zu Klaus Manns 60. Geburtstag am 18. November," *Frankfurter Allgemeine Zeitung,* Feuilleton No. 268 (November 18, 1966), p. 32.

3,999. Weber, Werner. "Späte Prosa von Th. M.," *NZZ,* Vol. 177, Morgenausgabe No. 2858 (October 13, 1956), Bl. 1. [*Nachlese*]

4,000. ———. "Erinnerung an Th. M.," *NZZ,* Vol. 186 Morgenausgabe No. 2697 (June 19, 1965), Bl. 1.

4,000a. Weigand, Hermann J. "Th. M's *Gregorius: Der Erwählte,*" in A. Leslie Willson's *ed.* of H. J. Weigand, *Surveys and Soundings in European Literature,* pp. 243-289. Princeton University Press, 1966. [Cf. I, #2,933]

4,000b. ———. "Thoughts on the Passing of Th. M.," in item #4,000a, pp. 290-307. [Obit. — Cf. #3,428]

4,001. Welzig, Werner. "Th. M's 'Der Erwählte,' " in Rudolf Henns und Hugo Moser, *eds., Germanistik in Forschung und Leben,* pp. 178-183. Berlin: E. Schmidt [1965]

4,002. Wenzel, Georg. "Uber Leben und Werk Th. M's," *Börsenblatt für den Deutschen Buchhandel,* (Leipzig), 133 (November 8, 1966), 822-823. [Review of E. Hilscher, item #1,420]

4,003. Westphal, Gert. "Th. M. spricht," *S. Fischer Almanach: Das 80. Jahr,* pp. 40-47. [Frankfurt a. M.] 1966.

4,003a. Wien, Werner. "Der Zauberer und seine Kinder," *Bremer Nachrichten,* August 8, 1956. [Review of Klaus Mann, *Der Vulkan;* Monika Mann, #2,100; Erika Mann, #2,059; Th. M., "Versuch über Tschechow," *Thamar, Betrachtungen eines Unpolitischen*]

4,004. Wilson, John R. "Tuberculosis and the Creative Writer," *JAMA,* Vol. 196, No. 1 (April 4, 1966), pp. 161-164. [*The Magic Mountain*]

4,005. Wohlgemuth, Rolf. "Ein unveröffentlichter Brief Th. M's," *Marginalien,* No. 19 (1965), pp. 67-68. ["Schwere Stunde"]

4,006. Wolff, Kurt. "Th. M.," in Bernhard Zeller und Ellen Otten, *eds., Kurt Wolff: Briefwechsel eines Verlegers 1911-1963,* pp. 432-442. Frankfurt a. M.: H. Scheffler [1966] [K. Wolff's correspondence with Th. M., 1941-1947]

4,007. Wolfskehl, Karl. "An Th. M.," in Margot Ruben's *ed.* of his *Briefe und Aufsätze*, pp. 37-38. [Hamburg] Claassen [1966] [Letter of November 14, 1929]

4,008. Wysling, Hans. "Aschenbachs Werke: Archivalische Untersuchungen an einem Th. M.-Satz," *Euphorion*, 59 (1965), [272]-314. [See also #3,550, *Felix Krull*].

4,009. Zeller, Bernhard [and] Werner Volke. "Th. M.," in their *ed.* of *Buchkunst und Dichtung: Zur Geschichte der Bremer Presse und der Corona*, pp. 142-143 et al. [Passau] 1966.

4,009a. Ziolkowski, Theodore. "German Literature and the Prize," *Books Abroad*, 41 (Winter 1967), 13-17. [Th. M. and the Nobel Prize — also deals with Hauptmann, Hesse et al.]

4,010. Zuckmayer, Carl. "Th. M.," in his *Als wär's ein Stück von mir*, pp. 54, 170 et al. [Frankfurt a. M.] S. Fischer [1966]

4,011. Zweig, Arnold. "Abschied von Th. M.," in item #660, pp. 8-10. [*See also* #3,616]

PART C

RESEARCH IN PROGRESS

4,012. Birch, Joan (University of Texas). Statistical Study of the Prose Style of Th. M.

4,013. Bruhn, Gert (Princeton). The Self-Quotation in the Works of Th. M.

4,014. Diefenbach, Horst (University of Queensland, Australia). Anthorial Intrusions in Th. M's Third-Person Novels.

4,015. Dill, Heinz (University of Illinois). Spiel und das Spielerische bei Th. M.

4,016. Hannum, Hildegarde Drexl (Harvard University). The Will in Th. M's Fiction.

4,017. Herminghouse, Patricia (Washington University). Th. M's Theory of the Novel in Relation to the Early German Romanticists.

4,018. Hughes, Kenneth (Rutgers University). Structural Elements of the Joseph Novels of Th. M.

4,019. Jospe, Susan (Indiana University). The Structure of *Doctor Faustus*.

4,020. Mahoney, Dennis (Indiana University). An Analysis of Th. M's *Königliche Hoheit.*

4,021. Musinsky, Christiane (University of California, Los Angeles). Th. M's Formal Essays.

4,022. Prusok, Rudi (Washington University). The Use of Scientific Knowledge in the Works of Th. M.

4,023. Riesenmann, Patricia (Indiana University). The Criticism of Th. M's *Doctor Faustus.*

4,024. Simón, Mercedes (Barcelona). La Montaña mágica de Th. M.: Problemas de traducción al español.

4,025. Steinmetz, Donald (University of Minnesota). Th. M's Views of the Social Responsibilities of the Artist: An Inquiry into the Origin of a Political Ideology.

4,026. Sullivan, Mary (University of Pennsylvania). Th. M. and the Middle Ages.

4,027. Sumichrast, Marika (Ohio State University). Th. M. and Czechoslovakia.

4,028. Ternes, John (University of Pennsylvania). The Grotesque in the Works of Th. M.

Indices

A.

INDEX OF JOURNALS AND NEWSPAPERS

ABBREVIATIONS

MFS	*Modern Fiction Studies.*
MLF	*Modern Language Forum.*
MLJ	*Modern Language Journal.*
MLN	*Modern Language Notes.*
MLQ	*Modern Language Quarterly.*
MLR	*Modern Language Review.*
MP	*Modern Philology.*
NDH	*Neue Deutsche Hefte.*
NDL	*Neue Deutsche Literatur.*
NZZ	*Neue Zürcher Zeitung.*
NMQ	*New Mexico Quarterly.*
NYHT	*New York Herald Tribune.*
NYT	*New York Times.*
PBSA	*Papers of the Bibliographical Society of America.*
PLL	*Papers on Language and Literature.*
PQ	*Philological Quarterly.*
PEGS	*Publications of the English Goethe Society.*
PMLA	*Publications of the Modern Language Association of America.*
QQ	*Queen's Quarterly.*
RLC	*Revue de Littérature Comparée.*
RLM	*Revue des Langues Modernes.*
RLMC	*Rivista di Letterature Moderne e Comparate.*
SRL	*Saturday Review of Literature.*
SAQ	*South Atlantic Quarterly.*
SZ	*Stimmen der Zeit.*
TLS	*Times Literary Supplement.*
VQR	*Virginia Quarterly Review.*
WB	*Weimarer Beiträge.*
YULG	*Yale University Library Gazette.*
ZDP	*Zeitschrift für Deutsche Philologie.*

Aachener Post, Aachen. 3,738
Aachener Volkszeitung. Aachen. 2,770
Aargauer Tageblatt. Aargau. 194, 196

Bulletin of the Leo Baeck-Institute. London. New York. Tel Aviv.
   3,305-3,306
Bund, Der: der kleine Bund. Bern. 195, 617-625, 1,169, 1,546,
   1,710, 2,390, 2,964, 2,996-2,997, 3,184, 3,311, 3,490, 3,728,
   3,755, 3,833-3,835
BZ am Abend. Berlin. 215
BZ am Mittag. Berlin. 305

Cahiers des Saisons. Paris. 651, 1,704
Cahiers du Sud. Marseille. 381, 461, 709, 2,824
Cahiers Pologne-Allemagne. Warsaw. 2,499
Cambridge Journal. Cambridge, England. 2,764
Canadian Forum. Toronto. 585
Candide. Paris. 639
Capitolium. Rome. 2,624
Carleton Miscellany. Northfield, Minn. 2,380
Casopis pro moderní filologii. Prague. 24, 2,144, 2,574, 3,041. *See
   also Philologica Pragensia.*
Cela zimes. London. 3,574, 3,579
Chicago Jewish Forum. Chicago, Ill. 3,476
Chicago Natural History Museum Bulletin. Chicago, Ill. 2,086
Chicago Review. Chicago, Ill. 915, 1,679
Christengemeinschaft, Die. Stuttgart. 3,515
Christ und Welt. Stuttgart. 66, 944, 950, 1,068, 1,070, 1,072, 1,462,
   1,464, 1,565, 1,578, 1,733, 2,971b, 3,254-3,255
Christian Science Monitor. Boston, Mass. 1,509
Christliche Sonntag, Der. Freiburg i. Br. 1,079
Church Quarterly Review. London. 3,072
Ciba-Symposium. Basel. 2,580
Civis. Marburg a.d. Lahn. 3,333
Claremont Quarterly. Claremont, Calif. 2,074
Cobden. London. 871
College English. Chicago, Ill. 577, 2,357
College Language Association Journal. Springfield, Ill. 1,639
Colloquium. Berlin. 2,687, 2,707
Comedia. Paris. 3,699

Deutsche Literaturzeitung. Berlin. 1,058, 1,184, 1,608, 2,312, 2,550, 3,044-3,045, 3,460, 3,885
Deutsche Medizinische Wochenschrift. Leipzig. 1,961
Deutsche Presse. Prag. 3,734
Deutsche Rundschau. Baden-Baden, Darmstadt, Zurich. 823, 1,113, 1,790, 1,932, 1,937-1,939, 2,497, 2,612, 2,769, 2,934, 3,499
Deutsche Sprache—Deutsche Literatur. Tokyo. 3,339
Deutsche Tagespost. Berlin. 3,604
Deutsche Tageszeitung. Berlin. 1,136, 3,733
Deutsche Universitätszeitung. Frankfurt a. M. 1,142, 2,952, 3,177, 3,179-3,180
Deutsche Vierteljahrsschrift für Literaturwissenschaft und Geistesgeschichte. Stuttgart. 383, 538, 1,259, 1,879, 2,254, 2,699, 3,021, 3,855, 3,910-3,911, 3,932, 3,960, 3,990
Deutsche Warte—Atalaya Alemaña. Barcelona. 3,607
Deutsche Woche. München. 1,488, 1,491, 2,639, 2,667
Deutsche Zeitung. Berlin. 984
Deutsche Zeitung und Wirtschaftszeitung. Köln, Stuttgart. 173, 777, 1,071, 1,338, 1,982-1,983, 2,936, 3,004, 3,209, 3,214, 3,343
Deutscher Forschungsdienst. Bad Godesberg. 2,914
Deutscher Kurier. Berlin. 1,190.
Deutsches Ärzteblatt. Düsseldorf. 3,996b
Deutsches Gesundheitswesen. Berlin. 49
Deutsches Medizinisches Journal. Berlin. 953
Deutsches Volksblatt. Stuttgart. 3,193
Deutsches Volksecho. New York. 515
Deutschunterricht, Der. Berlin. 182, 1,847, 1,849, 2,549
Deutschunterricht, Der. Stuttgart. 117, 1,089, 1,177, 1,788, 1,864, 2,771, 3,331
Dichten und Trachten. Berlin. 2,913
Dietsche Warande en Belfort. Antwerp. 497, 2,465
Dinge der Zeit. London. 798-802
Diplomatischer Kurier. Köln. 13-14
Direction. Darien, Conn. 2,719
Diskurs: Frankfurter Studentenzeitung. Frankfurt a. M. 1,838
Documents. Offenburg, Paris. 46, 2,780, 3,507-3,508

Doitsu Bungaku—Die deutsche Literatur. Tokyo. 127, 498, 1,244, 2,134-2,134a, 2,146-2,148, 2,284-2,285, 2,338, 2,361, 2,364, 2,454, 2,468, 2,821, 2,829, 3,023, 3,025, 3,099, 3,241, 3,317-3,318, 3,554-3,555, 3,561, 3,563, 3,565
Dokumente. Köln. 852, 1,273
Domino. Zürich. 2,349
Du: Schweizerische Monatsschrift. Zürich. 316, 340, 601, 960, 1,499, 1,991, 2,055, 2,074, 2,236, 2,384, 2,736, 2,993, 3,137
Duemila. Hamburg, Rom. 1,604
Duitse Kroniek. Amsterdam. 506, 1,609, 2,064, 2,946, 3,087-3,089, 3,968
Dunántúl. Pécs. 124
Düsseldorfer Hefte. Düsseldorf. 2,007, 2,518
Düsseldorfer Nachrichten. Düsseldorf. 377, 2,785

Echo, Das. Wien. 2,585
Echo der Zeit. Recklinghausen. 1,077
Eckart. Witten, Berlin. 427, 440-441, 691, 1,820, 2,668-2,669
Eckart-Jahrbuch. Witten, Berlin. 1,541
Eclair, L'. Paris. 69, 2,753, 3,313
Ecole Bernoise—Berner Schulblatt. Bern. 3,553
Edda. Oslo. 261-262, 445
Edioth Hayon. 947
Effort Libre, L'. Poitiers. 39
Eichendorff-Blätter. See Neisser Zeitung.
Einheit, Die. Berlin. 319
Eisenacher Tagespost. Eisenach. 2,558, 2,560
Eiserne Blätter. München. 584, 3,582
Eklektisches Bundesblatt. Frankfurt a. M. 3,681
Encounter. London. 793, 1,278b, 1,279, 2,651, 3,299
Englische Rundschau. Köln. 1,122, 1,422, 3,298, 3,300-3,301
Epoca. Milano. 2,280, 2,571
Erasmus. Bruxelles. 253
Erasmus. Darmstadt. 123, 268, 322, 324, 795, 1,106, 2,778, 2,786
Erdkreis. Würzburg. 3,061
Erlanger Universität, Die. Erlangen. 2,998

Fremden-Blatt. Wien. 724
Fuldaer Volkszeitung. Fulda. 519
Fundo. Tokyo. 2,283
Furche, Die. Wien. 347, 864

Gaceta literaria. Madrid. 3,740
Ganze Deutschland, Das. Detmold, Stuttgart. 359-360, 1,265, 1,810
Gazeta literara. Bucharest. 1,424, 1,536, 2,331, 2,817
Gazeta lwowska—Lemberger Zeitung. Lemberg. 3,709
Gazette de Lausanne. See Gazette littéraire. 2,232
Gazette littéraire. Lausanne. 2,231, 2,232, 3,260
Gazzetta del Mezzogiorno. Bari. 1, 2,372, 2,619
Gazzetta del Popolo. Torino. 1,006, 2,616, 3,248
Gegenwart, Die. Frankfurt a. M. 72-73, 486, 701, 932-933, 1,110, 1,138, 1,813-1,814, 2,665-2,666, 3,049, 3,142
Gehört-gelesen. 1,576
Geibun-Kenkyu. Tokyo. 824
Geist der Zeit. Berlin. 1,656
Geist und Tat. Hamburg. 1,396
Geist und Zeit. Darmstadt. 74, 2,549, 3,361
General-Anzeiger der Stadt Wuppertal. Wuppertal. 729
Genossenschaft, Die. Basel. 1,545
German-American, The. New York. 1,645
German Life and Letters. Oxford. 391, 431, 523, 1,347, 1,972, 2,485-2,487, 2,650, 2,680-2,681, 3,201, 3,497, 3,500-3,501, 3,513, 3,520-3,521, 3,877, 3,992
German Quarterly, The. Appleton, Wis. 303, 370-371, 432, 438, 715, 728, 753, 817, 820, 859, 861, 967, 1,164, 1,216, 1,232, 1,351, 1,384, 1,431, 1,609-1,610, 1,861, 1,926, 1,976, 2,074, 2,498, 2,763, 2,951, 2,988, 3,115, 3,139, 3,166, 3,436, 3,540, 3,831a, 3,874a
Germania. Berlin. 408, 673
Germanic Review, The. New York. 352-353, 369, 372, 483, 804, 912, 1,084-1,087, 1,209, 1,220, 1,225, 1,526, 1,719, 1,855, 1,872, 1,875-1,876, 2,493, 2,540, 2,761, 2,950, 3,102, 3,320-3,320a, 3,428-3,430, 3,493, 3,873-3,874

Heidelberger Student, Der. Heidelberg. 1,524, 2,073
Heidelberger Tageblatt. Heidelberg. 1,038-1,040, 2,813
Heim und Leben. Zürich. 1,919-1,920
Hellweger Anzeiger. 1,448
Hersfelder Volkszeitung. Hersfeld. 3,541
Hessische Blätter für Volksbildung. Giessen. 1,728
Hessische Nachrichten. Kassel. 2,536
Hessische Post. Kassel. 2,279
Heute und Morgen. Düsseldorf. 517, 678, 1,264, 2,028, 2,433
Hilfe, Die. Berlin. 610, 1,368
History of Ideas Newsletter. New York. 1,212, 2,768
Hobbies. Chicago, Ill. 587
Hochland. München. 476, 1,082, 1,334, 1,460, 2,019, 3,156
Hommes et Mondes. Paris. 412-414
Hopkins Review. Baltimore, Md. 576
Horen, Die. Berlin. 767, 1,677
Horisont-Horisonts småskrift. Vasa, Finland. 1,166, 3,867
Horizon. London. 875
House and Garden. New York. 725
Hudson Review. New York. 246, 3,735a
Hufvudstadsbladet. Helsingfors. 775
Humanitas. Brescia. 3,242
Humboldt. Hamburg. 3,095
Hungarian P. E. N., The. Budapest. 2,704

Iasul literar. Iasi. 2,506-2,507, 3,951
Idea. Rome. 2,013
Indépendance belge, l'. Bruxelles. 3,775
Indice de Artes y Letras. Madrid. 1,549
Industriekurier, Der. Düsseldorf. 162, 490
Inostrannaja literatura. Moscow. 843
Insula. Madrid. 3,297
Intermountain Review. Utah State College. 2,416
International Forum. Berlin. 2,347
International Literary Annual. London. 2,496, 3,374
Internationale Literatur—Deutsche Blätter. Moskau. 1,530

Labyrinthe. Genève. 2,228
Land und Leute. Ludwigslust. 217, 1,241
Landbote, Der. Winterthur. 2,693
Landfall. Christchurch, N. Z. 2,332
Landschäftler. Basel-Liestal. 2,812
Larousse mensuel. Paris. 53
Lehrgang Deutsche Sprache und Literatur. Berlin. 1,413
Leipziger Tageblatt. Leipzig. 1,036, 3,328, 3,700
Lemberger Zeitung. See *Gazeta lwowska.*
Leserzeitschrift. Reutlingen. 229
Lesestunde, Die. Berlin. 2,843, 3,062
Letteratura. Rome. 2,593
Letterature Moderne. Bologna, Torino. 889, 2,737, 3,605
Lettere Italiane. Arosa. 536
Lettres. Genève, Paris. 2,229
Levende Talen. See *Revue des Langues Vivantes.*
Librarium. Zürich. 2,875-2,876
Libri del Giorno, I. Milano. 2,183
Lions: Internationale Mitteilungen im Dienste der Menschheit. Kassel. 2,006, 3,425
Listener, The. London. 522, 907, 1,275, 2,411, 2,479, 2,488-2,489, 2,614
Literarische Blätter. Geneva. 3,031, 3,340
Literarisches Echo, Das. Berlin. 3,726
Literarische Revue. München. 1,069
Literarische Welt, Die. Berlin. 435, 591, 603, 934, 1,117, 1,627, 1,643-1,644, 1,843, 2,868, 2,900
Literární rozhledy. Prague. 3,701
Literatur, Die. Berlin, Stuttgart. 696, 1,012, 1,252-1,254
Literature and Psychology. New York. 607-608, 2,237, 3,020
Litterär kritik. Copenhagen. 250
Los Angeles Daily News. Los Angeles. 854
Lübecker Freie Presse. Lübeck. 3,591, 3,593
Lübecker Morgen. Lübeck. 1,583, 2,907
Lübecker Nachrichten. Lübeck. 163, 1,162, 1,335, 1,337, 1,394-

1,395, 1,606, 1,738-1,740, 2,018, 2,375-2,376, 2,861, 2,953-
2,954, 3,742, 3,828
Lübecker Volksbote. Lübeck. 306
Lübeckische Anzeigen. Lübeck. 630
Lübeckische Blätter. Lübeck. 125, 231, 273, 275-276, 278-279, 282,
    418-419, 780, 788, 976, 1,326-1,329, 1,694, 2,072, 2,154-2,155,
    2,157-2,161, 2,744, 2,751, 2,879-2,880, 2,989, 3,097b, 3,830,
    3,849, 3,966
Luceafarul. Bucharest. 1,537
Luminar. Mexico City. 3,438
Lundagård. Lund. 657
Lunds Veckoblad. Lund. 2,458
Luzerner Neueste Nachrichten. Luzern. 831, 1,604, 1,606, 3,144
Luzerner Tagblatt. Luzern. 825

Ma' arib. Tel Aviv. 480
Maatstaaf. Amsterdam. 663
Mädchenbildung und Frauenschaffen. Berlin, Hannover, Hamburg.
    683
Main-Post. Würzburg. 3,208
MD. New York. 79
Manchester Guardian. Manchester. 80, 880, 1,371-1,372
Mannheimer Morgen. Mannheim. 395, 1,638, 2,568
Marburger Presse. Marburg. 400
Marginalien: Blätter der Pirckheimer-Gesellschaft. Berlin. 1,568,
    1,809, 3,459, 4,005
Marianne. Paris. 996
Matin, Le. Paris. 81
Mattino, Il. Napoli. 2,044, 2,743, 3,791
Medizinische Welt, Die. Berlin. 1,313
Menschen. Dresden. 3,146
Mercure de France. Paris. 11, 52, 54, 634, 3,108 3,675
Merian. Hamburg. 3,925
Merkur: Deutsche Zeitschrift für europäisches Denken. Stuttgart,
    Köln. 243, 363-366, 488, 1,318, 1,388, 1,390-1,392, 1,457,
    1,485, 1,503

Merkur am Sonntag. See *Münchner Merkur.*

Messaggero, Il. Roma. 2,370-2,371

Mindener Tageblatt. Minden i. W. 1,080, 3,081

Mittag, Der. Düsseldorf. 202, 489, 493, 505, 812-814, 1,830-1,831

Mittagsecho. Berlin. 3,019

Mitteilungen des Instituts für Orientforschung. Berlin. 1,410

Mitteilungsblatt. Tel Aviv. 277, 281, 797, 1,045, 1,049-1,050, 3,200, 3,303-3,304

Mitteilungsblatt. Deutsche Akademie der Wissenschaften zu Berlin. 2,043

Modern Fiction Studies. Lafayette, Ind. 2,286, 3,995

Modern Language Bulletin. Boston, Mass. 3,781a

Modern Language Forum. Los Angeles, Calif. 1,083, 2,257

Modern Language Journal. Milwaukee, Wis. 456, 3,585, 3,971

Modern Language Notes. Baltimore, Md. 304, 1,339, 1,527, 1,999, 2,001-2,002, 2,128, 2,352, 2,355, 3,015, 3,365

Modern Language Quarterly. Seattle, Wash. 1,020, 1,213, 1,217, 2,655, 2,695-2,696, 2,891-2,892, 3,191

Modern Language Review. London. 42, 667-669, 959, 1,214, 1,219, 1,222, 2,261-2,262, 3,078, 3,227, 3,498

Modern Philology. Chicago, Ill. 2,408-2,409, 3,859

Moderna språk. Saltsjö-Duvnäs. 271, 290, 566

Molad. Tel Aviv. 2,816

Monat, Der. Berlin. 385, 1,278f, 1,558-1,559, 1,711, 2,807

Monatsbericht für die Ausgewählten Werke Storms. Tokyo. 2,335

Monatshefte. Madison, Wis. 7, 289, 375, 437, 499, 718, 783, 986, 1,088, 1,153, 1,221, 1,432, 1,525, 1,607-1,608, 1,611, 1,681, 1,720, 2,095, 2,167, 2,354, 2,430, 2,457, 2,579, 2,683-2,684, 2,698, 2,887, 2,889-2,890, 2,893, 2,979, 2,987, 3,302a, 3,502, 3,538, 3,584, 3,825-3,825a, 3,901, 3,904-3,905, 3,963, 3,969-3,969a, 3,985

Monatsschrift Polen. Warschau. 1,670, 3,509

Monde, Le. Paris. 785, 2,502, 3,827-3,827a

Mondo, Il. Rome. 1,051, 3,572-3,573, 3,805

Mondo Occidentale, Il. Rome. 2,369

Morgen, Der. Berlin. 154, 161

Morgenblatt für Freunde der Literatur. Frankfurt a. M. 1,359
Morgon-Tidningen. Social-Democraten. Stockholm. 1,947-1,950
Moscia. 2,015
Motor im Bild. München. 1,042
Münchner Illustrierte. München. 2,054, 2,056
Münchener Medizinische Wochenschrift. München. 43, 2,613, 2,846
Münchner Merkur. München. 745, 747, 849, 989, 1,715, 2,533-
    2,535, 3,741
Münchner Neueste Nachrichten. München. 1,103, 1,714, 2,713,
    3,721, 3,723-3,724, 3,771, 3,776
Münchner Sonntagszeitung. München. 3,762
Münchner Zeitung. München. 2,279, 3,269, 3,782
Music Library Association News. Washington, D. C. 2,091
Music Review, The. Cambridge, England. 2,091
Music Survey. London. 1,189, 2,941
Musica. Kassel. 829, 2,565, 3,372, 3,528
Musica d'oggi. Milano. 2,592
Musikrevy. Stockholm. 786
Mutiny. New York. 1,009
Muttersprache. Lüneberg. 966, 1,196, 1,815, 2,718, 3,529

Nagyivilág. Budapest. 2,702
Names. Madison, N. J. 1,718, 2,163-2,164
Nation, Die. Berlin. 397, 1,780, 3,316
Nation, The. New York. 169, 592, 858, 991, 2,289
Nationaltidende. Copenhagen. 2,243
National-Zeitung Basel. Basel. 82-83, 185-190, 192-193, 672, 831,
    938, 1,918, 2,481, 2,559, 2,561-2,562, 2,830, 2,858, 3,007, 3,682,
    3,712, 3,737, 3,768
National-Zeitung. Berlin. 210
National-Zeitung Berlin. Berlin. 2,113
Nazione Italiana, La. Firenze. 2,482
Neckar-Echo. Heilbronn. 3,780
Nederlands Tijdschrift voor Geneeskunde. Haarlem. 3,793
Neisser Zeitung. Neisse. 3,802

York. 227, 532, 860, 1,878, 1,881, 2,429, 2,656-2,664, 2,697, 3,959, 3,974

Quatre Dauphins, Les. Paris. 2,825
Queen's Quarterly. Kingston, Ont. 226, 468
Quelle. Osaka. 1,676
Querschnitt. Berlin. 3,422-3,423
Questo e altro. 11
Quotidiano Sardo, Il. Cagliari. 553

Radiojournal. Prague. 3,033
Reclams Universum. Leipzig. 3,726a, 3,779
Réforme. Paris, 883, 901
Renascence. Milwaukee, Wis. 2,836
Reporter. New York. 1,691
Resto del Carlino, Il. Bologna. 3,773
Revista de Filologia Romanica si Germanica. Bucharest. 2,494, 2,512
Revue Bleue. Paris. 987
Revue de Genève. See *Bibliothèque Universelle.*
Revue de l'Enseignement des Langues Vivantes. Paris. 1,964
Revue de Littérature Comparée. Paris. 662, 2,287
Revue des Cours et Conférences. Paris. 321
Revue des Deux Mondes. Paris. 464, 467, 1,008, 2,346
Revue des Langues Modernes. Paris. 1,906, 2,122
Revue des Langues Vivantes—Tijdschrift voor Levende Talen, Bruxelles. 508, 962-963, 1,242, 1,758, 2,012, 2,424, 3,090
Revue du Caire. Cairo. 3,571
Revue Générale. Bruxelles. 1,031
Revue Hebdomadaire. Paris. 3,342
Revue Nouvelle. Paris. 44, 2,273
Revue Rhénane—Rheinische Blätter. Mainz. 1,863
Rhein-Echo. Düsseldorf. 1,735
Rhein-Neckar-Zeitung. Heidelberg. 234-241, 2,170, 2,302, 2,308, 2,854
Rhein-Pfälzische Rundschau. 3,477
Rheinisch-Westfälische Zeitung. Essen. 604

Urania. Leipzig. 3,427

Vaderland, Het. The Hague. 421, 687
Vanguardia, La. Barcelona. 3,608
Värld och vetande. Stockholm. 267
Vårlösen. Stockholm. 259
Vaterstädtische Blätter. Lübeck. 1,921, 2,373-2,374
Velhagen und Klasings Monatshefte. Bielefeld. 3,167-3,168
Verger. Paris. 903
Versicherungswissenschaftliches Archiv. 2,611
Viata-româneasca. Bucharest. 1,537a, 2,014a, 2,611, 2,818
Vierteljahrsschrift für Philosophische Pädagogik. Osterwieck/Harz.
   3,526
Vierteljahrsschrift für Zeitgeschichte. Stuttgart. 3,096
Világirodalmi Figyelö. Budapest. 1,161, 2,360, 2,701
Vinduet. Oslo. 1,437
Virginia Quarterly Review. Charlottesville, Va. 1,099, 1,163
Vita e Pensiero. Milano. 530-531
Volksblatt. Salzburg. 2,857
Volksbühne, Die. Hamburg. 330
Volksecho. New York. *See Deutsches Volksecho.*
Volksstimme. St. Gallen. 865, 867-868, 3,707, 3,853
Volksstimme. Stuttgart. 214
Volks-Zeitung. New York. 1,731
Voprosy Literaturny. Moscow. 694
Vorhof. Dessau. 2,590, 2,638
Vorwärts. Bonn. 348, 700, 1,797, 2,977
Vossische Zeitung. Berlin. 760, 763, 958, 1,521, 1,922, 3,695, 3,739,
   3,760, 3,765, 3,784, 3,794
Vrij Nederland. Amsterdam. 1,261

Waage, Die. Wien. 1,487
Wandlung, Die. Heidelberg. 1,023
Washington Post. Washington, D. C. 2,241
Washington Square College Review. New York. 811, 913-914
Wege zueinander. Stuttgart. 1,726

Wirkendes Wort. Düsseldorf. 130, 402, 808, 1,076, 1,226, 1,440, 2,529, 2,714, 3,512, 3,530, 3,587

Wirtschaftskorrespondenz für Polen. 773, 3,702-3,704

Wisconsin Studies in Contemporary Literature. Madison, Wis. 3,439

Wissenschaft und Fortschritt. Berlin. 2,500

Wissenschaftliche Annalen. Berlin. 689, 2,386

Wissenschaftliche Berichte der Präfektur-Universität. Osaka. 1,672-1,673, 3,978

Wissenschaftliche Zeitschrift der Ernst Moritz-Arndt-Universität. Greifswald. 2,915

Wissenschaftliche Zeitschrift der Friedrich Schiller-Universität. Jena. 1,800

Wissenschaftliche Zeitschrift der Humboldt-Universität zu Berlin. 1,651, 2,139

Wissenschaftliche Zeitschrift der Martin-Luther-Universität. Halle-Wittenberg. 1,723

Wissenschaftliche Zeitschrift der Pädagogischen Hochschule Potsdam. Potsdam. 2,615

Wissenschaftliche Zeitschrift der Tbilisser Universität. 3,902

Wissenschaftliche Zeitschrift der Universität Rostock. 1,143, 1,145, 1,147

Woche, Die: Wiener Montags-Zeitung. Wien. 3,544

Wochenpost, Die. Stuttgart. 220, 2,278, 3,137

World Review. London. 1,260

Wort, Das. Moscow. 135, 1,823, 3,358

Wort in der Zeit. Graz. 1,730

Wort und Wahrheit. Freiburg i. Br. 1,276, 2,219-2,220, 3,109

Württembergische Abendzeitung. Stuttgart. 1,579-1,580

Xavier University Studies. New Orleans, La. 3,135

Yale Review. New Haven, Conn. 1,694, 1,852, 1,857, 3,403

Yale University Library Gazette. New Haven, Conn. 51, 1,606, 2,642

Zagadnienia rodzajów literackich. Lódz. 3,114a

Zahnärztliche Rundschau. Berlin. 3,539

Zeichen der Zeit, Die. Berlin. 350-351, 513, 1,004

Zeit, Die. Berlin-Schöneberg. 128, 2,107, 2,238

Zeit, Die. Hamburg. 598, 656, 716, 806, 1,030, 1,517-1,518, 1,577, 1,585, 1,587, 1,750, 1,962, 2,120, 2,209, 2,214, 2,872, 2,922, 3,049, 3,116-3,123, 3,590, 3,919a, 3,982, 3,983a

Zeit im Buch, Die. Wien. 2,716

Zeitschrift des Vereins für Lübeckische Geschichte und Altertumskunde. Lübeck, 420

Zeitschrift für ärztliche Fortbildung. Berlin. 122, 1,996, 3,127

Zeitschrift für Bücherfreunde. Leipzig. 3,767

Zeitschrift für deutsches Altertum und deutsche Literatur. Wiesbaden. 3,872

Zeitschrift für deutsche Bildung. Frankfurt a. M. 2,436

Zeitschrift für deutsche Literaturgeschichte. See Weimarer Beiträge.

Zeitschrift für deutsche Philologie. Berlin. 1,768, 1,770, 2,317, 2,621

Zeitschrift für Germanistik. See Sung Kyun Kwan.

Zeitschrift für Menschenkunde. Heidelberg. 748

Zeitschrift für Slawistik. Berlin. 1,451, 3,351

Zeitschrift für Theologie und Kirche. Tübingen. 3,128

Zeitwende: Die Neue Furche. Hamburg. 2,999, 3,857

Zürcher Student, Der. Zürich. 3,131

Zürcher Woche. Zürich. 784, 1,995

Zürichsee-Zeitung. Stäfa. 3,962

Zwiebelfisch, Der. München. 2,125, 3,408

B.

SUBJECT INDEX

1. WORKS BY THOMAS MANN*

Achtung, Europa [Bü I, # 54] 16, 533, 996

Addresses . . . 1942-1949. Washington, D. C.: Library of Congress, 1963. 119, 371

Adel des Geistes [Bü I, # 107] 138, 253, 583, 2,473

Altes und Neues [Bü I, # 93] 188, 537, 867, 936, 2,020, 2,219, 2,304, 2,786, 2,794, 2,898, 3,050, 3,136, 3,173, 3,742, 3,783

An die Redaktion von 'Svenska Dagbladet' [in Bü I, # 11] 500

Appell an die Vernunft. See Deutsche Ansprache

Der Bajazzo [in Bü I, # 1] 3,584

Die Begegnung [Bü I, # 94] 2,154, 3,411. See also *Bekenntnisse des Hochstaplers Felix Krull*

Bekenntnis zum Sozialismus [Bü V, # 414] 3,765

Bekenntnisse des Hochstaplers Felix Krull (including *Die Begegnung*). [Bü I, # 99] 1, 6, 15, 29-30, 36, 135, 140, 152, 169, 176, 199, 246, 280, 414, 426, 439, 468, 529, 531, 551, 585, 599, 617, 643, 648, 678, 683, 705-706, 716, 722, 744, 803, 808, 823, 830, 854, 894, 907, 983, 1,007, 1,038, 1,060, 1,075-1,076, 1,082,

---

* After each of Thomas Mann's works, described in Hans Bürgin's *Das Werk Thomas Manns*, mention is made of the reference number in his bibliography, abbreviated as Bü.

392 THOMAS MANN STUDIES

1,089, 1,099, 1,150, 1,174, 1,198, 1,255, 1,276, 1,278-1,278a,
1,338, 1,372, 1,376, 1,390, 1,402, 1,431, 1,473-1,474, 1,535,
1,558, 1,568, 1,620, 1,630, 1,679, 1,709, 1,722, 1,729, 1,738,
1,749, 1,841, 1,854-1,855, 1,879, 1,888, 1,949, 2,026, 2,044,
2,049, 2,086, 2,134a, 2,155, 2,191, 2,220, 2,266, 2,290, 2,293,
2,314, 2,325, 2,348, 2,450, 2,486, 2,515, 2,533, 2,539, 2,551,
2,558-2,559, 2,567, 2,574, 2,591, 2,604, 2,615, 2,669, 2,706,
2,725, 2,796-2,797, 2,814, 2,836, 2,874, 2,887, 2,889, 2,891,
2,905, 2,965, 2,998-2,999, 3,002, 3,004, 3,011, 3,049, 3,078,
3,116-3,117, 3,147, 3,162, 3,192, 3,206, 3,261, 3,279, 3,281,
3,299, 3,303, 3,322, 3,333, 3,379, 3,398, 3,410-3,411, 3,450,
3,505, 3,529, 3,550, 3,625, 3,628, 3,672, 3,700, 3,736, 3,738,
3,741, 3,747, 3,759, 3,790, 3,799, 3,805, 3,807, 3,886, 3,888,
3,935, 3,956, 3,974
Bemühungen [Bü I, # 28] 562, 2,004, 2,634, 3,103, 3,796
Betrachtungen eines Unpolitischen [Bü I, # 12] 325, 390, 478, 584,
609, 626, 933, 1,110, 1,278b, 1,289d, 1,352, 1,480, 1,515, 1,589,
1,696, 1,732-1,733, 1,750, 1,761, 1,795, 1,879, 1,891, 1,893,
2,000-2,001, 2,058, 2,218, 2,258, 2,282, 2,592, 2,916, 2,934,
2,968, 3,146, 3,167, 3,329, 3,353, 3,408, 3,536, 3,633, 3,942
Die Betrogene [Bü I, # 95] 10, 162, 189, 228, 413, 549, 619, 657,
666, 937, 1,062, 1,173, 1,264, 1,371, 1,375, 1,448, 1,517, 1,581,
1,737, 2,007, 2,237, 2,257, 2,265, 2,305, 2,384, 2,427, 2,449,
2,479, 2,486, 2,519, 2,529, 2,603, 2,631, 2,646, 2,699, 2,705,
2,748, 2,757, 2,785, 2,795, 2,950, 2,956, 3,112, 3,199, 3,287,
3,364, 3,444, 3,463, 3,604, 3,675, 3,712, 3,990
Bilse und ich [Bü I, # 5] 734, 853
Ein Briefwechsel [Bü I, # 52] 74, 598, 2,436, 2,455, 2,775, 3,743,
3,764
Buddenbrooks [Bü I, # 2] 136, 186, 202, 298, 305, 420, 489, 491,
524, 600, 635, 659, 676, 679, 691, 756, 759, 779, 782, 806, 824,
932, 942, 954, 1,036, 1,141, 1,190, 1,231, 1,273, 1,370, 1,455,
1,507, 1,583-1,584, 1,640, 1,714, 1,769, 1,780, 1,788, 1,835,
1,914, 1,960, 1,975, 1,977, 2,011-2,012, 2,072, 2,161, 2,244,
2,326, 2,342, 2,375-2,376, 2,424, 2,478, 2,507, 2,523, 2,570,
2,611, 2,625, 2,677, 2,720-2,723, 2,728-2,729, 2,765, 2,855,

2,864, 2,871-2,872, 2,875-2,878, 2,895-2,896, 2,903, 2,930, 2,961, 2,990, 3,009, 3,075, 3,081, 3,175, 3,241, 3,439, 3,539, 3,544, 3,569, 3,627, 3,676, 3,721, 3,757, 3,849, 3,925, 3,964, 3,996

Chamisso [in Bü I, # 20] 632

Children and Fools [Bü IV, # 475] 18

The Coming Victory of Democracy [Bü IV, # 490] 1,866, 2,766, 3,113. See also *Vom Zukünftigen Sieg der Demokratie.*

Correspondence—Th. M's Collected Letters

Amann, # 3,426: 103, 355, 363, 389, 623, 1,081, 1,087, 1,178, 1,594, 1,733, 2,291, 2,483, 2,647, 2,689, 2,807, 3,118, 3,306, 3,808, 3,994

Bertram, # 1,575: 208, 363, 385, 493, 498, 638, 827, 839, 1,081, 1,088, 1,293, 1,576, 2,225, 2,691, 2,806-2,807, 2,922, 3,052, 3,254, 3,419, 3,535, 3,542, 3,850, 3,979

Faesi # 833: 120, 173, 448, 1,268, 1,301, 1,319, 1,601, 1,907, 2,809

Kerényi, # 1,700c: 358, 363, 769, 1,081, 1,088, 1,294, 1,326, 1,502, 1,954, 2,308, 2,423, 2,690, 2,740, 2,789, 2,805, 3,084, 3,120, 3,254, 3,418, 3,534, 3,808, 3,986

Mazzucchetti, # 2,210: 837, 2,838

Briefe I, # 2,062: 104, 118, 208, 364, 370, 373, 386, 467, 520, 573, 625, 787, 951, 1,049, 1,069, 1,077, 1,081, 1,097f, 1,128, 1,267, 1,271, 1,299, 1,344, 1,379, 1,467, 1,476, 1,516, 1,541, 1,577, 1,867, 1,955, 1,968, 2,298, 2,685, 2,808, 3,053, 3,058, 3,214, 3,221, 3,255, 3,979

Briefe II, # 2,066: 120, 196, 365, 370, 374, 379, 387, 573, 590, 1,045, 1,050, 1,071, 1,097g, 1,131, 1,262, 1,269, 1,309, 1,337, 1,344, 1,379, 1,467, 1,477, 1,499, 1,543, 1,585, 1,836, 2,331, 2,453, 2,461, 2,810, 2,937, 3,055, 3,109, 3,217, 3,309, 3,402, 3,487, 3,833, 3,979

Briefe III, # 2,071: 106, 361, 366, 1,072, 1,135, 1,263, 1,587, 2,848, 3,822-3,823, 3,835, 3,862-3,864, 3,866, 3,878, 3,920, 3,941, 3,962, 3,987

Deutsche Ansprache [Bü I, # 39] 306, 586, 927, 1,136, 1,254,

1,524, 1,643, 1,706, 1,734, 1,910, 2,274, 2,920, 3,683, 3,703, 3,733, 3,778

Deutsche Hörer [Bü I, # 68] 82, 252, 1,716, 2,145, 2,939, 3,522

Deutschland und die Deutschen [Bü I, # 74] 2,445, 2,465

Doktor Faustus [Bü I, # 76] 17, 26, 45, 107, 111, 158, 175, 177, 180, 183, 225, 256, 261, 282, 286, 289, 291-292, 332, 335, 341, 343, 346-347, 369, 391, 404, 411, 417, 458-459, 483, 507, 516, 521-522, 532, 536, 542, 548, 558, 564, 579, 595, 635, 661-662, 675, 694, 701, 707, 757, 783, 786, 790, 799, 801, 845, 851, 863, 869, 873, 915, 918-919, 997-998, 1,029, 1,047, 1,073, 1,113, 1,140, 1,155, 1,170, 1,180, 1,189, 1,203, 1,218, 1,234, 1,259, 1,270, 1,273, 1,278a, 1,278e, 1,323-1,324, 1,331, 1,345, 1,359, 1,365, 1,443, 1,453, 1,471, 1,484, 1,486-1,488, 1,527, 1,632, 1,642, 1,666, 1,672-1,673, 1,684, 1,686, 1,690, 1,705, 1,721, 1,723, 1,742, 1,759, 1,782, 1,793, 1,799, 1,824, 1,828, 1,936, 2,003, 2,040-2,041, 2,091-2,092, 2,148, 2,169, 2,175, 2,185, 2,207, 2,221-2,223, 2,239, 2,256, 2,283-2,284, 2,300a, 2,301, 2,313, 2,321, 2,359, 2,379, 2,385, 2,400-2,401, 2,425, 2,446, 2,459, 2,500, 2,516, 2,523, 2,531, 2,564, 2,577, 2,579, 2,587, 2,592, 2,594, 2,610, 2,621, 2,692, 2,697-2,698, 2,732, 2,745, 2,747, 2,760, 2,762, 2,779, 2,787, 2,792, 2,816, 2,828, 2,843, 2,860, 2,913, 2,918, 2,925, 2,941, 3,000, 3,019, 3,064, 3,072, 3,076, 3,083, 3,088, 3,114a, 3,157-3,158, 3,166, 3,171, 3,204, 3,239, 3,245, 3,278, 3,307, 3,317, 3,320a, 3,338, 3,340, 3,361-3,362a-b, 3,403, 3,446, 3,449, 3,477, 3,480, 3,485, 3,497, 3,499, 3,509, 3,518, 3,528, 3,554a, 3,560, 3,562, 3,565, 3,569, 3,605, 3,636, 3,643, 3,667, 3,670, 3,798, 3,879, 3,883, 3,910, 3,917-3,918, 3,927, 3,938, 3,967, 4,019, 4,024

Die Ehe im Übergang [in Bü I, # 40] 1,943

Das Eisenbahnunglück [Bü I, # 103] 1,744, 3,009

Die Entstehung des Doktor Faustus [Bü I, # 84] 54, 117, 466, 650, 735, 792, 839, 876, 943, 1,735, 2,292, 2,463, 2,489, 2,793, 2,854, 3,065, 3,551, 3,909

Der Erwählte [Bü I, # 89] 3, 12, 66, 149, 201, 407, 412, 430-432, 717, 721, 741, 808, 813, 910, 959, 969-970, 1,000-1,001, 1,039,

1,172, 1;388, 1,398, 1,414, 1,460, 1,472, 1,630, 1,725, 1,758,
1,817, 1,824, 1,829, 2,001, 2,016, 2,042, 2,147, 2,302, 2,354,
2,447, 2,544, 2,700, 2,737, 2,927, 2,948, 3,048, 3,051, 3,066,
3,087, 3,090, 3,111, 3,149, 3,159, 3,180, 3,232-3,233, 3,384,
3,409, 3,492, 3,515, 3,530-3,531, 3,547, 3,586, 3,627, 3,643,
3,890, 3,919, 3,921, 4,001

Erzählungen. See Sämtliche Erzählungen
Essays of Three Decades [Bü IV, # 508] 1,852

Fiorenza [Bü I, # 4] 125, 313, 724, 841, 906, 1,061, 1,103, 1,702,
 1,825, 2,187, 2,641, 3,154, 3,253, 3,424, 3,479, 3,632, 3,758
Die Forderung des Tages [Bü I, # 40] 512, 893, 1,816, 1,843, 2,856
Freud und die Zukunft [Bü I, # 50] 1,823, 2,585, 3,545
Friedrich und die Grosse Koalition [Bü I, # 11] 1,043, 1,191,
 1,312, 1,521, 1,923, 2,231, 2,744, 2,910, 3,348
Der Frühlingssturm [Bü III, # 1] 2,272, 3,474

Gedanken im Kriege [in Bü I, # 11] 1,355, 2,754, 3,348
Gefallen [in Bü I, # 116] 731, 2,189-2,190, 2,336, 3,047
Geist und Kunst, 3,552
Gesang vom Kindchen [in Bü I, # 14a] 418, 622, 2,251-2,252,
 2,317, 3,416, 3,726
Das Gesetz [Bü I, # 67] 1,097e, 1,183, 1,500, 1,985, 2,139, 2,142,
 2,228, 3,009
Gladius Dei [in Bü I, # 3] 1,702, 3,154, 3,721, 3,983
Goethe und die Demokratie [Bü I, # 82] 156, 185
Goethe und Tolstoi [Bü I, # 23] 162, 2,558, 2,730, 3,756, 3,846

Herr und Hund [Bü I, # 14] 418, 422, 437, 524, 1,370, 1,426,
 1,796, 2,095, 2,251-2,252, 2,317, 2,771, 3,200, 3,726

Joseph und seine Brüder (including *Der Knabe Henoch*) [Bü I,
 # 47, 48, 51, 66] 7, 33, 59, 129, 139, 154, 161, 221-223, 342a,
 350, 353, 530, 534, 553, 648, 671, 805, 816, 861, 871, 888, 920,
 975, 1,004, 1,094, 1,169, 1,186, 1,211, 1,238, 1,331, 1,351,

1,366, 1,391, 1,399, 1,410, 1,431, 1,459, 1,542, 1,579, 1,599,
1,776, 1,785, 1,802, 1,824, 1,850, 1,873, 1,916, 1,930, 1,934,
2,019, 2,037-2,039, 2,042, 2,149, 2,170, 2,303, 2,306, 2,443,
2,467, 2,567, 2,576, 2,628, 2,636, 2,700, 2,710, 2,767, 2,834,
2,868, 2,889, 2,897, 2,944-2,945, 3,012, 3,015, 3,033, 3,123,
3,150, 3,172, 3,197, 3,229, 3,242, 3,300, 3,319, 3,342, 3,345,
3,405, 3,555, 3,577, 3,581, 3,626, 3,630, 3,638, 3,720, 3,857,
3,868, 3,880a, 4,018

Der Kleine Herr Friedemann [Bü I, # 1] 3,047
Der Knabe Henoch. [From *Joseph und seine Brüder*—Bü V, # 427]
154
Königliche Hoheit [Bü I, # 7] 151, 401-402, 444, 524, 635, 1,048,
1,243, 1,334, 1,370, 1,507, 1,769, 1,813-1,814, 2,023, 2,188,
2,343, 2,713, 2,811, 2,905, 3,009, 3,365, 3,431, 3,597, 3,776,
4,020

Last Essays. New York: Alfred A. Knopf, 1959. 592, 723, 1,011,
1,377, 1,856, 2,241, 2,353, 3,029, 3,993
Lebensabriss. A Sketch of My Life. [in Bü I, # 109; IV, # 79]
1,746, 2,647, 2,665, 3,702, 3,994
Leiden an Deutschland [Bü I, # 72] 95, 3,525
Leiden und Grösse der Meister [Bü I, # 49] 1,363, 1,367, 2,024,
2,442, 2,963, 3,691
Leiden und Grösse Richard Wagners [in Bü I, # 49] 773, 1,166,
2,688, 2,820, 3,723-3,724
Lotte in Weimar [Bü I, # 58] 239, 608, 667, 672, 730, 917, 925,
1,008, 1,060, 1,097c, 1,137, 1,167, 1,208, 1,242, 1,397, 1,428,
1,572, 1,665, 1,712, 1,777, 1,827, 1,846-1,847, 2,015, 2,042,
2,050-2,051, 2,184, 2,191, 2,229, 2,245-2,246, 2,444, 2,759,
2,859, 2,869, 2,901, 3,205, 3,263, 3,359, 3,750, 3,766
Lübeck als geistige Lebensform [Bü I, # 30] 2,112, 3,234, 3,757,
3,788, 3,826

Mario und der Zauberer [Bü I, # 37] 441, 460, 557, 718, 742,
1,091, 1,102, 1,413, 1,693, 2,121, 2,128, 2,133, 2,138, 2,150,

1,507, 1,513, 1,591, 1,762, 1,878, 1,880-1,881, 1,991, 2,014,
2,125, 2,128, 2,131, 2,133, 2,167, 2,254, 2,257, 2,319, 2,355-
2,357, 2,469, 2,522, 2,542, 2,573, 2,616-2,617, 2,894a, 2,915,
3,009-3,010, 3,018, 3,020, 3,027, 3,085, 3,115, 3,135, 3,138,
3,236, 3,272, 3,283, 3,305, 3,331, 3,335, 3,366, 3,368, 3,444,
3,488-3,489, 3,554, 3,904, 3,995, 4,008

Tonio Kröger [in Bü I, # 3] 275, 460, 635, 870, 962, 976, 1,006,
1,195, 1,507, 2,013, 2,468, 2,573, 2,616, 2,837, 2,866, 2,919,
3,009, 3,024, 3,032, 3,085, 3,223, 3,283, 3,380, 3,433, 3,495,
3,503, 3,596, 3,772

Tristan [Bü I, # 3] 109, 460, 635, 760, 978, 1,064, 1,066, 1,339,
1,714, 1,719-1,720, 2,238, 2,528, 2,616, 2,635a, 2,731, 2,915,
3,009, 3,016, 3,085, 3,328, 3,369, 3,435, 3,543, 3,610, 3,775,
3,939, 3,968

Unordnung und frühes Leid [Bü I, # 31] 435, 1,252, 1,627, 1,774,
2,042, 2,112, 2,183, 2,317, 2,339, 2,840, 3,259, 3,519, 3,698,
3,713-3,714

Versuch über das Theater [in Bü I, # 20] 2,253
Versuch über Schiller [Bü I, # 101] 477, 540, 726, 868, 1,096,
1,461, 1,810, 2,307, 2,509, 2,781, 2,946, 3,169, 3,587
Versuch über Tschechow [in Bü I, # 108] 1,283
Die Vertauschten Köpfe [Bü I, # 62] 424, 479, 739, 1,016, 1,168,
1,200, 1,556, 1,624, 1,700a-1,700b, 2,981-2,983
Vom Zukünftigen Sieg der Demokratie [Bü I, # 53] 2,124, 2,456
Von Deutscher Republik [Bü I, # 24] 471, 1,532, 2,201, 2,466,
2,543, 2,558, 3,478, 3,782

Wälsungenblut [Bü I, # 18] 105, 146, 455, 508, 563, 639, 968,
1,149, 1,514, 2,336, 2,340, 2,441, 2,596, 2,607-2,608, 2,676,
3,105, 3,188, 3,216, 3,394, 3,434, 3,785
Der Weg zum Friedhof [in Bü I, # 3] 1,864
Der Wille zum Glück [in Bü I, # 1] 2,881, 2,929
Das Wunderkind [in Bü I, # 10] 1,922, 3,767

Der Zauberberg [Bü I, # 25] 7a, 26a, 43, 110, 137, 147, 157, 287, 295, 307, 314, 318, 334, 344, 392, 399, 440, 454, 509, 511, 561, 570, 615, 635, 652, 658, 734, 748, 753, 776, 780, 789, 807, 835, 873, 898, 909, 946, 965, 974, 980, 985, 1,097d, 1,107, 1,109, 1,158, 1,160, 1,164, 1,196, 1,205-1,206, 1,212, 1,228, 1,233, 1,277, 1,278c, 1,278f, 1,313-1,314, 1,331, 1,364, 1,380, 1,413, 1,447, 1,501, 1,507, 1,527, 1,550, 1,574, 1,674-1,675, 1,698, 1,700d, 1,717, 1,731, 1,761, 1,768-1,769, 1,815, 1,870, 1,879, 1,947-1,948, 1,961, 1,973, 1,996, 2,036, 2,093, 2,128, 2,163, 2,171, 2,233, 2,246-2,247, 2,260, 2,294, 2,356, 2,378, 2,430, 2,490, 2,493, 2,503, 2,567, 2,572, 2,605, 2,613, 2,643, 2,672, 2,822, 2,844-2,846, 2,894, 3,034, 3,041, 3,061, 3,102, 3,127, 3,168, 3,191, 3,231, 3,247, 3,294, 3,312, 3,330, 3,370, 3,422, 3,432, 3,480, 3,510, 3,512, 3,526, 3,576, 3,598, 3,627, 3,629, 3,644, 3,656, 3,659, 3,681, 3,692, 3,697, 3,706, 3,718, 3,728-3,730, 3,748-3,749, 3,752, 3,760, 3,763, 3,768-3,769, 3,774, 3,779, 3,781, 3,784, 3,793-3,794, 3,797, 3,801, 3,825, 3,848, 3,963, 3,968, 3,985, 4,004, 4,024

2. SUBJECTS—THEMES

Allegory, 2,095, 3,657
America, 90, 120, 941, 1,606, 1,612, 1,615, 1,689, 1,926, 2,609, 2,726, 3,646, 3,954
Antike, 1,582
Anti-Semitism, 269, 1,348
Artist, 677, 811, 862, 905, 914, 1,018-1,021, 1,276, 1,442, 1,445, 1,536, 1,573, 1,806-1,807, 2,250 2,286, 2,511, 2,620, 2,695, 3,025, 3,335, 3,339, 3,517, 3,561, 3,978, 3,989, 4,025
Awards, Honors, 61, 191, 210, 217, 263, 889, 935, 1,121, 1,129, 1,496, 2,311, 3,452. *See also* Nobel Prize

Berlin Archive, 172, 2,043, 2,057,

2,386-2,387, 2,440, 3,459, 3,468, 3,612
Bibliographical Items, 296, 502-503, 572, 794-795, 859, 891, 1,023, 1,161, 1,605, 1,628, 1,753-1,756, 1,932, 2,141, 2,151, 2,153, 2,338, 2,341, 2,389, 2,429, 2,612, 2,629, 2,655-2,664, 3,230, 3,265-3,266, 3,304, 3,395, 3,467, 3,563, 3,710, 3,809, 3,818, 3,899, 3,906, 3,911, 3,912, 3,959
Bildungsroman, 160, 3,659
Biography, 37, 55, 65, 68, 75, 79, 90, 94, 101, 236-237, 297, 311, 320, 340, 405, 504, 546-547, 580-581, 647, 814, 834, 874, 885, 890, 947, 960-961, 1,033, 1,040, 1,080,

1,681, 1,863, 1,905, 1,964, 2,435,
2,524, 2,569, 2,753, 2,831, 3,071,
3,094, 3,267, 3,313, 3,315, 3,380,
3,727, 3,957
Freemasons, 1,569, 3,681

German Literature, 160, 793, 1,097i,
1,275, 1,282, 1,411, 1,484, 2,541,
2,869-2,870, 3,130-3,131, 3,557
Germany, 992, 1,093, 1,201, 1,265,
1,427, 1,928, 1,940, 2,134, 2,709,
2,780, 3,091, 3,097, 3,623, 3,671

Hermes, 1,261, 2,260
History, 380, 818
Homosexuality, 2,014, 3,339
Humanism, 251, 254, 351, 356, 433,
631, 797, 908, 1,095, 1,175, 1,439-
1,440, 1,455, 1,808, 1,850, 1,995,
2,130, 2,239, 2,310, 2,362, 2,484,
2,622, 2,626, 2,749, 2,851, 3,008,
3,219, 3,247, 3,254, 3,556, 3,566,
3,989
Humor, 178, 201, 1,186, 1,419, 1,803,
2,495, 3,042, 3,046, 3,624, 3,868,
3,949
Ideology, 1,282
Interviews—Conversations, 57, 78,
171, 240, 294, 311, 332-333, 558a,
603, 896, 989, 1,017, 1,434, 1,792,
1,811, 1,976, 2,135, 2,347, 2,370,
2,391-2,392, 2,433, 2,462, 2,530,
2,584, 2,586, 2,719, 3,074, 3,100,
3,346, 3,360, 3,381, 3,685, 3,699,
3,720, 3,739, 3,744-3,745, 3,761-
3,762, 3,777
Irony, 28, 163, 165, 178, 204, 221-
223, 384, 717, 902, 1,244, 1,278,
1,419, 1,440, 1,685, 1,718, 2,474,
2,668, 2,671, 2,761, 2,862, 3,012,
3,025, 3,222, 3,241, 3,375, 3,510,
3,564, 3,624, 3,627, 3,810, 3,813,
3,967

Italy, 55, 289, 320, 488, 491, 642,
713, 771a, 1,604, 1,701, 2,101,
2,212-2,214, 2,328-2,329, 2,337,
2,624, 2,734, 2,971a, 3,018, 3,321,
3,524, 3,641, 3,847, 3,907, 3,932,
3,934

Jews and the Jewish Problem, 269,
284, 1,348, 1,510, 1,544, 2,815,
3,022, 3,139, 3,189, 3,282-3,282a,
3,683, 3,903

Language, 798, 877, 966, 1,089,
1,196, 1,405, 1,492, 1,526, 1,550,
1,586, 1,791, 1,815, 1,988, 2,139-
2,140, 3,367, 3,442, 3,492, 3,529,
3,631, 3,635, 3,646, 3,907, 3,996,
4,008
Later Work of Th. M., 247, 501, 606,
1,078, 1,215, 1,225-1,226, 1,343,
1,439, 2,588, 2,630, 2,725, 3,622
Literary Affiliations, 323, 341, 353,
522, 675, 977-978, 1,452, 2,970,
3,625, 3,636, 3,904, 3,938, 4,017
Lithuania, 3,344
Lübeck, 191, 231, 263, 305, 340, 630,
806, 815, 1,121, 1,129, 1,162,
1,741, 1,921, 1,975, 2,018, 2,160,
2,373-2,374, 2,751, 2,855, 2,861,
2,943, 2,953-2,954, 2,961, 3,082,
3,373, 3,423, 3,592, 3,594, 3,964,
3,966
Lyrical Poet—Th. M. as a Lyrical
Poet, 2,272, 3,902

Music, 291, 458-459, 545, 575, 662,
689, 695, 701, 786, 829, 863, 869,
1,014, 1,189, 1,256-1,259, 1,345,
1,446, 1,800, 2,091, 2,156, 2,268,
2,271, 2,321, 2,359, 2,439, 2,471,
2,493, 2,593, 2,606, 2,715, 2,860,
2,924, 2,947, 3,114a, 3,231, 3,318,
3,514, 3,528, 3,569, 3,600, 3,609,
3,660, 3,746, 3,968

3. PERSONAL NAMES

4. REVIEWS OF CRITICISM

Admoni, Vladimir G. [and] Tamara
I. Silman, # 8: 2,550, 2,777
Alberts, Wilhelm, I, # 99: 958,
2,250
Altenberg, Paul, # 34: 777, 1,154,
1,298, 1,767, 1,770, 1,902, 1,972,
2,593a, 2,684, 3,163, 3,460

Bauer, Arnold, I, # 113, II, # 200:
1,292, 1,845, 3,694
Baumgart, Reinhard, # 204: 669,
1,232, 2,324, 2,712, 3,595
Berendsohn, Walter A., # 283:
3,811; # 284: 1,596, 3,903, 3,983a
Bergsten, Gunilla, # 292: 17, 282,
605, 668, 1,105, 1,184, 1,570,
1,957, 2,458, 2,892, 3,133, 3,224,
3,302a, 3,546, 3,856, 3,859, 3,872,
3,898, 3,992
Blume, Bernhard, I, # 1,700: 3,682
Brennan, Joseph Gerard, I, # 140:
499, 2,540, 3,585
Brüll, Oswald, I, # 145: 2,558
Bürgin, Hans, Walter A. Reichart
[and] Erich Neumann, # 502:
271, 922, 1,161, 1,593, 1,608,
1,784, 1,809, 1,896, 2,914, 2,971,
3,043, 3,118
Bürgin, Hans [and] Hans-Otto
Mayer, # 504: 897, 1,135, 1,595,
1,969, 2,389, 2,413a, 2,849, 3,106,
3,386, 3,811, 3,901, 3,941, 3,952,
3,983a, 3,987

Cleugh, James, I, # 148: 1,508,
2,635

Deguy, Michel, # 649: 839, 1,903

Devescovi, Guido, # 661: 2,198
Diersen, Inge, # 677: 1,087, 1,146,
1,286, 1,899, 3,044, 3,202

Eichner, Hans, I, # 159, II, # 750:
190, 1,869, 1,887, 2,911, 2,978,
3,553
Eloesser, Arthur, I, # 619: 408,
1,469, 3,687

Faesi, Robert, # 831: 1,566, 2,021,
2,312, 2,967, 2,996
Flinker, Martin, # 887: 103, 656,
1,087, 1,290, 1,998, 3,965
Fougère, Jean, I, # 1,127: 1,885
Fourrier, Georges, # 905: 1,897

Golik, I. E., # 3,859b: 3,972
Gray, Ronald, # 1,059: 3,873
Grosser, J. F. G., # 1,090: 329,
1,151, 1,304

Hamburger, Käte, I, # 2,450, II,
1,186: 1,845, 2,261, 3,056,
3,874a, 3,888a; II, # 1,183: 2,142,
3,887
Hatfield, Henry, I, # 199: 113, 720,
2,498; II, # 1,229: 1,861, 2,893
Havenstein, Martin, I, # 201: 393
Helbling, Carl, I, # 1,063: 2,558
Heller, Erich, # 1,278: 103, 115,
207, 268, 290, 481, 487, 523, 723,
791, 1,010, 1,086, 1,179, 1,224,
1,462-63, 1,485, 1,551, 1,691,
1,767, 1,839, 1,857, 1,937, 2,614,
2,651, 2,696, 2,764, 3,028, 3,107,
3,118, 3,301, 3,498
Hellersberg-Wendriner, Anna, #

Sandberg, Hans-Joachim, # 2,835: 3,969a
Sato, Koichi, # 2,842: 126
Saueressig, Heinz, # 2,844: 99, 122, 3,983a
Scarpa, Roque Esteban, # 2,852: 708, 3,201
Schaar, P. J. van der, # 2,853: 3,123, 3,882
Scherrer, Paul, # 2,877: 1,291, 1,898, 2,158, 3,045
Schröter, Klaus, # 2,971: 279, 1,152, 1,246, 1,308, 1,578
Sonthcimcr, Kurt, # 3,097: 208, 447, 839, 1,300, 1,328, 1,659, 2,152, 3,059, 3,122, 3,126
Sós-Endre [and] Magda Vámos, # 3,101: 3,606
Stresau, Hermann, # 3,181: 276, 1,307, 2,553

Thirlwall, John C., # 3,271, 3,874, 3,913

Thomas, R. Hinton, # 3,273: 114, 1,222, 1,893, 1,999, 2,010, 2,312, 2,488, 2,980, 3,152, 3,521

Venohr, Lilli, # 3,350: 1,087, 1,289

Weigand, Hermann J., # 3,432: 3,086
Weimar, Karl S., # 3,435: 438, 1,720
Weiss, Walter, # 3,442: 3,860a
Wenzel, Georg, # 3,461: 1,303, 1,416; # 3,472: 3,900
White, Andrew, # 3,483: 2,763
Wolf, Alois, # 3,531: 430, 432, 3,969
Wolff, Hans M., # 3,532: 32, 1,430, 1,844, 2,002, 2,683

Žmegač, Viktor, # 3,600: 1,058, 1,287, 1,900, 2,949, 3,513

C.

INDEX OF AUTHORS, COLLECTORS, EDITORS, AND TRANSLATORS

A BIBLIOGRAPHY OF CRITICISM

423

Heumann, Fred S., 1,366
Heuschele, Otto, 3,888a
Heuss, Theodor, 1,367-1,369
Hewett-Thayer, Harvey Waterman, 1,370
Hewitt, Douglas, 1,371-1,372
Heym, Stefan, 1,373-1,374
Heymen, Walter, 2,687
Hicks, Granville, 1,375-1,377
Hiehle, Kurt, 1,378
Hildebrandt, Dieter, 1,379
Hildebrandt, Wolfgang, 1,380-1,381
Hildenbrandt, Fred, 1,382, 3,889
Hill, Claude, 1,383-1,385
Hill, Roland, 1,386
Hillard-Steinbömer, Gustav, 1,387-1,395, 3,890-3,892
Hiller, Kurt, 1,396; p. 27
Hilscher, Eberhard, 1,397-1,421, 3,892a
Himmel, Adolf, 1,422
Himmel, Helmuth, 1,423
Hîncu, Dumitru, 1,424
Hindus, Milton, 1,425
Hines, Jack, 1,426
Hinton Thomas, R. See R. Hinton Thomas.
Hirsch, Felix E., 1,427
Hirsch, Karl Jakob, 1,428
Hirschbach, Frank Donald, 1,429-1,433
Hirschfeld, Hans E., 3,961
Hiss, Walter, 1,434
Hocke, Gustav René, 1,435-1,436
Höllerer, Walter, 3,893
Hølmebakk, Gordon, 1,437
Hoentzsch, Alfred, 1,438
Hof, Walter, 1,439-1,440
Hoffa, Lizzie, 3,729
Hoffman, Frederick John, 1,441
Hoffmann, Fernand, 1,442-1,445
Hoffmann, Gerd, 1,446-1,447
Hoffmann, Paul, 1,448

Hoffmann, Wilhelm, p. 29
Hoffmeister, Werner G., 1,449
Hofman, Alois, 1,450-1,456, 3,893a
Hofmiller, Josef, 1,457, 3,894
Hogestraat, Erich, 1,458
Hohmeyer, Jürgen, 1,459
Hohoff, Curt, 1,460-1,467
Holländer, Friedrich, 3,730
Hollander, Jürgen von, 1,468
Holmberg, Olle, 1,469-1,478, 3,731
Holmqvist, Bengt, 1,479-1,482
Holthusen, Hans Egon, 1,483-1,486
Holthusen, Wilhelm, 1,487
Holz, Hans Heinz, 1,488-1,492
Hommel, Friedrich, 1,494-1,495
Honsza, Norbert, 1,497-1,498, 3,640, 3,895
Hoppe, Manfred, 1,499
Horst, Karl August, 1,500-1,505
Høst, Gerd, 1,506
Hotes, Leander, 1,507
Hotzel, Curt, 3,732-3,733
Howard, Brian, 1,508
Huddleston, Sibley, 1,509
Hübinger, Paul Egon, 1,510
Hübner, Arthur, 434
Huebner, Friedrich Markus, 1,511-1,512
Hübner, Fritz, 1,513
Hübner, Paul, 1,514
Hübscher, Arthur, 1,515-1,516, 3,734
Hühnerfeld, Paul, 1,517-1,518
Hülsen, Hans von, 1,519-1,523; p. 23
Hülsmeyer, Ernst, 1,524
Hughes, Kenneth, 4,018
Hughes, William M., 1,525
Hugin, pseud. See F. von Schleswig-Holstein.
Hunt, Joel A., 1,526-1,528
Hupka, Herbert, 1,529
Huppert, Hugo, 1,530-1,531
Hussong, Friedrich, 1,532-1,533, 3,735

Katzin, Winifred, 1,677
Kaufmann, Alfred, 1,678
Kaufmann, Edward, 1,679
Kaufmann, Fritz, 1,680-1,684
Kauz, F., pseud. *See* Kuno Fiedler.
Kawahigashi, Shoji, 1,685
Kaye, Julian Bertram, 1,686
Kayser, Rudolf, 1,687-1,689
Kayser, Wolfgang, 1,690
Kazin, Alfred, 1,691
Keim, H. W., 1,692
Keister, Don A., 718
Kejzlarová, Inge, 1,693
Kellen, Konrad, 1,694
Keller, Erkme, 3,644
Keller, Ernst, 1,695-1,696
Kellerson, Germaine, 1,697
Kelsch, Wolfgang, 1,698
Kerényi, Karl, 1,699-1,703
Kern, Alfred, 1,704
Kern, Irmgard, 1,705
Kerpel, Eugen, 1,706
Kersten, Kurt, 1,707
Kessler, Harry Graf, 1,708
Kesten, Hermann, 1,709-1,713, 2,886, 3,903
Keyssner, G., 1,714
Kiaulehn, Walther, 1,715, 3,741
Kiefer, Margrit, 3,645
Kiewert, Walter, 1,716
Kihlmann, Erik, 1,717
Kim, Dschae-Min, 1,718
Kirchberger, Lida, 1,719-1,720, 3,904-3,905
Kiremidjian, Garabed D., 1,721
Kirkwood, Henry, 3,646
Kirn, Richard, 1,722
Kirsch, Edgar, 1,723
Klapheck, Anna, 1,724
Klatt-Krieser, Charlotte, 1,725
Klausing, Helmut, 1,726
Klein, Johannes, 1,727-1,728
Kleinberg, Helmut, 3,647

Kleine, Don W., 1,729
Klemm, Reinhold, 1,730
Klemperer, Felix, 1,731
Klemperer, Klemens von, 1,732
Klessmann, Eckart, 1,733
Klöckner, Albert, 1,734
Klose, G. Johanna, 1,735
Kluft, Ernst, 1,736-1,737
Klugkist, Kurt, 1,738-1,741, 3,742
Klynne, Hilding, 3,648
Knaus, Albrecht, 1,742-1,744
Knipowitsch, J., 1,745
Knittel, Jean, 3,743
Knoertzer, C., 1,746
Knopf, Alfred A., 1,747-1,748; pp. 19, 21
Koch, Thilo, 1,749-1,751
König, Otto, 3,744-3,745
Koeppen, Wolfgang, 1,752
Köttelwesch, Clemens, 1,753-1,756, 3,906
Kogon, Eugen, 1,757
Kohler, Marlyss, 1,758
Kohlschmidt, Werner, 1,759, 2,492
Kohn, Hans, 1,760-1,761
Kohut, Heinz, 1,762-1,763
Kokemüller, Klaus, 3,649
Kolb, Annette, 1,764-1,765
Komor, Ilona, 1,765a
Konelev, A., 1,766
Konrad, Gustav, 1,767
Koopmann, Herbert, 1,768-1,771
Koppen, Erwin, 3,907
Korlén, Gustav, 3,908-3,908a
Korn, Karl, 1,772-1,773
Korrodi, Eduard, 1,774-1,779
Kortüm, Albrecht, 1,780
Kracauer, Siegfried, 1,781
Krämer-Badoni, Rudolf, 1,782
Kraft, Irma, 1,783
Kraft, Werner, 3,958
Krammer, Jenö, 1,784
Krammer, Marie, 1,785

Kranz, Gilbert, 1,786
Kratz, Henry, 1,787
Kraul, Fritz, 1,788
Kraus, Fritz, 1,789-1,790
Kraus, Karl, 1,791
Kraus, René, 1,792
Kreft, Jürgen, 1,793
Krekeler, Heinz L., 1,794
Krell, Max, 1,795-1,798
Kreuzer, Helmut, 1,799
Krey, Johannes, 1,800
Kristensen, Tom, 1,801-1,804
Kroepfle, Hans Herbert, 1,805
Kroll, Hans, 3,238
Krüger, Heinz, 1,806-1,808
Krueger, Joachim, 1,809
Kudszus, Hans, 1,810
Kücking, Marlies, 3,650
Kühn, Karl Herbert, 1,811
Küntzel, Hans, 1,812
Küsel, Herbert, 1,813-1,814
Kufner, Herbert L., 1,815
Kuhn, Friedrich, 1,816
Kuhn, Hugo, 1,817, 2,544
Kunert, Günter, 1,818
Kunisch, Hermann, 1,185
Kunz, Josef, 1,819-1,821
Kunz, Ludwig, 1,822
Kurella, Alfred, 1,823
Kurzweil, Baruch, 1,824
Kutscher, Arthur, 1,825
Kyyrö, Kauko, 1,826

Laaths, Erwin, 1,827-1,831
Laborde, Jean, 1,832
Lämmert, Eberhard, 1,833-1,835
Lamm, Hans, 1,836
Lamprecht, Helmut, 1,837-1,839
Landau, E. M., 1,840
Landquist, John, 1,841-1,842
Landry, Harald, 1,843
Landsträsser, Ludwig, 1,844
Lang, Hans Joachim, 1,845

Lange, Gerhard, 1,846
Lange, I. M., 1,847-1,850
Lange, Sven, 1,851
Lange, Victor, 1,852-1,861
Lask, Thomas, 3,909
Lasso de la Vega, José S., 1,862
Lauret, René, 1,863
Lauschus, Leo, 1,864
Lawrence, D. H., 1,865
Lean, Tangye, 1,866
Leber, Hugo, 1,867
Lederer, Joe, 1,868
Leemans, Paul, 1,869
Lehner, Horst, 3,098
Lehnert, Herbert, 1,870-1,883, 3,910-3,911a
Leibholz, R. N. P., 1,884
Leibrich, Louis, 1,885-1,907, 3,912
Leip, Hans, 1,908
Lem, Stanislaw, 1,909
Lemke, Karl, 1,910
Lennartz, Franz, 1,911
Lennert, Rudolf, 1,912
Lenz, Renate, 1,913
Leonhardt, Rudolf Walter, 3,913
Leonhardt, Wilhelm, 1,914
Leopold, Keith, 1,915-1,916
Leopoldi, Hans Heinrich, 1,917
Leopold, Martha, 761
Lepel, Hermann, 1,918
Lepman, Jella, 1,919-1,920
Leppert, Günter Fred, 1,921
Leppmann, Franz, 1,922-1,923
Leppmann, Wolfgang, 1,924-1,926
Lernet-Holenia, Alexander, 1,927
Lervik, Kaare, 1,928, 2,431
Leschnitzer, Franz, 1,929
Lesser, Jonas, 1,930-1,941
Lessing, Theodor, 1,942-1,943
Lestiboudois, Herbert, 1,944
Leuteritz, Gustav, 3,746
Leutner, Karl, 1,945
Leuzinger, Peter, 1,946